The Ordeal
of Thomas Barton

Studies in Eighteenth-Century America and the Atlantic World

co-sponsored by
The Lawrence Henry Gipson Institute for Eighteenth-Century Studies, Lehigh University

General Editor: Scott Paul Gordon, *Lehigh University*

Publishing rich, innovative scholarship that extends and enlarges the field of early American studies, *Studies in Eighteenth-Century America and the Atlantic World* embraces interdisciplinary work in eighteenth-century transatlantic literature, history, visual arts, material culture, religion, education, law, and medicine.

Other Titles in This Series

http://www.lehigh.edu/~inlup

The Rev. Thomas Barton. (From the original canvas portrait, now lost, in Leach's Philadelphia Portraits, The Historical Society of Pennsylvania.)

The Ordeal
of Thomas Barton

Anglican Missionary
in the Pennsylvania Backcountry, 1755–1780

James P. Myers, Jr.

Lehigh
University
Press

Bethlehem: Lehigh University Press

Associated University Presses
2010 Eastpark Boulevard
Cranbury, NJ 08512

The paper used in this publication meets the requirements of the American National Standard for Permanence of Paper for Printed Library Materials Z39.48-1984.

Library of Congress Cataloging-in-Publication Data

Myers, James P., 1941–
    The ordeal of Thomas Barton : Anglican missionary in the Pennsylvania
backcountry, 1755–1780 / James P. Myers, Jr.
        p.   cm. — (Studies in eighteenth-century America and the Atlantic World)
    Includes bibliographical references and index.
    ISBN 978-0-9821313-4-3 (alk. paper)
        1. Barton, Thomas, 1730–1780. 2. Missionaries—Pennsylvania—Biography.
3. Church of England—Missions—Pennsylvania. 4.
Pennsylvania—History—1775–1865.   I. Title.
    BV2803.P4M94   2010
    266'.3092—dc22
    [B]

                                                                    2009031200

It behoves those who are placed as Watchmen on the Walls of our HOLY ZION, to cry aloud and spare not the approach of every Thing that can hurt or make us afraid. . . .

—Rev. William Smith, 1755

Contents

Preface

THIS DISCUSSION OF THOMAS BARTON'S AMERICAN ADVENTURE HAS ITS genesis in 1987 when my wife and I acquired property on Chestnut Hill in Tyrone township, Adams county, Pennsylvania. Concealed in woods on the land was a small graveyard of unmarked fieldstones, the origins of which no one seemed to possess any accurate information. Local speculation identified it as the resting place of Native Americans or escaped African-American slaves who had found protection in the Quaker community nearby. After over a year's research at the Adams County Historical Society and discovery of some old deeds carefully preserved by a neighbor, we began to obtain a more accurate understanding of its origin: the burial ground, dating from the 1760s and early 1770s (but possibly as early as the 1740s), held the remains of the Church-of-England McGrews, a large Ulster Scots-Irish family which had migrated to Chester county, Pennsylvania, most probably from Aughnacloy, county Tyrone, c. 1729, and which had finally settled in Tyrone and its adjacent townships, Menallen and Huntington, in then western York county. The McGrews took possession of and cultivated their land during a time troubled by conflict with the French and Native Americans who raided the Pennsylvania frontier. Profound discord within the frontier communities also prevailed, for the largely Ulster Scots-Irish and Anglo-Irish who settled the new lands "over Susquehanna" brought with them many of the rivalries and factional disputes that had distinguished their troubled existence in northern Ireland, a cultural turbulence fueled by religious friction among the Anglican, Quaker, and Presbyterian faiths by which they defined themselves. With the removal of the French-and-Indian threats after 1763, the denominational conflicts intensified, often contributing to the evolving political antagonisms that dramatically climaxed just before and during the American Revolution.

I discovered that during the years 1755–59 Thomas Barton, hitherto a relatively obscure figure in local history, actually had played a key role on the trans-Susquehanna frontier. As itinerant missionary for the Society for

the Propagation of the Gospel in Foreign Parts, Barton was assigned spiritual leadership of members of the Church of England who had organized
themselves into three small parishes in Carlisle, Huntington township, and
York-town. Barton's itinerancy thus embraced a large portion of Pennsylvania's western frontier in land today defined as Cumberland, Adams, and
York counties. He sited his home strategically in the middle of what was
then termed the "Conewago settlement," named for the great creek cours-
ing through the area occupied by many of his Anglican communicants. Although his local log church—Christ Church—and its graveyard lay about
two miles east of Chestnut Hill, Barton lived even more easterly, in Reading township, on a "plantation" just north of today's Rt. 234 or what was
known during Barton's time as the "Great Road to York," thus placing his
residence closer to York than to Carlisle.

Performing last rites would have brought Thomas Barton to our graveyard, then a piece of Finley McGrew's plantation, which he had named
"Aughnacloy." Finley's brothers Alexander and John (both Barton's parishioners) held property abutting Finley's, while another brother, James, and a
nephew, Archibald (son of John) lived at some distance. It was a complicated family arrangement, for Finley and James were Quakers, while Archibald, John, and Alexander were communicants of Christ Church. A William
McGrew, a shadowy figure and brother or nephew of Finley, lived on the
southern side of Conewago Creek, a Presbyterian in a community of Presbyterians who farmed the rich bottom lands of Tyrone and Straban townships, several of whom owned slaves. In the event, the one-half acre
graveyard on Quaker Finley's plantation, perhaps originating before Christ
Church and its burial ground were established in the early 1750s, served the
needs of the Anglican McGrews, and did so until at least 1801, the date on
a face-down gravestone I discovered one morning near the barn, not far from
the burial ground. After most of the McGrews moved westward early in the
nineteenth century—they had commenced migrating in the 1770s—the Anglican graveyard was gradually allowed to become overgrown, its origin
and identity lost.

Research on the Scots-Irish McGrews led to deeper investigations into
the religious and ethnic contentions in the area. Internal hostilities among
the early settlers evolved into confrontations between independent-minded
Presbyterians and Anglicans who supported the Penn proprietary, with
Quakers generally endeavoring to remain aloof from the factionalism, but
sometimes siding with the more tolerant Anglican proprietary. Inevitably,
this conflict acquired a patriot-Loyalist character when Pennsylvania
emerged as one of the principal centers for resistance to Britain's efforts to
bring her North American colonies under greater control after the Seven

Years' War. One of the frontier's leading representatives of both the Penn proprietary and the Church of England, Thomas Barton occupied a central position during the years 1755–78, after which he was expelled from Pennsylvania for refusing to forswear his ordination oath to Britain's royal family. Significantly, he also matured as the patriots' net tightened around him, embracing in the end the tragic destiny he had come to perceive as inevitably his. In part, this book traces that evolution.

Drawing upon Barton's published works and his large, invaluable legacy of correspondence, his 1758 journal of the Forbes expedition, as well as letters to and about him, this appreciation initially surveys the beginnings of his incumbency as Anglican missionary and proprietary placeman in then western York county. The third chapter examines his participation in the 1758 Forbes campaign against Ft. Duquesne, bringing into focus his many insecurities and his disillusionment with frontier life. Chapters 4, 5, and 6 explore Barton's career in Lancaster—the role he successfully assumed as mediator within that town's teeming religious diversity; the part he played as a forceful cultural leader in the community, reflecting the Enlightenment values that inspired him in many ways; and his reluctant participation in the turbulent controversy spawned by the Paxton Boys' vigilante murdering of Christianized Conestoga Indians in Lancaster. The last chapters, 7 and 8, suggest how the growing conformity and repression imposed by the die-hard patriots who had seized control of the new state during the early years of the Revolution steeled Barton's resolve, driving him to translate his earlier esteem for exemplars of uncompromising Stoic resolution—esteem even for enemies—into the defining heroism of his last years. Long an admirer of those who embraced heroic martyrdom, Barton, in his death, uniquely dramatized the very words he had employed in 1756 to describe the death of the feared and hated Delaware war-chief Captain Jacobs: "he was born a Soldier, & would not die a Slave."

Acknowledgments

T<small>HE COLLECTIONS OF SEVERAL INSTITUTIONS, TOGETHER WITH THEIR</small> helpful staffs, provided essential primary materials which made this biography of Thomas Barton possible: the American Philosophical Society (of which Barton was a member); Special Collections in the Waidner-Spahr Library of Dickinson College, which preserves many of the records relating to St. John's Episcopal Church; the historical societies of Lancaster and York counties; St. James's Episcopal Church in Lancaster, Pa.; the Adams County Historical Society, with its rich, comprehensive collection of early land records; the Archives of The United Society for the Propagation of the Gospel (Oxford, U.K.); and the Archives of the Episcopal Church, U.S.A. Words cannot sufficiently stress the importance of the Historical Society of Pennsylvania, with its treasure-trove of letters and documents crucial to illuminating Barton's career. During my many years of researching and writing on Barton, Gettysburg College made my project feasible with its financial and moral support.

As important as all of these proved, many individuals played incalculable roles in assisting my efforts. Don Schlegel of Columbus, Ohio, has investigated the history of the Barton family of Carrickmacross, county Monaghan, Ireland. Earlier editors of *Pennsylvania History,* Michael Birkner and William Pencak, and of the *Pennsylvania Magazine of History and Biography,* Ian Quimby, helped me negotiate difficult disciplinary boundaries when time came for me to publish my initial research on Barton. Susan Roach, of the interlibrary loan department of the Musselman Library, Gettysburg College, often undertook extraordinary efforts to locate hard-to-find materials. Arthur Weaner, associate director of the Adams County Historical Society, always found time amidst his farming duties to share with me his extensive knowledge of the early land surveys of York and Adams counties and to provide me with copies from his collection of aerial property maps. And Charles Glatfelter, emeritus professor of history, Gettysburg College, and, at the time, executive director of the Adams County Historical Society, whose knowledge of Pennsylvania's early religious history is unequaled, provided me with encouragement and direction and not a little of his understated humor throughout the years I investigated Barton. Finally, I reserve special thanks to Scott Paul Gordon of Lehigh University Press without whose urging appreciation of Thomas Barton's ordeal would be little more than footnotes and a few academic articles on the history of colonial Pennsylvania.

The Ordeal
of Thomas Barton

Introduction

*I now began to consider myself (as the Rev^d. M^r. Provost Smith expresses it in
a Letter to me), "As One who had advanc'd to the very Frontiers of the Messiah's Kingdom, & among the first who had unfolded his ever-lasting Banners
in the remotest Parts of the West."*
                                                              —Thomas Barton

*I think of . . . men born into our Irish solitude, of their curiosity, their rich dis-
course, their explosive passion, their sense of mystery as they grew older, their
readiness to dress up at the suggestion of others though never quite certain
what dress they wore, their occasional childish worldliness.*
                                   —William Butler Yeats, on the Anglo-Irish

IF HISTORICAL PERSONALITIES REQUIRE SPECIAL KEYS TO UNLOCK THEIR
ambiguities and obscurities in order to draw the latter into the full light of
conscious appreciation, then one of the essential keys to Thomas Barton's
character lay in his ethnic and religious origin. Barton (1728–80) descended
of a north-of-Ireland family which had immigrated to Ulster during Crom-
wellian times. The Bartons of county Monaghan in due course became
landed gentry, identified themselves with the Church of Ireland, and suffered during the Williamite wars when their castle of Carrickmacross was
sacked by Catholics fighting in the cause of James II. Members of the Anglo-Irish Ascendancy class, the Bartons lost their lands and fortune early in
the eighteenth century, although it is not altogether certain how.

Notwithstanding his family's reduced circumstances, Thomas Barton
was still able to study at Trinity College, Dublin (at that time, a kind of fin-
ishing school for male children of the Ascendancy), after which he emi-
grated to America about 1751. Following a brief teaching career and
marriage in Philadelphia, he took divine orders in the Church of England,
receiving certification as a missionary in the Society for the Propagation of
the Gospel in Foreign Parts (the "SPG").

19

When the Anglicans of Pennsylvania's western-most counties needed spiritual and secular direction following Braddock's defeat in 1755, Thomas Barton provided it, marshalling and even leading the militia, and promulgating the Church of England's doctrines of enlightened moderation and latitudinarian toleration in the face of fanatical proselytizing by Calvinist dissenters. Had Barton succeeded only in championing the Anglicans of York and Cumberland counties, his legacy most likely would be indistinguishable from those of other SPG missionaries who labored in the frontier's stoney Church of England vineyard. But, as member of a missionary society favored by the Pennsylvania proprietary and the British Crown, and as the product of an elite ruling class inspired by ideals of sacrifice and leadership, he conspicuously executed in his person and office the colonial policies of both the Penns and Westminster. He acted, as well, as a conduit through which trusted intelligence concerning the frontier was channeled to Philadelphia and thence to London. The great number of Barton's surviving letters and reports reveal an informant tirelessly apprising his superiors of events, feelings, possibilities, and threats—details which put before the modern reader a picture of frontier life virtually unparalleled. Only in the writings of Barton's SPG colleague, the Reverend Charles Woodmason of South Carolina, can we find more detailed description of conditions in the pre-Revolutionary American backcountry.

Barton, however, possesses significance beyond his invaluable depictions of border warfare and the trials of the trans-Susquehanna frontier. His Anglo-Irish origins in Ulster ideally equipped him for dealing with the explosive conflicts generated among the Ulster Scots-Irish Presbyterians, the Anglo-Irish Quakers, and the Anglo-Irish Anglicans who overwhelmingly dominated Pennsylvania's western counties. He was in fact one of the most articulate of a virtual network of Anglo-Irish and Anglicized Irish (that is, Irish Catholics who had conformed to the Church of Ireland and English principles) who were recruited to help stabilize the centrifugal turbulence of the American backcountry. As such, he sheds considerable light on the ethnic and cultural identity of that relatively uncharted class of officeholders which included, among others, the tireless Charles Woodmason,[1] whom he may have known, and his own friends Sir William Johnson, born in county Meath, and George Croghan, born in county Roscommon. Revealed through his extensive correspondence and other writings, Barton illuminates a group that several commentators have begun to appreciate as important—far more important than its numbers would intimate—in the ethnic mix of pre-Revolutionary America.[2]

Barton's allegiance to his Anglo-Irish traditions, combined with his vocation in the Church of England, predisposed him to embrace an essentially conservative position in politics. Unlike colleague and friend, the Anglo-Scottish provost of the College of Philadelphia, William Smith, moreover, Barton was not an opportunist trimming his sails to take advantage of the prevailing political winds; he was in fact condemned and subsequently punished in 1778 by the new revolutionary government of Pennsylvania for Tory sympathies and, presumably, activities. The last several years of his life delineate the downward swing of a career that had been, until the 1770s, moderately successful. As the mounting revolutionary forces increasingly inflicted their tragic momentum on him, Barton came to perceive that he was evolving into the martyr figure he had long admired. He appears, in fact, to have consciously shaped his life to conform to that ideal as his end drew near. And it is with the emergence of a tragic identity that Barton's life achieves poignancy. Propelled by cultural forces he only half-recognized and mindfully embarking upon an end the precedents for which he knew well from tragic literature and such homiletic compilations as Foxe's *Book of Martyrs,* Barton aspired to the more-than-ordinary sacrifice we associate with the cultural-religious hero. Like many before and after him, he proved indeed that life often imitates art.

For all of his varied accomplishments, the received historical estimation of Barton has relegated him to the shadows cast by several of his friends, for example, Sir William Johnson and William Smith. This should not, however, mark him out as less deserving for study, for the obscurity into which his repute fell in great part resulted from his having joined the side that lost the Revolution. As several studies have argued, historians all-too often pay tribute to the victors and to the movements that succeed, ignore the defeated, and silently pass over causes the latter championed. Such an emphasis is as faulty, the critics insist, as it is narrow. In his study of Thomas Hutchinson, Loyalist governor of Massachusetts, Bernard Bailyn appeals to our need to recover "a whole area of the Revolution that has been almost completely submerged and that hardly enters at all into our general understanding of what that formative event was all about."[3] To explore the lives of American Loyalists is "to explain the human reality against which the victor struggled and so to help make the story whole and comprehensible." The articulate, sustained, and indeed impassioned record Barton has left us does much to exhume that hitherto hidden world of Tories and Loyalists, and of those who simply, if naively, endeavored to remain neutral.

Irish historian Ciaran Brady advances a similar justification for studying "losers in history" that might have appealed to Anglo-Irishman Barton: the defeated, the losers, the martyrs—these significantly intimate what might have been; they permit us momentary glimpses into alternate realities that now lay buried under the detritus of Time. For Brady, moreover, men like

Thomas Barton "are significant because they demonstrate in their different ways the complexity of the process by which historical change is effected. They offer proof that history moves not through slowly unfolding, unilinear patterns, nor through cyclical revolution, but through contingencies of force and circumstance, whose conjuncture could not have been predicted and could never be repeated."[4]

To historians like Bailyn and Brady, then, the recovery of Barton's record would be a salutary advance toward rescuing from obscurity the Tory and Loyalist attitudes that compellingly fueled pre-Revolutionary America, indeed, that paradoxically helped to drive the engine of revolution itself. For it is one of the tragic ironies of Barton's career that his roles and philosophy contributed to the very instability it was his task to allay. Largely unrecognized by commentators is Barton's participation in the Enlightenment which distinguished Pennsylvania from most of the other colonies. Ironically, however, although Pennsylvania's tradition of pluralism and liberty inspired the formation of a free and tolerant nation, the revolution that took place within its own borders subverted Pennsylvania's older latitudinarian structures and ideals because of their identification with the "British way of life."[5] In the post-Revolutionary years, that state, once the vanguard of those provinces fostering Enlightenment values, sadly fell to the rear.

Early associated with the College of Philadelphia, described by John F. Woolverton as "the most 'secular' center of higher education in colonial America,"[6] and with that institution's first provost, William Smith ("one of the major figures of the Moderate Enlightenment"),[7] Barton carried the cultural and political legacy of Anglo-Irishmen like Dean Jonathan Swift, Bishop George Berkeley (also a member of the SPG), and Edmund Burke into the Pennsylvania backcountry. As a botanist, mineralogist, classicist, educator, relatively broad-minded missionary, and Anglican minister who defended Pennsylvania's tolerant pluralist commonwealth, like a lightning-rod he attracted to himself the far less liberal, coercive power of the Presbyterian-dominated Constitutional party once it obtained effective control of the state in 1778.[8] Long a trenchant critic of Scots-Irish Presbyterian dominance of the frontier, Barton was gradually deprived of friends, livelihood, family, home, and even health, dying in 1780 in New York City, less than a year and a half after the new government hounded him into exile. In many ways, the relatively libertarian and enlightened society he had supported and defended during his incumbency as an SPG missionary ultimately drew upon him the repressive, vengeful energies he had fought for twenty-three years.

Thomas Barton of Carrickmacross, Philadelphia, Reading township (then York county), and Lancaster, was a man of many faces: husband, father, teacher, minister, soldier, naturalist, proprietary man. Positioned at the very heart of Pennsylvania's pre-Revolutionary, Enlightenment society, he was also one of its most eloquent apologists. By recovering a sense of his now obscured life and an awareness of his neglected writings, we should in turn be able to obtain a deeper appreciation of that lively and vital world that was turned upside-down by the events of the 1770s.

1

Watchman on the Walls

If the people of the Frontiers were duly sensible of our inestimable Privileges, and animated with the true Spirit of Protestantism, they would be as a Wall of Brass round these Colonies, and would rise with a noble Ardour to oppose Every attempt of a Heathen or Popish Enemy against us. For none were Ever brave without some Principle or another to animate their conduct; and of all Principles, surely a rational sense of British Freedom & the Purity of our Holy Religion, is the noblest.

—William Smith

Idealism must always prevail on the frontier, for the frontier, whether geographical or intellectual, offers little hope to those who see things as they are. To venture into the wilderness, one must see it, not as it is, but as it will be.

—Carl Becker

In the year 1755, two events left their impress upon the history of Pennsylvania. One was momentous, an upheaval of the first order, and its consequences, like concentric ripples produced by a large stone hurled into a still body of water, continued to move and shape the history of the colony's frontier long afterward. By comparison, the other was insignificant, the mere, almost undetectable slipping of a pebble into the rushing torrent of Time. Initially unrelated, the first-mentioned of these calamitously impacted upon the second, making the latter eventuate in ways that have profoundly enlarged our appreciation of life on the Pennsylvania frontier during the years 1755–9.

The more minor of these occurrences had its genesis in the religious needs of a people often neglected in accounts of colonial Pennsylvania, of the Anglicans[1] who dwelt along the western frontier and who, as it fell out, were largely Anglo-Irish, reinforced with a scattering of Scots-Irish. Numerically outnumbered by their Presbyterian neighbors clustered to the north in Cumberland county and to the south in the settlements of Marsh Creek,[2] the people of the Church of England had informally staked out an area for themselves along the Conewago and the Bermudian Creeks in Huntington, Tyrone and Reading townships in western York, today's Adams, county. A shoal precariously situated in a sea of Presbyterians, Seceders, and Covenanters, and cut off from the nearest Anglican church, St. James in Lancaster, by the triple geographic barriers of dense forest, broad river, and great distance, they felt the survival of their religion an uncertain thing indeed. "We Are in A Starving Condition for ye Spiritual Nourishment, of our Souls," the "Inhabitants of . . . Conniwaga" wrote in a petition of October 3, 1748, "Nor can we Ever hear Divine Service without traveling Many Miles. . . . we Dread to think of our Children being brought Up in Ignorance as to all Divine Knowledge and [it] Cuts us to ye very harte, to See our poor Infants Dye without being Made Members of Christ, by Baptism."[3] Desperate to attract a resident minister, they had already set aside 180 acres of glebe land "for ye Use of ye Minister" and erected "A small Church . . . which we have Called Christ Church of thirty foot Long & twenty wide."[4]

The Society for the Propagation of the Gospel in Foreign Parts, to which the settlers directed their petition, could not send them a resident missionary until the spring of 1755.[5] In that year, the Reverend Mr. Thomas Barton, newly ordained by the Bishop of London and commissioned by the SPG, made his arduous way "over Susquehanna" to the Conewago settlements and there took charge of his Anglican flocks, which were dispersed over a vast area stretching from west of Carlisle to York-town, from Sherman's Valley to Marsh Creek.

In many respects, his parishioners could hardly have obtained a more suitable minister. A former schoolteacher, a naturalist with a special attraction to botany and mineralogy, and a militant defender of king and their Protestant faith, Barton became their fierce and eloquent advocate. He employed his considerable literary and rhetorical energy in their cause, producing a rich legacy of letters, reports, and pamphlets that open a unique window into the lives of those who dwelt within the shadow of the frontier's edge during the years 1755–59.

The second, more momentous event alluded to occurred during the summer of the same year. In July 1755, a British army commanded by Major General Edward Braddock set out to seize Fort Duquesne, the French stronghold situated at the junction of the Allegheny and the Monongahela Rivers, on the site of present-day Pittsburgh. As every schoolchild knows, Braddock's army, moving north along the Monongahela, was ambushed and all-but annihilated on July 9, a few miles south of Ft. Duquesne. A disaster for Braddock's combined colonial and royal army, the massacre also plunged Pennsylvania's frontier into chaos, for the French and their Indian allies subsequently were able to use Ft. Duquesne to raid with im-

Sketch of the second log church, Christ Church, Huntington township, Adams county, Pennsylvania. (Drawn in the 1860s by the Rev. Francis Clerc. Courtesy of St. John's Episcopal Church and Dickinson College, both in Carlisle, Pennsylvania.)

punity the settlements recently established along the western margin of the Susquehanna.

In the wake of Braddock's debacle, the new itinerant missionary Mr. Barton directed a stream of letters to Philadelphia and London voicing the panic and terror that swept through Cumberland and western York counties like wild fire. One of these, dated "3 o'clock in the Morning, November 2nd, 1755," registers vividly the near-hysteria that gripped the backcountry after the French-and-Indian victory:

> I am just come from Carlisle. You may see by the inclosed in what a Situation I left it. The great Cove is entirely reduced to ashes. Andrew Montour charged Mr. Buchanon last night at John Harris' to hasten home & remove his wife and children.[6] I suppose by to-morrow there will not be one Woman or Child in the Town.
>
> Mr. Hans Hamilton marches this morning with a party of Sixty men from Carlisle to Shippen's Town. Mr. Pope and Mr. McConaughy came over with me to raise Reinforcements in order to join Mr. Hamilton immediately.[7]

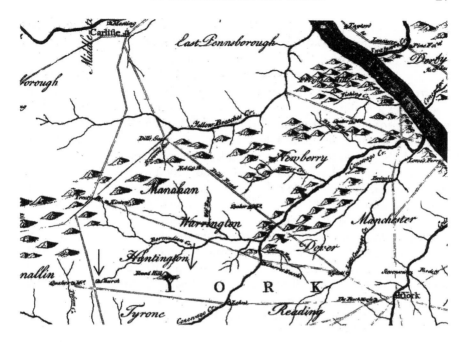

Detail from Nicholas Scull's Map of the Improved Parts of the Province of Pennsylvania, 1759, illustrating the approximate area encompassed by Thomas Barton's SPG mission (1755–59), Carlisle—Huntington township—and the town of York. Christ Church is designated simply as "Church," situated to the right (east) of the "Quaker M^g.," lower left-hand corner, indicated by an arrow. The second arrow, to the right of the first, roughly identifies the site of Barton's plantation. (MG-11, Map Collection, map no. 630; courtesy of the Pennsylvania Historical and Museum Commission, Pennsylvania State Archives).

I intend this morning to return to Carlisle with a Party of men to guard that Town; the Gent^n. there desire me to request your assistance without Delay.[8]

Barton's long November 8, 1756, official report, or *notitia parochialis,* to the society, however, is perhaps more valuable to us (reprinted in Appendix A below). Missionaries of the SPG were required to report yearly on their activities to the society in London. Typically, the annual account enumerated parishioners, baptisms, and marriages, and summarized the more significant problems and conflicts that had challenged the missionary during the year. Thomas Barton's reports, however, were atypical, for they elaborated and analyzed to a much greater extent events that most of his colleagues would normally only have mentioned, if even that. His first *notitia parochialis,* November 8, 1756, runs to no less than twenty-two quarto pages and accordingly preserves a wealth of detail relating to the problems besetting the Anglican communities of the Pennsylvania back-country. Pertinent to this discussion, it also records at length the crisis that confronted Barton and his people as a consequence of Braddock's defeat, conveying a feeling of precipitous, catastrophic reversal, of buoyant expectancy drowned in a riptide of irrepressible fear and anguish: "Just when I was big with the Hopes of being able to do Service . . . we receiv'd the melancholy News, that our Forces under the Command of General Braddock, were defeated. . . . This was soon succeeded by an Alienation of the Indians in our Interest: —And from that Day to this, poor Pennsylvania has felt incessantly the sad Effects of Popish Tyranny, & Savage Cruelty!—A great Part of five of her Counties have been depopulated & laid waste; & some Hundreds of her sturdiest Sons either murder'd, or carried into barbarous Captivity!"[9] Daily, he witnessed the sufferings of the frontier-people who, abandoning their homesteads, now fled eastward "groaning under a Burden of Calamities; some having lost their Husbands, some their Wives, some their Children,—And all, the Labour of many Years! In this Condition (my Heart bleeds in relating what I am an Eye Witness to) they now wander about, without Bread of their own to eat, or a House to shelter themselves in from the Inclemency of the approaching Winter!"[10]

Barton was both religious leader of his people and de facto representative of the Penn proprietary. He therefore lost no time meeting the emergency. In the autumn of 1755, responding to widespread appeals that he do so, he published his sermon *Unanimity and Public Spirit.* Reinforced with a prefatory essay by friend and colleague, the Reverend William Smith, provost of the College of Philadelphia and one of the colony's leading intellectual lights, the pamphlet exhorted the frontiersmen, irrespective of religious affiliation, to set aside their factional interests to meet the common threat of a merciless, tyrannical enemy. More pragmatically, and not to be outdone by his Presbyterian colleagues, John Steel of Cumberland county and Andrew Bay of the nearby Marsh Creek settlement,[11] Barton organized his parishioners into work parties to improve the fortifications at Carlisle and to defend against attacks. Writing from Huntington township (site of Christ Church) to the Reverend Richard Peters, friend, Anglican minister, and secretary of the province, he described the new militant role fate had compelled him to embrace:

> I was oblig'd more than once *to call* together the Inhabitants to meet in a Body at my House,[12] in Order to encourage them under their present fearful Apprehensions.—Some skulking Indians which were seen to pass towards the South-

Mountains, have rais'd such Commotions among them, that they are ready to quit their Habitations, & flee to preserve their Lives. . . . what a poor, defenceless Situation this is. Not a Man in Ten is able to purchase a Gun.—Not a House in Twenty has a Door with either Lock or Bolt to it. So that a very small number of Indians might totally destroy the whole Inhabitants (in their present Circumstances) without the least Opposition.[13]

Barton's contemporaries praised his seizing the initiative. William Smith, for example, commended him as one of those preachers "who are placed as Watchmen on the Walls of our HOLY ZION, *to cry aloud and spare not* on the Approach of every Thing that can *hurt us or make us afraid.*"[14] Smith wrote the Bishop of Oxford in 1756 that "poor M^r. Barton has stood . . . upwards of a Year at the Risk of his Life, like a good Soldier of Jesus Christ, sometimes heading his People in the character of a Clergyman, and sometimes in that of a Captain, being often obliged, when they should go to Church, to gird on their Swords and go against the Enemy."[15] The people of the backcounties fortunately found in Barton the martial strength and expertise they required. Together with Andrew Bay and John Steel, he provided the frontiersmen with the immediate leadership and inspiration they looked for in vain to Philadelphia. Smith makes this clear in the same letter. If Barton, he continued "and two worthy Presbyterian Ministers had not stood it out, I believe all the parts beyond Susquehanah, where his Mission lies, would have been long ago deserted."[16] When Barton described his congregations' new martial attitude, he did so with an enthusiasm and pride that he must have shared with Bay and Steel: "Tho' my Churches, are Churches militant indeed, subject to Dangers & Trials of the most alarming Kind; yet I have the Pleasure every Sunday (even at the worst of Times) to see my People coming crowding with their Muskets on their Shoulders; declaring that they will dye Protestants & Freemen, sooner than live Idolaters & Slaves.[17]

Barton's actions were important, for the Anglican clergyman tirelessly labored to surmount doctrinal and ethnic differences in the interest of the colony. His making common cause with his Scots-Irish Presbyterian colleagues thus ratified not only the exhortation of his own published sermon *Unanimity and Public Spirit,* but it also reflected yet another qualification that equipped him well for the ecclesiastical rigors of York and Cumberland counties—his common Hibernian origin with most of the other settlers. Because this distinction has ramifications that extend far beyond the issue under immediate discussion, we need to explore briefly Barton's earlier Irish upbringing.

Unlike most of the proprietary representatives who resided in the eastern part of the province, Barton was an Ulsterman. He was thus intimately acquainted with the history, the problems, and the rivalries that distinguished the north-of-Ireland Scots-Irish, Anglo-Irish, and "mere" or pure Irish; and the Presbyterian, Quaker, Anglican, and Roman Catholic immigrants on the Pennsylvania frontier. He came from a social class which, in Ireland, had acquired experience in governing the various ethnic groups that complicated that island's turbulent social and political life—the native Irish; the substantial remnants of the earlier, pre-1689 English settlement; Huguenots; great numbers of restless, malcontended Scots-Irish colonists; and the more recent immigrants from England. Unfortunately, while his background might have qualified him in the eyes of those officials who guided church and state in Pennsylvania, it seriously disadvantaged him insofar as the Ulster Scots-Irish Presbyterians had inherited a smoldering, long-enduring distrust of Ascendancy landowners, Anglo-Irish churchmen, and the traditions they promoted. Hence, Barton ironically helped nurture the cultural ferment and instability of border life, and in several respects, his cultural identity and sundry public roles contributed to the very turmoil he sought to allay.

Our principal source for details of Barton's years in Ireland is his eldest son. In 1813, William Barton published a biography of his distinguished uncle, Thomas's brother-in-law, the mathematician, astronomer, clockmaker, and American patriot David Rittenhouse. In the course of the book, William frequently digresses on the life of his own father. In one such excursion, he speaks of his father's derivation from an Anglo-Irish Ascendancy family which had fallen on hard times. His father, he writes, "was a native of Ireland, descended from an English family; of which, either two or three brothers settled in that kingdom, during the disastrous times in the interregnum of Charles I. Having obtained very considerable grants of land in Ireland, this family possessed ample estates in their then adopted country. . . . Through one of those untoward circumstances, however, by means of which the most unexpected revolutions in the affairs of families and individuals have been sometimes produced, the expectations of an independent patrimony which our Mr. Barton's father had entertained, were speedily dissipated."[18] Notwithstanding this misfortune, Thomas obtained schooling "in the vicinity of his family residence in the county of Monaghan . . . and at a suitable age, he was sent to the university of Dublin, where he finished his academical education."[19]

Although William does not here elaborate further on the "untoward circumstances" that frustrated his grandfather's expectation of a financially secure life, another document sheds some additional light on the family's loss. In 1778, William Barton, studying law in England, recorded his pedigree at the College of Arms,[20] testimony providing several additional facts about Thomas Barton's ancestry: namely, that the latter's grandfather, a Captain William Barton, had suffered at the hands of Catholic troops during the Williamite wars in 1688; that his father, another William, had married Susanna Bashford; and that he had been born of that union in 1728 in the castle of Carrickmacross, county Monaghan.

Historical documents and other genealogies confirm that Capt. William Barton's castle was sacked by Jacobites sometime in 1688–89.[21] This, however, was not the principal event whereby Thomas's father William lost his "expectations of an independent patrimony." It appears from the account of Thomas's son William that another male offspring of Captain William "gave by Will his Est[ate] to an illegimate Dau[ghte]r who it[']s s[ai]ᵈ M[arrie]ᵈ . . . Richard . . . Tenison . . . which family has the Estate of Barton."[22]

Recent inquiry, however, suggests that the supposedly illegitimate daughter might have been in fact the only legitimate issue of Capt. William Barton, thus implying that if illegitimacy can explain how the Barton estate passed out of the male line into the Tenison family through a female, Margaret, then probably Thomas's father, if not Thomas himself, was the illegitimate.[23] The sketchy family history in the *Memoirs* and the recorded pedigree, together with what strikes one as either confusion or lying, intimates that Thomas or his son William or both suppressed or misrepresented details of their connection with the family of Capt. William Barton of Carrickmacross Castle.

The history of the various Barton lines in Ireland is vague. It is clear, however, that, descended of a ruling, landowning family, albeit fallen upon hard times, Thomas finished his schooling at Trinity College, Dublin, the institution which educated Ireland's Anglo-Irish elite. Recollected by son William, Thomas, "destitute of fortune . . . arrived in Philadelphia soon after he had completed his scholastic studies."[24] Following in the footsteps of many indigent but well-educated young immigrants, he set up school in 1751 in Norriton township. There he made the acquaintance of young David Rittenhouse, whom he tutored, and his sister Esther. In 1752, he secured an appointment to the faculty of William Smith's Academy of Philadelphia. In December 1753, he married Esther Rittenhouse, their first child, William, being born in April of 1754. Then, on August 17, 1754, he resigned from the Academy in order to return to England, there to undergo ordination and licensing as a missionary in the SPG. What occurred to bring on this apparently sudden redirecting of his life?

Why Barton in 1754 decided to join the SPG is not clear. His recent marriage, followed by the birth of his son, must surely have dramatized to him the inadequacy of his salary. William Smith, moreover, had recently returned from England, on May 22, 1754, as a newly ordained Anglican priest and certified SPG missionary. Inspired by the heady wine of Enlightenment ideals[25] and animated with fresh ideas from recent discussions with the archbishop of Canterbury and Thomas Penn, Smith had succeeded in obtaining the proprietor's agreement to support the fledgling college with both his name and substantial annual monetary gifts. He had also explored plans to strengthen the cause of the charity school movement.[26] It is fairly probable, then, that this organizer and mover played a critical role in persuading Barton to sail for England a few months following his own return to Philadelphia. It is also likely that Smith proved instrumental in obtaining a promise of support from Thomas Penn, assistance that Barton gratefully acknowledged in a letter to the proprietor in 1757.[27] Supplementing the King's Bounty of £20 that new missionaries could count on, Penn's support would have made the long, expensive trip feasible.

To these possibilities might be added Barton's determination to turn his life about. We may observe in this respect that his son William was born four months after his marriage to Esther Rittenhouse, implying perhaps a union not made altogether freely, or if freely, then certainly not timely. Additionally, we have a piece of teasing criticism suggesting that Barton's reputation was far from exemplary. Writing to Charles Ridgely on September 5, 1754, Samuel Chew of Philadelphia remarks on Barton's departure "that Holy Order is fallen into great Contempt, when such Fellows as he are made Parsons."[28] Had he, as seems likely in the case of Charles Woodmason of Charleston, South Carolina, experienced a sudden conversion? Had Barton established something of a reputation as a man-about-town? That his character prompted Samuel Chew to gossip in this way implies, if little else, that the lowly schoolmaster hardly inhabited the shadows of academic obscurity.

Barton's need to improve his circumstances, his desire to help promote the "great work" of the SPG, his intention to put behind him a possibly morally dubious life—all these would have been reinforced by his certain knowledge that a great many of the Irish, and not a few of the English, Bartons had obtained livings in the Anglican church. Although not all the Bartons who took holy orders were necessarily directly related, several probably were. The most intriguing among the Irish Bartons was the Reverend Richard Barton (*fl.* 1739–51). Son of a vice-provost of Trinity College, Dublin (the Reverend John Barton), Richard served as curate of Lurgan, near Belfast, and authored several works on moral philosophy, natural history, and geography, the latter revealing, like Thomas, a special interest in mineralogy and gemstones.[29] He died the same year Thomas sailed for Philadelphia—was there some link between the two events? Whatever the possible connection here, something of a traditional Anglican vocation among the Irish Bartons would have naturally inclined Thomas in that direction as a means of obtaining greater security and the possibility of future advancement.

The process for obtaining ordination was by no means perfunctory. A candidate had to undergo thorough examination to determine his intellectual and doctrinal fitness in the classical languages, the Bible, the history of the Church, the book of Common Prayer, and the Creeds.[30] SPG records show that in 1755 Barton produced the recommendations required for admission to candidacy—"a Certificate from the Trustees, and from the Professors of the Academy of Literature and Useful Knowledge lately erected at *Philadelphia,* that he had been more than two years employed as an Assistant in that Academy."[31] The society appointed him missionary to Pennsylvania on January 17, 1755, pending his ordination by the bishop of London. Ordained January 29, 1755 and receiving the King's Bounty February 7, he returned to Philadelphia on April 10, 1755.[32] From 1755 on, Thomas Barton lived as a member of an Anglican brotherhood vigorously opposed to both Roman Catholicism and Quakerism, of an order that in the words of John F. Woolverton, demanded of its members "equality, frugality, simple dress, dignified and grave deportment."[33] Because Barton's life was from this point on intimately tied to the society, we need to examine briefly its history and character.

The Society for the Propagation of the Gospel in Foreign Parts had been founded in 1701 to execute missionary work in Great Britain's overseas colonies, particularly the American provinces. Ironically inspired in part by the Society for the Propagation of the Gospel in New England, officially founded in 1649, and by the Roman Catholic Congregation for the Propagation of the Faith, the SPG evolved out of the more domestically focused Society for the Propagation of Christian Knowledge in order to strengthen the Church of England in the colonies, convert "the Natives" and unbaptized African slaves, and bring Christianity to those Whites settled in areas slighted by organized religion.[34] In several important ways, it revealed the impetus of eighteenth-century Enlightenment ideals.[35] To support its activities, it drew upon a coalition of ecclesiastical, educational, business, and social interests. In time it evolved into the principal institution by which the Church of England carried out its American mission and by which the Crown endeavored to extend its imperial authority beyond the purely secular. In the American provinces, the SPG tried both to counter the great energy and popularity of the dissenting sects, particularly in colonies where the Church of England had not been established as the official religion, and to neutralize Roman Catholic missionaries. Frequently, it appropriated strategies already effectively employed by the Society of Jesus, prompting Thomas Jefferson to remark that its missionaries were "Anglican Jesuits."[36]

The SPG brought to its mission an energetic discipline and commitment that inspired suspicions, accusations, and jealousy among the dissenters. Quakers and Presbyterians, who especially feared the official establishment of the Church of England in such colonies as Pennsylvania, stridently opposed the creation of an American episcopate, one of the aspirations of the Pennsylvania missionaries. The specter of the hated tithe laws whereby members of all creeds would be taxed to support the established church also haunted the darker fantasies of the dissenters. All of these very real possibilities in Pennsylvania—official establishment of one sect, episcopacy, and tithing—had earlier driven great numbers of the sectarians from such locales as Ireland and the German Palatine. With the conversion of William Penn's descendants to the Church of England and their political alliance with that church, the SPG, along with the Church itself, came in Pennsylvania to enjoy power and influence far in excess of its numbers, a strength reinforced with the rechartering in 1755 of the Academy of Philadelphia as the College of Philadelphia, as an essentially Anglican institution.

Responding to the crisis brought on by Braddock's defeat, in 1756 the SPG published for its American missionaries its *Instructions from the Society, for the Propagation of the Gospel in Foreign Parts, to Their Missionaries in North-America.*[37] In almost all respects, this pamphlet reflects the main ideas of Barton's *Unanimity and Public Spirit* and the example he had already set in seizing leadership on the frontier in 1755–56. Its first several points unequivocally stress the society's secular program. Missionaries were charged "to endeavour, with the utmost Care and Zeal, in this critical Conjuncture, to support His Majesty's Government; and to promote the Welfare and Safety of His Majesty's *American* Subjects."[38] In the cause of civil unity, they were next instructed to extend their activities "among *all* Protestant" believers within the areas embraced by their missions in order "to prevent a *gradual* Sacrifice to the . . . implacable Ambition" of the French and their Indian allies. The tract exhorted missionaries to become catalysts for helping people to organize "those Means of Defence and Opposition, with which Divine Providence has intrusted them, for the Preservation of themselves, their Families, and their Country."[39] This third provision pointedly challenged such pacifist ideals as those of the Quakers, for the missionary was further charged to "represent, with all due Force, that the Neglect of this natural and *now* necessary Duty of Defense, is nothing less than inviting and encouraging brutal Murderers to shed innocent Blood, and commit the most atrocious Outrages."[40] Not only would those who neglect this duty invite disaster, but they would also become "Accessaries and Partakers of the Guilt of Murder." Fourthly, the itinerant was enjoined to inculcate "Submission to Government and Obedience to Authority."[41]

The fifth and sixth instructions reflect the SPG's religious objectives, though always secular and sacred remain intertwined. The missionary was expected to avail himself of "every Opportunity of exerting your best Endeavours for the Conversion of the *Indians* to the Christian Faith."[42] For its sixth point, the society stressed the importance of assisting the people in the full performance of their religious observances and duties. Its final instruction drew sacred and secular emphases into a climactic, general affirmation of the organization's stabilizing role: the society, the *Instructions* read, directs and beseeches "That you earnestly exhort your People to offer up their most devout Supplications to Almighty God for his gracious Blessing and Protection from the perfidious and cruel Men, who lie in wait to destroy every Thing that is valuable to our commercial, free, and Protestant Colonies; . . . and that, as the only sure Means to obtain the Divine Blessing, you inculcate upon your People the Necessity of *breaking off their Sins* by sincere *Repentance,* and of *living Soberly, Righteously, and Godly in this present World; having always a Conscience void of Offence, towards God, and towards Man.*"[43] In every respect, the society insisted that its clergy maintain "sober discipline and strictness of life."[44] Not only were they to work for the education and spiritual welfare of others, but they were also to labor in the vineyards of self-growth.[45] The SPG provided no place among its members for the dissolute, pleasure-loving, lazy Anglican vicar who had effectively undermined the Church's integrity in the popular perception.

It was this order, then, that Barton entered in January of 1755. In effect, he bound himself to a union as indissoluble and soul-shaping as his recent marriage to Esther Rittenhouse.

∞

Returning to Philadelphia on April 10, 1755, Barton immediately sent word to the people of Christ Church, Huntington township, members of which journeyed to Philadelphia and conveyed his household goods to his new home. Thomas, Esther, and their first child, William, followed shortly after. The expeditious help of the Conewago congregation implies some prior arrangement. Possibly, they had contacted Barton through William Thomson, a student from that area who had enrolled in the college and himself went on to take orders and eventually become Barton's replacement after he moved to Lancaster in 1759.[46]

Much research needs to be undertaken to appreciate exactly how Anglo-Irish immigrants fit into the ethnic mix of frontier life. Several studies, however, offer some essential clarification.[47] About one-quarter of all Protestant immigrants from Ireland were members of the Church of Ireland.[48] Even though a great majority settled in cities along the coast, where they became the first to found Irish-American societies,[49] not a few gravitated to the backcountry, like those who composed Barton's congregations and like the Anglo-Irish Quakers nearby in the Warrington and Menallen Meetings of western York county. From what can be understood, Barton's life conformed to a general pattern we perceive in many other "mid-rank" Anglo-Irish. Social historian David Doyle observes that the Anglo-Irishman, or the Irishman who had conformed to the Church of Ireland, tended to enter a "high position in the English administration of North America,"[50] while those who failed to secure, say, governorships (as had William Cosby and Arthur Dobbs) or other prestigious offices (like Anglicized Irishman Sir William Johnson—the surname is a translation of the Gaelic *mac+ Shane,* i.e., "son of John"—superintendent of Indian affairs in the northern colonies), settled for roles as placemen and middlemen.[51] We might include among the latter Sir William Johnson's principal deputy George Croghan, an Irish Catholic who conformed to Anglicanism. Records show that not a few, like Barton, entered the clergy, thus reinforcing the authority of the Crown in Maryland, Virginia and the Carolinas where the Church of England had been officially established or of such proprietary governments as Pennsylvania's, where William Penn's descendants had become Anglicans.

A great proportion of the Irish who immigrated during the years 1717–76 originated in Ulster.[52] Invariably, these "Ulster immigrants sought livelihood and security . . . , independence, power and familiarity in the *relatively* exclusive settlement" "on the farming frontier of the Back Country," where their "significant leaders" were clergymen.[53] It becomes understandable, therefore, that a man of Barton's background, energy, and aspirations would have looked for welcome among the communities of fellow migrants from the north of Ireland being planted west of Susquehanna. The frontier communities were far from uniformly Scots-Irish Presbyterian, as was once believed: they reflected as well an admixture of Anglo-Irish Quakers,[54] Anglicans, and even native Irish Catholics.[55]

As we have seen, the trans-Susquehanna Anglicans had already petitioned for their own resident missionary as far back as 1748. Barton's decision to resign his teaching position at the Academy of Philadelphia and risk a dangerous sea voyage to be ordained soon after his marriage; his expeditious move to western York county; his later acknowledgment of support and assistance from Proprietor Thomas Penn—all these imply that he saw and seized an opportunity to improve his lot by becoming an SPG missionary and, in effect, a proprietary placeman. Later, he would seek to enhance his position further by attaching himself to the circle, essentially Anglo-Irish, that had Sir William Johnson for its center. In his own turn, Barton would recommend the advancement of fellow Anglo-Irishmen who had recently immigrated.[56] In both of these actions, he revealed another characteristic of his class, for, as Doyle reminds us, "wherever they gained patronage power in the colonies, or over colonial appointments, they created knots of Anglo-Irish expatriates."[57]

The consequences of Barton's appointment as a missionary on Pennsylvania's western frontier were as complex as far-reaching: in a way, his commission may even be construed as contributing twenty-five years later to his death. More immediately, however, it offered him more power and economic gain than he would have obtained as a teacher in William Smith's academy.[58] It opened to him an avenue whereon, like his influential colleagues the Reverends Richard Peters and William Smith, he might eventually garner greater prestige and reward. Unfortunately, that he chose to pursue his career, not in Philadelphia, but rather on the Pennsylvania marchland, and later in Lancaster, proved detrimental: for although he indeed served the Penn proprietary well in his position of spiritual and secular leader, Barton also collided headlong into the frontier's de facto fortress of authority, Scots-Irish Presbyterianism. In Ulster, the Church of Ireland was secure as a governing force; in western Pennsylvania, and colonial America more generally, however, the "miniscule Anglo-Irish minority lacked the coherence to establish a secure niche in American life, nor were the rest of the Irish inclined to grant it to them."[59]

Neither Anglo-Irish Quakers nor Scots-Irish Presbyterians had forgotten the old resentments fostered by the religious tyranny and excesses of the established Church of Ireland. Religious and tribal conflicts such as those shared among Ulster's Presbyterians, Quakers, and Anglicans translated themselves readily to the American frontier.[60] Even though economic and possibly social factors actually may have figured more importantly than religious oppression in instigating the great early eighteenth-century exodus from Ulster, many Scots-Irish apparently regarded the religious element at least as equal to the economic destitution they faced.[61] Certainly, the century-old legacy of religious/ethnic conflict partly explains Presbyterian hostility toward Anglican missionary Barton, a resentment he records throughout his career and one that climaxed three years after coming to Conewago in his clash with another important proprietary representative in the area, Colonel John Armstrong of Carlisle. The crisis years 1755–58, however, reveal Barton generally endeavoring to surmount the ancient rivalries by cooperating with his Presbyterian colleagues, John Steel and Andrew Bay, to inspire their people to meet the common French-and-Indian foe.

The response of the settlers in York and Cumberland counties to the emergency was immediate. Like the inhabitants of Pennsylvania's other exposed counties,[62] they lost little time in petitioning the provincial government to undertake such measures as would help them withstand the new threats. They particularly wished to see erected a chain of fortifications that would extend a defensive line beginning at the Delaware River and running west and southwest to the Maryland border. On October 30, 1755, Sheriff John Potter of Cumberland county summoned a meeting in Shippensburg. Augmented with "Assistant Members" from York county, among them Barton's neighbor the Reverend Andrew Bay, the General Council of Cumberland County resolved that "Five large Forts" should be constructed at the following locations: "Carlisle, Shippensburg, Collonell Chambers's [i.e., today's Chambersburg], Mr Steells Meetting House [near present-day Mercersburg], & at Willm. Allison's Esqr. [i.e., today's Greencastle]."[63] In short time, these and others, like Fort Granville, were in fact erected along the exposed frontier to reduce enemy infiltration and to provide protection during actual attacks.[64]

A second, more far-reaching response was also more controversial insofar as it required legislation to raise a militia and provide funds to pay for and supply an army and to build forts. The Pennsylvania Assembly was at this time dominated by the pacifist faction, principally Quaker, which initially thwarted attempts to pass militia and supply bills. In time, however, the measures were enacted. Until they were Governor Robert Hunter Morris in July 1755 authorized the setting up of "associated companies." In effect, these were voluntary associations of militia whose legality lay with royal charter rather than with provincial legislation.[65] Records show Barton's commission as a "captain," probably in one of these associations.[66] Additionally, to meet the emergency and later to augment the thin line of provincial forts, private individuals erected their own defenses, frequently little more than blockhouses. McCord's, McDowell's, and Chambers's originated as privately built forts intended to fill the urgent need. Tradition also has it that a number of such forts, probably blockhouses, were erected in western York, now Adams, county.[67]

These stop-gap defensive measures came in the nick of time. During the early spring of 1756, Indians struck as far east as present-day Chambersburg. On April 1, they attacked and destroyed a private fortification, Mc-

Cord's Fort, situated northwest of Benjamin Chambers's fortified mills. Retreating, they were pursued by militia from Lurgan township, Cumberland county. Reinforced by nineteen men from Hans Hamilton's company at Fort Lyttelton, the combined forces intercepted the war party at Sideling Hill on April 2, In a letter written two days later, Hamilton immediately reported news of the provincials' defeat: "These are to Inform you of the Malancholy News that Occurd on the 2nd Instant. . . . Our men Engaged about 2 hours, being about 36 in Number, & we should have had the better had not thirty Indians Came to their Assistance. Some of our men fir[d] 24 Rounds a piece, and when their Amunition Fail[d] were oblig'd to Fly."[68]

Of even greater strategic significance than the destruction of McCord's Fort, a French-and-Indian war party at the end of July 1756 captured and burned the provincial defense, Fort Granville, that stood on the site of today's Lewistown, Mifflin county. In the assessment of William A. Hunter, authority on Pennsylvania's French-and-Indian War forts, "the loss of this fort was a stunning blow."[69] Indeed, just how imperiled the settlers felt may be appreciated in the missive Barton sent to Richard Peters: "I came here this Morning, where all is Confusion. Such a Panick has seized the Hearts of People in general, since the Reduction of Fort Granville, that this Country is almost relinquished, & Marsh Creek in York County is become a Frontier. . . . I should be extremely glad to have the Pleasure of a Line or two from you. Your Advice would be of service to me at this Time, when I know not what to do, whether to quit this Place, or to remain a little longer, to see whether any thing favourable will turn out for us."[70]

The day before he wrote Peters, Barton had dispatched another communication to Governor Morris. In his tersely-worded covering letter, he explained that he was enclosing a "Petition at the Solicitation of a great number of People" in York county. He goes on to stress the urgency of the predicament faced by the frontiersmen of both York and Cumberland counties: "Marsh Creek is the now the Frontier, and such a Panick has seiz'd the Hearts of People in general, that unless we have soon some favourable Turn in our Affairs, I am affraid the Enemy need not long be at the Pains to dispute a Claim to those two Counties."[71] The petition itself pleads at length for military aid from the provincial government against "the outrages of [a] barbarous and savage enemy." It is an eloquently devised appeal, and its vocabulary and phrasing suggest that Thomas Barton, one of its 191 signatories, was also its principal author.

Evidently, Barton occasionally assumed responsibility for delivering petitions of this sort, in addition to writing and sending them. We see him the following year in Easton traveling "Express with an Application . . . for a further Protection," on this occasion to the new governor William Denny.

Sending the petition on its way, Denny remarked of Parson Barton that he "waits only for an Answer, and is very much wanted at home."[72]

Beyond the immediate demoralization that it precipitated, Ft. Granville's destruction revealed the weaknesses of what later became known at the outbreak of World War II as the "Maginot mentality," i.e., of passively relying upon a line of fortifications that were "widely spaced, lightly garrisoned, and difficult to supply and to reinforce."[73] This realization seems dramatically to have inspired the settlers to supplement their defensive passivity with offensive measures. This they did by carrying the war into Indian country itself and eliminating the Delaware stronghold of Kittanning.

The raid upon Kittanning was for the most part executed by the Pennsylvania Regiment's Second Battalion, commanded by Barton's rival-to-be, Lieutenant Colonel John Armstrong of Carlisle. The story of the attack has been well told by others.[74] Briefly, after moving across the Alleghenies undetected, Armstrong's men completely surprised the Indian town on the dawn of Wednesday, September 8, 1756. Nonetheless, by the time they broke off their assault, they had lost seventeen known dead, with as many wounded, including Armstrong himself. The settlement, however, was put to the torch, its dreaded Indian leader Captain Jacobs killed.

Although Barton did not march with the Second Battalion, he knew men who had, and at least one of them, perhaps his parishioner in Carlisle, Lieutenant Robert Callender, the officer Armstrong employed as his secretary after he had been wounded, possibly forwarded to him details omitted from Armstrong's official report written at Fort Lyttelton. Barton's February 28, 1757, guardedly optimistic report to Proprietor Thomas Penn on post-Kittanning events is remarkable for several reasons. Most obviously, it establishes that Barton perceived one of his roles as that of an intelligencer or news-correspondent/spy. His tone, however, implies that his relationship to Penn was something other than that of a mere client addressing his benefactor and thus explains why he did not express the more general euphoria voiced by other writers once they realized that Kittanning and the threat it represented had been destroyed. Former governor Morris's assessment typifies the favorable appreciation: "I think the Expedition will be of great use to the Publick as it will raise the spirits of the People and serve to remove that Dread and Panick which has seized the generality of the People."[75] Indeed, the corporate fathers of Philadelphia struck a medal commemorating the victory, and Thomas Penn presented a sword and belt to Armstrong.[76]

As one who had met Penn in London in 1754 and who would continue to count on the latter's generosity—Thomas Penn was not usually acclaimed for his largesse—Barton, however, wrote more candidly than most. Thus, although he acknowledges that "Since the Reduction of the Kittanning under Colonel Armstrong, we have not been much disturb'd," he also fears that "the approaching Spring will again make us tremble. We have a great deal to do, & but little done."[77] He perceives that "the killing [of a] few Indians & burning their Huts at the Kittanning is an Action not very considerable in itself." His coolness may reflect the rivalry already developing between himself and the proprietary's placeman in the Carlisle area, the "Hero of Kittanning"; more importantly, Barton's intuition that "the approaching Spring will again make us tremble" proved altogether well-taken.

In addition, Barton used the opportunity to inform his benefactor of Callender's bravery, a fact curiously, perhaps pointedly, omitted by Armstrong in his official account. Callender, who copied down Armstrong's report, might well have mentioned the omission to his minister. Barton wrote the following: "One M^r. Callender . . . distinguish'd himself by the most uncommon Bravery & Resolution. It is asserted that when Jacobs took to a House, out of which he kill'd & wounded Many of our Men—Callender undertook to fire it, which he accomplish'd at the infinite Hazard of his Life;—And that when our People precipitately retreated upon a Report prevailing that the French were to be up that Day from Fort-du Quesne, Callender not content to leave the Houses standing, went back with a small Party of Men, & set Fire to them all."[78]

Very possibly, Barton's supplying this detail concerning the performance of one of his communicants might have been an initial shot in his conflict with Armstrong. His bringing this instance of Callender's heroism to the notice of the proprietor might not be that unusual, but his apparent respect for Captain Jacobs's death must certainly stand out as unique in a cleric and a settler who had witnessed first-hand the sufferings everywhere evident on the Pennsylvania frontier. Rather than predictably turning the killing of Jacobs into a pious homily on the evil pagan receiving his just deserts, Barton in another letter finds in the *sachem*'s end intimations of the Stoic deaths celebrated in ancient epics and plays of Greece and Rome, and in John Foxe's popular *Book of Martyrs:* "the famous Captain Jacobs fought, & died, like a Soldier. He refus'd to surrender when the House was even on Fire over his Head; And when the Flame grew too violent for him, he rush'd out into the Body of our Men flourishing his Tomahawk, & told them he was born a Soldier, & would not die a Slave."[79] Throughout his career, Barton expresses a fascination with Stoic heroism and martyrdom, and it is no exaggeration to note that this tragic and religious ideal ultimately shaped his own evolution and end.[80]

As Barton foresaw, the French-and-Indian raids resumed. In the following year Delaware and Shawnee once more attacked the backsettlers frequently and with impunity. The April 5, 1758, attack on Buchanan Valley is well-known, for it was this incursion that carried Mary Jamieson, the so-called "White Squaw," off into a world she came eventually to prefer to the one from which she had been forcibly abducted. Not quite so famous was the raid that occurred eight days later and which Barton described with an urgency we can feel to this day: "I have the misfortune to acquaint you that we are all Confusion. Within 12 miles of my House, two Families consisting of 11 Persons were murder'd & taken. . . . The poor Inhabitants are flying in numbers into the interior Parts. I prevail'd yesterday upon the Inhabitants of Canawago & Bermudian to assemble themselves together, & forming themselves into Companies, to guard the Frontiers of this County. . . ."[81] This attack occurred in the vicinity of present-day Virginia Mills in Hamiltonban township, south of today's Gettysburg. Fortunately, Richard Baird, who had been taken prisoner, later made his escape to Ft. Lyttelton and left us a particularly vivid eye-witness account.[82]

By the spring of 1758, Brigadier General John Forbes had arrived in Philadelphia to set into motion plans for a major campaign against Ft. Duquesne. By employing a combined army of both provincial and royal forces, he planned to drive the French from Pennsylvania, thereby depriving the Delaware and Shawnees of their major support.

The Pennsylvania Regiment was eventually reorganized, with Colonel Commandant John Armstrong given actual leadership of the regiment, although Governor William Denny enjoyed nominal command as colonel-in-chief. In turn, although Armstrong, as colonel, theoretically still commanded the First Battalion, Lt. Colonel Hans Hamilton was de facto commander of that unit. Colonel Commandant James Burd led the Second Battalion.[83] To increase the strength of the regiment and to exploit untapped reserves of manpower in the trans-Susquehanna settlements, provincial authorities undertook to raise still a third battalion. Most of the men in four of the new companies being formed came from Barton's area in western York county, with one, commanded by his parishioner Captain Archibald McGrew, raised in Conewago itself.

On April 30, 1758, the proprietary land agent and surveyor for the county of York, George Stevenson, wrote of two important concerns. He records—"what is most remarkable"—that four leading York county Quakers finally made common cause with the imperiled settlers and recently supported their efforts to raise a local militia of "45 men." Secondly, Stevenson suggests the possibility that "four or five good Companies could be rais'd in a very short Time here if proper Officers are chosen, & that in a Short Time. If the Governor & Council should think my Services necessary, I mean in recommending Officers & raising Men, &c., &c., all Fatigues of that kind will be a Pleasure to me."[84]

Stevenson's pleasure was soon to be great, for Richard Peters replied forthwith, observing that he and John Armstrong had already been exploring the possibility of raising new companies.[85] Although nothing seems to have come of that particular plan, Peters also stressed the desirability of commissioning "one full set of Officers of German Farmers and Freeholders." An ordained Anglican priest himself, he further advises Stevenson to urge the "Ministers . . . in different and proper parts of the Country . . . to appoint Meetings, and animate the People to raise Levees with all possible Dispatch."[86]

Stevenson reported later on his success in enlisting local clerics, Barton among them, to whip up support for the war: "The Rev[d] Mr. Craddock gave me the Pleasure of a Visit, & preach'd an excellent War Sermon from Mr. Listry's Pulpit, on Friday last, in the hearing of Messrs. Barton, Bay, & Listry; he went with Mr. Barton yesterday, is to deliver another Sermon to the same Purpose to day from Mr. Barton's Pulpit."[87]

Influential Maryland Anglican clergyman Thomas Cradock had apparently been invited by the proprietary to preach what in effect was a ecumenical sermon to a congregation which included Anglican Barton, Presbyterian Andrew Bay, and the German Reformed John Jacob Listry or Lishy, who served congregations in or near the new town of York and what is now the Upper Bermudian Church in Huntington township, close to Barton's Christ Church. Thematic similarities to Barton's 1755 sermon *Unanimity and Public Spirit* imply that the latter might have helped inspire Cradock's exhortation to unify against the French and Indian threat.[88] Barton's friendship with Cradock was evidently close enough for the latter to stand during the same visit as godfather to Barton's second son, David Cradock Barton, born in 1758. Later, after Barton had removed to Lancaster, he invited Cradock to visit the town so that Barton's new parishioners might see "that Mr. Cradock was my friend, . . . [and that therefore they] will think me a Man of Consequence."[89]

In the event, Stevenson's efforts to recruit a new battalion bore fruit. Three fresh companies from western York county commanded by Thomas Hamilton, Robert McPherson, and Archibald McGrew soon marched north to Carlisle along the Oxford Road to become integrated into the new Third Battalion, while a fourth, David Hunter's, joined the First.[90] Before the Pennsylvania Regiment was deemed ready as a fighting unit, however, a tactful decision had to be made on who would be commissioned its chaplain, or, refocused, how diplomatically to accommodate the proprietary's religious representative, Anglican itinerant minister, the Rev. Mr. Thomas Barton.

∞

Of all the controversies which must have occurred during those busy preparations for the campaign and which we know of, it is perhaps surprising that one of the most heated should involve the position of chaplain in the Third Battalion. That it did is surely the measure of gravity with which Church of Englanders and Presbyterians, particularly Anglo-Irish Anglicans and Scots-Irish Presbyterians, regarded the role of spiritual advisor. Additionally, it dramatizes the degree to which the old tribal animosities, spawned in Ulster, continued to divide the frontier.

The full conflict has been detailed elsewhere, permitting us here to note only its general character.[91] Suppression of details by the principals, John Armstrong and Thomas Barton, and missing documents obscure fully what actually transpired during July 1758. It appears that Barton, although initially appointed chaplain to the Pennsylvania Regiment,[92] had for some reason to settle for the chaplaincy of the Third Battalion.[93] The overwhelming numbers of Presbyterians in that unit, however, instead petitioned General Forbes to commission for them one of their own creed, as was the case in both the First and Second Battalions.[94] In a further attempt to undermine Barton's prestige and authority, Armstrong provoked Deputy Quartermaster General Sir John St. Clair to stop Barton "in the time of reading prayers."[95] So extraordinary was this aggressive interference with the practice of their religion that Barton's congregations addressed a remonstrance to Forbes, petitioning the general to investigate the matter. Written in Barton's distinctive hand and set forth in his characteristic prose style, the remonstrance in part reads that

> we are sensibly affected with the extraordinary & unprecedented Treatment given our Reverend & worthy Incumbent M[r]. BARTON on Sunday the second Day of this Instant July, by having an armed Messenger sent him, while he was performing Divine Service in his own Parish—ordering him to desist & dismiss the People.—As this Proceeding seems unhappily calculated to propagate Dissension & Animosity among us at a Time when Protestants of every Country & Denomination should join Heart & Hand to repel the common Enemy of all; & is a high Insult to the National & establish'd Church:—We pray that your Excellency would be pleas'd to enquire into this Affair, & restore us to that Ease & Satisfaction, which we have long enjoy'd under the Ministry of our laborious & very worthy Teacher."[96]

Because he had been denied supreme spiritual authority of the entire regiment and because great numbers of Presbyterians in the Third resented him, Barton evidently refused the governor's commission to the Third. Instead, he requested that Forbes employ him as a kind of Anglican chaplain-at-large for the entire royal and colonial expeditionary force, thereby eluding the acutely censorious eye of Presbyterian and rival Colonel Commandant John Armstrong. Forbes agreed, and on July 9, 1758, he commissioned the Anglo-Irishman: "you are hereby invited & authoriz'd to the Discharge of all Ministerial Functions belonging to a Clergyman of the Church of England amongst the Troops under my Command."[97] Forbes unequivocally assured his new chaplain that "all & sundry, are hereby order'd and requir'd to pay due Reverence & Respect to you & the Reverend Function you are invested with." Barton's victory must certainly have rankled Armstrong, but, had he any doubts earlier, the latter now saw that Barton enjoyed powerful support and accordingly refrained from openly attacking him in his correspondence. We see this reticence during the campaign, for example, when he alludes vaguely to Barton's character but then pulls back from denouncing him more forcefully to Peters: "as for Mr. B———n, I have not had the least Communication with him since I saw you, nor Never intend to have. I have never been mistaken of the that Gent[n], but shall Leave his Character to Persons of his own Community."[98]

This episode is instructive. It reveals to us the insecurity of those seeking advancement and courting the power brokers. John Armstrong had already established himself in the good graces of the Penns by efficiently executing his duties as land agent, surveyor, commander of militia in Cumberland county, and leader of the 1756 expedition that destroyed Kittanning. Nonetheless, his fervent Presbyteriansim must have made his allegiance to the Anglican-dominated proprietary at times suspect. The tone of some of his letters, particularly during the disturbances involving the Paxton Boys, Frederick Stump, and the Black Boys,[99] strikes the reader as overly unctuous and smooth, thus implying some degree of insincerity. At several other times, his allegiance and use of power were openly questioned.[100]

For different reasons, Barton also had to tread carefully. His correspondence during these years frequently speaks of rumor mongering against him, real or imagined. As we saw, even before he received ordination, Philadelphian Samuel Chew teasingly alluded to his dubious reputation.[101] Recently discovered correspondence between Barton and William Smith, furthermore, establishes that Barton had recently survived a potentially explosive scandal and must therefore have been at that time under close scrutiny by his superiors, sacred and secular. Because this near-disgrace derived from his 1755 war sermon, *Unanimity and Public Spirit,* we need to examine that tract and its genesis in some detail.

2
"Threaten'd, Abus'd, & Treated like a Criminal"

At a Time when Murder & Desolation crowded the aching Sight, & our poor back Settlers were daily forsaking their Habitations, & flying from the destroying Hands of barbarous Savages; . . . . I intended to write for the Pulpit & not the Press [and] . . . borrowed, (or if you please, stole) such Extracts as were applicable to my Purpose.—

—Thomas Barton

BARTON ADDRESSED HIS 1755 SERMON *UNANIMITY AND PUBLIC SPIRIT* TO ALL the Protestants on the frontier, Church of Englanders as well as Dissenters. He exhorted them to set aside their factional bickering and make common cause against their foe. So popular did the sermon prove, he remarked to William Smith, that "Many who heard it, importun'd me . . . to make it publick."[1] After securing a prefatory endorsement from Provost Smith in August, Barton saw the sermon through the press the following month.[2]

If Barton is to be credited, his exhortation contributed significantly to stabilizing the frontier by inspiring many of those still living in Cumberland and York counties to resist the Delaware and Shawnee war parties rather than flee eastward. Writing to Smith, he stressed that "When I preach'd this Sermon, it had a good Effect upon all that heard it. . . . were it not for the Pains I took, few Inhabitants would have remain'd in these Parts.—This, Sir, is not boasting. Hundreds can testify it.—"[3] Not without self-interest, Smith sent the archbishop of Canterbury a copy of his own prefatory epistle, at the same time describing Barton's timely militant tone: "This Letter was soon after published & dispersed by the rev[d] M[r]. Barton, together with a Sermon of his suited to the Times. . . . It had a good Effect."[4]

Recent rediscovery of a long-overlooked epistolary exchange between Smith and Barton, however, reveals that Barton's zeal to meet the crisis inspired him in dubious ways. Beyond simply exhorting the people of the frontier to unify against their common enemy, in writing his sermon he plagiarized another, fairly well-known tract written ten years earlier and then convinced the apparently unsuspecting Smith to introduce the soon-to-be-

46

The Rev. William Smith, provost of the College of Philadelphia, at about the age of 30. (From an engraving by John Sartain, based on Benjamin West's portrait of Smith, in Horace Weymiss Smith, *The Life and Correspondence of the Rev. William Smith,* 2 vols. [Philadelphia: S. A. George, 1879–80].)

published sermon with an elaborate endorsement. That Barton's career and friendship with Smith survived the scandal following exposure of his plagiarism raises several significant questions concerning not only Barton's identity as an Anglican itinerant missionary, but also his tacit role as a mid-level representative of the Penn proprietary. Soon after his exposure, why did William Smith, angry and personally injured, nonetheless defend Barton? Why did Smith and, apparently, provincial secretary Richard Peters, instead of distancing themselves and their church from their disgraced colleague, participate in suppressing the evidence and rumors pertinent to Barton's plagiarism? Why did Thomas Penn (who must surely have known of Barton's transgression) continue to support and reward the Anglo-Irish cleric, even forging with him a friendship beyond the bounds of the conventional patron-client relationship? And more broadly, what do Barton's plagiarism, its publication, and its ultimately successful concealment imply about the roles of proprietary agents during the turbulent period following Braddock's defeat? Before actually exploring these issues, however, we need to examine a more fundamental question: what circumstances motivated the Reverend Thomas Barton essentially to pilfer a popular sermon and then brazenly publish it under his own name?

∞

We have already seen that Barton's log church in Huntington township became a rallying point during times of danger, and that day and night, his little plantation south of Mud Run in Reading township succored his people. Writing to Richard Peters, he described the new martial role fate had thrust upon him:

> I was oblig'd more than once *to call* together the Inhabitants to meet in a Body at my House,[5] in Order to encourage them under their present fearful Apprehen- sions.—Some skulking Indians which were seen to pass towards the South-Mountains, have rais'd such Commotions among them, that they are ready to quit their Habitations, & flee to preserve their Lives. . . . what a poor, defenceless Situation this is. Not a Man in Ten is able to purchase a Gun.—Not a House in Twenty has a Door with either Lock or Bolt to it. So that a very small number of Indians might totally destroy the whole Inhabitants (in their present Circumstances) without the least Opposition.[6]

From what we can infer, Barton's militancy invited censure from many of Pennsylvania's pacifist factions.[7] To justify and clarify Barton's martial stance, his two colleagues in Philadelphia explained his new role. English-born Richard Peters, in a letter possibly to Thomas Penn, stressed that Barton's combative readiness, far from undermining his religiosity, actually augmented it: "Mr Barton in a more particular manner deserves the commendations of all lovers of the Country, for he has since November last put himself at the head of his Congregations and Marched by Night or by Day on every Alarm. Had others imitated his Example Cumberland would not have wanted Men enough to defend it, nor has he done anything in the Military way but what has increased his Character for Piety and that of a sincerely Religious Man and Zealous Minister. In short, Sir, he is a most worthy, active and serviceable Pastor and Missionary, and as such please mention him to the Society."[8] From the hand of one of the province's most powerful men, Peters's commendation trenchantly underscores Barton's value to the proprietary. It also reveals, as does Reverend Peters's own career, how closely allied the interests of the Church of England and the proprietary were.

William Smith undertook a more elaborate and extended justification. The provost of the College of Philadelphia wrote to the bishop of Oxford in 1756 that "poor Mr. Barton" has withstood the dangers on the frontier "upwards of a Year at the Risk of his Life, like a good Soldier of Jesus Christ, sometimes heading his People in the character of a Clergyman, and sometimes in that of a Captain, being often obliged, when they should go to Church, to gird on their Swords and go against the Enemy."[9] Smith's testimonial is consistent with the defense he published prefacing Barton's sermon the previous year. Himself frequently attacked for being meddlesome and all-too worldly,[10] Smith described to the archbishop of Canterbury the quandary SPG missionaries such as Barton and himself often found themselves in: "If we exhort to a manly Defence of our inestimable Liberty, we are said to be Dabblers in Politics, & not Ministers of the meek and blessed Jesus. [The Quakers] are afraid of seeing a Spirit of Virtue and Freedom raised among the People, which would spurn those Quietest & non-resisting Principles which at present sway the Government of this Province."[11] Inspired by his "Conscience, & Charity to our poor suffering back-Inhabitants," Smith refused to be cowed by pacifist scruples. Instead, he "wrote to the Missionaries on the Frontiers . . . exhorting them to make a noble Stand for Liberty."[12] With this, he acknowledges that he had inspired Barton to embrace the aggressiveness so controversial among their detractors. He intimates as well that his letter influenced Barton to write the 1755 sermon urging unity and public spiritedness: his own letter, he reports, "was soon after published & dispersed by the rev^d M^r. Barton, together with a Sermon of his suited to the Times."[13]

At least in part, then, Barton wrote his sermon in response to Smith's exhortation "to make a noble stand for Liberty." That he eventually published it had apparently little to do with his original motives. He simply wrote his appeal, he explains in his own preface, in order to contribute his *best Endeavours towards the Support of our* common Protestant Cause, *according to the Duties of my Station, in this Time of public Danger.*"[14] Repeated requests, especially from his distinguished friend the Reverend Provost William Smith, however, persuaded him to commit it to the press and

The Rev. Richard Peters, Pennsylvania's provincial secretary. (From the portrait by John Wollaston, c. 1758. Courtesy of the Pennsylvania Academy of the Fine Arts, Philadelphia; gift of Mrs. Maria L. M. Peters.)

thereby set it before a far greater audience than he had originally envisioned. Before he agreed to its publication, Barton prevailed upon Smith to introduce it with something from his own pen. In the event, Smith produced an augmented version of his earlier exhortatory missive to Barton in order to introduce the sermon to a larger and more scattered readership, especially to those Philadelphians who might not appreciate fully the trials and dangers that had inspired Barton's appeal. Because it is prefatory and introductory to *Unanimity,* it might be useful to consider it before examining Barton's sermon.

Reflective of a man who, with all his faults, must be ranked as one of eighteenth-century America's foremost educators,[15] Smith's epistle surpasses in sophistication and rhetorical skill the sermon it introduces and rivals in length. Smith begins by stating his reservations concerning Barton's "Want of Method," which has resulted in a somewhat loosely organized piece: "the Parts are not strictly arranged[;] you have fallen," the rhetorician gently chastises Barton, "into several Repetitions."[16] Conceding the character of Barton's special audience and the imminent danger to which the missionary spoke, Smith himself prefers the "Art of making one Part rise gracefully out of another."[17] Accordingly, he subtlely transforms what begins as an apology for and reassurance to Barton into a thinly veiled attack upon those political factions which naïvely behaved as though the human race still inhabited an unfallen world. First, he rebuts already voiced objections to the paradox of "a Minister professing the Doctrine of the meek and blessed JESUS. . . . blowing the Trumpet of War, and declaiming against *Popery.*"[18] He then maintains that people be realistically governed for the mixture of good and ill that they are: we no longer live in an Eden "where the *Rose* bloomed without its *Thorn;* and, till we are admitted into the KINGDOM OF UNIVERSAL RIGHTEOUSNESS, we must not look for the Blessings of Peace, entirely free from the Miseries of War."[19] National sins beget "national Chastisements." Indeed, he affirms that "it behoves [sic] those who are placed as Watchmen on the Walls of our HOLY ZION, *to cry aloud and spare not* on the Approach of every Thing that can *hurt or make us afraid,* either in our civil or religious Capacity; surely no Warmth can be unseasonable at a Time when all that we account dear or sacred is threatened with one indiscriminate Ruin."[20]

His rhetorical fire now burning white, Smith discards the last vestiges of reserve. In this public forum, he does not refer to his Philadelphia Quaker readers directly, but he patently attacks their principles. He reminds Barton's critics of the great distance, spatial and moral, separating their city from that western landscape haunted daily and nightly by unimaginable horrors, from an infernal marchland where panicked backsettlers flee their habitations and the mutilated corpses of their loved ones. How, he asks, can anyone "be silent to avoid the Imputation of being thought too warm?"[21] "Shall we expose ourselves to worse than Persecution," he continues, layering rhetorical question upon question, "for Fear of stirring up a Persecution of others?"

Barton's unseemly meddling in public affairs, his call for unity, and his martial valor—all actions the pacificists excoriated—are thus not only defensible: they are also virtually obligatory, morally necessary. "Most certainly, my Friend," he assures his colleague, "all this may be done; and I think it has been clearly shewn that all this ought to be done by every *Minister,* and more especially those of our national *Church,* which is the great Bulwark of the *Protestant Interest."*[22]

With this, Smith launches into an impassioned, sustained apology for the Anglican church as the sword and buckler of civil authority, an argument that Barton in his more ecumenical appeal had avoided and that the Quakers must have received as sobering confirmation of their worst forebodings of Anglican tyranny and that certainly supports Thomas Jefferson's insight into the Jesuitical inspiration of the SPG. Although it occurs near the conclusion of his epistle, we suspect it was one of Smith's principal motives for writing, a corrective to Barton's diplomatic omission. Indeed, it builds upon Smith's earlier premise that a "CHIEF RULER" administers law and superintends the *"public Weal":* ". . . the *Priesthood* rests on the same Foundation with *Society* itself, and takes its Rise from the Necessity of human Affairs, which requires some Institution for assisting the *Busy,* rousing the *Indolent,* and *informing* ALL. Without this, every other Institution for the Good of Mankind would be but of little Avail; and there never was a Society of any Kind, which did not find it necessary, under some Name or another, to appoint certain Persons, whose particular Business it might be, to study and explain what was conceived to be the great Interests of that Society."[23]

The priestly calling thus secularly justified, Smith can then gently lecture the inexperienced Barton on how best to execute his very special role: "if we exert ourselves manfully in such a Cause, who knows, but at last, thro' Almighty Grace, a Flame may be kindled which shall not only exalt the meanest Bosom among us, equal to the foremost of our Neighbours; but which shall also burn and catch and spread, like a wide Conflagration, till it has illumined every Part of this immense Continent, with the *sublime Spirit of* TRUTH AND FREEDOM?"[24]

Thomas Barton's impassioned sermon was well tailored to the perilous challenges in Cumberland and York counties. It required, however, this vision of someone distant from the immediate danger and local rivalries, and addressing a larger readership, to bring the sermon's martial resonance into a more broadly persuasive perspective. Although he does not fully seize the Quaker bull by its theologically blunted horns, William Smith's prefatory letter justifies his colleague's religious militancy in order to lay bare the great threat that he and the Anglican Proprietary perceived imperiling the colony's survival. As detrimental as Barton's "Race of *Priests,* and *Monks,* and *Inquisitors,* and other Tools of a foreign Yoke" might have been,[25] Smith attacked the political impotency and ethical dubiousness of a policy founded simplistically and spuriously upon the pacificism of the Quakers and some other German creeds such as the Mennonites, Moravians, and Amish.

Barton's sermon is in many ways a noteworthy effort. Not only does it eloquently and resonantly exhort his congregations to the defense of "our pure *Protestant Faith,* our equitable *Laws,* and our sacred Liberties, . . . When such a dark and dismal Cloud hangs over our Heads,"[26] but it also trenchantly exposes a major weakness in the fabric of Pennsylvania's frontier life—its disabling factionalism and dependence upon a government unable or unwilling, or both, to defend its citizens living on the frontier. Although it is sometimes maintained that the Paxton disturbances of 1763–64 first signaled how factionalism, along with a seeming legislative indifference to the French-Indian threat, was eroding the frontier's fragile security,[27] Barton's sermon, coupled with its prefatory epistle by William Smith, publicly identified both problems at least as early as 1755.

Barton took for his principal theme the passage from 1 Corinthians in which Paul pleads *"that there be no Divisions among you; but that ye be perfectly joined together in the same Mind, and in the same Judgment."* What Barton calls *unanimity* is the fountainhead of those benefits nurturing the flourishing commonwealth—justice, honesty, truth, and those other "humane and generous Affections, all the soft and endearing Actions, which alone can render Man useful and *sociable* to Man!"[28] Each day offers up, he elaborates, ample proof of the "pernicious Consequences of Divisions and civil Discord,"[29] evidence that he urgently summarizes in all of its horror and fear. But far worse than their everyday misery will be their future torments should the inhabitants of the backcountry fail to withstand the enemy and thus be "obliged to exchange our holy Protestant Religion for Popish Error and Delusion" which will "hold our Souls and Bodies in miserable Bondage!"[30] After he vividly catalogues present sufferings and the even more harrowing outrages to come should the settlers suffer defeat, he appeals to all his readers—i.e., "MEMBERS OF THE CHURCH OF ENGLAND, AND PROTESTANT DISSENTERS *of all Denominations"*—to "lay aside every idle Division and Distinction, and be heartily united for the future in *the same Mind, and the same Judgment"* that Paul had celebrated.[31]

After the threat had moderated a year later, Barton wrote out his first official report to his superiors in the SPG.[32] Along with a general description of his missionary activities in his new home, Barton acknowledges receiving a copy of the recently published *Instructions from the Society, for the Propagation of the Gospel in Foreign Parts, to Their Missionaries in North-America* (London, 1756).[33] In several respects the society's charge to the missionaries conforms so closely to what Barton had already been about on the frontier that it is likely reports of his successful undertakings influenced the formulation of those instructions. One of these, the third, reflects almost perfectly the spiritual, hortatory, and military leadership he had provided: "in order to prevent . . . dreadful Calamities, . . . exhort the People to employ, with a true Christian Zeal and Courage, those Means of Defence and Opposition, with which Divine Providence has intrusted them, for the Preservation of themselves, their Families, and their Country; and for the just Punishment of wicked and barbarous Aggressors."[34] This transparently appeals for exactly the action Barton had performed in writing and then publishing his sermon. In addition, the society enjoined its missionaries to oppose forcefully the pacificism that attracts violence and brings wars upon the inhabitants of a province or country:

> in the Spirit of *Meekness instructing those that oppose themselves,* . . . represent, with all due Force, that the Neglect of this natural and *now* necessary Duty of Defence, is nothing less than inviting and encouraging brutal Murderers to shed innocent Blood, and commit the most atrocious Outrages. . . . all, who omit this important Branch of their Duty, become Accessaries and Partakers of the Guilt of Murder, by wilfully delivering up honest, innocent, quiet Subjects, with their whole Country, to the Fury of our avowed Enemy, or the unrelenting Violence of single Assassins, or of associated rapacious Murderers."[35]

Although Barton might have been executing informal society policy in 1755, this official document published less than a year after the printing of *Unanimity and Public Spirit* tacitly ratifies the motives that inspired him. Consequently, it is puzzling that in his November 8, 1756, report to the society he never details his military actions at this time nor acknowledges in any of his extant official communications the writing and publishing of his sermon.[36] His official reports were intended in part to provide his superiors with information they needed to evaluate and reward him. If he were to obtain the favor essential to his advancement, he needed in effect to boast. Additionally, all of Barton's correspondence show him to have been a man who enjoyed writing about himself and explaining his actions. The closest he comes to revealing his recently embraced combativeness occurs when he acknowledges that his "Churches, are Churches militant indeed" and describes his pleasure "every Sunday" in beholding his "People coming crowding with their Muskets on their Shoulders; declaring that they will dye Protestants & Freemen, sooner than live Idolaters & Slaves."[37] Of his sermon or its publication he says not a word. His uncharacteristic silence is perplexing; it invites speculation.

Recently rediscovered evidence of Barton's plagiarism explains this reticence.[38] In a letter of October 9, 1755, Smith angrily demands of Barton "by next Post without Evasion a Categoric Answer" to five questions. These center on the latter's knowledge of "a Sermon preached by M[r] Roberts to the dissenting Congregation at Salisbury in the late Rebellion" and, more importantly, on Barton's abuse of his friendship with Smith.[39]

After an impassioned opening outburst, the Philadelphian detailed how he came to discover Barton's misdeed. Hearing rumors of Barton's literary theft, he set out one day to vindicate his friend's reputation in the "Coffee house" where his detractors were busily comparing the two sermons page by page. Unhappily, the evidence compelled Smith to acknowledge the plagiarism—"great was the Power of Truth." And greater was Smith's sense of betrayal and outrage. In his eyes, Barton, exploiting their friendship, had persuaded him to introduce, without his knowledge of course, a shameless plagiarism. His personal reputation as a scholar was thus called into question: in the perception of their detractors, either he condoned Barton's theft, or he had ignorantly failed to recognize a fairly popular work.[40] Feeling used and betrayed, Smith nonetheless promised to do what he could to suppress the gossip and to "strive to prevent any ill-natured Exposure of you in the Prints." In this, he succeeded well.

Smith's remarks obliquely intimate that he suspected Barton had written out of profound naiveté and tactlessness—the latter had not even eliminated anachronistic details from Roberts's original, glaring irrelevancies that the puzzled Smith had deleted when he edited Barton's manuscript for publication. For example, he had found such references as the "Tool of France," i.e., the Pretender (focus of the 1745 rising), to denote "no Meaning here." Smith's incredulity was total: "Could you think it possible that a Sermon so famous among Dissenters as Roberts's was not in the Hands of many here?" And indeed, a comparison of Barton's *Unanimity* with Samuel Roberts's *Love to Our Country, and Zeal for Its Interest . . . Preach'd to a Congregation of Protestant Dissenters at Salisbury on Sunday, October 6, 1745 . . .*[41] reveals such wholesale and undisguised theft from the earlier tract, far beyond the contemporary practice of preachers "borrowing" from one another's sermons, that Smith's disbelief almost strikes us as understated.

Broadly, Barton's original contribution to the 1755 exhortation consisted of an introduction and a conclusion to Roberts's sermon. *Love to Our Country* had been inspired by similar circumstances during the Great Rebellion of 1745, but it needed to be adapted to the present, local emergency. In addition to refocusing it, Barton shifted some paragraphs about, improved Roberts's style, deleted some of the more glaring anachronisms and irrelevancies, although, as we have seen, it remained for Smith to identify and remove still others. In other respects, he simply lifted whole paragraphs from Roberts. Indeed, it might be accurate to say that Barton essentially updated *Love to Our Country* by providing it with a new frame. The following comparison illustrates how closely Barton followed his original:

There is no Perfon here, I imagine, but who will eafily conceive to what End thefe Reflections are directed, and to what Purpofe they naturally lead. The prefent Circumftances of this Nation, threatned with Evils of the moft formidable Kind, and alarmed with Apprehenfions of the moft horrible Danger, neceffarily call upon us to quicken the Ardor of public Spirit, to ftir up every latent Spark of Love for Liberty, and mutually to receive and fpread the glorious Flame of Zeal for the common Caufe, which at the fame time that it warms only and enlivens ourfelves, will effectually fcorch and confume our Enemies.	THERE is no Perfon here, I imagine, who does not eafily conceive to what End thefe Reflections are directed, and to what Purpofe they naturally lead. The prefent Circumftances of this Province, threatened with Evils of the moft alarming Nature, neceffarily call upon us to quicken the Ardor of public Spirit; to ftir up every latent Spark of Love for Liberty; and mutually to catch and fpread the glorious Flame of Zeal for the common Caufe, which, at the fame Time that it warms only and enlivens ourfelves, will effectually fcorch and confume the Difturbers of our Peace.
Samuel Roberts, *Love to Our Country*, 5th ed. (London, 1745), 10	Thomas Barton, *Unanimity and Public Spirit* (Philadelphia, 1755), 4

Textual comparison, Roberts and Barton.

To his credit, Barton replied to Smith's queries without delay, albeit lamely.[42] In all of his rationalizations, it becomes clear that he was inspired by little beyond the frontier's wildfire of fear and anguish. Fame, reward, advancement—these had no meaning to one who had witnessed the terrible suffering in Carlisle and Huntington. If he sinned, it was not in the cause of personal gain. Those who criticized his thefts, he explained, simply ignored the impending catastrophe: "At a Time when Murder & Desolation crowded the aching Sight, & our poor back Settlers were daily forsaking their Habitations, & flying from the destroying Hands of barbarous Savages;—I thought it no *Crime,* in a Protestant Country, to stand up in Defence of a Protestant Cause; and beseech them "with one Mind & one Judgment," to guard against Popery & popish Tyrants. . . . I borrow'd, (or if you please, stole) such Extracts as were applicable to my Purpose.—In all this I could not imagine there was any *Crime.*"[43]

Barton's October 28, 1755, letter to Smith is crucial to appreciating his guilelessness and the degree to which he regarded his use of Roberts as something transcending issues of honesty. After he tries to excuse his theft, as we have seen, on the grounds of its relative inconsequence when appreciated within the context of the crisis that inspired it, he reminds Smith that he, Barton himself, had earlier objected to publishing it. Originally, he had intended it only for the ears of his congregations. In a conversation the two had had in York, he had forthrightly acknowledged the sermon's two principal defects: "ill Nature was predominant, & . . . many Thoughts in it were borrow'd." He recalled to his friend how he, Smith, first promised to "prevent" criticism of its rhetorical inelegancies and then dismissed Barton's second reservation by insisting that "there was no such Thing in the World as new Thoughts." Even after Smith had rather glibly set aside Barton's half-hearted, understated confession of his debt to others, Barton considered "throwing away Roberts's Part" (although we must conclude that that would have left a very abbreviated sermon indeed). To have done so, however, would have disappointed those who had requested that he publish exactly "that very one, they [had] heard me preach. . . . From this Dilemma, I freed myself, chusing rather to venture it as it was, than not Oblige my People, & shew my Concern for my injur'd King & Country.—"44

Following their earlier exchange in York, on August 15, he sent Smith a copy of the sermon. His cover letter shows his continuing reluctance to set it before a larger audience. As earlier, he tries to shift at least part of the decision for publishing it to Smith's scholarly and critical judgment. "I submit it entirely to your Direction," he wrote, "to suppress, or publish it, at your Discretion."45 He offers Smith another opportunity to delete any potentially offensive or inappropriate material when he requests a testimonial from Smith's hand: "If you think it worth an Impression; I must beg the Favor of you to add Something in Behalf of it: And whatever Corrections, or Amendments you shall be good enough to make, I shall thankfully acknowledge; And without such I should never venture to send it to the Press.—"46

Unanimity and Public Spirit was printed by Franklin and Hall in September 1755, to be sold for 9 pence.47 Most immediately, it seems to have produced the intended effect of galvanizing the collective will of the frontiersmen. Left to their own devices, the inhabitants of the backcounties united to meet successfully the threats that daily imperiled their lives. Barton's insistence on his pamphlet's salutary effect carries with it the ring of truth: "When I preach'd this Sermon, it had a good Effect upon all that heard it. . . . were it not for the Pains I took, few Inhabitants would have remain'd in these Parts.—This, Sir, is not boasting. Hundreds can testify it.—"48

In other respects, the discovery of the plagiarism threatened to undermine the proprietary's and the Church's twin efforts to discredit Quaker opposition to the war and to mount an effective counteroffensive following Braddock's defeat. Barton's opening paragraph in the October 28 letter reveals his appreciation of the plagiarism's negative impact: "I am equally surprized & sorry that the *Interest of the Church,* my *Character,* & *your Engagement* should be *in Danger of suffering,* by Means which might be thought insufficient to disturb any one of them."

The plagiarism also spawned rumors that tarnished Barton's career and fed his uncommonly profound insecurity. Throughout his life, gossip-mongers readily targeted Barton, and he even occasionally suspected evil-doers when apparently none was active;[49] but in 1755 some of the charges at least were genuine enough. Barton informed Smith that on October 19 he had "receiv'd a scurrilous, & anonymous Letter much upon the Subject of *robbing M^r. Roberts* &c." Of greater concern, he continues, were charges by the "uncharitable Author" that he, Barton, despised "*the Dissenters,*" an accusation patently designed "to make me odious in these Parts, where the Dissenters are many.—And indeed the Propagation of such a Falsehood would soon have that Effect."[50]

Apparently, this assault on Barton's character contributed significantly to his distress, for we find the missionary's tenuous self-assurance collapsing under the rumor campaign: "I am threaten'd, abus'd, & treated like a Criminal!—I cannot bear it.—"[51] The opprobrium under which he had to continue in his priestly offices must certainly have fueled Barton's determination to leave the Carlisle-Huntington-York circuit.[52] His exposure, moreover, cannot have but further exacerbated his worsening relationship with Presbyterian John Armstrong.

Before Barton and Smith succeeded in interring the plagiarism "in the dark backward and abysm of time," the former referred to it once more. Laconic and teasing, Barton discloses in a letter of November 2, 1755, that "M^r. Bradford is the Gent^n who has been so industrious to injure me. More of this in my next."[53] Although either the promised letter has been lost or Barton failed to provide further information, we may infer several possibilities from the remark. The Mr. Bradford identified here was clearly behind the apparently successful effort to discredit Barton. He may, furthermore, have authored the anonymous letter Barton referred to in his October 19 communication. In citing only the surname, Barton implies that Mr. Bradford is known to both himself and William Smith—his detractor is no obscure malcontent lurking in the shadows and requiring further identification. That the accuser was the Presbyterian Philadelphia printer William Bradford (3rd), is reinforced by one datum that Smith himself preserved. In his October 9 missive, Smith rehearses how he first learned of Barton's misdeed: "Your Sermon & Robert's [*sic*] were both put in the Coffee house, page confronted to page & your Name in the Title stigmatized both as *Thief & Murderer.*"[54] Smith's particularization "in the Coffee house" must surely denote William Bradford's London Coffee House, the print shop/gathering place he opened in 1754 on the corner of Market and Front Streets.

That Smith could enter the shop, view the indisputable evidence, manuever to remove "the Sermons from the Coffee-house," and promise Barton to "strive to prevent any ill-natured Exposure of you in the Prints" was the measure of his authority in Philadelphia at that time. "I shall strive to wipe off the Reproach wherever my Influence extends," he promised. Achieving that end, of course, would also erase any blame that might have attached itself to his own reputation. The silence into which the controversy subsided intimates that Smith's influence indeed must have extended far and wide.

Judging by the correspondence that has survived, Smith never faltered in his support for Barton. Whether or not he discussed the plagiarism with anyone else cannot be determined. Beyond Barton's reputation, of course, Smith had his own image, already under rather constant attack, to preserve. The most likely person in whom Smith might have confided, Richard Peters, never appears to allude to Barton's transgression. But because it is probable that Peters would have heard the same rumors bruited about Philadelphia that also found their way to Smith, it seems likely that he too participated in the suppression undertaken by Smith. It may be significant that, following the autumn of 1755, both Smith and Peters wrote letters warmly commending Barton's efforts on behalf of church and province.[55]

Barton, too, drew the veil of silence over his misdeed. Shaken, as we have seen, by Bradford's rumor-campaign, he informed Smith that he would "lay the whole Affair before the Archbishop & Society, by whose Decision I shall stand or fall.—"[56] Either he thought better of this and never apprised the Society or whatever communication he did dispatch has disappeared. After November 1755, he never alludes to the dubious use he made of Samuel Roberts.

This episode helpfully illustrates several noteworthy points. It shows us a mid-level proprietary Anglican agent responding to the frontier's crisis by freely, if ingenuously, pilfering the writing of another cleric, ironically a Dissenter. Vilified by at least one critic in Philadelphia as a "*Thief & Murderer,*" Barton, through his association with William Smith, the Anglican Church, and the Penn Proprietary, potentially exposed them all to censure and discredited the causes they advocated. William Smith's, and very probably Richard Peters's,[57] suppression of the rumor-mongering and the evidence implies a semi-official effort to shore-up the damage wrought by Barton's literary theft. Smith's triumphant spiriting away from the coffee house the pamphlets being compared and his having "the Prints" expeditiously censored succeeded not only in salvaging the images of all the parties at risk, but also in virtually burying the episode from historical scrutiny until modern times.

Instead of destroying his exchange with Barton, however, Smith reserved the correspondence for later examination or perhaps for adding to the list of whatever misdeeds Barton might enact in the future. His annotations on the cover of his emotional October 9, 1755, letter suggest that, for all that he later seemed to turn his back on the affair, Barton's plagiarism was far from being a dead thing in his own mind. Describing the packet's contents, he wrote: "To M^r. Barton, on finding [a] great Part of his Sermon taken from Mr Roberts. W^t his unsatisfactory Answers. Oct. 19th 1755–." And below this, with unintended historical irony that later readers may now savor, he added: "Correspondence to be preserved & re-examined on some future occasion." Indeed, the epistolary exchange was preserved and examined centuries later.

In addition, the affair also intimates that persons highly placed on the proprietary hierarchy—Richard Peters and Thomas Penn, most probably—identified Barton's potential usefulness as a propagandist and polemicist. Instead of sacrificing him to his detractors, the officials silenced the strident criticisms, or allowed them to subside, and rewarded the plagiarist.

Having just recently flirted with disgrace, Barton ironically soon found himself enjoying the modest favors that befell those who served the proprietary. For example, notwithstanding his potentially explosive conflict with Presbyterian John Armstrong, the Penns' able and powerful land-agent, surveyor, and leader of militia in Carlisle, Barton as we have seen succeeded in obtaining his commission as Anglican chaplain-at-large to the combined royal and provincial army preparing to march on Ft. Duquesne.[58] In 1759, he was transferred to a more rewarding and secure living in Lancaster, where he soon emerged as one of the principal intellectual influences in that community. Thomas Penn awarded him monetary gifts, and the SPG increased his salary. And his anonymous contribution to the pamphlet war ignited by the Paxton disturbances of 1763–64 brought him further rewards, the choicest being a lifetime right to farm on the Conestoga Manor.

In 1758, however, he had yet to prove that the apparent faith in him expressed by Smith, Peters, and Thomas Penn was not without foundation. Enjoying a prestigious position in the overwhelmingly Scots-Irish Pennsylvania Regiment, Barton, always prepared to report and interpret, would presumably be appreciated by a proprietary ever-vigilant of the prestige and power being accumulated by the Presbyterian faction. He would serve as the proprietary's eyes and ears, as its strategically placed informant and agent-of-influence. Additionally, he would represent proprietary interests against the potentially aggrandizing policies of Pennsylvania's rivals, Maryland and Virginia, which were also greedily eyeing the western lands disputed with France.

3

Memento Mori

You who live in this Land of Liberty—whose Fathers pass'd thro' the Dangers of an immense Ocean, & experienced many happy Deliverances—who early planted the Gospel in this remote Wilderness—who have shared Blessings & Privileges, never felt or enjoy'd by many Natives of the World—"Why will you die? . . ."

—Thomas Barton

BARTON'S WRITINGS COME DOWN TO US WITH A GREAT MANY MYSTERIES. Each of his long, major works provokes questions or is associated with some controversy. As we have seen, *Unanimity and Public Spirit* impeached his very integrity and judgment and continues to challenge our conception of the roles of eighteenth-century Anglican itinerant missionaries. The pamphlet *The Conduct of the Paxton Men, Impartially Considered,* published anonymously in 1764 and later attributed to him, invites searching inquiry into the evidence supporting his authorship; indeed, his supposed writing of a tract which audaciously contradicts what we know of his oft-expressed feelings for Native Americans and Scots-Irish Presbyterians demands explanation. Additionally, a long, untitled and unsigned epistemological work in his handwriting, now in the archives of St. James's Episcopal Church, Lancaster, leads one to wonder if Barton actually wrote it or simply transcribed it from some other source. Although the scholarly uniqueness of the treatise among Barton's writings makes valid stylistic comparisons difficult, style often being a function of content, it does occasionally sound like him, leading us to speculate further on his essaying such a philosophical, arcane subject.

Pivotal to this chapter, his manuscript 1758 war journal confronts us with an altogether different set of challenges. For one thing, in its present form it is unfinished, and that fact, together with its disillusionment with certain aspects of military life, invites us to suspect that he abruptly withdrew from the Forbes expedition altogether and returned to Conewago.[1] Secondly, the surviving journal manuscript is clearly a later, edited draft of Barton's original diary or notes.[2] In culling the journal for evidence of Barton's life and ideas, we must never forget this: what we have is an edited, revised, and possibly uncompleted version of the now-lost original.

Why did he start revising his journal? And why did he apparently fail to carry his account any further than September 26, 1758 (Forbes's army took possession of Ft. Duquesne at the end of November 1758)? Unless lost correspondence comes to light to fill us in on unknown events of the last months of 1758, we shall never know the truth beyond one certain probability: Barton experienced either at the time he wrote the journal or when he revised it some profound frustration or significant setback, if not reversal. Two unsigned letters, clearly in his exuberant style, intimate that he indeed remained with the Forbes expedition at least until the destruction of Fort Duquesne on November 24, 1758 and the burial of Braddock's dead on November 28.[3] Whatever might have prompted him to stop writing, granted that his original notes ceased with the September 26 entry, did not, therefore, persuade him to resign his commission. Several innuendos and allusions by Barton and John Armstrong, moreover, suggest that both men by that date had fallen under a cloud or clouds. Lacking evidence to the contrary, we may infer some ideological or religious conflict inspired questions or suspicions sufficient to put both men on the defensive.

The last extant reference by Barton to his participation in the Forbes campaign occurs in his short letter to the SPG written December 21, 1759, a full year after the reduction of Fort Duquesne. In it, he discusses his recent move to Lancaster, describes his new congregations, and details his clerical activities. Then, without transition, he concludes the letter: "I went into the Army for the Reasons which I gave General Forbes in a Letter, a Copy of which I enclose you, with his answer.— As it has always been my Aim thro' the Course of my Ministry to do every Thing that might tend to the Honour of Religion & the Credit of the Mission, I hope the Hon[ble]. Society will not disapprove of this Part of my Conduct.—"[4]

Two points are significant here: Barton's abrupt shift into a defensive tone strongly implies that he is responding to some earlier request from the SPG that he explain his behavior during the campaign, including perhaps his motives for accompanying Forbes—hence his forwarding copies of the original correspondence between himself and the general. Secondly, whatever motive or action might have been under scrutiny, it belongs to some larger pattern that provoked controversy, and is the part, moreover, he feels above censure—"I hope the Hon[ble]. Society will not disapprove of *this Part* of my Conduct" (my emphasis). His motivation for volunteering beyond question, what had Barton done that, even after a year, he feels no need to explain or rationalize?

Several allusions and misrepresentations of fact by both Barton and Armstrong intimate that Barton from the beginning of his maneuvering for Forbes's favor had behaved in a way inconsistent with his role as defined by others. Armstrong in fact employs the intriguing adjective *extraordinary* to register his contempt. Anticipating some accusations from Barton, who never appears to have made them, the colonel wrote on July 8, 1758: "I doubt not parson Barton will write you some very high Charge against me like Sacrilege, &c. *I have neither time nor inclination to trouble you with a detail of his Conduct, only that it is Still very extraordinary;* for the Publicks and your Sake, I have not Open'd his Conduct nor Character to the General—he is at present quiet, & I don't trouble my head with him."[5] In spite of his stated disinclination to trouble his correspondent, probably Peters, with "a detail of" Barton's "extraordinary" behavior, Armstrong, typical of people who feign such indifference to save face, goes on to elaborate what was probably distressing him: Barton, he says, "won't suffer himself to be Call'd a Chaplain to the [Third] Battalion, nor act under the Governor's Commission, but has procur'd a kind of Liberty from the General to go on the Expedition a Volunteer."[6]

Barton's first journal entry reveals that he himself may have come to regret his maneuvering for the special, voluntary role of Anglican chaplain-at-large in Forbes's army (rather than province-commissioned chaplain to the Third), for his journal entry suppresses what had actually transpired and instead misrepresents the circumstances under which he came to accompany the expedition: "Friday, 7th of July, receiv'd the Governor's Commission appointing me Chaplain to the 3rd Battalion of the Pennsylvania Regiment, commanded by Colonel Mercer; with a letter from the Secretary [Richard Peters] apologizing for my not having the Preference of the other two."[7] That is all Barton sets down. Missing here and later in the journal is his refusal of the governor's commission to the Third Battalion and his request for and receipt of the more prestigious chaplaincy Forbes later granted him. Indeed, even as the army began to march, Barton was already tailoring his own account of what had transpired. In another letter, after thanking Peters for the latter's recent communication, which included the commission to the Third authorized by Governor William Denny, he complains how "Bigots & Enthusiasts" [that is, New Side Presbyterians] have tried to prevent his going on the expedition and, more generally, obstructed his "Discharge of . . . [my] Duty in this Place" (that is, Carlisle).[8] More pointedly, he laments that the governor's commission (which he had in fact declined) "subjects me to the Power of a Man [that is, Colonel John Armstrong], who has already shewn himself an Enemy to that Cause which I am bound by every Tye of Conscience, Duty & Inclination to support."[9]

Barton uses strong language here—"a Man, who has already shown himself an Enemy" to his church. But for the survival of the astonishing, plagiarized *Unanimity* and evidence of the abuse to which it exposed him, we would have no insight into what might have prompted him to write in this way.

On July 5, 1758, the Anglican congregations of Cumberland and York counties addressed a remonstrance to general Forbes. In it they petition the commander to investigate an occurrence of several days earlier, for which they, as did Amstrong, employ the adjective *extraordinary:* "we are sensibly affected with the extraordinary & unprecedented Treatment given our Reverend & worthy Incumbent Mr. Barton on Sunday the second Day of this Instant July, by having an armed Messenger sent him, while he was performing Divine Service in his own Parish—ordering him to desist & dismiss the People."[10] In language recalling Barton's *Unanimity* and set down in Barton's hand—the remonstrance was clearly authored by Barton—the petitioners remind Forbes that they live in "a Time when Protestants of every Country & Denomination should join Heart & Hand to repel the common Enemy of all," not "propagate Dissension & Animosity among us." Accordingly, they ask Forbes "to enquire into this Affair, & restore us to that Ease & Satisfaction, which we have long enjoy'd under the Ministry of our laborious & very worthy Teacher."

Three days later, in his July 8, letter, Armstrong implies that he was the ultimate, if not the immediate, source for this impropriety. Describing a quarrel he had had with Forbes's Deputy Quartermaster General Sir John St. Clair, he lays direct blame on St. Clair for invading Barton's church: "a Quarrel ensu'd betwixt us, in the Course of which, Sir John, after appointing parson Barton to preach, he Stop'd him again in the time of reading prayers, but soon found his Error, & he and the parson join their Forces to England."[11] Evident from this is that Armstrong must have said something to provoke the notoriously temperamental St. Clair into interrupting the service that he, St. Clair, had originally authorized. Armstrong thus had every reason to anticipate that Parson Barton would indeed make "some very high Charge against me like Sacrilege," and must have been taken off guard when Barton shrewdly decided to write nothing explicit about the event.

In his reply to Peters, Barton never details what had recently taken place, nor does he even mention his having rejected Governor Denny's commission to the Third Battalion, a refusal Armstrong had already commented upon ten days earlier.[12] Rather, he deceptively maintains that he is "well pleas'd" with the governor's appointment to the Third and then pushes on, implying that he has reason to entertain loftier aspirations.

At the letter's conclusion, Barton observes that General Forbes had recently written him, in proof of which he supplies Peters with a copy of the former's "polite Letter." In almost all respects, the copy matches the one he sent the SPG a year later. The difference between the two, however, is that he deletes from the Peters copy Forbes's opening clause establishing that the general was actually responding to Barton's letter of the previous day: "*I am favour'd with yours of the 8th,* and am sorry to find that the Troops of the Communion of the Church of England are not properly provided with a Clergyman of their own Profession" (the italicized text identifies the part Barton deleted in the copy of Peters).[13] Also omitted by Barton is mention of his July 8 letter to Forbes professing eagerness to serve as Episcopalian chaplain to the "great Number of the Forces under your Command [who] are of the Communion of the Church of England."[14] Clearly, Barton edited and suppressed part of the correspondece between Forbes and himself to persuade Peters that the general had gratuitously sought out his, Barton's, services. Moreover, as already noted, nowhere in his July 18, 1758, letter to Peters does Barton speak of his refusal of Governor Denny's commission to the Third.

This episode reveals several significant facts about Barton. He capably out-manuevered the Presbyterians of the Pennsylvania Regiment from preventing his joining the expedition, for although they blocked his chaplaincy in their unit (opening the way for his less prestigious appointment to the Third Battalion of that regiment, which he subsequently refused), he obtained in the end greater honor as Anglican chaplain-at-large for Forbes's entire army. Additionally, both to the powerful Richard Peters and in the journal he was revising (presumably to be read by others) he sought to conceal the cunning with which he had carried the contest. As with his professions of urgent, ingenuous concern for the frontiersmen when trying to excuse his plagiarism in 1755, throughout his reconstruction of this episode he sets before us a persona whose only aspiration was to serve "the Honor of the Church, [and] the Satisfaction" of the people.[15] Thomas Penn himself seemed to confirm that Barton's recreation of himself in the most flattering light succeeded: "*Your consenting to go with General Forbes,* was much to your honour, and greatly conducive to the Public Service, & I do not at all wonder at the reception General Forbes gave you whose good understanding and conduct has proved of so great advantage to his Country."[16]

Armstrong, on the other hand, apparently withdrew into bitter reticency. Not only had Anglican Barton out-flanked him, but he must also have perceived how their mutual patrons had unhesitatingly supported his rival. Even with Richard Peters, he found it prudent to swallow his venom, and we should recall in this respect that Peters was more a worldly politician than an Episcopal priest, a man to whom Armstrong, for example, could freely voice his hope in the same letter that Pennsylvania's governor "will Castrate" a certain officer who had not acted with sufficient aggressiveness. Months later, Armstrong still referred to Barton only allusively: "as for Mr. B——n, I have not had the least Communication with him since I saw you, nor never intend to have. I have never been mistaken of that Gent^n, but shall Leave his Character to Persons of his Own Community."[17] Whatever had earlier angered Armstrong about Barton's character still obtained. In fact, two clues in the same letter, when set alongside Barton's abruptly breaking off his journal, offer possible insight into what might have occurred.

Immediately before denying having spoken with Barton, Armstrong tries to refute gossip concerning his participation in some unspecified religious conflict: "If any person has inform'd you that I have had any religious dispute . . . they have injur'd themselves & imposed upon you, for upon the strictest truth, tho' there has been a great deal of reason for Such Altercation yet have I had none, nor any body else that I know of."[18] That he mentions Barton's name immediately after employing the evasive "any person" tacitly associates the chaplain with the accuser he fears. It stands to reason as well that these two unyielding upholders of their faith would continue to collide over religious issues. Indeed, as though to confirm that Barton is the "any person" denoted here, Armstrong, as noted, had already unequivocally (in July 1758) accused Barton of readying some religious rumor-mongering: "I doubt not parson Barton will write you some very high Charge against me like Sacrilege, &c."[19] In both instances, one overt and the other inferential, Armstrong identifies Barton as the source for vague accusations of sacrilege or religious contentiousness to be lodged against him, Armstrong.

It might be significant that Armstrong's second letter (October 3, 1758) was written only one week after Barton's journal stops. Barton breaks off at the conclusion to one of the most vividly rendered episodes in his journal, the execution of John Doyle for desertion. Although he never explicitly criticizes what occurred during that autumn evening of Tuesday, September 26, 1758, his word choice, syntax, and selection of details make two things clear. Barton admired the unindulgent heroism with which "Papist" and presumably Irishman John Doyle unflinchingly faced his executioners; and he was mortified, if not outraged, by the purposeful desecration the firing squad inflicted on Doyle. To appreciate the complexity of Barton's reactions, the passage needs to be cited in full:

I walk'd with him to the Place of Execution, surrounded by a strong Guard.— He behav'd with uncommon Resolution;—exhorted his Brother-Soldiers to take Example by his Misfortunes;—To live sober Lives;—to beware of bad Company; to shun pretended Friends, & loose wicked Companions, "who, says he, will treat you with Civility & great Kindness over a Bottle; but will deceive & ruin you behind your Backs:—" But above all he charg'd them never to deser^t. When he saw the Six Men that were to shoot him, he enquir'd if they were good Marks-Men; and immediately strip'd off his Coat, open'd his Breast, kneel'd down, & said "Come Fellow-Soldiers, advance near me—do your Office well, point at my Heart, for God's sake do not miss me, & take Care not to disfigure me."—He would suffer no Handkerchief to be ty'd over his Face, but look'd at his Executioners to the last, who advanc'd so near him that the Muzzles of their Guns were within a Foot of his Body.—Upon a Signal from the Serjeant Major they fir'd, but shot so low that his Bowels fell out, his Shirt & Breeches were all on Fire, & he tumbled upon his Side;—rais'd one Arm 2 or 3 Times, & soon expir'd. A shocking Spectakle to all around him; & a striking Example to his Fellow Soldiers.—

Barton's unconcealed esteem for John Doyle's determination to die well reminds us of his unusually respectful description of the Delaware war-chief Captain Jacobs's epic-like death at Kittanning in 1756.[20] For all that they might have deserved their ends, Barton felt that the stoicism of each merited his memorializing how each death fulfilled, as it were, the ancient Greek ideal of *areté,* the art of dying with excellence.

The executioners' deliberate disembowelling of Doyle, their inflicting upon him an agonizing, humiliating death, on the other hand, might well have determined Barton to write or revise no further. This "shocking Spectakle" might even have inspired him to object strongly to the deliberate desecration of human life and thus place himself uncompromisingly against the rough exegencies of martial justice. In 1756, he had detailed a somewhat analogous episode wherein Indians attacked a young woman's funeral procession, drove off the mourners, "And what is unparallel'd by any Instance of Brutality, they even open'd the Coffin, took out the Corps and scalp'd her."[21] If any trait consistently stands out in Barton's character, it is that, for all his flaws, he could honestly identify what was ignoble and estimable in both Indians and Whites.

We shall never know what event or events might explain Armstrong's anticipation of accusations of "Sacrilege." Nor can we determine why Barton ceased revising his journal with his completing the narrative of John Doyle's terrible end. But certainly, the behavior of soldiers (most, if not all, Presbyterians) under the command of the Scots-Irishman Colonel John Armstrong might well be the cause: by desecrating and torturing an Irish Catholic who had confessed his sins and offered himself as an exemplar of Christian repentance and stoic heroism, they would have profoundly angered a cleric for whom death was one of life's defining rites.

∞

To anyone living on the Pennsylvania frontier in the 1750s and 1760s, violent death was an inescapable sight. Barton, however, reveals an enduring, almost medieval fascination with dying and death as a subject of recurrent meditation. A sketch of his seal displays a traditional iconic death's head and thigh bones. These are surrounded with royal regalia of the scepter, crown, and orb, all garlanded with the venerable Latin tag *Memento Mori,* "remember that you must die."

Thomas Barton's seal. (Stauffer Collection, the Historical Society of Pennsylvania.)

Some of his letters from this period resonate with the stark choric power of Greek tragedy and medieval *memento mori* literature:

Within three miles of Patterson's Fort was found Adam Nicolson and his wife, dead & scalp'd, his two Sons & a Daughter are carried off; William Wilcock & his wife, dead & scalp'd; Hugh Micheltree, & a Son of s^d Nicolson, dead & scalp'd, with many Children, in all about 17.

The same Day, one Sherridan, a Quaker, his wife, three Children & a Servant, were kill'd & scalp'd, together with one W^m. Hamilton, & his Wife, his Daughter, & one French, within Ten Miles of Carlisle, a little beyond Stephen's Gap.

It is dismal, Sir, to see the Distresses of the People; Women & Children screaming & lamenting, Men's Hearts failing them for Fear under all the Anguish of Despair.

> . . . now we know that our Danger hastens with the Encrease of the Moon, & we expect nothing but Death & Ruin every night.[22]

One of the most resonant of his surviving sermons is based on Ezekiel 18:31: "For why will ye die?"[23] What is noteworthy about his stopping the journal after the narrative of John Doyle's execution is that the episode appears to climax several earlier vignettes also illustrating Barton's absorption with death.

The less grave of these incidents occurred while Barton was visiting Fort Cumberland, Maryland. In the midst of his observations on unusual geographic features, always a source of fascination to him, and on the fort, which disappointed, he transcribed an inscription on a lead tablet memorializing four soldiers of the First Virginia Regiment killed Nov. 1756. The last part of the tablet celebrates their "Noble Ambition to distinguish Themselves: They engag'd a Party of the Enemy hard by Fort Du Quesne And fell gloriously fighting bravely, being greatly overpower'd by Superior Numbers."[24] Recognizing Barton's admiration of acts of desperate valor, we can appreciate his care in copying the inscription. As if to remind himself and his readers of the ironies which often undermine our existence, however, he adds that "some of those Men afterwards return'd, & are now Officers in the Virginia Service. They are perhaps the first who ever saw their own Monument, & read their own Epitaph."[25]

A more sobering episode took place on August 19. Barton begins simply enough: "Buried a Virginian Soldier this Day." After he watched the body "launch'd into a little Hole out of a Blanket, and there left naked," however, he "remonstrated against the Inhumanity as well as Indecency of it." The sergeant would do nothing because he had orders "not to return without the Blanket." To finish the service, Barton "got some small Bushes cut, & thrown over him."

Before concluding the entry for that day, Barton observes that almost "400 Persons are now in the Hospital, sick of Fluxes, Diarhoas, Agues, Fevers, Small-Pox &C," a relatively alarming number for an army of some 6,000 men. His implication should be clear enough: the single example of inhumanity and indecency he had recorded is being replicated on a scale involving hundreds. "Why will ye die?" indeed.

On September 25 Barton was ordered to attend a group of five prisoners sentenced to be executed. He found them in tears "under terrible Apprehensions of approaching Death," but was apparently more greatly distressed to perceive "very little Sense of Religion in any of them." His mortification was reaffirmed when four of them, learning that they had been pardoned, "seem'd more affected and more pentitent at the Thoughts of Living than the Thoughts of dying."

Why the fifth, John Doyle, was not pardoned with the others remains unclear. Possibly, his commanding officer, Captain James Patterson of the Pennsylvania Regiment's First Battalion, did not plead for him as the officers of the other men had for their men.[26] Or perhaps his being Roman Catholic lessened his value. We do not know. What we do learn from Barton, however, is that Doyle displayed a true Christian humility and resolution that distinguished him from the pardoned soldiers. "Brought up a Papist," Doyle had confided, "his Conscience never supply'd him with sufficient Reasons to renounce that Profession, he was resolved to dye one." For Barton, such uncommon resolution was evidence of heroism.

Doubtless, if Doyle's commitment appealed to Barton's idealism, what the condemned soldier said next must have struck an even greater sympathetic response in the Anglican chaplain: "As he made no Doubt but the Prayers of good Men would avail much, he beg'd of me to stay with him the few Minutes he had to live, & attend him to the Place of Execution; to which I agreed.—"[27] Although a Catholic and therefore an outsider—and Barton's writings consistently disclose that he detested and feared Catholics, as much as, if not more than, marauding Indians—the deserter John Doyle exhibited a far greater mastery of the art of dying, the age-old *ars moriendi,* than the pardoned men, whose "very little Sense of Religion" had so mortified Barton. That the man should continue to evince up to his death the ennobling stoicism Barton describes in this passage and then be viciously debased through torture might have proved intolerable. If the "indecent" burial of the Virginian drove Barton to remonstrate against the indifference accorded the dead man, then we must credit that Doyle's execution would have produced a proportionately greater revulsion.

It is possible, furthermore, that Barton and Armstrong once more confronted one another across religious trenches dug a hundred years earlier. Of all the five men sentenced to be shot, John Doyle alone was a soldier in the Pennsylvania Regiment. Unlike the commanders of the other men, Captain Patterson evidently did not appeal to Forbes for a pardon.[28] Colonel Hugh Mercer, moreover, commander of the regiment's Third Battalion, to which Barton had been originally commissioned, presided over the general court-martial that condemned Doyle. It is possible, therefore, that Colonel John Armstrong might have been drawn into a fray involving several men under his command. Even if he did not, as he maintained, exchange words with Barton—"I have not had the least Communication with him"—he would not have dispassionately tolerated Barton's scruples undermining his regiment's military discipline. Hence his sharp words on Barton and his suspicion of accusations against him of "religious dispute" in the letter to Peters a week after after Doyle's execution. That October 3 missive may indeed allude to such a fray when Armstrong admits to there having been "a great deal of reason for Such [a religious] Altercation."[29]

After Barton's entry under September 26, we have no formal writing that can be identified as his with absolute certainty until the December 21, 1759, letter to the SPG, sent from Lancaster. At least two anonymous letters (dated November 28 and December 6, 1758) published in Benjamin Franklin's *Pennsylvania Gazette* after the fall of Fort Duquesne, however, are probably his.[30] A fuller analysis of Barton's style appears below in the discussion of his authorship of the 1764 pamphlet *The Conduct of the Paxton Men, Impartially Considered.* The attribution of the two letters to Barton depends upon some of the same arguments elaborated later. The brevity of these communications, however, will not allow the same kind of thorough comparison with other known specimens of his writings. Nevertheless, several points may be advanced.

Barton was familiar to Franklin's printing business. Franklin had already published his *Unanimity and Public Service* in 1755. The *Pennsylvania Gazette*'s printing in 1763 of an anonymous letter dated "Lancaster, July 28" which closely echoes and parallels one Barton had sent to Richard Peters on July 5,[31] confirms Barton's practice of writing anonymous letters for publication in the *Gazette.* Also to be recognized is his letter to Thomas Penn, wherein he admits to having written a long justification for more roads in Pennsylvania that appeared anonymously in the *Pennsylvania Gazette.*[32] Additionally, other missives or paraphrases of letters, published in the newspaper anonymously, detailing the troubles in the trans-Susequehanna counties for the years 1755–58, occasionally recall phrasing and syntax characteristic of Barton's writing.[33] There is little question, then, that he served the *Gazette*'s readers as a kind of on-the-scene, anonymous correspondent.

Beyond this, the two letters in question simply sound to this reader like Barton. Barton possessed a very distinctive epistolary voice, one readily recognizable for its energetic rhythms and cadences; its predilection for parenthetical phrases and hendiadys (that is, a linking together of words expressing the same idea by means of a copulative conjunction); its fondness for personification and other figures of speech such as synecdoche and metonymy; and its reliance on a formulaic, almost predictable vocabulary when treating certain subjects. What confirms the attribution is not only a focus on death, unusual in most military writing of the period, but also outrage over the enemy's disrespect for the British dead, a desecration of human remains that we have also seen distressing him in the journal, as well as some other writings.

If, as seems likely, the November 28, 1758, letter published in the *Pennsylvania Gazette*[34] announcing the fall of Fort Duquesne is Barton's, then that communication helps reinforce our appreciation of Barton's insistence on coupling death with issues of respect and honor. In all of its resonant indignation, the passage reads as follows: "To-day a great Detachment goes to *Braddock's* Field of Battle, to bury the Bones of our slaughtered Country-men, many of whom were butchered in cold Blood by (those crueller than Savages) the *French,* who, to the eternal Shame and Infamy of their Country, have left them lying above Ground ever since. The unburied Bodies of those killed since, and strewed round this Fort, equally reproach them, and proclaim loudly, to all civilized Nations, their Barbarity."

The second report (December 1758) expresses more graphically the writer's feelings that such abuse is tentamount to blasphemy, and it does so with cadences and syntax unmistakably Barton's. This letter's principal motive is to convey vividly how the French abandoned themselves to or supported their Indian allies in purposely desecrating British soldiers through torture and dismemberment, thereby defiling human life itself. Barton writes that the remains of "our dear brave Fellow Soldiers who fell" when Major James Grant's force of some 300 was massacred on September 14, 1758, are still strewn over three miles of ground "to within 100 Yeards of" Fort Duquesne.[35] While the Indians were burning alive prisoners taken at that defeat, the French officers laughed at "the cruel Sight, and . . . inhuman Scene." Rising to his climax, Barton like a priest-prophet from another epoch unleashes his solemn curse on the French desecrators: "No wonder then that they should dread the just Resentment of the Army. From this Time let the applauded Titles of Polite and Humane, no more honour the Savage Frenchmen. Hands, Feet, Skulls, and Bones were picked out from the Ruins of the Fort. After such (more than savage) Usage, what might they not expect from an enraged Army?"

This voice is distinctive. It is the cry of anguish and wrath, and it inhabits a realm alien to exegencies of military discipline and political expedience. It is the same indignant voice that excoriated British soldiers who dumped the body of one of their own, naked, into a hole for want of a blanket and who set afire and disemboweled a repentant Roman Catholic resolved to die nobly and manfully.

∞

During the months after the fall of Fort Duquesne, Barton disappears. His activities and whereabouts are unclear. How long did he stay with the western expedition? Did he return, disenchanted and disgusted, to his plantation in Reading township shortly after he wrote the *Pennsylvania Gazette* of the French atrocities at the Forks of the Ohio? H. M. J. Klein and William F. Diller maintain that "Chaplain Barton remained with the troops until some time after the forces under General Forbes had taken possession of Fort Duquesne on Nov. 25, 1758."[36] They offer no support for this, but indeed he might well have stayed in the west for a while. A letter of Thomas Penn implies as much.

Over the course of his career, Barton often sent the proprietor detailed descriptions of unsettled parts of Pennsylvania, identifying features of agricultural, geological, and mineralogical importance that would assist Penn in determining how best, if at all, to open them for settlement. In March of 1761, Penn thanked Barton "for your account of the Lands in the back parts of the Province."[37] In this letter, he apologetically answers a missive of Barton, one he, Penn, had not adequately responded to in his earlier communication of May 10, 1760. Barton's "account of the lands," therefore, might have been sent late in 1758 or during the first months of 1759 and must have described the new territories he had travelled through in 1758. Evidently, Barton had urged opening the newly secured area to colonization because Penn takes exception to Barton's earlier enthusiasm. I "believe," he replied, "we must not think of making Settlements on the Ohio 'til the next Age."[38] To obtain the information Penn referred to, Barton would have needed opportunity to explore the newly conquered territory about Fort Pitt, where Colonel Mercer of the Pennsylvania Regiment's Third Battalion was overseeing that fort's construction on the ruins of Fort Duquesne. The journal reveals him frequently satisfying his curiosity by undertaking other exploratory trips in already settled areas. Investigating the Ohio River lands would have been for him a natural way to occupy his time during the idle days of garrison duty at Fort Pitt or Fort Ligonier.

By January, however, he had probably returned home. Surviving parts of his church record book for the years 1755–59 in York county record that he began performing marriages again at least by January 29, with another on March 29.[39] Although fragmentary, this documentation implies that he seems to have been carrying out minimal duties in the Bermudian-Conewago settlements, possibly biding his time as he readied himself to move.

If we scrutinize his correspondence for the period 1755–59 carefully, we will perceive that he had been laboring for many years to escape the dangers and poverty of his missionary life on the frontier. On the surface, Barton struck the assuring stance of a man energetically and resolutely committed to upholding the twin causes of church and proprietary. Many letters repeat his determination to serve. In March 1757, for example, he wrote to the bishop of Oxford of his hope "that God will give me Grace to persevere in the Worst of Times & the worst of Circumstances, with all my Endeavours to advance the Interest of his true Religion & of my King and Country."[40] With some variation Barton often iterated this formula. Despite the bold front, however, several clues reveal that he was in fact already maneuvering for a transfer shortly after he assumed his incumbency on the frontier. As we have already seen, his November 8, 1756, report to the society recorded the magnitude of his disappointment and feeling of reversal after Braddock's massacre: "Just when I was big with the Hopes of being able to do Service . . . , we receiv'd the melancholy News that our Forces under the Command of General Braddock were defeated."[41] Distressed by the far-reaching consequences of that disaster, he nonetheless reassured his superiors of his "happiness," because by "being plac'd here. . . . God has enabled me to do some Service to our pure Protestant Religion in spite of its most inveterate Enemies." The rationalization sounds overstated, and his qualified disappointment is reinforced throughout the letter, not in the least by the report's disorganization, suggesting his uncertainty of how to confront the sundry, once unforeseen challenges now besetting his ministry.

That Barton had come to regret the conditions he and his young family found themselves in is stressed in a letter written merely seven days before this November 1756 report by his friend William Smith to the SPG secretary, Dr. Philip Bearcroft. Smith unequivocally puts the society on notice that all is far from well with their missionary in Conewago. Barton's and Smith's letters at this time, in fact, may embody a concerted plan by the friends to force some improvement in Barton's career, for Smith, after praising his colleague's work—"he is the Darling of his People"—observes, in proof of his valuation, that "I have just been up among them."[42] This also tells us that he had opportunity to confer first-hand with Barton and perhaps formulate a mutual strategy. What Smith says next became a leitmotif throughout Barton's career. Stressing that his congregations "do all they can for M^r. Barton," he pointedly warns that "if the Society do not grant him some Gratuity over his Salary in these direst Times, I fear he must leave them & seek a Living elsewhere." As time was to prove again and again, the SPG, hard put to field capable missionaries, could not ignore this threat to leave.

On the next day, Smith received from Barton's people a supportive testimonial on their minister's behalf, which he promptly forwarded to the society on November 5, reinforced with still another letter of his own. The timing of his three congregations' testimonial suggests that Barton or Smith, or both, might have encouraged its writing. In his second letter, Smith elaborates on his friend's dire situation once more, implicitly emphasizing the prudence and desirability for providing him with some additional material compensation: "I observe M^r. Barton's several Congregations have modestly hinted at their Inability to perform their Engagements. Yet I am sure they will do their best & M^r. Barton does not complain; tho' when I was lately in back Company with our Governor to the Frontiers, I could learn that he was much pinch'd."[43] Smith concludes with the hope that the society will "kindly consider what I hinted at in" his earlier letter.

William Smith's November 5 communication is a noteworthy effort on his friend's behalf. It reveals, moreover, that he has put the unpleasant business of Barton's plagiarism behind him. It also sheds light on Barton's apparent role as both proprietary agent, as well as Anglican missionary. Smith's opening paragraph, the letter's longest, elaborately urges the need for maintaining missions in the unstable backcountry, where "They will be so many Watch-Towers" planted against "the bloodiest of all Enemies, a Race of merciless Savages," as well as to offset the estimable militant spirit of "the Presbyterians and other Dissenters."[44] Beset from every quarter, the frontier's, indeed, the province's, very survival requires nothing less than the civilizing influence of a capable and dedicated Anglican teacher-warrior like Barton. Smith writes: "Our People now, inspired by their zealous Missionary, & kept constantly in mind of their holy Protestant Religion & inestimable Privileges, exert themselves manfully for the Cities of their God against a Popish & Savage Enemy; and I am sure were not the Sense of these Blessings to be extended backwards, as far as our Settlements extend, nothing could prevent our People from being seduced by busy Jesuits, & mixing gradually with our French Foes."[45] Smith thus argues that Barton and his work will help guarantee a Protestant Pennsylvania. "The *whole Country*," he summarizes, "is, therefore, under the highest Obligation to the Society for this New Mission, *both in a civil & religious Light*" (my emphasis). If we have reason to speculate on why the SPG and Thomas Penn unhesitatingly supported Barton's mission in York and, later, Lancaster counties, Smith articulates their reasoning: for all his insecurity, and, indeed, his idealism and naive bungling, the Anglo-Irishman had proven resourceful in helping stabilize the frontier and in advancing the cause of the Church of England. His loyalty was beyond question. And unlike his two predecessors, the Reverends Richard Locke and George Craig,[46] he was not inflexible, uncompromising. Indeed, as we shall see, his insecurity, a weakness bordering at times on paranoia, opened him to various kinds of manipulation.

Smith was not alone in his campaign to improve Barton's lot. Richard Peters, too, championed his cause. On September 16, 1756, he wrote that "Mr Barton . . . deserves the commendations of all Lovers of the Country. . . . In short, . . . he is a most worthy, active and serviceable Pastor and Missionary."[47] It is apparently to this letter that Thomas Penn refers when he thanks Peters for "the account you have given me of M[r]. Barton's conduct."[48] Although Penn did not at that time reward Barton, as he would later, he did send him a short personal letter, commending Barton's "behaviour, in the dangerous Situation" he inhabited and closing with the desire that "you will accept my hearty thanks for these Services" and a promise to communicate his pleasure to the society.[49]

The SPG responded favorably, if modestly, to the concerted urging of Smith, Peters, and Penn. In 1757 it awarded Barton a gratuity of £20 and following his return from the western campaign, it increased his annual salary another £20.[50]

In addition to struggling to obtain a living wage, however, Barton had been quietly campaigning for reassignment, probably to the Anglican paradise of Maryland or Virginia, where the Church of England enjoyed the prestige of a wealthily established church, although he would willingly have accepted other locations. In April 1758, immediately before Forbes's army left Carlisle, he explained to Thomas Penn that he had already written to "the Society some Time ago, requesting to be remov'd."[51] Having heard not a thing, he continues, "I am oblig'd to renew my application." His situation seemed desperate indeed. Beyond everything else, for some reason he feels betrayed. His people's failure or inability to provide his living has left him unable "to maintain my family or support the Interest of Religion in these Parts." What precisely he intends in his full explanation is obscure, but it seems related to a point he had made earlier in the same letter: "had they stood their Ground, I would have cheerfully combated Danger & Distress in their Service." Beyond their financial impoverishment, had his congregations failed to follow his attempts to rally them against their enemies? Had they not supported him in his conflict with the dissenting majority? Is he alluding to some weakness or desertion by them in his skirmish with Armstrong? Their failure remains ambiguous, but Barton is prepared to abandon whatever efforts he had undertaken on their behalf: "I hope the Ven[ble]. Society will permit me," he repeats, "to remove to some other Mission."

In subsequent, now missing, communications to Thomas Penn, Barton asked his friend and patron to bring the matter before the SPG himself, for in January of 1759 Penn indicated that he had mentioned to Archbishop Thomas Secker "what you wished me to do." Again Barton failed to obtain permission to relocate; nonetheless, he was given every reason to appreciate the esteem with which men like Penn, now his advocate, and Secker regarded him. Penn continued: "I found he did not approve of your contemplated removal; but he proposed, that twenty pounds sterling per annum should be added to your salary: for, his grace observed, that a person so capable as you are, to advise and assist the people in your neighbourhood, could not be spared for any other mission: And, on that consideration, the society had agreed to this augmentation of your salary."[52]

Missing documents once more conceal exactly what occurred next. Having been told he must continue to serve the Conewago mission, albeit with a higher salary, Barton next turns up in Lancaster performing the Easter service at St. James's and taking up residence in that same town. Discovered on the inside cover of "an old book . . . in the hand of M[r]. Barton" is the following inscription: "Arrived and settled at Lancaster, May 15, 1759, but first preached there as minister of the place, on Easter Day, the 15th of April, 1759."[53] Had Barton's friends prevailed upon the society to relent? or had Barton, too demoralized by years of penury, Indian attacks, and religious conflict and by his recent experiences with Forbes's army, simply decided to resign, thereby forcing the SPG to agree to his relocation at some remove from the frontier rather than lose him altogether? This last might well be the explanation, for an analogous situation in 1764 produced a rather similar resolution—disillusionment resulting in threats to resign or leave Pennsylvania, followed by the giving of considerable material rewards, bribes actually, if he agreed not to leave the province.

It also seems likely that Barton's success in the Conewago mission, coupled with the Anglo-Irishman's proven flexibility and adaptability, impressed the SPG as skills suited to resolve long-standing difficulties in the mission serving Pennsylvania's second-most important city. On December 21, 1759, for example, Barton wrote the society that on moving to Lancaster, he "found the Mission in great Confusion, occasion'd by some unhappy Disputes, which long subsisted between the Gentleman I have the Honour to succeed & the People—If I can be instrumental in putting an End to them, I shall think myself happy."[54] Actually, both of Barton's predecessors, Englishman Richard Locke and Scot George Craig, unaccustomed to the assertiveness of the St. James vestrymen, requested transfer from Lancaster. Although Craig was actually given a new assignment in 1758, he continued to minister to the Lancaster congregation.[55] Barton's stubborn determination to leave his frontier mission must have inspired a compromise whereby he accepted transfer to Lancaster as a troubleshooter of established credentials. What neither Barton nor the SPG could anticipate, however, was that problems would soon evolve in colonial America's largest inland town that would prove as demoralizing as any of the adversities he had survived over Susquehanna.

4
"A Swarm of Sectaries"

The County of Lancaster contains upwards of 40,000 Souls;— Of this Number not more than 500 can be reckon'd as belonging to the Church of England; The Rest are German Lutherans, Calvinists, Mennonists, Moravians, New-Born, Dunkars, Presbyterians, Seceders, New Lights, Covenanters, Mountain-Men, Brownists, Independents, Papists, Quakers, Jews &c.— Amidst such a Swarm of Sectaries, all indulg'd & favour'd by the Government, it is no Wonder that the National Church should be borne down.—

—Thomas Barton

OCCASIONALLY, IT IS CONVENIENT TO PERCEIVE BARTON'S LIFE IN PENN-sylvania as a connected sequence of beginnings. Coming to Norriton about 1751, he set up his own school. He then moved to Philadelphia to teach at William Smith's academy. Shortly after, he married, resigned his post, sailed to England and there received ordination into the Anglican ministry and authorization as an itinerant missionary in the SPG. It must have seemed to Barton that when he and his family took up residence in western York county they would be able to settle into assured places in the small, albeit struggling, Church-of-England society that had never enjoyed a resident minister during its brief period of existence. The French and Indian War, however, so disrupted life in the Conewago settlements that within three years Barton was on the move again, marching to the Forks of the Ohio as a chaplain in John Forbes's powerful army. Then, while Colonel Henry Bouquet carried the campaign westward after the reduction of Fort Duquesne, Barton returned east, eventually taking charge of new congregations in Lancaster county and a life, he hoped, secured from the uncertainties of Indian warfare and the tensions generated by the New Awakening and stridently intractable Scots-Irish Presbyterians and other religious "enthusiasts."

Within four years of taking up residence in Lancaster, however, he became embroiled in the so-called Paxton affair or controversy (1763/4), an upheaval which must have impressed him as barely short of a nightmare.

79

From about 1764 on, he explored several opportunities to relocate to happier, more remunerative circumstances, but after the Revolution erupted, he boarded up his churches after he was forbidden to preach. As the end approached, he watched his patrons die off, and his friends either join the patriots, return to England, or suffer far worse than he. It became clear to him then that there was no place left in the American colonies where he might enjoy the life he aspired to. When, in 1778, he was expelled from the new state, he hung on in poverty and ill health for almost two years, awaiting for a ship to return him to the island where he had begun and thereby allow his life to achieve the symmetry of closure. But even there, his expectancy eventuated in defeat only, for he died in the city of New York as his ship prepared to leave.

Many beginnings, then, with few decisive endings or even, and certainly, fewer sustained periods of stability. As with the Scots-Irish who everywhere challenged him, Barton consistently revealed in his letters an inexorable restlessness, an implacable disposition to move on. In part, his existence as a client dependent on the good graces of the Penn proprietary fueled his insecurity and restlessness. One wonders if this "unrootedness" was in fact part of a universal legacy shared by migrants from the north of Ireland or even all Irish, rather than simply a characteristic we have come to associate with the Scots-Irish.[1] Additionally, his very vocation put him constantly on the horse trails and roads linking his churches, thus reinforcing his disquiet.[2]

Much of his discontent derived also from the impecuniousness that defined the missionary's life. Even with occasional monetary gifts from Thomas Penn and salary increases from the society, Barton, like most SPG itinerants in the colonies, had a hard time surviving. With his parishioners themselves so impoverished that they could not provide the agreed-upon allowance, maintaining life and family became nearly impossible. For example, notwithstanding their fair promises and their having set aside glebe lands in Huntington township hard by the newly erected log church, Barton's Conewago/Bermudian parishioners, even before the frontier collapsed, had failed to clear the glebe of its forest. Hence, at the outset of a new career, joined with a young wife and a child, Barton found himself "under a Necessity of purchasing a small Plantation, & building on it at my own Expense; by which Means I embarras'd myself in Debt, in Hopes the People would assist me in in paying for it, . . . But [the] dismal Turn in our Affairs renders it impracticable."[3] The farm, situated two townships' distance from Christ Church, forced upon him additional disadvantages and hardships.

The unmarried SPG itinerant for Reading, Mr. Alexander Murray, has left us a particularly accurate appraisal of the challenges faced by himself

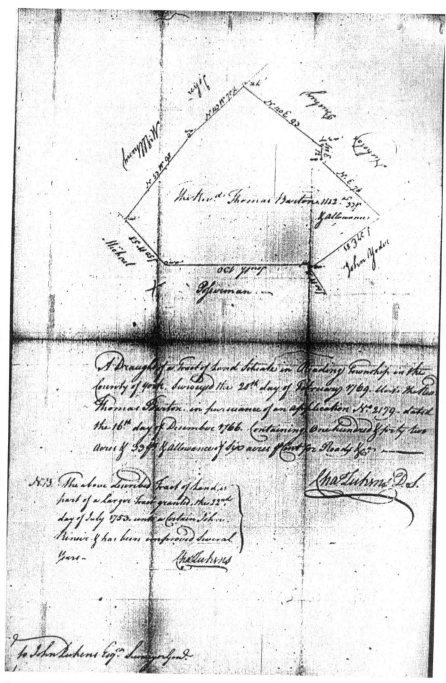

Survey, February 20, 1769, of Thomas Barton's plantation in Reading township, York (now Adams) county. (From the copy in the Adams County Historical Society, Gettysburg, Pa.)

and his two backcountry colleagues, Thomas Barton and William Thomson. As late as 1764, he advised the society's secretary that all three missionaries were "obliged to itinerate to our different congregations which are distant 30, 20, 18, 15 Miles from our respective places of residence and that in the severest Seasons of extreme heat and cold . . . So that I am often surprised how such of my Brethren subsist, who have large famiilies, as M[r]. Barton whose singular merit I humbly think deserves the notice of the Venerable Society."[4] Contemplating the straitened livings of Barton and Thomson makes Murray appreciate the comparative ease of his own charge: "I am still a Single Man and it will be prudent for me to continue such in my present circumstances."

It should not surprise us, then, that Barton's letters often allude to indebtedness and disclose him borrowing against his salary. His perennial impoverishment drove him to look into more promising circumstances elsewhere and soon eroded whatever improvement to his situation he might have immediately obtained in moving to the town of Lancaster in 1759.[5]

One small group of letters dating from 1759–61 sadly illuminates how powerfully indebtedness and near-poverty had ensnared Barton. His formal announcement to the society that "A few Weeks ago I remov'd my Family to Lancaster,"[6] was also accompanied by the report that he had begun to put his accounts in good order, for he wrote of trying to set right a two-year old claim against him and begs the society to pay "my Bill in Favour of M[r]. West." Like most of his brethren, Barton had to borrow in advance against his yearly allowances in order to survive the gap created when his stipend for one fiscal year ran out before the next started. It was near-poverty that Alexander Murray also noted in the letter cited above: we must, Murray complained, receive "at the year's end . . . so much as would satisfy an ordinary mechanic."[7] This annual need was to cause Barton great anguish the following year.

Visiting Philadelphia during the first week of December 1760, Barton borrowed £50 against his allowance, dating the note the 25th of December, when repayment was due. He post-dated the debt because he would have no opportunity to return in the dead of winter from Lancaster, over sixty miles away, to attend to the debt in person. Bad weather apparently prevented the bill from reaching the SPG treasurer, Mr. Pearson, until about two weeks after it fell due. Whatever his motive—he may have suspected forgery because of the irregular dating[8]—Pearson refused to accept the claim in January 1761 and again thirty days later after Barton resubmitted it.

Barton protested his treatment. Not only had Pearson insulted Barton's calling, but his stubbornness, Barton wrote, also "affected my Credit & Usefulness."[9] Under provincial law creditors who claimed "non Acceptance [and] Protest[ed] non Payment" made Barton liable for another ten guineas in penalties. His situation had become untenable: "I enclose you an Account of the Damages of the protested Bill, which I am sorry to tell you I was oblig'd to pay with *Borrow'd Money.*—This matter has injur'd me no little in Mind, Reputation, & Interest."[10]

Barton officially remonstrated his mistreatment on July 6, 1761. An annotation on the same letter reveals that it was "Read at the Committee Oct. 12, 1761." Evidently, the SPG did nothing, forcing William Smith to enter the fray on his friend's behalf. The following year, Smith painstakingly described the events that had occurred, and did so in language free of Barton's characteristic hyperbole and emotion. He incisively defined the problem faced by all the missionaries when he observed that they had to execute their responsibilities within an essentially materialistic society. Allowing that "M[r] Barton was wrong" to post-date the original bill, common enough practice among the society's itinerants, Smith insisted that it should in no way have opened him to the abuse he had endured from Mr. Pearson or from the merchants who clamored for repayment. The penalties indeed compounded Pearson's insult with further injury because in Pennsylvania a missionary with poor credit became a pariah. Smith explained: "This Province is a Country of Merchants, & the Usefulness of a Missionary can no way be more effectually destroyed with them than by such a *Slur* upon his Credit. M[r] Barton is a Man of very tender & delicate Feelings, & I am sure the affair has robbed him of many an hour's rest. Nor indeed is he yet in Circumstances to bear such a Loss."[11] Smith did more than protest his friend's unkind usage, however: "I have just," he wrote, "settled the Matter for M[r] Barton . . . without suffering it to make Noise & have paid the Damages."[12] He now hopes the society will put the matter to rest agreeably. With Smith's intervention, the "Pearson affair," although not Barton's impecuniousness, disappears from sight.

If Barton's indebtedness continuously eroded his peace of mind, the financial realities of St. James's Church during those early years reinforced his frustration. He discovered that his new church lacked even a library— "if there is any . . . I have never been able to find it."[13] Accordingly, he requests that he be allowed "to keep the Library which I receiv'd from them." The antecedent of *them* is ambiguous, but Barton may refer to the trans-Susquehanna congregations he mentions in his previous paragraph as still benefitting from his continuing visits. In this reading, then, he petitions the society for permission to retain books given to him by his earlier parishioners as personal gifts; he does not desire to make off with whatever parish library the society might have provided for Christ Church. Surely, he would not dispossess that church of its books just as his friend, William Thomson, as financially pinched as Barton, if not more so, was about to commence his incumbency in the Conewago settlements. Without a sound library, teacher Barton would be hard put "to propagate Religion & Virtue" in a town where his small congregation was beseiged by "such a Swarm of Sectaries."[14] His immediate perception of the need for a church library also eventuated, as we shall see, in his playing a central role in founding the town's first public library.

Many dissenters resented or feared even a minimal Anglican presence among them. The Church of England's official ties to the Penn proprietary, the Pennsylvania mission's manuevering to establish an American bishopric, and its potential to become an established church supported by mandatory, universal tithes—practices that the Scots-Irish remembered from Ireland as abusive and oppressive—these threats often alienated most of the other Protestants, for many of the German pacifist sectarians had also fled the oppression of state-supported churches. The only denominations not profoundly apprehensive already shared with the Church of England a history of episcopacy and of government support in their places of origin and a strong tradition of liturgical worship, the Swedish and German Lutheran and the German Reformed churches.

In 1760 Barton again confronted a financial crisis involving his Lancaster mission. He pointedly stressed that the Church must find ways of appealing to Lancaster's "principal Inhabitants," the Germans, and the means he proposed exposed both the fiscal straitjacket crippling his missionary effort and the ingenious skill with which he struggled to improve his church's standing.[15]

The many Lutherans who would happily send their children to St. James's, indeed, who would attend the church themselves, failed to do so because, great lovers of church music that they were, they knew that his church had no "Instrument to celebrate the Praises of God in the Manner that they have been us'd to." For want of an organ, in other words, the Church of England would lose potential converts in Lancaster. One of his parishioners, a physician highly esteemed in Lancaster and a man who appreciated the predilections of the German community, came to the church's rescue. Barton wrote: "Dr. [Adam Simon] Kuhn . . . has propos'd to us to purchase a small Organ of about £60 sterl[ing] Price, & that he would not only give us five Pounds towards it, but play for us gratis.— Besides this Benefaction, I have obtain'd £15. more, and shall use my best Endeavours to obtain the whole."[16]

The decision about 1761 to replace the old, undersized church building taxed the resources of St. James's congregation far beyond the challenge of raising money for an organ. Barton's December 6, 1760, letter, in fact, records that something of the bad feelings that had driven his predecessors, Richard Locke and George Craig, from Lancaster still lingered about his rectory. In previous communications he had lamented that his people in the rural satellite parishes of Pequea and Caernarvon exhibited a more estimable and authentic Christianity than their brothers and sisters in Lancaster: "the Misfortune here is, that some People puff'd up with a Notion of their superior Knowledge, Fortunes & Families, seem apprehensive of ranking with the meaner Sort, if they shew'd that Respect to Religion which is due to it."[17] The poor condition of the old log church and the missing library also bespoke a stinginess that the financial difficulties of building of a new church later confirmed.

Embarrassed by being unable to complete construction, Barton and his vestry were compelled to resort to the extremity of a kind of public appeal. The *Pennsylvania Gazette* for March 12, 1761, announced a fundraising lottery to benefit St. James's. It began:

The Members of the Church of England in the Borough of Lancaster, sensible of the Honour due to Religion and the Service of GOD, have hitherto, without any Aid from the Public, exerted their utmost Abilities to erect a Church in this Place; but finding themselves unable, from the Fewness of their Numbers, to finish and compleat it, are oblig'd, in Imitation of many of their pious and sensible Fellow-Christians in this and the neighbouring Provinces, to have Recourse to a small Lottery, to enable them to do it, or to leave the Building, begun (they humbly hope) with a good Design, unfinished.[18]

When the lottery failed to bring in the amount hoped for, the church officers tried another tactic. Once again they advertised in the *Gazette,* but this time they included the notice as part of a larger "scheme" (the word used by the *Gazette* to attract attention to a lottery advertisement) being offered by Lancaster's "High Dutch Reformed Congregation": ". . . . And the Wardens and Vestry of St. James's Church return their Thanks to the Public, for the Favours they received; but as the Money arising from the Lottery for the Use of said Church will not compleat the Work by them begun, they chose this Method of joining with their Neighbours and Fellow Christians, rather than set up a Lottery by themselves, for so small a Sum as above mentioned [i.e., £565]; and they flatter themselves, they shall meet with further Indulgence from the Public."[19]

Between the two lotteries, sufficient funds were raised to finish construction on the church. The officers had next to find a way to purchase a bell to be hung in the new but empty steeple and to undertake other improvements. This they did by applying directly to the SPG.[20]

Under the impetus of their enlightened minister, the congregation was drawn into working closely with sympathetic German Lutherans and Reformed in the town. This cooperation reveals Barton's willingness to act in concert with kindred Protestant groups, whatever his feelings toward other dissenting sects. Indeed, on May 4, 1766, he was invited to preach at the dedication of the new Trinity Lutheran Church, and did so, even reading from the English prayer book.[21] If only on this level involving Protestant communities of similar organization and liturgical practice, Barton appears in the center of limited ecumenical activity in pre-Revolutionary Lancaster. We need, however, to recognize that this evidence of cooperative spirit also had roots in a more devious SPG strategy developed some years earlier to undermine the independence and autonomy of the German-speaking population and bring it under the paternal wing of the Church of England.

In 1751, Chief Justice James De Lancey and Henry Barclay, both of New York, discussed points of doctrinal agreement and practice with the influential Lutheran minister the Reverend Henry Melchior Mühlenberg. Anglicans and Lutherans moved even closer in 1756 when the Reverend William Sturgeon of Philadelphia forwarded to the SPG "some undigested thoughts" of an unidentified Lutheran minister (probably Mühlenberg).[22] The designs of the SPG and the proprietary actually ranged considerably deeper than the free and amiable exchange of ideas and courtesies suggested here. British educators like William Smith and Thomas Barton felt that by teaching their children English ways and the English language, the Germans, no longer isolated from the language and customs of the British, would not fall easy prey either to Catholic missionaries or to Quaker dissenters intent on extending their power in the Pennsylvania Assembly.

Building upon the earlier discussions, several German clerics in 1754 joined what came to be known as the charity school movement. Among them were Henry M. Mühlenberg, Michael Schlatter, and Peter Brunholtz.[23] Schools were established, and funds, raised largely by the SPG in Great Britain, were channeled into the cooperative enterprise. Doubtless, when Barton wrote in his first *notitia parochalis* (November 8, 1756) that "M^r. Provost Smith has been lately up here to settle Free-Schools," he was possibly referring to plans to establish at the very least schools for the English and the handful of German children of York and Cumberland counties.[24]

William Smith pressed on. In 1753 he had argued that educating the children in English would greatly benefit the province:

The English language and a conformity of manners will be acquired, and they may be taught to feel the meaning and exult in the enjoyment of liberty, a home and social endearments. And when once these sacred names are understood and felt at the heart;— when once a few intermarriages are made between the chief families of the different nations in each country, which will naturally follow from school acquaintances, and the acquisition of a common language, no arts of our enemies will be able to divide them in their affection; and all the narrow distinctions of extraction, etc., will be forgot—forever forgot—in higher interests.[25]

In 1756, he stressed the urgency for increasing the missionary effort among the Germans. Smith urged that "till we can succeed in making our Germans speak English & become good Protestants, *I doubt we shall never have a firm hold of them.* For this Reason the extending the means of their Instruction as far [as] they extend their Settlement is a matter that deserves our most attentive Consideration."[26] Smith makes clear that his educational vision was at least as much political and social as intellectual.[27]

Not surprisingly, Smith's colleague and friend in the backcountry advocated the same program and for many of the same reasons.[28] Barton reported in 1764 to Daniel Burton how the "German Lutherans have frequently in their Coetus's propos'd a Union with the Church of England; & several of their Clergy, with whom I have convers'd, are desirous of addressing his Grace, my Lord Archbishop of Canterbury, & my Lord Bishop of London, upon this Subject."[29] Much less diplomatically, he advocated legally coercive measures to guarantee the program's success: "The Germans in general are well affected to the Church of England, & might easily be brought over to it— A Law obliging them to give their Children an English Education (which could not be deem'd an Abridgement of their Liberty, as British Subjects) would soon have this Effect."[30]

Initially successful, the charity school movement soon encountered opposition. Intelligent, suspicious Germans began to read between the lines of the Church of England's public-relations statements. Led by the Germantown printer Christopher Saur, they recognized that behind the movement's altruistic professions of trying to improve the intellectual lives of Pennsylvania Germans there lurked religious, political, and social motives that targeted the continued existence of their very culture and identity. Gradually, Saur's editorials turned many of his fellow Germans against the entire educational effort. Himself identified with pacifist sectarians and their Quaker supporters, he led his readers to see that "organized" religions such as the Lutherans and the Church of England were attempting to neutralize the strength of German religious groups having no church organization and sharing with the Quakers common principles of nonviolence.[31] Saur argued as well that the charity school movement was ultimately intended to deprive Germans of their very language,[32] a motive that both Smith's and Barton's letters confirm. When, therefore, Barton writes in his December 1760 letter that "Many . . . Lutherans who gladly embrace every Opportunity to teach their Children in the Religion, Manners, & Customs of England, would come to our Church,"[33] we need to keep in mind the deeper political implications when he further recommends purchasing an organ to attract sympathetic Germans.

Apart from supporting the charity school movement and its broadly socializing program, Barton acknowledged that German power in Lancaster had to be turned to the advantage of the Church of England. He wrote Philip Bearcroft unambiguously on this point: "Indeed if the Church in Lancaster ever flourishes, it must be by Means of the Germans, who (as I formerly mention'd to you) are the principal Inhabitants of the Place."[34] He therefore had reason to be pleased with the amiable relationship he had established with Lancaster's German Lutherans and Reformed.

As we might expect from his experiences with the Presbyterians of York and Cumberland counties, Barton was distressed by the stubborn presence of various other dissenting congregations in Lancaster. Echoing the alarm sounded thirty years earlier by provincial secretary James Logan,[35] Barton feared that "the Sectaries are likely to overrun us." "Their Colleges in New England & the Jerseys," he explains, "are continually sending out Preachers; who are always not Men of the most catholic Principles." SPG missionaries must therefore be ever watchful of the "Prejudice & Influence of these Gainsayers."[36] In 1762, he again recorded how "we are surrounded by multitudes of Dissenters of every Kind who are all brought up in such narrow principles that they can be no friends to the National Church."[37]

Apparently, he made some advances against their opposition, winning converts from their ranks, and feeling thereby assured that he had achieved much "amidst all the mad Zeal & Distractions of the *Religionists* that surround me."[38] It would not be until later in 1763 and the year after that that he would experience bitter confirmation of his worse forebodings about the largely Scots-Irish Dissenters.

Concerning the Catholic presence in Lancaster, Barton seems curiously ambivalent. The man who had in 1755 passionately railed against the menace to Protestant religion from ungodly French "Papists" found little evidence to support those fears in his new home. Although "Popery," he wrote in 1762, "has gained considerable ground in Pennsylvania of late years," the Catholics of Lancaster, ministered to by a German Jesuit, have caused little trouble: "Their behaviour in outward appearance is quiet and inoffensive." *Outward appearance* is, of course, a carefully applied qualifier that allows Barton to anticipate his parting shot that "they have been often suspected during this war of communicating intelligence to the Enemies of our Religion and Country."[39] Setting down rumors and hearsay is the best he can do with Lancaster's Catholics.

∞

The early years in Lancaster saw Barton fighting the stranglehold of poverty and putting the affairs of St. James's Church onto a more secure footing than he had found them. Always civic-spirited, he also worked to improve the welfare of the entire community and to advance the cause of his patron, Thomas Penn. His earlier scientific curiosity in mineralogy, botany, and geography now acquired a commercial edge as well. Barton's correspondence with Penn reveals that he watched for opportunities whereby Penn and Lancaster county might mutually increase their wealth through exploiting the riches of the land. In addition to sending his benefactor curiosities such as fossils and other natural specimens, he saw to it that the proprietor could examine first-hand in England examples of marble and proposed methods for refining iron ore.[40] He explored with Penn the feasibility of improving hemp cultivation, of starting silk production, and of raising indigo. That his interest was not altogether selfless becomes clear when Penn cautions him against undertaking economic ventures: "As to your engaging in the Manufacture [of hemp], I think you had better decline it; so far as raising any commodity on your Land [it] is certainly very proper; but I think your Ecclesiastical friends here would not approve of your engaging publickly in such a concern."[41]

Barton seems to have lacked the combination of intuition, political connections, unscrupulous energy, and simple good fortune that benefitted his friend William Smith. Few of his land speculations came to anything, while Smith succeeded in amassing immoderate amounts of real estate. In time Smith even became a proprietor himself when he turned some of his property into the community that evolved into the town of Huntingdon along the Juniata River. Assisted by his half-brother, Thomas, who faithfully acted as his agent and by the tirelessly enterprising George Croghan who acquired clear title to cheap land that he in turn sold to Smith, the latter came to own "seven thousand acres in Bedford county, not to mention sixty-five hundred acres in Northampton and Northumberland counties, and about ten thousand acres in Tryon county, New York, and the seven thousand acres around Huntingdon."[42]

Few of Barton's speculations came to anything. His hope for military bounty lands, awarded for service on the Forbes campaign, never materialized, and his dreams of becoming a big landowner in Pennsylvania's Wyoming Valley were dashed with the eruption of border warfare with Connecticut, which claimed ownership of that territory. Frustrated as a land speculator, he naturally turned to commerce, only to be warned away by Penn and other considerations. The Board of Trade, for example, charged with protecting the home country's industry, would move to thwart any industrial competition from the colonies, and Barton's colleagues, to say

Thomas Penn, Proprietor of Pennsylvania During Barton's Earlier Years. (Society Collections, Historical Society of Pennsylvania.)

nothing of his detractors among the dissenting sects, would object, as Penn foresaw, to commercial, worldly ventures. Certainly, in his February 1762 letter, Penn was tacitly recalling how even Barton's successful military leadership in 1755 had opened him to attacks of meddling in public affairs and worldliness. Had he been as unconcerned with public opinion as Smith, Barton might have obtained some measure of material prosperity.

For all that he succeeeded in diverting Barton from business activities, Penn nonetheless expressed gratitude for Barton's interest in both the proprietary and the province. In one typical instance, he commended Barton's proposal for improving the poor transportation and communication network in Pennsylvania: "I am greatly pleased with the Scheme formed for making the River Schuylkil Navigable, tho' it is not to be supposed they will succeed at first, experience must shew the Undertakers the best method of proceeding in difficult cases; to send People over from hence that are able, would be an immense Expence, and to send pretenders would not answer any good purpose."[43] Much later, in 1772, when Barton publicly submitted a detailed argument for building a turnpike linking Lancaster with Philadelphia, he did so pseudonymously under the name *Clericus*.[44] Only after a full year did he admit privately to Penn that he had authored the "well received" tract.[45]

As a measure of his gratitude, Penn promised in 1762 to send Barton a soon-to-be-published edition of a "most curious Journal of several Journeys a very honest worthy Friend of mine has made from Petersburgh to Pekin, from the same place to Ispahan, and Constantinople."[46] The gift was intended not so much as a personal gesture to his loyal servitor in Lancaster as a contribution to the institution Barton had played a major role in founding, the Library Company of Lancaster, a role Penn perhaps acknowledges when in the same letter he refers to "your Library."

Ever the teacher, Barton may well have initiated the founding of that insitutition. As early as the year he moved to Lancaster, the Library Company records show that "the reverend Mr. Barton, one of the Directors of the Library," had given it "some curious Mines, Minerals and Fossils."[47] One speculates whether or not St. James's missing books had inspired Barton to help establish this library. Clearly, he became one its most energetic directors. It was also probably because of his connection to the proprietary family that Thomas Penn and his wife Juliana, after whom the library was later renamed, supported the institution with gifts of money, books, and such educational equipment as a pair of "M^r. Adams' Globes," "a Palantarium," and a "Reflecting Telescope."[48]

When in 1760, the College of Philadelphia awarded Barton an honorary master of arts degree, it certainly did so in part to recognize his many efforts to advance the intellectual and spiritual life of Pennsylvania's backcountry.[49] Notwithstanding the disheartening economic circumstances he had to contend with, it must have seemed to him that since leaving his virtually defenseless and impoverished trans-Susquehanna congregations, the future looked promising indeed. St. James's and especially its satellite parishes were beginning to prosper. His conciliatory gestures toward the German Lutheran and Reformed churches had produced a measure of har-

mony between the proprietary party and Lancaster's most influential religious factions. Barton had, moreover, assumed a leading role in the cultural life of the community. With the end of the Seven Years' War and the
resulting pacification of the frontier, he could anticipate resuming his missionary work among the Native Americans, an effort that had come to an
abrupt end in July of 1755.

The halcyon days following the signing of the Treaty of Paris in 1763
did not last long. The charismatic Indian leader Pontiac succeeded in exploiting a religious intensity and general unrest among his people, with the
result that the nightmare of border warfare was once more unleashed upon
the entire frontier and its adjacent areas during the early summer of 1763.
Interpreting Barton's life from the convenience of historical hindsight, it is
possible to see that this fresh upheaval, more particularly the consequences
it produced, ultimately affected him in ways that forever prevented his re-
alizing whatever hopes he might have nurtured when he decided about
1750 to seek his fortune in the new world.

Like his letters dating from 1755–57, Barton's correspondence during
the summer of 1763 reflects his consciousness that the recent revolution of
Fortune's Wheel (more in her role of Nemesis than of Opportunity) had
traumatically and unexpectedly, and perhaps capriciously, all but annihilated civilization's opportunity to survive in the western-most counties.
At the conclusion to his report of June 1763, he laments that his long set-
aside plans to "go for a few Months among the Indians" to open a mission
"among those miserable unenlightened People" have been destroyed by the
renewal of warfare. It is the old story of fury and blood, and of dreams destroyed that he had written of so often before: "our Country bleeds again
under the *Savage Knife!* The dreadful News of Murdering, burning &
scalping is daily convey'd to us, & confirm'd with shocking Additions . . . .
Above 50 Miles of the finest Country in America are already deserted—
And the poor People, having left their Crops in the Ground, almost ready
for the Sickle, are reduc'd to the most consummate Distress—and all this
unfortunately happens at a Time when our Soldiery is discharg'd— Our
Province is in a defenceless State."[50]

A week later, as the borderland reported new horrors being visited upon
soldiers and settlers, Barton wrote his friend Richard Peters, summarizing
the recent intelligence: "*Presque Isle* & *Venango* are taken—Cap[t]. Coch-
rane has been burnt to ashes, & all his brave men tomahawk'd."[51] It is noteworthy that although he adds his voice to the general clamor—"Vene-
geance cries aloud"—he seems to insinuate into his letter his awareness
that a communal hysteria is about to sweep everything before it—discipline, the rule of law, the redeeming gift of Christian grace. "The People,"

he writes, "have Spirit enough to act, *were they directed by proper Authority*" (author's emphasis). He elaborates on this caution when he admits that the "general Cry & Wish . . . for . . . a Scalp-Act" might indeed "put a final Stop to those Barbarians," but he maintains that "this Method" should "be reconcil'd with *Revelation* and the Humanity of the English Nation." Events were soon to show that Barton's guarded insistence on the importance of preserving civil and compassionate values was well-taken.

For all his tempered alarm at the incipient anarchy, Barton's disappointment was greater, and nowhere perhaps was it so bitterly evident than in his perception that the terrible reversal of 1763 fell at the very moment "when We imagined ourselves going into the Arms of Peace to sing a lasting REQUIEM!"[52]

5

"A Stark Naked Presbyterian"

An Episcopalian minister in Lancaster wrote to vindicate [the Paxton Boys] bringing scripture to prove that it was right to destroy the heathen and very many were of of the same opinion. . . .

—Rhoda Barber, 1830

BARTON'S LETTERS DURING THE TIME OF PONTIAC'S WAR SPEAK WITH ANguish of the miseries revisited upon the people of the frontier. And even though Lancaster was well-removed from the scenes of war, rumors of attack still threatened the security of those living near Susquehanna's eastern shore. Ironically, however, not Pontiac's scalp-hunting warriors, but embittered, frustrated Scots-Irish settlers invaded the streets of Lancaster to terrorize and murder. On December 27, 1763, even while Barton celebrated the birth of the Prince of Peace—he had been on circuit earlier in the week—irate and alienated frontiersmen tomahawked and shot the small band of baptized Conestogas who had sought government sanctuary in the town after the Paxton Boys had murdered six of their tribe on December 14. Feeling betrayed by the provincial government's apathy and resenting the protection extended to the reservation Indians, additional back settlers joined the vigilantes. The rioters then marched on Philadelphia itself in February 1764 to obtain redress and to kill the some 140 Indian refugees from Northampton county harbored in that city.[1]

Oddly, Barton left little explicit testimony of his feelings and thoughts on the atrocities enacted during the actual "rebellion" and on the energetic pamphlet war that the Paxtonians' actions provoked. If he did correspond on the subject, his letters have been lost. This silence is puzzling and most uncharacteristic for two reasons. Significantly, he may himself have actually contributed clandestinely to the paper war ignited by the Paxton Boys' vigilantism. But more importantly, existing documents invite us to infer that his possible contribution, if not the events that inspired its writing, dramatically damaged Barton's perception of himself in the world of politics.

94

The tract now commonly attributed to him, *The Conduct of the Paxton-Men,* appeared in 1764, its title page bidding for wide appeal and advertizing that it was to be sold by Lancaster shopkeeper John Creaig. Like most of the many pamphlets published on the Paxton disturbances,[2] this essay also appeared anonymously. Only in 1873 did George Maurice Abbot write on the verso of the title page of the copy now in the Library Company of Philadelphia the following attribution of authorship: "The Author of this pamphlet (Paxton-Men) was the Rev. Thomas Barton of Lancaster. G. M. A. Oct. 29th 1873." Not only was Abbot librarian of the Library Company, but he was also Thomas Barton's great-great-grandson, descended through the latter's firstborn son, William. On the basis on Abbot's scholarly credentials and family connection, most scholars have accepted his identification.[3] Notwithstanding Abbot's identification and the scholarly agreement accorded it, a careful reading of the tract, set against what can be established of Barton's life and outlook, raises significant questions about this attribution.[4]

Because the tract is typical of the position taken by other pro-"Paxton-Boys" pamphlets, we need to inquire whether Thomas Barton was truly its author: for why would Barton, whose correspondence consistently expresses aversion to both mob rule and intractable dissenters, especially New Side Presbyterians, advocate the cause of the largely Scots-Irish Presbyterian vigilantes? An SPG itinerant missionary sincerely committed to Christianizing and educating the Native Americans, both before and after the Paxton emergency, why would Barton defend the slaughter of twenty baptized, peaceable Conestogas who had sought protection in Lancaster? A writer whose numerous extant letters disclose a man eager to explain his life and ideas, a correspondent always ready to comment on contemporary happenings, why did he leave no report on the massacres? If we accept that he wrote *The Conduct of the Paxton Men,* improbable as that may seem, how are we to interpret his personal evolution and the new, disturbing path he took in the political labyrinth of colonial Pennsylvania? Finally, if he did author an essay so transparently out of character with his other writings, what inferences may be drawn concerning the motives of the proprietary government whose client he was and which, it appears, he served so faithfully?

∞

A few of these perplexities hinge upon relatively minor points of historical fact and probability. If George M. Abbot had known of a family tradition identifying Barton as the author, that tradition would most likely have

THE CONDUCT OF
The PAXTON - MEN,
Impartially reprefented ;

The DISTRESSES of the FRONTIERS, and the COMPLAINTS and SUFFERINGS of the PEOPLE fully ftated ; and the Methods recommended by the wifeft Nations, in fuch Cafes, ferioufly confider'd.

WITH SOME
REMARKS upon the NARRATIVE,

Of the Indian-Maffacre, lately publifh'd.

Interfpers'd with feveral interefting Anecdotes, relating to the MILITARY GENIUS, and WARLIKE PRINCIPLES of the People call'd QUAKERS : Together-with proper Reflection and Advice upon the whole.

In a LETTER from a GENTLEMAN in one of the Back-Counties, to a FRIEND in Philadelphia.

——— ——— Si tibi vera videtur,
Dede Manus ; et, fi falfa eft, accingere contra.———
LUCRET.

The impious Man who fells his COUNTRY's FREEDOM,
Makes all the Guilt of Tyranny his own.———
His are her SLAUGHTERS, her OPPRESSIONS His.———
MARTYN's TIMOLEON.

Whoever will pretend to govern a People without regarding them, will foon repent it.——Such Feats of Errantry may do perhaps in ASIA :—But in Countries where the People are FREE, it is Madnefs to rule them againft their Wills.——They will know that Government is appointed for their Sakes, and will be faucy enough to expect fome Regards and fome Good from their own DELEGATES.——Thofe Nations who are govern'd in Spite of themfelves, and in a Manner that bids Defiance to their Opinions, their Interefts, and their Underftandings, ——are either SLAVES, or willfoon ceafe to be SUBJECTS.
CATO's LETTERS.

PHILADELPHIA:

Printed by A Steuart, and fold by JOHN CREAIG, Shopkeeper in Lancafter. 1764.

Title page of *The Conduct of the Paxton-Men. . . .*, 1764, attributed to Thomas Barton.

derived from Abbot's great-grandfather and Thomas's eldest son. Yet William Barton, eight years old at the time of the December murders, never once alludes in his biography of his uncle, David Rittenhouse, to his father's attitude toward the rioters.[5] Furthermore, William frequently and gratuitously digresses elsewhere to offer considerable detail on his father's life. He quotes Rittenhouse's eye-witness description (recorded in a 1764 letter to Thomas Barton) of the Paxtonians' march on Philadelphia[6] and expends over three pages on the disturbances themselves without referring at all either to his father's activities at that very moment or to his supposed authorship of the tract. Either, and more unlikely, William Barton knew nothing of his father's relationship to the Paxton affair, or, more probably, he suppressed the information.

There exists an outside chance that William Barton knew nothing of his father's association with the pamphlet, and perhaps of the pamphlet itself. Nevertheless, he had to have known of Benjamin Franklin's anonymously published *A Narrative of the Late Massacres,* to which *The Conduct of the Paxton Men* replied.[7] That the acclaimed Franklin had authored *A Narrative* was, in fact, an open secret alluded to and passed around by most of the subsequent pamphleteers. William revealed his awareness of the fact in discussing Rittenhouse's reactions to the Philadelphia riots when he quoted from Franklin's June 2, 1765, letter to Henry Home the former's admission: "I wrote a pamphlet, entitled *A Narrative,* &c. to strengthen the hands of our weak government, by rendering the proceedings of the rioters unpopular and odious."[8] Yet William ignores the relationship between Franklin's attack and the pamphlet supposedly authored by his father, one of the most cogent of several rejoinders. Had he known of his father's rebuttal of Franklin's pamphlet, he presumably would have said so. William otherwise larded his biography with references and allusions to the famous and the revered. For example, in recalling his father's participation on the Forbes expedition, he could not withstand the invitation to sprinkle a handful of glittering names before his reader: "In that campaign [Mr. Barton] became personally acquainted not only with the commander in chief [i.e., John Forbes], but, among others, with colonel (afterwards general) Washington; colonel (afterwards general) Mercer; colonel Byrd of Virginia; colonel Dagworthy; colonel James Burd of Pennsylvania; . . . besides colonel (afterwards general) Bouquet; sir John St. Clair, sir Peter Hackett, major Stewart, and other gentlemen of worth and distinction."[9] From this, it should be obvious that William would not have declined the opportunity to link Franklin's name with his father's, had he been aware of the relationship, even if adversarial, between the two tracts. We must, however, return to this issue later.

Another factual challenge to Barton's authorship comes with the pamphleteer's teasing closing reference to his residence: "*Dated from my FARM-HOUSE, March 17th, 1764.*" This may represent an attempt to conceal further the tract's authorship. For one thing. it may suggest merely that the author wrote from his "Farmhouse," not necessarily that he resided there. But more significantly, the fact is that, so far as can be determined, Barton did not reside on or even own a farm in 1764. Only after 1768 did Barton begin to cultivate what appears to have been his first and only farm in Lancaster county, ironically located on the Conestoga Manor, the former reservation of the murdered Conestogas. Before 1768 he lived in the town of Lancaster. Barton sought a house in town and had to pasture and board his horse soon after his appointment to St. James's Church in 1759.[10] Moreover, in November 1763, the month before the murders, he acquired a residence on the southeast corner of North Lime and East Orange Streets.[11] In 1768, requesting assistance from Sir William Johnson in securing authorization to farm the Conestoga Manor,[12] Barton stressed the site's convenience to Lancaster: "I live in a town, where I have no Land of my own near."[13] Even after he acquired the Conestoga farm, he continued residing in Lancaster. In a letter of 1770 written in Lancaster to Sir William Johnson, he says of his town property (known to the townspeople as "Barton's Garden") that "I have a snug, little Garden . . . —My Spot is well cultivated, & yields me Variety of Vegetables, Fruit, & Flowers—I don't know whether Plato or Seneca (Diogenes, I am sure, had not) [had] as much Ground as I have.—Why then should I not be contented?—Only because my Stock of Philosophy is not as large as theirs was."[14] Several letters written by an in-law and his second wife, Sarah, also make clear that in 1776 Barton lived in the town.[15]

Another argument against Barton's authorship turns on the glaring disparity between the pamphleteer's expressed feelings toward the Paxtonians and the Indians, and Thomas Barton's known attitudes. At least one other contemporary polemicist perceived that the *Conduct* was executed in a spirit far from the title's self-publicized impartiality, so shrill was its defense of the rioters and its villification of the Indians.[16] Indeed, following a carefully orchestrated, point-by-point rebuttal of the earlier tract, the writer of *An Answer to . . . "The Conduct of the Paxton Men"* strips away his target's "spotted garment" to reveal nothing less than "a *Stark Naked Presbyterian.*"[17]

This exposure of the earlier pamphleteer's duplicity and political sympathies is important. In his introduction, the author of *The Conduct* pointedly disavows having any "political Ends to serve . . . [and] nothing to hope or fear from Party Connections."[18] He insists, rather, that his purpose is simply "to rescue the miserable Frontier People, who lately rose in Arms, from the Infamy and Odium thrown upon them, by *those* whose unfeeling Hearts have never suffered them to look beyond their own private Interest and Party."[19] Professing objectivity, he pointedly dissociates himself from any incendiary or insurrectionist impulse, unequivocally repudiating vigilantism: "Such violent Steps can never possibly be productive of any thing, but Wild Uproar and Confusion." He swears "to bear his Testimony against, and to discountenance by every Means in his Power" whatever might offer "the *least Insult* to the Laws and Government of his Country."[20] His argument, however, trenchantly defends the Paxton Volunteers and criticizes all Indians and the Quaker party's political position.

That the writer's initial professions of impartiality are perfunctory, almost pro forma, soon becomes evident. After quoting at length from the remonstrance/petition submitted by the rioters,[21] he refocuses his subject, employing the same phrasing he used on the tract's first page, but now arguing that the insurgents need to be appreciated as other than "Rioters, Rebels, Murderers, White Savages." Rational men, he elaborates, "are sensibly concern'd that [the Paxtonians] were reduced to the Necessity of having Recourse to such Methods *as might be deem'd* an Insult to the Government and Laws of their King and Country."[22] "As might be deemed"—the Paxton Boys only appeared to defy the state. What has been popularly interpreted as rebellion actually laid "bare the Pharasaical Bosom of Quakerism, by obliging the Non-Resisting Quality to take up Arms, and to become Proselytes to *the first great Law of Nature,*"[23] that is, self-preservation. The Quaker instinct to defend hearth-and-home is the very same motive that drove the Paxtonians to kill the protected Conestogas and march on Philadelphia. Hence, the murder of peaceful, government-protected Indians and the riotous demonstrations in the capital benefitted all true Pennsylvanians by driving the Quaker hypocrites from their holes to defend their city by force of arms. What detractors would label *insurrection* was actually an expression of natural law (self-preservation) and was directed against a hypocritical faction (the Quakers of Philadelphia and in the legislature) guilty of destroying the frontiersmen by means of spurious, duplicitous pacificism.

The author's insistence upon a distinction between the legislative and the executive components of government underlies his remarkable casuistry: "the *executive Part* of the Government, at least, deserves [the frontiersmen's] Esteem and Affection. I trust therefore, they will never do any Thing that may bring their Obedience and Regards to the Laws and Magistracy of their Country in Question."[24] The indifference of the Quaker faction to the frontiersmen and its protection of the Indians, on the other hand, invited defiance. By insisting that important political and ethical differences separated the proprietary from the assembly, the pamphleteer tries to deflect accusations of sedition.

Barton's oft-expressed support of the proprietary, his hostility toward Quakers, and his empathy for the backcountry settlers are consistent with the argument thus far. The anonymous writer, however, also advances a libertarian defense of rebellion alien to Barton's known beliefs. Additionally, he expresses such hostile and unfeeling attitudes toward the Christianized Conestogas that, for this reason alone, one feels uncomfortable accepting Barton's authorship.

A pivotal passage occurs on page thirteen, where the writer once more dissociates himself from rebellious intent: "I solemnly declare I have as great an Aversion to Mobs, and all riotous Proceedings, as any Man can have, as any Man ought to have." But this presumably straightforward affirmation of civil obedience permits the author to allow an exception. "At the same Time," he stipulates, "I must own, I shall never be for sacrificing the Lives and Liberties of a free People to the Caprice and Obstinacy of a destructive Faction." With this transition, he begins to justify an oppressed populace's right to rebel against tyranny. Basing his argument upon historical and biblical antecedents, parliamentary debates, and English Whig theorists such as Algernon Sidney, the writer argues that a government which ignores the just grievances of its people—like the frontiersmen's complaints—incites the people to rebellion. To reinforce his position, he cites the popular journalistic collection *Cato's Letters:* "The Author[25] of Cato's *Letters* very justly observes, that 'It is a most wicked and absurd Position, to say, that a People can ever be in such a Situation, as not to have a Right to oppose a *Tyrant,* a *Robber,* or a *Traitor,* who, by *Violence, Treachery, Rapine,* infinite *Murders* and *Devastations,* has deprived them of Safety and Protection.'"[26] To epitomize this principal thesis, he concludes the essay by associating his writing of the tract on St. Patrick's Day with the Irish or Scots-Irish passion for liberty: "*Dated from my* Farm-House, March 17th, 1764.—A Day dedicated to LIBERTY and ST. PATRICK."[27]

The most telling argument against Barton's authorship, however, rests upon the pamphleteer's unmitigated hatred for all Indians. Throughout his entire missionary career, Barton distinguished between hostile and "friendly" Native Americans. Generally, he criticized those allied to the French and eager to attack the British settlers. "Barbarous Savages," "the rude Spoiler," "Heathens or Infidels," "Barbarians," "a Cruel Enemy"—these are the more common nouns and adjectives he uses to describe the hostiles.[28] More typically, Barton employs the neutral term *Indians* to denote the Delaware and Shawnee warriors who were attacking the backcounties. In describing Colonel John Armstrong's destruction of the Indian stronghold of Kittanning, we have seen that he even praises the enemy sachem Captain Jacobs who evoked uncommon, epic heroism in his death.[29] Such esteem is inconceivable from the writer of the *Conduct*.

Barton predictably views the proposed beneficiaries of his missionary activities with a mixture of condescension and compassion—"poor ignorant Creatures," "tawny People," "miserable unenlightened People," "barbarous Nations who are immersed in the grossest Idolatry," "those poor Heathen who 'sit in Darkness & the Shadow of Death,'" and "rude & barbarous creatures."[30] When he writes in his own voice of the murdered Conestogas, he once again expresses himself as we would anticipate. In his 1764 report to the SPG, in a rare allusion to the disturbances, he praises his congregation for having had no part "in *the Murder of the Indians* in this Place and the different Insurrections occasion'd by *this inhuman Act*."[31] He also castigates the Paxton Volunteers in a letter to Sir William Johnson when he refers in passing to "the Assassination of those hapless Wretches."[32] Common sense insists that we credit the benevolence of his numerous proposals for improving the Indians' conditions, and that we believe a missionary so disposed would not freely defend, let alone derive vindictive satisfaction from, the slaughter of twenty defenseless and baptized Conestogas who were peacefully, if pathetically, settled into a life of poverty on their reservation near Lancaster.

Yet, naked hatred of the baptized Conestogas defines the author of *The Conduct of the Paxton Men*. The following may be cited as among the more outstanding instances of his bigotry and loathing: "a Handful of *Freeman* and the *King's Subjects,* who thought it their Duty to kill a Pack of villainous, faithless Savages" (12); "a Parcel of treacherous, faithless, rascally Indians, some of which can be proved to be Murderers" (14); "140 idle Vagabonds" (i.e., the Indians given sanctuary in Philadelphia; ibid.); "murdering Savages" (ibid.); "a mighty Noise and Hubbub has been made about killing a few Indians" (17); "they were a *drunken, debauch'd, insolent, quarrelsome* Crew" (ibid.); "the killing of a few treacherous Savages, who by their Perfidy, had forfeited their Lives" (24); "perfidious Wretches" (28); and "Shall *Heathens,* shall *Traytors,* shall *Rebels* and *Murderers* be protected?" (29). In one short passage, the writer admits—the reader might suspect here that he does so in a face-saving strategy—that he wished "the *Women* and *little Ones* at least, could have been spared." More troubling than this cruelty to the writer, however, was the Paxton Volunteers' "Insult to the Civil Magistrates, and . . . Encroachment upon the Peace and Quiet of that Town" (17).

The essay's libertarian emphasis and its simplistic, baseless denunciation of the twenty pacified and Christianized Conestogas as murderous savages deserving the annihilation meted out to them echo commonplace attitudes voiced by the more radical Scots-Irish Presbyterians.[33] Virtually the only terrain the pamphlet shares with the Anglican Thomas Barton was the mutual distrust, sometimes hatred of, the pacifist faction dominating the Assembly. Considerations of content and tone, therefore, make Barton's authorship improbable.

Complicating, indeed, strongly challenging, this rejection, however, are several other particulars. The pamphlet's epistolary form, its patriotic appeal to an Irish readership, its distinctive prose style, its rhetorical duplication of parts of an earlier Barton tract—all these combine with external evidence to suggest that, notwithstanding the essay's moral emphasis, Thomas Barton must in fact have authored it. *The Conduct of the Paxton Men* confronts the contemporary reader with an extremely complex, puzzling—indeed, Swiftian—polemic, the genesis of which needs to be appreciated within the labyrinthine circumstances of Barton's life and political world. Before exploring these historical details, however, the evidence pointing to Barton's authorship requires closer examination.

∞

Although *The Conduct of the Paxton Men* combines an apology for the Paxtonians with a polemic against Benjamin Franklin's *Narrative,* it also relies upon the convention of the letter. Both the title page and the initial headnote claim to be: "A Letter from a Gentleman in one of the Frontier-Counties, to his Friend in Philadelphia, relating to the Paxton-Men."[34] In August, 1755, William Smith also used the letter-polemic convention to preface Barton's *Unanimity and Public Spirit:* Smith might well have provided Barton with a convenient precedent. Certainly, Barton found the epistolary form congenial, as his many surviving letters indicate.

Furthermore, David Rittenhouse might have been the "Friend in Philadelphia" Barton addressed. Generally, the addressee is forgotten once the essay gets fully underway, but in one notable passage the author implies that his missive should correct his friend's ignorance of frontier life. The pamphleteer writes: "I am no Stranger to your Fellow-feeling and Humanity:—I well know that you have a Tear for Distress, and a Sigh for Misery."[35] He then diplomatically reminds his friend that "if it were not criminal, I should envy you your happy Lot, in being placed by Providence at some Distance from the Scenes of Destruction and Desolation, of which, I and my Neighbours have been Melancholy Eye-Witnesses." With that, he elaborates a full page of graphic description of recent frontier atrocities.

If the apologist is to be believed, if it is not a further effort to conceal his identity, he wrote his letter on March 17, 1764, one month following Rittenhouse's epistolary condemnation of the Paxtonians' march on Philadelphia. William Barton does not quote Rittenhouse's letter in full, his purpose having been apparently to illustrate that his uncle "was zealously disposed to support the legitimate authority of the government, in order to suppress illegal and disorderly proceedings, subversive of the laws and dangerous to the public peace and safety."[36] We do not, consequently, know what beyond the descriptions of mob behavior Rittenhouse might have said of the demonstration or the murders that preceded it. And because the actual Barton/Rittenhouse correspondence has been lost or destroyed, we cannot examine whatever letters Barton may have penned to Rittenhouse on this subject. One thing about the pamphlet is nevertheless clear: it was written in part to defend the desperate actions of a people who felt that government apathy had abandoned them to the Indian threat. It was also written to exonerate the backsettlers from such criticism as Rittenhouse expresses in his February 16, letter, when, for example, he writes: "I have seen hundreds of Indians travelling the country, and can with truth affirm, that the behaviour of these fellows [the frontiersmen] was ten times more savage and brutal than theirs."[37]

The concluding patriotic invocation of St. Patrick raises another problem concerning Barton's presumed authorship. In his biography, William Barton stresses the English contribution to his father's Irish upbringing. Thomas was "descended from an English family" that once possessed "considerable grants of land in Ireland," although the family had lost its wealth by way of some unnamed "untoward circumstances." In spite of this, the family still managed to see that Thomas received an education befitting his class "under the direction of the Rev. Mr. Folds, a respectable English clergyman" and, later, at "the university of Dublin," that is, Trinity College, Dublin, the Ascendancy insitution established during the reign of Queen Elizabeth.[38] Granted this emphasis upon Barton's Ascendancy identity, the pamphlet's defense of the Scots-Irish and its concluding appeal to St. Patrick and freedom might tempt us to dismiss Barton's authorship. However, that would involve overlooking too much other evidence.

The pamphleteer ends with a final, rousing appeal to the Irish, or Scots-Irish, passion for freedom: "*Dated from my* Farm-House, March 17, 1764.—A Day dedicated to LIBERTY and ST. PATRICK." In eighteenth-century America, St. Patrick appealed as an ethnic symbol to *all* immigrants from Ireland, Protestant and Catholic, Scots-Irish, Anglo-Irish, and "pure" Irish alike.[39] Barton, moreover, not only maintained ties with many of his countrymen and recommended recent Irish immigrants for teaching and ministerial positions,[40] but he also numbered several of his countrymen among his closest friends, particularly George Croghan and Sir William Johnson. Both figures, especially the Irish Catholic who had converted to Episcopalianism and the son of Anglicized Irish gentry whose original name had been *McShane* ("the son of John"), were well-known for their fondness for elaborate St. Patrick's Day celebrations.[41]

Barton did more than champion and maintain close relationships with fellow Irishmen: he apparently defined himself as Irish. This seems remarkable in light of the extremes to which many other eighteenth-century Anglo-Irish (for example, William Congreve, Oliver Goldsmith, Edmund Burke, and Richard Sheridan) publicly distanced themselves from their Irish origins. As late as 1779, one year before his death and while living as an exile in dire straits in New York city, Barton still discovered the resources to refer humorously to his ethnic identity. Writing to the Reverend William Frazer, he apologizes: "I have not receiv'd the Letter which you address'd to me . . . & therefore (tho' an *Irishman*) cannot undertake to *answer* it."[42]

Beyond these considerations of content and attitudes, inescapable similarities in prose style suggest Thomas Barton wrote *The Conduct of the Paxton Men.* Not unlike handwriting, style offers extremely useful evidence of identity, even in instances where an author might try to alter it.[43] Style is like one's fingerprints or an emotional-intellectual-rhetorical DNA code. Trained to detect nuances of vocabulary use, patterns of phrasing and syntax, and strategies for organizing and developing ideas, literary critics can frequently identify a particular author's writing, especially when that individual produced a considerable body of work over a substantial period of time and focused upon a relatively limited number of subjects. Thomas Barton is such a writer.

Apart from his extant manuscript sermons, which share the specialized analytic and exegetical strategies of homiletic literature, the remainder of his known writings—letters, epistolary reports to the society, war journal, and the published exhortation *Unanimity and Public Spirit*[44]—all disclose distinctly similar features. Difficult to characterize in a phrase, his style might be described as eighteenth-century journalistic rather than academic, political or philosophical.[45]

Barton's prose stands out for its energetic, spirited, if at times glib, "flow"; its numerous parenthetical, interruptive, and exclamatory statements; its predilection for hendiadys (often alliterated), and for similarly paired adjectival (rather than adverbial) modifiers; its frequent use of metonymy and synecdoche in emotionally stressful descriptions.[46] Perhaps reflecting the fast pace with which his ideas move and at which he often writes, Barton also reveals a fondness for the dash or the dash combined with a period to mark a sentence's end.[47] Any or a few of these would scarcely serve to particularize Barton's prose, but combined with one another and set forth with rhythms and cadences as distinctive as the grain patterns that define oak, cherry, maple, or walnut, his style announces itself readily.

Space prevents extensive comparisons, but a few examples may be cited to establish recurring stylistic patterns. Two, possibly three, Barton letters describing atrocities during the summer of 1763 survive, one a report to the Society and one to Richard Peters. The other, an anonymous report written in Lancaster to the *Pennsylvania Gazette,* so closely reproduces phrasing, structure, and details of the Peters letter that it must have been written by Barton. If indeed his, the last invaluably confirms how he tended to draw upon a ready-made stylistic repertoire from letter to letter.[48]

One of Barton's favorite figures of speech involves a synechdoche employing the image of blood/bleeding. It invariably occurs in his descriptions of Indian atrocities and of his heart's reactions thererto. As early as his November 8, 1756, *notitia parochialis,* or annual report to his superiors, he writes: "my Heart bleeds in relating what I am an Eye Witness to."[49] He tells Thomas Penn that "My Heart bleeds for the poor People."[50] The author of *The Conduct* expresses himself similarly: "My Heart has often bled" (3) and "what good Man is there, whose Heart does not bleed . . . ?" (30).

An analogous personification helps Barton express the magnitude of suffering sweeping the frontier: "our bleeding Country"; "their bleeding Country."[51] *The Conduct's* author rebukes the Quakers "who have so long suffer'd the Province to bleed beneath the *Savage Knife*" (16). This extended figure also recalls the personification-metonymy Barton employed in the June 28 letter to the Society—"our Country bleeds again under the *Savage Knife!*"[52]

The image of fire offers another natural, powerful way of conveying war's destructiveness. The letter in the *Pennsylvania Gazette* speaks of the country's seeming "to be one general Blaze," anticipating the pamphlet's "all burnt to Ashes in one general Flame" (31). In addition, this peculiar phrasing echoes similar descriptive usage elsewhere—the pamphlet's "their Country rescued from total Ruin" (34) and an earlier letter's lament that all is "ready to sink together in one general Ruin!"[53]

The author of *The Conduct of the Paxton Men* shares with Barton a fondness for hendiadys. Compare the following characteristic examples from the pamphlet and Barton's earlier writings. *The Conduct:* "Distresses and Sufferings . . . Infamy and Odium . . . wild Uproar and Confusion

(3, n.); "Lenity and Mercy" (12); "meek and peaceable . . . Protection and Security. . . Vengeance and Destruction" (16); "Noise and Hubbub" (17); "Vassalage and Slavery" (22); "Ruin and Desolation" (23); "Cruelty and Inhumanity" (27); "Laws and Magistracy" (32); and "Liberty and Freedom" (33). Barton's earlier works: "The general Cry & Wish"; "Miseries and Distresses"; "Beggary and Despair"; "Objects of Charity and Commiseration"; "Sighs and Groans"; "Calamity & Distress"; "Dangers & Trials"; "barbarous & cruel"; "Affluence & Plenty"; "Support & Maintenance"; "Difficulties & Impediments"; "Customs & Manners"; "Hardships or Distresses."[54]

Barton and the author of the pamphlet also like to alliterate their doubled nouns and modifiers. A sampling from Barton's known works: "Cries & Confusion"; "the Pulpit & not the Press"; "sudden and savage Death"; "Division and Distinction"; "Advice and Assistance"; "Grand & Glorious work"; "Danger & Distress"; "an Interest with, & an Influence upon"; "all Health & Happiness."[55] As late as 1779, his letters still reveal this predilection: "my Children & Churches"; "Pilgrimage & Poverty"; and "present Passions & Prejudices."[56]

Even though The Conduct's author discloses a greater inclination for simple descriptive hendiadys, he also employs alliteration to achieve added emphasis: "Application and Addresses" (n., 8); "drunken, debauch'd" (17); "Discord and Dissention" (22); "Gallows or the Gibbet" (23); "Honour and Hospitality" (27); "Destruction and Desolation" (30); lawful and loyal Methods" (33); and "Quakers and Don Quixotes" (34).[57]

Barton's frequent use of the verb and the verbal noun groan finds its parallel in the pamphlet. Compare "groaning under a Burden"; "miseries they now sadly groan under"; "calamities under which they have groan'd"; "Sighs and Groans"[58] with the pamphlet's "Groans of the People" (34).

In all of this, Barton, who consistently portrays himself as an "Eye Witness,"[59] emphasizes the ultimate ineffability of the anguish and suffering he has seen: "The complicated Distresses of these poor Creatures are beyond Expression"; the inhabitants are "distressed beyond Expression or Conception"; "the Distress of the Back Inhabitants is beyond all Description"; "the Miseries and Distresses of the poor People were . . . beyond the Power of Language to describe."[60] The pamphlet's author closely echoes the same hyperbole: "the Miseries of the back Inhabitants are really beyond the Power of Description" (30).

Stylistically, then, Thomas Barton and the writer of The Conduct of the Paxton Men favor certain recurring rhetorical turns and figures of speech, synecdoche and metonymy. Both rely upon a specific, predictable vocabulary and rhetorical strategy for describing certain kinds of events. The two authors, moreover, show a predilection for the flexible and supple form allowed by the epistolary convention. Less open to analysis is the similar rhythm, cadence, and syntax that characterize each as journalistic at times, hortatory at others, and generally flamboyant in an almost baroque, seventeenth-century, rather than eighteenth-century, way. On a level of appreciation admittedly subjective, reading aloud certain passages from Barton and *The Conduct* produces kinesthetic ratification of the argument that we are reading the same writer.

∞

Separated by two wars and nine years, Barton's *Unanimity and Public Spirit* (1755) and the anonymous *Conduct of the Paxton Men* were written for different ends, the one to urge the faction-ridden frontier to unite before a common enemy, the other to vindicate the backcountry vigilantes. Yet each pamphlet exhorts a people, abandoned to adversity by an indifferent assembly, to employ its own resources to survive. More than anywhere else perhaps we can detect in the two pamphlets' respective conclusions the same mind urging a people betrayed to protect their natural freedom.[61]

In the final pages of *Unanimity and Public Spirit,* Barton refocuses his sermon on the contemporary emergency that inspired it. He appeals to his readers' terror of enslavement to a foreign, "Romish" tyrant: "who . . . would not rather die a *Protestant* and a *Freeman,* than live an *Idolater* and a *Slave.*"[62] To reinforce his call to positive action, he cites "the Author of *Cato's Letters*" and Algernon Sidney on the ignominy of tyrannical rule: "As Mr. Sidney observes, [tyrants] *use their Subjects as Asses and Mastiff-Dogs, to work and to fight, and to be oppressed and to be killed for them.*"[63] In uniting to fight the French and their Indian allies, the divided frontiersmen—"Members of the Church of England and Protestant Dissenters *of all Denominations*"—will boldly give the lie to those critics who argue that we "have degenerated from [our] Virtue, or lulled ourselves into inglorious Ease to the utter Ruin of our Posterity! But where Freedom points the way, 'whether to Life or to Death,'" he concludes, "may we dare to follow, and to our latest Breath dare to continue what we are, *Protestants and Freemen!*"[64] Left to their own devices, the settlers in Cumberland and York counties must use their freedom to defend their religion and liberty, for "once extinct in Pennsylvania, whither, or into what Region, shall we flee in Search of them?"[65]

Although focused a bit differently, the concluding argument to *The Conduct* also invokes "the Spirit of a free People . . . [who] have a Right to *demand,* and to *receive* Protection."[66] The French oppressor in *Unanimity*

has become the Philadelphia Quaker, and accordingly the very same earlier citation from Algernon Sidney can be turned against that faction: "But
it seems that there are Men in PENNSYLVANIA, who (to use the Words
of the great ALGERNON SIDNEY) look upon the People 'like *Asses* and
Mastiff Dogs,['] who ought 'to *work* and to *fight,* to be *oppress'd* and *kill'd*
for them.'"[67] As before, supportive passages from and allusions to *Cato's
Letters* are introduced, including one prominently set forth on the title page.
British subjects—that is, a "free People"—their lives and liberties jeop-
ardized by a government which has long-ignored their grievances, need no
longer "crouch beneath their Sufferings"; rather, they may draw upon "a
proper Spirit of Jealousy, and Revenge" to achieve the protection that
is their right.

The writer of each pamphlet, then, armed with the authority of *Cato's
Letters* and Algernon Sidney, advocates the freedom of a people to adopt
extreme, even violent, measures to defend their lives and liberty when the
higher civil authority fails to do so. Each relies upon similar and identical
passages from *Cato's Letters* and Algernon Sidney to advocate a libertarian position in the face of governmental apathy or tyranny.

Reinforcing this analysis is the attribution of *The Conduct of the Paxton
Men* to Barton by his own great-great-grandson George Maurice Abbot, librarian of the Library Company of Philadelphia. Although we cannot determine what prompted Abbot to assign the tract to his distinguished
ancestor, he might have possessed a piece of now-lost family history that
indeed passed down to him through his great-grandfather William. If
Thomas, as now seems likely, wrote the pamphlet, William must have
known of it and suppressed or helped suppress the fact of authorship. The
oldest of Thomas's children, a lawyer, a co-designer (with Charles Thompson) of the Unites States Great Seal), a scholar who demonstrated in his
biography of his uncle intimate acquaintance with the vast, now-lost Bar-
ton/Rittenhouse correspondence, he is the most probable source for a piece
of family tradition like this.[68] If so, his failure not to disclose it publicly in
his 1813 biography may reflect either his father's attempt to distance himself from the tract or his, William's, own embarrassment. The Paxton
killings were very much alive in the oral memory of Lancaster county, and
the recollection was far from salutary, not at all the kind of skeleton a man
in the public eye would exhume.

As late as 1830, Rhoda Barber set down in a school exercise book the
history of the founding of Wrightsville, Pennsylvania, a community where

her family had long resided. Born three years after the Paxton Boys had stopped at her father's farm, she recalls her father's conversations with them and her brothers' seeing bloodied tomahawks lashed to their saddles. She also reports the following significant detail: "an Episcopalian minister in Lancaster wrote to vindicate them [i.e., the Paxtonians] bringing scripture to prove that it was right to destroy the heathen and very many were of the same opinion."[69] Forty-three years before Abbot's annotation, Rhoda Barber testified to the persistence of an oral recollection which in effect identified Barton as an apologist for the Scots-Irish vigilantes, a recollection which would have reinforced a Barton family tradition Abbot was partner to.

An oral tradition recorded in 1830, a scholarly judgment probably founded on family knowledge and set down in 1873, parallels in style, tone and attitude, and in the use of authoritative support—these persuasively reinforce Thomas Barton's candidacy as the author of *The Conduct of the Paxton Men*. Yet that pamphlet's unabashed, de facto defense of Scots-Irish vigilante justice and its unmitigated loathing of the converted Conestogas disturbingly contradict both Barton's long-standing sentiments and the few · remarks he offered on the affair. We therefore need to ask what might have inspired him to write such a polemic, publish it anonymously, and then, possibly, persuade his son William (granted he knew) to respect that anonymity.

The one known Barton letter dating from the same year as the publication of *The Conduct of the Paxton Men,* his November 16, 1764, report to the SPG, needs to be examined carefully. After some preliminaries, he notes the miniscule number of Anglicans (about 500) in a population of about 35,500 in Lancaster county, a veritable Babel of Dissenters and others: "German Lutherans, Calvinists, Mennonists, Moravians, New-Born, Dunkars, Presbyterians, Seceders, New Lights, Covenanters, Mountain-Men, Brownists, Independents, Papists, Quakers, Jews, &c."[70] The hotly contested county elections for the General Assembly and local positions on October 1 sadly reflected this disproportion, with not one Anglican church member in Lancaster "elected into any of these Offices."[71] At this juncture, Barton reassures the society of his several congregations' good behavior during the recent turmoil. His observations, tone, and focus are significant enough to warrant quoting the passage in full:

I have the satisfaction to assure the Hon[ble]. Society that my People have continued to give Proofs of that Submission & Obedience to civil Authority, which it is the Glory of the Church of England to inculcate: and whilst Faction & Party Strife have been rending the Province to Pieces, they behav'd themselves as became peaceable & dutiful Subjects, never intermeddling in the least— Suffer me to add, Sir, that in the Murder of the Indians in this Place & the different Insurrections occasion'd by this inhuman Act, not one of them was ever concern'd—Justice demands this Testimony from me in their Favour; as their Conduct upon this Occasion has gain'd them much Credit & Honour—Upon the whole, the Church of England visibly gains Ground throughout the Province—The Mildness and Excellency of her Constitution, her Moderation & Charity, even to her Enemies, And (I hope I may be indulg'd to say), the indefatigable Labours of her Missionaries, must at Length recommend her to all except those who have an hereditary Prejudice & Aversion to her.[72]

Barton bears witness here to his people's respect for "civil authority" and their aloofness from the strife, the faction-fighting, the murders. Their discipline throughout December 1763 and the whole of 1764 earned for them "much credit and honour." His word choice, moreover, patently registers his disapproval of the rioting and atrocities—"the murder of the Indians," "insurrections," and "inhuman act."

When compared with his previous reports, what should impress us about this account is Barton's silence on his own role(s) during the recent emergency. With this exception, his official communications to the SPG describe not only conditions and attitudes among his parishioners as a threatened minority in their communities, but also his own activities among them—his riding the circuit to marry, baptize, bury, and conduct services; his building of new churches and repairing of older structures; his missionary and educational work among the Native Americans and, indeed, British dissenters and German sectarians; his rallying his congregations against the French and Indian menace and leading them on raiding parties and work details to improve fortifications; and his attempts, while suffering from gradually failing health, to survive on an insufficient income. In all other respects, this *notitia parochialis* fully details his actual activities and efforts to advance Episcopalianism. It is, therefore, noteworthy that had he inspired his people to obey the "civil authority, which it is the glory of the Church of England to inculcate," he would certainly have spoken of it. To obtain recognition, advancement, and reward, he needed to publicize his achievements. The closest he comes to doing this, however, is in the vague, generalized, and evasive allusion to the "indefatigable labors of" the Church's missionaries.

Most noteworthy, he fails to mention writing *The Conduct*. Why? Did qualms of conscience override his responsibility to report to his superiors in London, an omission he compounded by publishing it anonymously?

Surely he had similar motives in 1755 for not acknowledging that he wrote the largely plagiarized tract *Unanimity and Public Spirit.*[73] Officially, then, he seems to have dissociated himself from two morally dubious publishing ventures; in 1755 he resisted concerted efforts to put into print his plagiarized war sermon, and, with and after publication, he failed to claim credit for it; in 1764 he employed anonymity to insure the illusion of his detachment from the turmoil.

Two other features of his November 1764 SPG report merit attention. Consistent with his earlier disapproval, he censures the Presbyterians more than any other dissenting denomination: "they are a People who are unsteady, and much given to Change, fond of Novelty, & easily led away by every kind of Doctrine. This Disposition will ever be a Bar to their Encrease— The Seceders are making great Havock among them & are proselyting[74] them by Thousands to their Opinions:— These last however, are a Set of Men who under a Monarchial Government, I think, cannot subsist long;— Their Interest upon their own Principles, must undoubtedly destroy itself."[75] Posing the greatest threat to the secure establishment of the Anglican church, in the long run the Presbyterians' anarchical energies will inevitably undo them: "The Church of England then must certainly prevail at last."[76]

In his reproof of the Presbyterians, as in his sympathy for the murdered Conestogas, Barton continues to express feelings which as an Anglican itinerant missionary he had already voiced in his earlier reports. What is different about the November 16 letter is a major, novel point: the entire concluding section elaborates a justification for his wanting to leave Lancaster county.

Barton begins casually by underscoring that he has always faithfully officiated at the several widely separated churches that were his charge: I "have never, to my Knowledge, been absent once, even in the severest Weather, except detain'd by Sickness; to which I was always happy enough to be a Stranger till of late."[77] He repeats in the following paragraph that his "Itinerantcy also bears heavy upon me in my present State of health."[78] Poor health had prompted him earlier to petition the SPG for removal, and because he has become even more ill, he now hopes the Society will assent to his relocating: "I return my most grateful Acknowledgments to the Society for their kind Indulgence in giving me Leave to remove to another Mission, for the better Preservation of my Health."[79] As if to plant an attractive possibility in the minds of his superiors, he expends considerable effort describing an area he has visited in nearby Delaware which "would soon make a flourishing & valuable Mission" if put into the charge of "a prudent Clergyman."[80]

Barton also cites extreme financial need. With "11 in [my] Family, a Wife, 7 Children & 2 Servants," his "Economy & Frugality" can do little to secure the necessities of life, "which must be purchas'd [here] at a most extravagant Rate."[81] Perennially the bane of missionaries in colonial America, subsistence income continues to exact its toll on Barton, as it had in Cumberland and York counties.

Failing health, insufficient income, and poor prospects for improving either of these in Lancaster justify Barton's desire to move. Yet interspersed among these oft-expressed explanations are new intimations of psychological or spiritual distress: "My Ambition aspires at Nothing more than what will purchase me a Freedom from Want, from low & abject Dependance."[82] Dependence—"low & abject Dependance"—on others he finds particularly humiliating; it circumscribes his freedom ("freedom from Want"). The infelicitous circumstances of his life in Lancaster have disrupted his inner harmony: "Peace of my Mind, & the Prospect of doing Good" are "dearer to me than any other Consideration." He cannot enjoy these where he resides, but is willing to gamble, even if moving from Lancaster may not bring him the relief he seeks. "Whether a Removal to another Mission would be of any Advantage to me," he concludes, "I know not."[83] But his desperation was profound enough for him, despite poor health, to consider risking all. It should not be surprising, therefore, that his despair momentarily drove him to threaten resigning: "I shall ever esteem it my highest Honour that I have been employ'd in the Society's Service; But if the Prospect of Indigence should at any Time compel me to retire, I would humbly hope that their Protection & Countenance will be continued to me."[84] Barton's humble hope for the society's future protection is the plea of a man face-to-face with the reality of his vulnerability, social and political as well as financial.

In November 1763, Barton purchased a residence convenient to St. James's and situated in a prestigious quarter, on the corner of North Lime and East Orange Streets, across from the Shippen mansion. One month before the first atrocity, therefore, Barton was evidently planning to remain in Lancaster. The events between December 1763 and sometime well before November 1764, when he refers to an earlier petition to remove, altered that intention. In 1765 he visited the Mohawk River valley, where he stayed at Johnson Hall, the guest of Sir William Johnson. The earliest reference to a correspondence between Barton and Johnson occurs in a note dated August 1763.[85] His first extant letter to Johnson, dated after his 1765 excursion, reveals that the two had become fairly close as friends, and their correspondence from this period indicates that Barton is exploring opportunities for himself in Mohawk country.[86] We also see him maneuvering for a chaplaincy in Canada,[87] letting it be known as well that he would gladly relocate to Maryland.[88] Clearly, the evidence points to a man doing his best to escape a locale where he no longer wished to live.

Tension and exhaustion gradually undermined Barton's consitution. Sometime between writing his November 1764 report and autumn 1765, he suffered the physical collapse he anticipated.[89] His circumstances worsened. On April 28, 1766, he sent a richly suggestive letter to Colonel James Burd complaining of scurrilous attacks by "a notorious Disturber of the Peace."[90] What, if anything, had Barton done to incite the abuse? Had it any connection with his supposedly clandestine writing of *The Conduct?* And why does he bother to notify one of the principal magistrates of Lancaster, further cautioning him at the same time to do nothing for the moment?

Barton's distress did not go unheeded. The SPG agreed to increase his annual allowance; Thomas Penn, never celebrated for financial liberality, offered him a personal gift of £50. The terms for both, however, were the same—that he promise to stay where he was, in Pennsylvania.[91] In addition, and with an irony he would not have ignored, Barton was given permission to farm the Conestoga Manor, which had ceased to be a reservation with the extermination of its Native American residents.[92] Because of his established value to church and proprietary and perhaps because of what he had achieved in writing *The Conduct of the Paxton Men,* the SPG, Thomas Penn, and Sir William Johnson handsomely rewarded Barton and obtained thereby his agreement to remain in Lancaster.

It is the contention here that Barton wrote *The Conduct of the Paxton Men* anonymously under some kind of pressure, or even coercion. With William Smith in Great Britain on a fund-raising venture for the College of Philadelphia, Barton was the only experienced propagandist, "agent of influence," as it were, readily available to the proprietary party.[93] Although it is improbable that the Penns and their leading supporters pressured him, people lower down, say, the Shippens or other officials in Lancaster, probably looked to him to respond to Franklin's *Narrative.* If so, they would perhaps have found a man not readily disposed to betray his principles in the cause of political expedience.[94] But Barton no longer enjoyed the high level of support he had relied upon earlier. William Smith was in Great Britain; Thomas Penn's nephew John, who did not know Barton as well as his uncle had, had taken up residence in Philadelphia in 1763; and Richard Peters had resigned the provincial secretaryship in 1762, allowing Joseph Shippen to replace him. Barton's world was changing for the worse, and with it his old network of alliances.

We do not know what compelled Barton to set aside his ideals, but it is likely that some powerful figures discovered a way to undermine his scruples. Possibly, he yielded to dire economic need, together with the promise of immediate financial remuneration, or even to threats to divulge publicly an earlier misdeed (e.g., his 1755 plagiarism of Samuel Roberts's tract), or to both of these. In the event, Barton suppressed his conscience and oft-expressed respect for Christianized Indians and his disdain for anarchic, intractable Scots-Irish Presbyterians to construct a virulent and effective rebuttal of Franklin's polemic and Quaker policy. Apparently, however, he had had enough of Lancaster county. Having violated his ethics, grown disgusted with regional politics, and teetering precariously on the edge of a breakdown, he desperately sought to leave Pennsylvania to obtain the peace of mind and opportunity to do good which to him "were dearer . . . than any other consideration." An easier living in Maryland or within Johnson's more congenial proprietorship (possibly recalling to Barton the felicities of Irish "Big House" culture), or even the bleak rigors of garrison duty in Quebec—all sang their Sirens' song to his distraught soul.

To appreciate the full political importance of *The Conduct,* we need to understand the tract as more than a simple pro-Paxton, anti-Indian, anti-Quaker polemic. Published in March, 1764, it was an early salvo in the proprietary's campaign to dislodge the Quaker faction from its domination of the General Assembly. As a number of commentators have observed, the proprietary sought to accomplish this in part by entering into a coalition with the numerically powerful but politically isolated and disaffected poor city dwellers and frontiersmen, who were for the most part also Scots-Irish Presbyterians.[95] During the period when the Paxtonians continued to disrupt the civil peace, challenging both the proprietary executive and the Quaker-dominated legislature, some of the proprietor's friends began to perceive how the strident malcontentedness of the Scots-Irish might be exploited against the Quakers. In a masterpiece of duplicity, the proprietary party moved in two contrary directions: on the surface and to all appearances, it continued publicly to denounce frontier vigilantism, issuing outraged proclamations against the Paxton Volunteers and general warrants for their arrests, even promising handsome financial rewards to those who would turn them in. Tacitly, the proprietary group looked the other way. Even though most of the Paxton ringleaders were known, not one was ever arrested. Some of them even settled on the former Indian reservation. What pleasure Barton must have experienced in deriding those squatters in his own voice: "several of the Paxton people took possession of this Farm—built Cabbins and settled upon it under the ridiculous notion of a *right by*

Conquest."[96] In time the proprietary faction expelled them, but otherwise did nothing. It should be no wonder, then, that its informal, tacit coalition with the Scots-Irish against the Quakers spawned rumors of collusion going back as early as the December 14 killings.[97]

Whether or not the proprietary's refusal to heed the early warnings of potential vigilantism from such respected, moderate Presbyterians as John Harris and the Rev. John Elder points to active collaboration with the Paxtonians we cannot determine.[98] Clearly, however, the Church of England, as religious arm of provincial, secular power, was drawn into the plot to wrest control of the Assembly from the Quaker faction. Exemplifying a new, profane, if perhaps cynical, ecumenicalism, the doors of Philadelphia's Episcopal churches were even thrown open to the local Presbyterian ministry.[99] In addition, after Benjamin Franklin published his attack on the Paxtonians, the Reverend Thomas Barton, itinerant SPG missionary to Lancaster, was apparently directed to neutralize Franklin's cogent criticisms by defending the rioters, discrediting the Conestogas, and exposing the shallow hyprocrisy of the Philadelphia Quakers, many of whom actually took up arms in February 1764, to defend their city and the Indians sheltered therein from the frontiersmen's wrath. But lest he betray proprietary strategy, Barton had to write as someone other than the most eloquent and literary Anglican divine then in the colony. Anonymity, of course, also assuaged his personal scruples. He succeeded in remaining unknown. So cunningly did Barton's pamphleteering persona ape the Scots-Irish voice that the tract's author was believed to be, as we have seen, "a *Stark Naked Presbyterian.*"[100] Although Barton's hand might have been suspected by some, his authorship generally remained secret until his own great-great-grandson identified him in 1873.

The coalition of poor city dwellers, Presbyterian backcountry settlers, and proprietary politicians proved short-lived. After the anti-Quaker groups failed to obtain control of the Assembly, the old animosities among them resurfaced. Faction-ridden Pennsylvania resumed stumbling along the path to the upheavals of the mid 1770s.[101] Later, when historical circumstances once again confronted Barton with unscrupulous politicians attempting to bend his will and coerce his allegiance, however, he refused to compromise. Locked out of his churches, accused of preaching against the new republic and of being "privy" to a plot to seize arsenals in Lancaster, York, and Carlisle in 1777,[102] he accepted painful separation from his children and banishment to New York City rather than forswear his oath to the king, thereby firmly setting his foot on the path to martyrdom.

6

No "Canting Parson"

. . . for your kind good Wishes I heartily thank you without Suspecting any thing of the meer Priest in your Prayer the sincerity of which I can have no doubt of, and whilst I am convinced of your possessing that Social disposition and goodness of heart for which you are pleased to applaud your friend, It is not in my power to conceive there is any of the Canting Parson in your Expressions.
—Sir William Johnson

AMONG THE MYSTERIES SURROUNDING BARTON'S LIFE, FEW ARE AS INtriguing as his friendship with the powerful, influential Sir William Johnson. Johnson, who lived on his manorial estate in New York's Mohawk River Valley, was the Crown's superintendent for Indian affairs in the northern colonies. The British government's principal negotiator with Native American tribes, particularly the Six Nations of the Iroquois, Johnson decisively helped shape policy and events involving the New York and Pennsylvania frontiers and the lands to the west recently won from France. One of his primary tasks was to insure that the Six Nations remained loyal toward British interests.

The Christianized Conestogas (remnants of the Susquehannocks, which people the Iroquois had effectively destroyed as a nation) near Lancaster had enjoyed the protection of the Iroquois. Their murder by the incensed Paxtonians and the latter's continuing threats against the other Native Americans settled in eastern Pennsylvania, therefore, put the province in an extremely awkward, dangerous position. For this reason, Governor John Penn wrote Sir William Johnson on December 31, 1763, explaining what had occurred earlier in the month and urgently requesting Johnson to "take the properest Method of acquainting [the Six Nations] with the Truth of this Transaction, and of removing any disadvantageous Impressions they may have received from an imperfect Account of the Matter."[1] An exchange of communications among Johnson, Thomas and John Penn, General Thomas Gage, and New York Lieutenant Governor Cadwallader Colden shows the two provinces trying to prevent the situation from deteriorating any further.[2]

Sir William Johnson, superintendent of Indian affairs for the northern colonies, c. 1760. (From the color miniature in the Library and Archives of Canada, Ottawa, copy no. C83491.)

It appears that Barton and Johnson first made contact sometime before the Paxton killings. In August 1763, Barton wrote the latter recommending the Lancaster gunsmith John Henry.[3] As noted in the previous chapter, a catalogue of letters among the Johnson papers destroyed by fire records the receipt on April 3, 1764 of what must be news of Barton's pamphlet, if not the tract itself.[4] As we have seen, the *Conduct* was presumably finished on St. Patrick's Day, March 17, 1764. Whoever mentioned the pamphlet or sent it to Johnson must have done so soon after it was published for its title to have been included in the catalogue for April 1–3, 1764. Because none of the other numerous Paxton pamphlets seems listed among the Johnson papers, we may infer that Johnson was himself not gathering or collecting a library of Paxton tracts. In all likelihood, the informant or sender simply wanted Johnson to be aware of that particular tract. Why?

Although not explicitly identified, the sender, if not Barton himself, was probably the Francis Wade mentioned immediately before the reference to Barton's pamphlet: "one [letter] of the 3d from Francis Wade, Philadelphia, telling of the wrecking on the French coast of the vessel which carried Mr Croghan and Colonel Armstrong, asking payment of a draft on Captain Clawes and mentioning a petition to the crown for a change of government and a pamphlet called the *Conduct of the Paxtoners*."[5] The reference is far from clear. Did Wade's letter only mention "a pamphlet called the *Conduct of the Paxtoners*"? or was the publication actually included? Furthermore, the lack of an explicit verbal before "a pamphlet" makes the relationship between Wade's letter and the tract even more ambiguous, for the entry may be construed as simply recording the receipt of *The Conduct* from some unidentified party (who might indeed have been Barton himself).

A subsequent Wade letter strongly implies he served as a source of news on Barton, if not in 1764, then certainly two years later. Wade wrote to Johnson from Philadelphia on March 31, 1766, indicating that he had spoken to Barton.[6] Because the letter has been badly mutilated, its content cannot be determined precisely. In it, however, Wade seems to refer to his disabusing Barton of a misperception the latter had entertained concerning a physician he recommended to Johnson.[7] In some way, then, Barton, Croghan, Wade, and Johnson might all have been known to one another in 1764.

One explanation sees two names, Croghan's and Armstrong's, coupled with the title of a pamphlet that some of the proprietary party knew to have been authored by Barton, himself a proprietary man and a friend to Croghan, and at one time at least a rival of Armstrong, another proprietary placeman. All three, moreover, having obtained renown in the conduct of Indian affairs would have been known to Johnson—Croghan and Amstrong certainly were. The possibility exists that someone, Wade or Barton, wanted Johnson to see or at very least know of this major proprietary coup in the Paxton-pamphlet war. Possibly, Barton later explained his involvement in the pamphlet war; or possibly Johnson initially queried Barton on his participation.

Whatever the intriguing notation may mean, the next and rather startling news of the two men dates from 1765 when Barton, from the city of New York, thanked Johnson for his recent hospitable reception at Johnson Hall. Insofar as his note announces a number of interests Barton and Johnson enjoyed and explored in their subsequent correspondence, it merits examining at length. Three emphases stand out. First, Barton promises to forward Johnson several scientific instruments appealing to the latter's interest in electrical experimentation, thus making clear that the two men enjoyed a common scientific curiosity: "I have given Directions to the best Workman in this Place to make a Conductor & some other Things for your *Electrical Aparatus*—Capt. Prevost has undertaken to see them pack'd, and will carefully forward them in a few Days— As soon as I return to Lancaster, I shall do myself the Pleasure to send you the proper *Leyden Bottles,* & the other Articles which I mentiond to you."[8] In his next communication to Johnson, Barton expresses hope that his friend received the scientific apparatus and "that they were so well executed as to answer the Ends propos'd."[9] At the end of the month, Barton once more speaks of sending Johnson "a few *Gimeracks*" and announces that "the Jet D'eau, & some other Things which I promis'd to send you are almost ready. . . . as they are really curious, I shall employ my best Endeavours to get them to you as soon as possible."[10]

These references to scientific apparatus and experimentation remind us of Barton's activities as a naturalist. The interest in botany and mineralogy he had expressed earlier also extended itself to physics and astronomy.[11] Indeed, he supported and assisted his brother-in-law David Rittenhouse in his construction of the Orreries that were acquired by the College of Philadelphia (now the University of Pennsylvania) and the College of New Jersey (now Princeton University). The "Correspondent, at Lancaster" who described a display of the Aurora Borealis on January 5, 1769, for the American Philosophical Society was probably Barton.[12] He also participated in the observations undertaken by the American Philosophical Society to record accurately the transit of Venus in 1769. In 1770, he contributed to discussions on the appearance of a new comet.[13] Unfortunately, however, the scientific excitement shared by Johnson and Barton soon became lost as they explored two other interests.

In a second matter, Barton writes of his eagerness to assist Johnson in any way that "might be agreeable" to him. He desires Johnson to know "that I shall at all Times receive a singular Satisfaction in having it in my Power to serve you. . . . If I can contribute to your Amusement, or do any Office that might be agreeable to you, you will make me happy whenever you honour me with your Commands." Later epistolary exchanges establish that Barton is speaking here to Johnson's roles as both the Crown's representative and the proprietor of one of America's largest manorial estates.

Finally, Barton's epistle dramatically seizes the initiative in drawing his new and powerful acquaintance into supporting the missionary work of the SPG: "The Rev^d. M^r. Auchmuty[14] Rector of the Churches of N. York . . . begs your Permission to propose you to the Society for the Propagation of the Gospel in Foreign Parts, as a Member of that Venerable Body—This Request I flatter myself you will not refuse, when you consider of what Advantage it might be in planting *proper Missions* in the Indian Country, which is an Object I am sure you have at Heart—."[15]

Johnson responded promptly on November 7, 1765, but Barton's long letter of November 9, reveals him too excited to wait for Johnson's response to make its way south: "I have transgress'd the Rules of Politeness in the Length of this Letter; but my Heart is so full of the Pleasure I receiv'd, and my Thoughts so carried away with the Remembrance of the agreeable & happy Moments I had the Honour to spend, in Johnson-Hall, that I have forgot my Duty, and indulg'd myself in a *Paper-Talk* with you—."[16]

In this letter, and true to his promise to assist Johnson settle his lands, Barton recommends several specialists for Johnson's projects—an iron-worker, "a Sadler, Collar-Maker, & Wheel-Wright . . . the Mechanicks you mention'd . . . Planters . . . a young Gentleman, regularly bred to Physick & Surgery."[17] Additionally, after explaining that he has shipped what scientific equipment "could be sent by this Conveyance," he then satisfies his own technical curiosity by requesting a description of Johnson's "simple Process" for manufacturing potash.[18]

Barton concludes the letter proper by asking to be remembered to Johnson's nephew Sir Guy Johnson and with a joking allusion to some now obscure event that occurred at Johnson Hall: "My Friend Mr. Burns, I hope, is still alive, & *unwedded*—He has my good Wishes."[19] The name *Burns* (i.e., Michael Byrne) is Gaelic and reminds us that Sir William Johnson was himself of an Irish-gentry, Catholic family which had conformed to the Church of Ireland, the McShanes of Smithstown, county Meath. The Johnson papers show Sir William consciously to have enjoyed cultivating the identity of an Irish landowner, elaborately celebrating St. Patrick Days, trying to secure the services of a harper, and expressing interest in pipers.[20] His most trusted deputy was George Croghan, another former Irish Catholic who had conformed. It might well be, then, that Johnson Hall possessed for Barton some of the nostalgic graces and traditional largesse of an Irish "Big House." His later correspondence repeatedly expresses determination to return to avail himself of its hospitality and its owner's good will. A year later, for example, explaining how his second son David Cradock's death to smallpox and his wife's illness from the same disease had delayed his writing, he affirms that "no Distance, or Length of Time will ever be able to cancel the pleasing Idea I retain of Johnson-Hall, & of the kind reception I met with there—I know no Wish at present which I would prefer to that of being able to spend a Week or two with you, & to assist you in fixing up some little philosophical Aparatus, that might amuse you in your Hours of Leisure & Retirement. If Mr. Croghan should visit you in the Spring, I shall endeavour to break thro' every Engagement to accompany him."[21] For all that Barton sincerely intended to return to Johnson Hall, the course of their two lives never again converged to make that reunion possible.

Significantly, Barton's postscript to the November 9, 1765, letter reminds us that Sir William Johnson remained securely behind a social barrier that no amount of Irish affability and goodwill could surmount fully. His authority and economic power conferred upon him the role of patron. Barton's postscript suggests such studied nonchalance that one suspects it discloses his reason for originally journeying the great distance to Johnson Hall. In it, he refers to his failure to obtain a tract of land in New York because of Governor Colden's "Situation with his Council."[22] Apparently, Barton had journeyed to the Mohawk to look over the prospects, his hopes high. Had the application succeeded, he says he would have been able to settle his land with "industrious & useful Persons." He might even have "been induc'd to have remov'd myself," a remark that, in light of his troubled circumstances in Lancaster, strikes us as understated. He concludes by asking Johnson's opinion on whether or not to renew the petition when the new governor arrives. Like other themes in these early letters, this desire to improve his situation by becoming a landowner and proprietor, or what we would today term a *developer,* also runs through Barton's later correspondence with Johnson.

The Anglican Church had carried out missionary work among the Mohawks, eastern-most tribe of the Iroquois Confederacy, during the years 1704–19.[23] When Sir William Johnson became interested in Christianizing the Iroquois, therefore, ground had already been broken. We need to remember, however, that consistent with the ideals of eighteenth-century British colonialism, his inspiration was both personal and political, religious and secular. Proprietor of a vast manor in the eastern Mohawk River Valley that included his fledgling towns of Canajoharie, Schenectady, and Johnstown, Johnson had a vested interest in seeing the neighboring Mohawks pacified and kept loyal to British interests. Following the end of the Seven Years' War, he perceived that the Iroquois, in the words of Frank J. Klingberg, could be used as "a weapon against French Jesuit penetration from Canada on the one hand, and later against revolutionary religious dissent on the other, as represented, for example, by [the Reverend Eleazer] Wheelock from New England."[24]

Throughout the 1750s, the SPG, strapped for funds and short of qualified missionaries, could only manage to support a mission in Albany and to educate a few Indian children at William Smith's College of Philadelphia.[25] The growing influence of New Englander Eleazer Wheelock, together with Johnson's deepening distrust of dissenting missionaries, gradually catalyzed a more ambitious program. Because of his friendship with the Irish baronet, we find Barton mediating between Johnson and the SPG authorities, his mysterious September 1765 visit to Johnson Hall evidently being the occasion by which the two parties formally came to join forces.

In that first note he sent Johnson following his visit, Barton urges his new friend to avail himself of Samuel Auchmuty's willingness to propose Johnson for membership in the SPG. He believes, moreover, that Johnson will not decline the opportunity "when you consider of what Advantage it might be in planting *proper Missions* in the Indian Country, which is an Object I am sure you have at Heart."[26]

Johnson expressed enthusiastic, immediate agreement with the proposal. Replying in November, he affirmed heart-felt concern for the welfare and happiness of the Indians and recalled the assistance he had always provided "Missionaryes sent amongst them." Accordingly, he said, I "shall not hesitate to agree to Mr Auchmutys kind proposal, . . . assuring him that I can have no Objection to becoming a member of so Venerable a body."[27]

It seems inconceivable that Barton and Johnson would not have spoken of this issue while the latter was being regaled amid the baronial pleasures of Johnson Hall, or even that Barton was not sent in part to sound Johnson out on the matter. Certainly, occasional phrases in both letters sound forced, as when Barton presumes that establishing *"proper Missions . . .* [is] an Object I am sure you have at Heart"; or when Johnson reminds the SPG, with which he had had contact since 1749, that he nurtures an interest and "sincere regard for" the "happiness" of the Indians. This part of their exchange, at least, sounds perfunctory, pro forma. In any case, the society's secretary, Daniel Burton, wrote Johnson in May 1766, announcing his acceptance into the SPG.[28] Additionally, Burton requested of Johnson "the favour of your advice & direction for some Scheme of a more extensive Nature" than had been put into practice during earlier times.

Johnson's exchanges with Daniel Burton, Samuel Johnson (president of King's College, New York), William Smith, Richard Peters, and Thomas Barton show the clerics and their most aggressive lay leader busily hammering out a program for bringing SPG missionary priests and schoolmasters into Mohawk country. The role of these latter would be two-fold: to Christianize and "civilize" the Mohawks and to insure their loyalty to Britain's cause. Although it is not germane to the present study to examine closely the society's missionary effort among the Iroquois, one issue does deserve attention. Based upon his many years of intimate contact with the Iroquois and a deep respect for their humanity, Johnson insisted until his death in 1774 that at least some of the Anglican missionaries should imitate the successful strategies of the French Jesuits by living among the Indians. This feeling opposed prevailing attitudes in the SPG: Smith, for example, particularly believed that civilizing the Indians would be achieved best by raising and educating their children in missions separated from the Iroquois towns or "castles."

Expectedly, the man whose educational plan had led to his being appointed provost of the College of Philadelphia[29] sketched out an initial "Scheme for Converting the Heathen Natives of America connected with the English Government."[30] His proposal, Smith claimed, was inspired by the successful policies instituted by the Jesuits in Paraguay. Its primary stress and novelty as a missionary program fell upon the priority of "Teaching the Arts of civil Life & Humanity . . . before . . . the Teaching of Christianity to them."[31] To achieve this, the Indians would be induced to settle among White families recently given special grants of land. Subsidized at first by the SPG, they would gradually be "brought to see & to feel with how much More Comfort, Ease and Security they can live in this Way, than in their own Vagrant unsettled Condition."[32] Once this objective has been achieved, "the Instruction of Children at Schools, and in all Sorts of manual or mechanic Employments will become easy."[33] At this point, the Indian parents, but more importantly, their children—future proselytizers to their own yet unsettled people—"will . . . be brought to listen to the Blessed Gospel." Unless "Settlements are made on some such Plan as this," Smith concludes, "the opening [of] a School or sending a Missionary here & there among vagrant Tribes . . . will be like Writing in the Sand."[34]

Sir William Johnson's response to Smith's proposal proves that he was a leader of vision as well as of immense practicality and humanitarianism.[35] Implied in his answer is the criticism that although Smith may possess expertise for running a municipal college, he had little pragmatic appreciation with the cultural needs of Native Americans. Johnson agrees with many points in the Smith-Peters plan, but he trenchantly argues that any missionary effort truly bent on success must respect the Indians' "unconquerable Aversion to Arts and Husbandry." The results in French Canada, rather than far-distant Paraguay, prove clearly that "a Civilized Member of Society & an Indian Hunter are not incompatible Characters," so that the transition from the life of nomadic hunter to that of settled farmer must be very gradual and must proceed by way of resident missionaries carefully screened to reflect in their dealings the highest of religious and humane ideals. Again, he argues, this is what gave "the french Jesuits . . .

so considerable an Advantage over us." At greater length and with transparent disdain for the zeal and ethnic arrogance that typified the usual missionary and White settler, Johnson wrote: "I have ever observed that those Ind^s. who have the least intercourse with us, have the most integrity, & possess the best Moral Qualities, & would be easily brought under the Conduct of a Good Resid^t. Teacher of exemplary Life to perceive the Sweets of a well regulated Society; which once effected they wo^d. soon adopt your Judicious plan without Umbrage or Jealousy."[36] He recognized further that by insisting that missionaries reside among their charges he would be raising obstacles to the SPG effort. "None of the Clergy of our Church," he wrote, "could Submit to sacrifice their friends hopes, & Connections, to bury themselves in an obscure Village Surrounded by a parcel of Indians." Nonetheless, he intuited that "nothing ever bade fairer for success if it could be put in practise."[37]

Barton had already sent off his proposal to the society before this exchange between Smith and Johnson. But for its earlier date, it might be interpreted as a compromise between visionary Smith's and realist Johnson's approaches. Like Johnson, he acknowledges that the Indians challenged the missionary effort in two ways: they regarded Europeans "*as Enemies & Intruders*" intent on depriving them of "their Rights & Property"; and "their erratic State of Life, wandering from Mountain to Mountain & from River to River, in Search of their Game," will frustrate any traditional proselytizing program.[38] In order to settle the Native Americans down to an agricultural way of life, one in which they could be of course watched and regulated, it will prove necessary to send among them "Missionaries formed from amongst the Indians themselves." In time, this initial phase can yield to one in which European missionaries, fluent in the native tongues, would gradually replace or supplement their Indian colleagues. "I make no Doubt," Barton concludes, "but such Missionaries would, in a little Time, perswade their wandering Tribes to incorporate with Civil Society, & to settle to Tillage & the Cultivation of their Lands, by showing them how much more comfortable, as well as advantageous, such a Life would be than that which they now lead.[39]

The central, key strategy to the success of this proposal lay in the training of the Indian missionaries who would make initial contact with their nomadic people. This education would be carried out in schools erected for the purpose. Although the College of Philadelphia and Barton in his own little school in Lancaster were providing the education suitable to future missionaries of Indian heritage, Barton envisioned a far more ambitious undertaking. He conceived a need for at least three major establishments "of at least ten Boys," the cost to be borne by the society, the provinces affected, and individual patrons such as Johnson. The Indian schools would be distributed throughout the colonies, one on the Mohawk River, attached to Johnson's free-school near Johnson Hall, another at Fort Pitt, and the third in "the back Parts of S. Carolina under the Care of the Superintendent of Indian Affairs for the Southern District, or some Missionary there."[40]

Having struck a balance between Smith's idealism and Johnson's practicality, it remains unclear why Barton himself never actively joined the missionary enterprise energetically undertaken by Johnson, particularly when he found the Mohawk baronet so congenial an acquaintance. One suspects that low salary and the rigors of frontier life—factors that in part drove Barton from western York county seven years earlier—combined together with the fact of his large family and, in Johnson's phrase, a disinclination shared with most missionaries to "bury themselves in an obscure Village Surrounded by a parcel of Indians," argued against his relocating in the north. Instead, as Smith makes clear to Johnson, their friend "seems determined to sollicit a Maryland Living."[41]

Newly ordained missionaries, young clerics without large families and less needful of a secure lifestyle were ideally suited to the challenges and the society's requirements. With those qualifications in mind, the services of John Stewart, Jacob Hall, William Andrews, and Harry Munro were finally secured through the untiring recruiting efforts of Barton and Smith.

Johnson showed high regard for his friend in 1767 when he sent his own son, William of Canajoharie, to Lancaster to be educated. The first clue that Barton and Johnson had been discussing such a possibility comes in June 1767, when Smith wrote that Johnson had already spoken of his willingness to commit to Barton's "Care, one or two Youths of Indian Extraction."[42] Highly commending Barton, Smith also hints that their friend would gladly undertake the effort "if his Income could be a little increased thereby," the support to come from both Johnson and the society.[43]

William, or *Tegcheunto,* the son of Sir William and his Mohawk mistress, Caroline Hendrick, niece of the powerful Chief Hendrick, arrived by July 22, when Barton wrote Johnson of the lad's progress. He notes that William's extraordinary "Application" or effort more than offset his "Deficiency" in "Genius, or Quickness of Apprehension."[44] He promises to spare no effort in educating Johnson's son. The early success of the experiment, moreover, already makes him hope that other Indians would "send about a Dozen of their most discreet & ingenious Boys to this Place—I should take Pleasure in the Education of them."

After receiving news of Johnson's pleasure over William's progress,[45] Barton replied on December 2, 1767, at greater length, detailing the boy's advances in writing, arithmetic, and reading. On the negative side, he describes William's "heavy . . . plodding" intellect and expresses concern over his reserved, bashful, even "unsociable" character.[46] The earlier pugnacity that William had brought with him now, fortunately, seems well in the past—"I have prevail'd upon him to lay [it] aside, So that he is now as peaceable a Lad as any in the Place." Barton also expresses gratitude over Johnson's readiness to recommend to the SPG that Barton be allowed to set up a small Indian school at the Lancaster mission.

The experiment with William ended abruptly in March 1768 when Barton had to send him back to New York. On January 10, 1768, Frederick Stump and his servant John Ironcutter (Eisenhauer) without apparent provocation slaughtered some ten Indians in Cumberland county, near Barton's old parish of St. John's in Carlisle.[47] As George Croghan remarked in a letter to Johnson, the Stump affair has "Revived y[e]. old Dispute About the Murder of the Conistoga Indians."[48] It was exactly this resurgence of the old animosities that unnerved the young William. Barton wrote: "ever since the turbulent & disordered State of the Back Counties, occasioned by the Murder committed upon several Indians by one Stump, & the Rescue of that Villain, & the lawless insolent Behaviour of some of the Inhabitants, in Consequence thereof . . . He immediately sollicitted Leave to return Home."[49] Living only a few blocks from the scene of the earlier massacre, it is no wonder that William "apprehended himself in Danger," as Barton put it in a later letter.[50]

Beyond his anxieties, William apparently experienced severe depression. He simply lost all interest in his studies: "he has relaxed in Application to Study, been uneasy in Mind; and from the most diligent, contented, happy Lad, is become the most dissatisfied, sullen, careless Creature imaginable."[51] With considerable patience, Barton futilely urged William to postpone leaving: "But notwithstanding his Situation in my own Family (which I hope he will do me the Justice to own, was comfortable & easy) I could not succeed with him."

The civilizing influences to which Sir William and Barton endeavored to expose William of Canajoharie and that appeared initially to produce positive effects must in fact have been superficial. Raised among the Mohawks and thrust into the White culture of Lancaster, he bore the cruel conflicts of two worlds on his soul. In the words of Johnson's biographers Arthur Pound and Richard Day, William "could not travel the white man's road in peace while his Indian cousins, the Delawares or Munseys, were being sacrificed in the back alleys."[52]

After William returned to the safety of Johnson's Mohawk Valley, Barton persevered with his plans for a school. Later records show that he succeeded in establishing one for the poor of Lancaster. On March 15, 1771, the SPG authorized Barton to hire a schoolmaster at an annual salary of £10. It is significant, however, that Joseph Rathel, reporting to the society, failed to mention the attendance of any Indians, although he did refer to the children of African-Americans: "I attend several Negroes belonging to different Families of the Church every Sunday Evening in the School House, and use my best Endeavours to instruct them in their Catechism and some of the plainest Duties of Religion and Morality, by which I hope these poor Creatures will be much benefitted."[53] A later schoolmaster, William Graham, stresses that Barton's school was primarily instituted to serve the needs of the indigent in his congregation. "The School," he wrote, "is in good order, and truly beneficial to a number of poor people (Members of the Church of England) whose children . . . are among the Catechumens whom the Rev. Mr. Barton examines publicly in the church, and can answer every question fully and distinctly."[54] Barton's school lasted until 1777, when Graham, an American patriot, resigned.[55]

∞

The Barton-Johnson correspondence opens an unexpected window for us into Barton's ministerial philosophy and preacherly style, and thus helps us glimpse some additional qualities in the man. As we saw, Johnson gradually came to object to dissenting missionaries when he learned that they were subversively undermining the authority of the British Crown and his own image among the Indians. He also felt that, coming as they did out of the puritanical heritage of New England, they soured and blighted the essentially happy dispositions of their converts. "Another objection," to the dissenting missionaries, he wrote in October 1766, "is that those brought up under the Care of Dissenting Ministers become a Gloomy race & lose their Abilities for hunting &ca[.,] spend their time in Idleness & hang^g upon The Inhabit^s. for a Wretched subsistence hav^g lost those Qualities wch rendr them usefull to us with^t acquir^g any others in their place worthy the Name of Christ^{ns}. to wch indeed they have little or no pretensions[,] all wch discountenances Religion with the rest of the Ind^s."[56] Johnson tended to view the Native American essentially as a "noble savage," an innocent child of nature.[57] A month later, he again asserted that the ideal missionary should be a man "as distant from Gloominess as from Levity."[58]

Barton concurred fully with Johnson's view on "The gloomy Priest," who does little but "whine, cant, cry, or sniffle."[59] In 1767, he elaborated on the ideal he himself must have endeavored to exemplify to his people: "The Religion of Christ is a Religion of Joy, and does not consist in a demure Phiz,[60] a sullen Aspect, a clouded stormy Face, that forebodes Nothing but Thunder & Lightning; or a narrow superstitious Observance of Trifles, attended with the Neglect of the weightier Matters of the Law & the Gospel—I hope & wish that you may obtain such a Man as you desire."[61]

The balance Barton praises here is evident throughout his extant sermons. It also inspired a little work, now rare, he published in 1767, *The Family Prayer-Book, Containing Morning and Evening Prayers for Families and Private Persons*. Printed by the Cloister Press at the Seventh-Day Baptist community in nearby Ephrata, it is based upon the Church of England's Book of Common Prayer and was intended for private use by his congregations to help them better prepare their hearts "for the social Worship of the Church." Although "*Family Worship*" may be "a Duty too little attended to," neither should it become something onerous, "a dreary observance." For this reason, he ends his short preface with the kindly hope that "every Happiness temporal and eternal . . . attend you" and recommends his reader "to God's Grace & the Love of Christ." He signs himself, appropriately, as "Your obliged Friend and affectionate Pastor."[62]

∞

The Barton-Johnson correspondence also offers further evidence of Barton's insecurity, even paranoia. Forced by circumstances of his role as a proprietary agent and a minister serving a minority, albeit powerful, denomination, Barton was often forced into confrontational situations with dissenters and had to execute his responsibilities from a vulnerable position that invited gossip and rumor-mongering. For a person apparently driven by a profound need to be liked, his public consciousness must not have been enviable. In respect to his private relationship with Johnson, his insecurity was often exacerbated by the long interval between letters, and even worse, by the rather frequent disappearance of communications.

A fairly typical expression of his fear that he has somehow failed Johnson opens his December 2, 1767, epistle. Even though Barton had but recently taken Sir William's son, William of Canajoharie, into his own home to educate, Johnson's recent long silence prompted apprehensions "that I had, by some unlucky Accident or other, forfeited the Honour of your Notice & kind Opinion. . . . my Fears began to persuade me, that my not hearing from you for several Months, proceeded from some Cause unfortunate, tho' unknown to me."[63]

Johnson speedily reassured Barton that he had "causelessly entertained" such suspicions. He reminds Barton what the latter must surely have known, namely, that Johnson's position of Indian superintendent often required him to travel about the frontier for long periods, as was indeed the case recently: "failure of Correspondence on my part can be attributed to [no] other causes than the nature of my Avocations and my having been far from home."[64]

Barton's apprehensions, however, continued to erode his peace of mind. Toward the end of 1769, he feared that some rumor-monger had turned Johnson against him. "I am afraid," he wrote, that "some ungenerous Person, who envied me the Honour of your Friendship, has endeavoured to interrupt it." He struggles to maintain a facade of gracious appreciation for those glimmers of true friendship he had recently and briefly enjoyed: "Be that as it may, I shall never cease to be grateful to remember the pleasing Hours I spent at Johnson-Hall."[65]

Barton wrote this some time after both his failure with William of Canajoharie and his successful campaign to obtain farming rights to the Conestoga Manor. It is therefore unlikely that his anxiety derived from any attempt to discredit him in either of those affairs. Significantly, his letter to the society written on the same day refers to his having authored a popular manuscript tract (now apparently lost) attacking dissenting enthusiasts. Very possibly, then, his conspicuous involvement in religious controversy might have attracted local gossip and verbal abuse, prompting him to suspect some local enemy of communicating unsavory accusations to Johnson.

By this point in their relationship, Johnson must have recognized Barton's oft-professed doubts for what they were—tacit appeals to be reassured regularly of Johnson's continuing esteem and friendship. In his reply to the 1769 letter, he labors at great length to assuage Barton's feelings of abandonment. "You may be Assured," he insisted, "that there is not the Least grounds for your attribut^g." his not writing "to the endeavours of any person w^h soever."[66] Illness and, once more, protracted negotiations had robbed him of the leisure to correspond. He closes by reaffirming the importance of their friendship: "I esteem your Correspondence so much that I would willingly say something to you, whenever I could, and this you may be assured of[,] that no attempts have been made to Lessen you in my Esteem, or if there had, my friendship is not to be so easily removed, on the Contrary I shall always be happy to See or hear from you whenever either is Convenient."[67]

With a breathlessness still evident today, Barton replied in a short note, relieved at Johnson's explanation: "It will ever be the Study and the Ambition of my Life to deserve your kind Regards; & you may therefore be assured that no Avocations whatever shall interrupt that Correspondence, with which you have been pleased to honour me."[68]

A few months later, Barton reversed roles with Johnson. Recuperating from a recurrent liver disorder that had prevented his writing earlier, Barton endeavors to head off imagined accusations from Johnson that his own silence intimates a rejection of his friend. His first several paragraphs explore the importance to Barton of their friendship and acknowledge the damaging roles that lost and delayed letters and illness have played in triggering anxieties. The profuse concluding paragraph in this opening section emotionally details the depth of his feelings and implies as well that, true or not, he continues to perceive their friendship under attack:

> I cannot express the Happiness I feel in being told by you, that I have such a Share in your Friendship & good Opinion, as *no Attempts can lessen.* May it be my good Fortune (as I am certain it will be the Endeavour of my future Life) to deserve them!—Permit me to assure you, from a Heart that dictates what I write, that my Attachments to you are such, as Make me daily regret the Distance of my Situation from you; in which Nothing, but the Prospect of educating a Number of Children, who have no other Inheritance to expect, could possibly detain me.[69]

The final surviving letter in their exchange dates from the following year. Once more, Barton apologizes for the continuing "Obstruction in my Liver . . . [that] prevented that Attention, which was due to your Letter."[70] His next paragraph, in light of this letter's being the last extant one from Barton, reads rather like an epilogue, recapitulating the deep feeling he had for his friend. Although it may be fanciful to speculate here, it almost sounds as though he foresaw that one of them would die shortly:[71] "I deem it no small Part of the Felicity of my Life that I have the Honour of Sir William Johnson's good Opinion & Friendship."[72] The great geographic spaces that separated them for the past nine years and their respective responsibilities have in no way undermined his affection and esteem. He concludes this section begging Johnson leave "to assure him, with great Sincerity, that no merely *selfish* or *mercenary* Consideration should detain me from the Pleasure of a nearer Communication with him—But tho' I am *for the present* depriv'd of this Satisfaction, yet I cannot relinquish the Hopes that I shall one Day enjoy it, & partake, Worthy Sir, of those 'pleasing Prospects,' which you have so elegantly represented."[73]

∞

The Barton-Johnson correspondence is important for several reasons. It confirms the portrait we have of Barton from his exchanges with Thomas Penn, namely, that of a loyal servant-counsellor contributing his expertise and drawing upon his contacts to advance the cause and opportunities of his patron. Recommending individuals for placement, advancing artisans and teachers for specific positions, commenting on events, and describing territories—these activities precisely helped him fulfill the client's expected role.

Whatever intimations of friendship may be evident in the Barton-Penn letters become more fully realized in Barton's communications with Johnson. A common origin in the Anglo-Irish, or Anglicized Irish, Ascendancy class of the north of Ireland; a compatability in outlook; a shared curiosity in scientific subjects such as electricity and horticulture; and a respect for each other's accomplishments and competency drew the two men spontaneously into a friendship that lasted until Johnson's death in 1774. The openness and warmth with which Barton declared his feelings make the modern reader wish more of his personal correspondence had come down to us, particularly the over twenty-year exchange with his brother-in-law, David Rittenhouse, from which Thomas's son William quoted so freely.

The Barton-Johnson letters reveal a frank, affectionate, and earnest man helping his friend settle his Mohawk estates and regularly affirming the importance of their bond. They also set before us vividly a Barton easily unsettled by suspicions of treachery and rejection, a man perhaps distrustful of his own capacity to please. His recurrently implied need to please, and Johnson's astute, sympathetic perception of that vulnerability, also help us appreciate why Barton may have enacted some of the questionable deeds he did or why he allowed himself to be used in ways that contradicted his principles, as in the Paxton-Boys pamphlet war. His apparently desperate need to be liked or loved and to obtain approval by performing well—all in excess of the usual paternalistic-filial implications of the patron-client relationship—these occasionally may have made him susceptible to erratic behavior and exploitation.

There is, however, a sense that as the forces building inexorably toward the American Revolution gathered momentum during the 1770s, Barton out of necessity gradually transcended his childlike need constantly to obtain approval and affection, that he matured in independence and inner strength as he confronted tests of character and challenges to his most deeply held beliefs. And it was to his credit that as the American SPG movement collapsed amid the chaos of the Revolutionary years, Barton's newfound resolve helped him avoid behaving in the dubious ways of many of his associates. Some colleagues, like William Smith, for example, managed for a time to straddle the political fence, though finally they slipped over to the American side and possibly did so more out of self-interest than political conviction. Others, like Daniel Batwelle, became increasingly strident in their defense of the Crown, fanatically, almost aggressively, eager to flaunt the gem-like flame of their Loyalist fervor. Barton, however, as unobtrusively as was possible for an Anglican cleric during such times, went his own way with the quiet heroism of a man committed more to personal conscience than to political expediency and expectation. One degree at a time, the new government found ways to punish this priest who would not conform, who refused to violate his sacred oath to his king but who would neither in deeds nor words provoke the vindictive retaliation readied for him. With each new turn of the screw, like the Jesuits his own Anglo-Irish forebears must have hunted down, Barton discovered strategies to execute his priestly vocation and at the same time elude those who would coerce his allegiance and punish his commitment. Finally, however, the new tyrants—whom Barton ironically addresses in his petition to Pennsylvania's Supreme Executive Council as the advocates of religious "as well as civil Liberty"[74]—devised a tool whereby they ejected him from Pennsylvania forever, conclusively slamming the door shut behind him.

7
"The Rage of the Times"

The Spirit of Violence & Outrage flames not only here, but throughout several of the Colonies, and bends its Fury at present against the Bishops & the Church of England:—where it will end, God only knows.
—Thomas Barton

PUBLIC EVENTS LEADING UP TO 1778, THE YEAR BARTON WAS EXPELLED from Pennsylvania, gradually deprived him of almost all those things by which he had confidently tried to measure his success—property, social approval, vocation, friends, children, and good health. One by one, each of these was robbed from him, directly or otherwise, punishment exacted by a vindictive revolutionary government for his refusal to capitulate fully to its will. And yet, obeying the formula sanctified in John Foxe's *Book of Martyrs* and immortalized in Hamlet, Oedipus, and Orestes, he uncovered within himself a resilience that had been aborning for most of a lifetime by embracing the dark paradox lying at the heart of all tragedy: to win, we must lose.

The years immediately preceding and during the American Revolution tested the integrity of the Anglican clergy and proved the nemesis for many of them. Generally, the Church of England's officially established status in such colonies as Maryland, Virginia, and South and North Carolina, and its close hand-in-glove association with other colonies such as Pennsylvania, provided radical American patriots with ready ammunition. The colonial Anglican clergy also tended to advocate episcopacy or the establishment of at very least one American bishopric and thus a hierarchical structure, together with increased efficiency and opportunities for obtaining greater privileges. American pluralism, the dominance of Puritan ideology, the Great Awakening, and the Anglican church's failure to unite the colonies and empire by way of her special activities—all these helped to fuel further suspicions and animosities toward the Episcopal clergy.[1] Simply put, many patriots regarded the Church of England as a very dangerous political institution.[2] Conversely, Anglicans, especially in Pennsylvania, feared

133

the Revolution as a Presbyterian plot to suppress the Episcopalian church completely. In the eyes of the Church of England clergy, national independence would expose them to the ruthless power of a Calvinist theocracy,[3] traces of which might still be found in many of the New England provinces.

The Episcopal clergy of Pennsylvania, however, confronted additional challenges beyond those generally occurring throughout the colonies. Unique geographic, political, and religious circumstances in that province combined to create for them an even more unenviable situation than what their other colleagues had to face. The many decades during which the Scots-Irish Presbyterians had been held in check by the Quakers and the Church-of-England proprietary were dramatically reversing themselves, vividly actualizing Anglican fears of a Presbyterian take over.[4] Between 1776–79, the radical constitutional faction of the American cause, largely Scots-Irish Presbyterian, obtained sufficient control of the Pennsylvania legislature to begin suppressing the remaining power of its traditional foes.[5] After years of struggling under the weight of an Anglican proprietary[6] and within a society often inspired by Quakers and similar German/ Swiss sects, the Calvinists of Pennsylvania successfully seized the main chance to reorganize the commonwealth. The intolerance, even bigotry, evidenced in such affairs as the Paxton Boys' disturbances and the handling of the Stump affair by the officials of Cumberland county now threatened to become institutionalized. Because the principal impetus for this revolution came from the Scots-Irish Presbyterians, the political faction for a time popularly acquired the title "Presbyterian Party."[7]

Straddling the border between northern and southern colonies, Pennsylvania reflected the extreme and contending forces that particularized the conflicts on either side of its boundaries, with the Church of England clergy in the northern colonies fiercely resisting the Revolution and those in the south generally, not merely acquiescing, but often enthusiastically supporting it.[8] The Pennsylvania clergy itself became divided into two groups, those who maintained Loyalist ties and those who joined the American cause. In each of the remaining colonies, on the other hand, the clergy generally inclined as a group in one direction or the other.

The bifurcation in Pennsylvania occurred for another reason, one founded on demographic factors. Economic and social vulnerability pressured the clergy of rural Pennsylvania to interpret their ordination vows strictly as pledging to both king and church a loyalty that allowed no abjuration. In turn, they had to confront increasing social and economic hardships as they struggled to execute their missions without reward and under the vigilant and censorious eyes of their powerful critics. Severed from their principal source of financial support in England, their lives became virtually unendurable.[9] Not a few died under the stresses and privations,[10] with the remainder, Barton among them, eventually being forced into exile.

Not so dependent upon funding from the SPG, the Philadelphia clergy, on the other hand, needed very much to obtain the approval of their local vestries. Hence, although rural missionaries struggled to disengage from the growing struggle, their urban colleagues could not remain aloof in a city that itself perennially functioned as *mise-en-scène* for a great part of the conflict, first as a convenient gathering place for the Congress, then as a city occupied by the British under General William Howe, and once more as the capital.[11] Less conservative than their rural brethren, necessarily more responsive to the will of their vestries, and constantly exposed to the demanding, shrill radicalism of the city, the Philadelphia ministers cautiously came to support the patriots.[12]

Notwithstanding their apparent acquiescence and later support, the Episcopalian clergy of Philadelphia joined with their rural colleagues in October of 1775 in affirming political neutrality. More importantly, all the Pennsylvania ministers pursued such measures as might reconcile Great Britain and her American colonies.[13]

In the event, Pennsylvania's increasingly powerful radical constitutional faction would not tolerate expedient aloofness and enlightened conciliation; it worked successfully to suppress what it defined as dissent by demanding unwavering, visible, repeated proof of patriotic commitment.[14] The aging SPG missionary to Apoquiniminck, Philip Reading, detailed the intimidation deployed against him. Intercepted, his letter was censored in Philadelphia as "being of dangerous tendency or at least as impeaching the propriety of the public proceedings."[15] Subsequently, however, the committee dismissed it as "not liable to . . . censure," thus allowing Reading to recopy and sent it once more on its way, together with an explanation of what had occurred.

Reading's original letter sharply pictures the kind of abuse he, and by implication his rural SPG colleagues, had to endure:

> It is hardly possible, especially since the commencement of the late unnatural hostilities, to avoid taking a part on one side or other of the dispute; and much industry has been used to render me obnoxious to popular resentment, by representing me as inimical to the measures prosecuting here in opposition to the parliamentary authority of the parent state. "No more passive obedience and non-resistance" had been scribbled with a pencil on my Church Door. It was lately urged as a just cause of complaint against one of the Captains of Militia, "that he had *lugged* his Company to Church, on a public occasion, to hear that *old wretch* preach, (meaning myself) who was always an enemy to the present

proceedings." Threats have been used to deter me from reading the prayers for the King.[16]

Nothing so graphic or moving as Reading's description can be found in Barton's letters of this time. It is evident, however, from the surprise he voices in March 1775 that several of his missives had gone astray, perhaps intercepted like Reading's but not ultimately released as unhurtful to the cause.[17] Hence he might well have detailed his trials in some earlier, now-lost letters. By 1775, he is clearly writing with great caution.

Like Reading, Barton was subjected to many kinds of coercion, and as the conflict gathered momentum, additional economic and health-related pressures also exacted their toll. That he was struggling to adjust to the death of his wife Esther in 1774 added to his difficulties.[18] His surviving letters speak of neighboring congregations within the circuits of other SPG itineraries left without any minister, people whose spiritual needs he tried to fill when opportunity permitted. So busy was he, he declared in 1775, that he had not been able to visit Philadelphia for the past three years. With no direction from the society, his salary cut off, and himself effectively isolated in the backcounty of Lancaster, Barton anticipated the worse: "The Rage of the Times is likely to ruin this once happy Country—Where it will end is uncertain."[19] Three months later, he once again laments that "the Temper of the Times forbid" him to detail specifics of his trials in Lancaster county.[20] Indeed, the dilemma facing Barton and his colleagues in the rural parishes was best described by William Smith, writing from the comparative safety of Philadelphia: "The case of the poor Missionaries is hard. To comply may offend their protectors and those that support them in the Parent Country. To refuse would leave them without Congregations every where; and perhaps it is more the wish of some that they should refuse than comply."[21] Following the signing of the Declaration of Independence on July 4, 1776, the rural clergy became even more isolated from their colleagues in Philadelphia, and as Smith feared they indeed began to lose their congregations. Essentially, to secure unanimity within their cause, the patriots successfully directed two strategic blows against the fragile underpinnings of the Anglican church of Pennsylvania.

The first of these attacks occurred spontaneously on the local level and targeted the prescribed Anglican prayers for the king (and the royal family) as supreme head of the Church of England.[22] The Declaration of Independence had effectively severed the old bonds of allegiance between subjects and king; no longer would the monarch's authority receive liturgical ratification. Replacing the earlier prayers for the king, the new government substituted one for the Congress itself: "Most gracious God, we humbly beseech thee as for the States of America in general, so especially for the high Court of Delegates in Congress at this time assembled."[23] All Anglican clergy were expected to comply with this requirement, and, surprisingly, many did. Among them, William White elaborated what he felt was trenchant justification for abandoning this part of the liturgy. Looking back, White in 1820 wrote: ". . . there occurs a case, in which there is an external necessity of omitting a few petitions, not involved in any Christian duty; so far as civil rulers are identified by name, or other personal description. In such a case, it seems evident, that the promise [taken at ordination to follow the *Book of Common Prayer*] is the most nearly complied with by the use of the liturgy to the extent which the external necessity permits."[24]

White's compliance was rewarded during the war with the chaplaincy of the United States Congress when it met in Philadelphia and with a bishopric after the war. William Smith and Jacob Duché followed White, with the result that the Episcopal churches of Philadelphia remained open.

The rural clergy did not capitulate before appeals to expediency. For them, the issue was far more complex than apparently for White and his Philadelphia colleagues. They recognized that it struck to the very heart of their integrity as priests. Again, Philip Reading of Apoquiniminck has left us one of the most carefully articulated analyses of the dilemma that challenged Barton and the other Pennsylvania clergy outside of Philadelphia. Noting the irony that the Church of England had been virtually suppressed in the supposedly "free and independent States," he justifies his refusal to expunge the offending prayers by citing "the Articles of religion and Canons of our Church," to which, as White acknowledged, all ordained Anglican ministers had to swear. Beyond issues of allegiance to the king's religious supremacy, Reading identifies the all-binding power of the fourteenth article that "leaves the Minister who officiates no room to alter the public service at his own discretion or to leave out parts of it to serve particular purposes."[25] He elaborates on this point as follows:

> The ordination vow which exacts obedience from the person to be ordained to his Bishop in all lawful matters has in view, I presume, those laws which have been enacted for the good Government of the Church and for regulating the conduct of Ministers in the ministrations in it. I can discover no one exception to answer special emergencies or to obviate difficulties that may arise on unforeseen occasions. Under these persuasions I could not consistently with my sense of the obligation, assume the danger even of reprehension from my superiors by deliberately and of purpose altering the Liturgy of the Church, much less would I subject myself and the people under my pastoral care to the severer censure of excommunication by disobeying the second Canon and contravening the points contained in it.[26]

More pointedly, Reading argues that repudiating the received Anglican liturgy leaves any person, clergyman or layman, "virtually excommunicated, separated or cut off from the communion of that Church, as it stands upon its legal basis tho' the sentence has not been actually pronounced against him."[27] Rather than expose himself and his family to the dangers everywhere evident should he not comply with the demands and thereby be thought to resist "the authority of the New Government," he closed his churches. As a priest, he would not perjure himself "by a breach of the most solemn promises" had made.[28]

Although Barton justified himself in 1776 with far less elaborate legalistic reasoning, he essentially agreed with Reading's analysis. He offered his last service in St. James's on June 23, 1776.[29] "To avoid the Fury of the Populace, who would not suffer the Liturgy to be us'd, unless the" passages for the king and his family were discontinued, he explained, he was "obliged to shut up my Churches."[30] Simply, conscience and integrity prevented his violating "the Declaration I made & subscribed when ordained." Consequently, "my Life & Property have been threaten'd upon mere *Suspicion* of being unfriendly to, what is call'd, the American Cause."

Denied opportunity to exercise his priestly calling publicly, Barton persevered as best he could in other ways. He visited his people "from House to House regularly; instructed their Families; baptiz'd & catechiz'd their Children; attended their Sick and perform'd such other Duties in *private* as aton'd for my Suspension from *publick Preaching.*"[31] He also obtained satisfaction in recognizing how his resorting to a secret ministry evoked "the Appearance of the Persecution of the primitive Christians. . . . it kindled & encreas'd their Zeal, & united them the closer together."[32] Characteristically, he found in adversity a compensating paradox: persecution anneals faith.

Barton's assurance is estimable in light of the energy and vehemence with which the commonwealth was beginning to coerce uniformity in political, and, implicitly, religious beliefs. It is also disturbing in a way, for an essential naiveté, the same guilessness that helped him justify his plagiarism in 1755, continued to shape his judgment. We can often detect in the same letter a contradictory attitude toward contemporary events. In his communication of November 25, 1776, for example, he records concrete knowledge of the cruel treatment meted out to some missionaries—for example, Daniel Batwelle was dragged from his horse in the town of York, stoned, and thrown into the water—and he acutely generalizes how "the Dreadful Conflict . . . has rent this once happy Country in Pieces."[33] At the same time, however, he fails to appreciate the powerful subterranean energies working to overthrow his world. He writes of "the calamities of America, brought on by *a few ambitious & designing Men* here, & which might have been prevented if Lord Howe's conciliatory Propositions had been accepted" (my emphasis). Additionally, even though he expends great effort in describing the "Infamy & Insult" to which he and his rural colleagues are everyday subjected, he confidently believes "that the Day is near at Hand, when the Churches will be open, & I shall again enter into my *publick Duties*" (Barton's emphasis). Indeed, he may, as the proverb has it, be whistling in the dark to reassure himself, but his feelings here reinforce other evidence we have already seen that Barton's judgment was often clouded by a deep-seated ingenuousness.

The new government irresistibly applied greater coercive pressure to nonconformists when it forbade white males over eighteen who had not sworn the oath to the new government to leave their counties of residence. This prevented Barton from visiting communicants who lived outside Lancaster county. He soon found a way around this prohibition by meeting women and their children from the other counties at the Lancaster county line: "under these melancholy Restrictions I have sometimes baptized above 30 in a Day.— In the last two Years [of his residency in Lancaster county] I baptized 347 Children . . . and 23 Adults."[34] One wonders if Barton perceived that he had become an Anglo-Irish hedge-priest, ironically following in the footsteps of those Roman Catholic priests proscribed and persecuted under Ireland's ruthless eighteenth-century penal codes. His use in one letter of the term *penal laws* in a parallel way makes one suspect that he did indeed: "In so melancholy a condition did the Edicts of Congress & the Penal Laws of the New Governm[t] place me, that I could have no communication with those who would have forwarded either Letters or Intelligence from me to England . . . prudence & my own safety directed me, at such times as were not employed in Visitations to my people, to confine myself entirely to my own house, which I did for two years."[35]

Throughout these troubles, Barton employed every strategy to avoid giving "Offence, even to those who usurp'd Authority & Rule, & exercised the severest Tyranny over us."[36] In this way he succeeded in escaping the cruel treatment meted out to those less prudent. Alluding to the fate of Daniel Batwelle, missionary to his old York-Huntington-Carlisle circuit, he notes that some offenders "have been drag'd from their Horses;—assaulted with Stones & Dirt;—duck'd in Water;—obliged to flee for their Lives;— driven from their Habitations & Families;—laid under Arrests, & imp,rison'd."[37] He nonetheless shared with his brethren the lot of those "mark'd out for Infamy and Insult" for daring "to act upon proper Principles."

Unable to provoke him into behaving rashly, into undertaking some act whereby he might be unequivocally charged with treason and disposed of accordingly, his enemies appear next to have resorted to embellishing wildly, if not inventing, grounds for punishing him further. Ironically, the blow was delivered by parties living, not in Lancaster, but in York and Carlisle, implying that old animosities against him in the heartland of Scots-Irish Presbyterianism still lingered on.

The center of the affair was SPG missionary Daniel Batwelle, alluded to earlier by Barton in the November 25, 1776, letter as the victim of especially vicious treatment. In 1773 Batwelle had replaced American-born William Thomson, Barton's friend and successor in the Huntington mission. English-born and a graduate of Oxford,[38] Batwelle was evidently popular with his congregations. He might, however, have resisted the Revolution both verbally and through his actions, for, as Barton wrote without mentioning him by name, he was beaten, stoned, ducked in Codorus Creek, and otherwise persecuted by incensed Germans in the town of York.

In 1777, Lancaster countian Daniel Shelly (or Schelley, Shelley) of Shelly's Island was arrested or kidnapped by men from Cumberland county and taken to Carlisle to give evidence in a supposed conspiracy to burn Lancaster and York.[39] In the event, Shelly, who appears to have been a Mennonite,[40] proved to have been little more than a messenger, if that, for the supposed conspirators of Cumberland, York, and Lancaster counties. During the investigation, William Beckworth and Adam Laughlin deposed that the Reverend Daniel Batwelle was "a principal Leader" in a plot "to destroy the publick Magazines at Lanc[r], York and Carlisle."[41] Additionally, and in the phrasing of George Stevenson, "M[r] Barton's Name is brought on the Carpet as being privy to the Tory Plot, and corresponding with our enemies."[42] In none of the extant depositions taken, however, was Barton accused of "being privy" to the conspiracy. Of the three who deposed, only Shelly even mentions him: "a Copy of a Letter written at New York, gave an Acc[t]. that Ticonderoga was taken. . . . that News first came to M[r]. Barton the Minister at Lancaster, and from him to Batwell."[43]

Forwarding a letter containing news that Shelly acknowledged as appearing in "the Phil[a]. News Papers" "ten Days" later hardly translates as being particularly "privy" to a plot. That Barton exchanged correspondence with his nearest backcountry Anglican cleric cannot be doubted. Every piece of evidence that has survived establishes that Barton was gingerly treading the straight-and-narrow, studiously avoiding words and acts that might be misconstrued as openly hostile. Unfortunately, however, legislation enacted by the assembly in June 1777, the so-called Test Act, made it criminal not to report knowledge of conspiracies and treasons.[44] Hence, the mere suspicion that Barton indeed possessed intelligence of the conspiracy—

albeit knowledge already publicized in "the Phil[a]. News Papers"—opened the way to so charging him.

Ostensibly in the interest of civil order, John Carothers of Carlisle and George Stevenson of York communicated the accusation to Lancaster justice of the peace William Henry, whom they seem not to have known,[45] so that he would "cause M[r] Barton to be secured in such manner as your prudence shall direct." In their expectation the two men miscalculated. Apparently, neither foresaw that Henry would prudently do nothing. Neither did the pair evidently know that Henry had been a member of the St. James's congregation, nor did they appreciate that even though many of Lancaster's notable patriots were also members of Barton's church, the latter generally esteemed their minister's integrity and behavior. They were not about to incarcerate on inflamatory hearsay a man who commanded their high regard, notwithstanding his acknowledged Tory sympathies. As nearly as we can determine, the plot hatched in Cumberland and York counties against Barton died silently in Lancaster.

The Lancaster of the 1770s was very different from the relatively homogeneous Scots-Irish town of Carlisle. America's largest inland city, Lancaster was of course Pennsylvania's most important urban center after Philadelphia, a major military, commercial, social, religious nexus and in its own right the gateway to the province's western counties. As we have seen, it also microcosmically reflected Pennsylvania's complex religious admixture, with German Lutherans and Reformed dominating—Holy Trinity Lutheran Church, consecrated in 1766,[46] was the largest Lutheran edifice in Pennsylvania. The Revolutionary period increased the city's importance and altered its character in ways significant for appreciating Barton's life during this troubled time.

Situated inland sufficiently to protect it from the enemy and located at the junction of several important roads and in the middle of a prospering agricultural and manufacturing area, Lancaster was ideally suited to serve as a military depot. Several federal and state arsenals and stockpiles of matériel were in fact maintained in the town.[47] In addition, Lancaster served as a detention center for British and Hessian prisoners of war.[48]

Swelling the numbers of garrison troops, commissaries, prisoners of war, and units of soldiers on the march, hundreds of refugees flooded the town from Philadelphia and the backcounties, the wealthier attended by servants and slaves. As the fortunes of war waxed and waned, so the numbers of government functionaries, federal and commonwealth, rose and fell, the entire Congress itself convening there on September 28, 1777. This was four days after Carothers and Stevenson sent off their accusations against Barton. Possibly, the letters were ignored in part, and then forgotten, because of the hectic activities occurring at that same time.

There may be other explanations for the evident indifference with which the Carothers-Stevenson charges were greeted. The city was fertile ground for all kinds of volatile rumors and wild gossip. Packed with thousands of extra people, located for a while fairly close to the battle lines and to British-occupied Philadelphia, providing temporary home to over a thousand prisoners of war who were often on the verge of rioting and escaping, and occasionally doing so,[49] and acutely responsive to the frequently shifting political and military winds, the steady diet of alarming reports, exaggerated rumor, and excited gossip could well have so inured men like Henry that they regarded the accusations as further evidence of one more groundless report. Diarist Christopher Marshall, for example, having fled occupied Philadelphia for Lancaster, recorded his feelings over Lancaster's prevailing climate of gossip: "there appears to be no kind of news to be depended upon, but as for Lyes this place is really pregnant and brings forth abundance daily, I might safely say hourly."[50] Similarly, writing to Jasper Yeates, Edward Burd complains that "It is really astonishing to hear the Number of contradictory & absurd Stories that are propagated thro' the Country."[51] In another communication, Burd admits of Dan Shelly himself that "I can hardly believe he could be guilty of so villainous a Design,"[52] helping us appreciate the skepticism with which news of Thomas Barton's supposed complicity might well have been received.

Such evidence as exists establishes that even during those years leading up to 1778 Barton was well regarded in Lancaster. In 1776, Sally Bard wrote her sister, Mrs. Mary Bard, of her recent visit to "uncle Barton." Even allowing for her favorable predisposition toward Barton by reason of family relationship,[53] her description of his life in the town depicts a minister genteel and cultured, one esteemed by his fellow townspeople. The night after their arrival, she related to her sister, "we were waked with a most delightful Serenade under the window consisting of two Violins one flute and a hautboy [oboe] played extreamly well, a Compliment to Mr. and Mrs. Barton."[54] She recorded that on "Saturday Mr. Barton was visited by all the Gentlemen of the place, its [sic] Customary here to send cards to all those you would wish to come and have an elegant Collation served up at twelve Clock with wine punch, &c."[55] Barton's new wife similarly testified to the congenial reception given her husband on the occasion of his second marriage: "On Saturday Mr. Barton was visited by all the gentlemen of the town of every denomination both Jews and Gentiles."[56]

Sally Bard also describes with great delight the singing in St. James's Church, performed presumably by British prisoners of war: "would you believe that our Church music at Lancaster exceeds any thing you have ever heard, It is entirely Vocal and performed by Soldiers who have been used to sing in Cathedrals. . . . when they begin to sing the whole congregation rise."[57] She portrays a Lancaster flourishing as a cultural oasis, with her uncle playing an appreciated and principal role in that community.

Although Bard in a second letter remarks on the great affection shared by Barton and his largely Welsh and Irish congregations in Caernarvon and Pequea, we can infer from other sources that he enjoyed good relations with his St. James's congregation as well.[58] This may be surprising insofar as the first two churches were largely Tory and St. James's conspicuously supportive of the American cause, with most of the latter's vestrymen, churchwardens and other notables active in the new government. Edward Shippen, for example, was president of the Lancaster Committee of Correspondence. George Ross became a member of the Pennsylvania Assembly and later a member of Congress, and signer of the Declaration of Independence. William Atlee became a justice of the first Supreme Court of Pennsylvania. Irish surgeon Edward Hand served as a colonel of the First Pennsylvania Regiment, later as brigadier general and adjutant general of the Continental Army, and a member of Congress. Judge Jasper Yeates later served as a delegate to the convention of 1787 which ratified the Constitution. Tavern keeper Matthias Slough held a position on the Committee of Correspondence. And William Henry, the talented inventor and gunsmith, served in several official positions, including one on the Pennsylvania Committee of Safety.[59]

No amount of warm regard, respect, and esteem on the part of his politically influential parishioners, however, could for long hold the inevitable at bay. Sarah Barton foresaw as much in 1776 when she wrote: "I do not know how it will be possible for him ever to leave congregations so much devoted to him tho it will probably come to that at last."[60]

The Pennsylvania Assembly's next decisive attack against political nonconformists, who included of course the rural SPG missionaries, fell in June 1777 when it passed its first Test Act. The legislation was so-called because its prescribed oath taking was intended to prove or "test" the subject's fidelity to the American cause. The legislation provided that all white males over the age of eighteen had to swear by July 1, of the same year an oath of allegiance to Pennsylvania, to renounce earlier oaths of allegiance of the king of Great Britain, to agree not to act in any way hostile to the independence and freedom of the commonwealth, and to report any treasons and plots against the government that they might discover.[61] Failure to take the oath exposed the offender to charges of treason and to being jailed without bail. Refusal also effectively placed the subject beyond the protection and enjoyment of the law: he could not hold office in the commonwealth, serve on juries, sue for debts, vote, buy or transfer land, or possess arms.[62]

Even among many American patriots, the Test Act was unpopular and deemed coercive in the extreme.[63] The more moderate republican faction widely perceived it as needlessly oppressive and ethically questionable. Pennsylvania had been founded by peoples endeavoring to escape exactly the kind of tyranny now being instituted by the legislation. Quakers had long refused on religious grounds to take oaths, as had some other dissenting denominations among the Germans. More significantly perhaps, the provision mandating the renunciation of earlier oaths to the king vitiated the very rationale for taking oaths in the first place: on what logical and ethical grounds can a person be verbally bound if the swearing of one oath requires the forswearing of an earlier one? Either an oath binds or it does not, and if not, what can be the point of swearing allegiance one day, to swear again to another cause the next?

Immigrants who had had to swear allegiance to the king to become naturalized were now required to forswear. Confusion among many new citizens of the commonwealth was accordingly widespread. Naturalized Germans were observed as objecting that "The world cant make them beleve they are clear of thire oath to the King, and they say to be obleged to Renounce their oath, & perhaps in a short time to be obleged [again] to swear to the King, is a matter seeming imposable for them to git over."[64]

Not only Quakers and kindred pietist denominations, but bewildered immigrants, and people who were simply unclear of where they stood were victimized by the law. Ignoring secular considerations, members of the Church of England, particularly the clergy, who, as we have seen, regarded the king as the head of their church, were also snared in the net broadly flung out by the radical-dominated Assembly. Among the Philadelphia clergy, all but Thomas Coombe gradually fell into line by taking the oath.[65] To a man, the ten remaining SPG missionaries to Pennsylvania (and Delaware, which the SPG still considered attached to Pennsylvania) resisted the law with, ultimately, sad consequences.

Whether he assumed the responsibility himself or was delegated to do it, on May 20, 1778, Thomas Barton set forth the "Case of the protestant Episcopal Missionaries of Pennsylvania" for "the Consideration of the Honorable Assembly of said State, now met in Lancaster" (see below, Appendix E). It is a lucidly eloquent, well-reasoned document, if oversimplified, for it suppresses such damning, contrary evidence as Daniel Batwelle's stubborn opposition to the patriots' cause. After stressing how their itineracy enforces great hardships on the missionaries, not the least of which is economic, Barton cites from the official SPG *Instructions, from the Society . . . to Their Missionaries* (London, 1756) to stress how he and his colleagues had reason "to inculcate Submission to Government and Obedience to Authority, *not only for Wrath but also for Conscience Sake.*"[66] Always, he argues, they took special pains (in the words of the *Instructions*) "to give no Offence to the Civil Government, by intermedling in Affairs not relating to their own Calling or Function." He emphasizes that they have never intermedled, "directly or indirectly, in the present melancholy contest, nor done any Act or Thing inimical to the Liberty or Welfare of America."

Having made clear the political neutrality and non-involvement of the SPG missionaries, Barton comes to the petition's center, the issue of the Test Oath and the penalties provided for refusing to take it. In light of their blameless record, the petitioners hope the Assembly will accept that they cannot, as stipulated in the legislation, abjure "the King of Great Brittain, his Heirs and Successors," nor totally dissolve their connections with the Countries that gave them Birth;— From which they have hitherto drawn their chief Support;— And to which alone they must look up for their future Maintenance."[67] To justify the indulgence they seek, Barton cites numerous international precedents whereby foreign states—even non-Christian nations like that ruled by the "Great Mogul"—have generously tolerated and protected the presence of Christian missionaries, "Men, set apart for the Purposes of Religion and Morality." Similar usage accorded by their own Protestant, Christian, state is not, therefore, so irrational an expectation. Irrational his expectation might not have been, but it was certainly naive, and Barton was soon made to perceive that any deviation would not be tolerated.

Barton set down his fullest account of the crisis which finally came to a head for him in a letter to John DeHart of Elizabeth-town, New Jersey. Trying to explain what had happened, he reported that "no choice was left me, but either to take the oath, or to suffer a painful separation from my dearest connexions; as well as from a country which always had, since I have known it, my predilection and best wishes. . . . and though my heart assures me, that many conscientious and good men have conformed to the test-act, yet my own conscience always revolted at the abjuration part of it, and prevailed with me to surrender every worldly consideration, that should come in competition, or tempt me to a violation of it."[68] Echoing his earlier "Case of the protestant Episcopal Ministers of Pennsylvania" (May 20, 1778), he maintains that none of his actions or words could have been construed as "intermeddling, directly or indirectly, in the present unhappy contest." His "scruples," he insists, "would be a stricter tie upon me, than any that could be made by oaths or tests."[69]

Thomas Barton's passport or safe-conduct, issued by Pennsylvania's Supreme Executive Council, September 17, 1778. (SPG Letter Books, Series B, vol. 21: 31. Courtesy of the United Society for the Propagation of the Gospel, United Kingdom.)

Barton made his fateful stand in May of 1778 (see below, Appendix F). On the 29th of that month, he formally declined, not without an ironic jab at the hypocrisy of the Supreme Executive Council, to forswear his earlier oath: "Your Petitioner, (who has the Happiness of addressing himself to the Advocates of religious as well as civil *Liberty,*) hopes he may be permitted to avow, that he cannot in Conscience *'adjure the King of Great Britain, his Heirs & Successors.'* "[70] Accordingly, he petitions for leave "to sell & convey" his property and "take at the earliest & most convenient Opportunity of returning to Ireland, the place of his Nativity." The council granted his request on June 4, 1778.[71] He and his wife conveyed their real estate in Lancaster to their daughter Esther and her husband Paul Zantzinger on August 26, 1778.[72] The council issued its passport on September 17, 1778: "the said Thomas Barton with his Wife, is hereby permitted to pass into the City of New York agreeable to resolve of Congress, not to return again."[73]

Barton's congregations in Lancaster, Caernarvon, and Pequea supplied him with testimonials to his having been nothing less than "a faithful, laborious and truely useful Minister," and "a peaceable, prudent, moral Man; never intermedling . . . with any affairs incompatible with his Calling or Function."[74] In further evidence of their love and esteem, the Caernarvon and Pequea congregations paid all the arrears due him, added an additional £50, and purchased a house where his children might live, free of troubles which might befall them in Lancaster.[75] This last provision proves that Barton's rupture with his life in Pennsylvania was total. Not only did he have to part company with his beloved congregations, but he was also required to leave the state without his children. Concerning this penalty, he wrote: "I was reduced to the very melancholy necessity of separating from 8 children (six of them helpless & unprovided for)."[76]

Mrs. Esther Atlee probably epitomized the feeling of loss experienced by most of Barton's parishioners when she wrote her husband, William, that "Our late parson set off yesterday with his lady; they have taken leave of us altogether. I can assure you that it affected me much when they called to bid me adieu. I could not help looking back upon many happy opportunities of doing my duty under his office; but I hope we shall find someone or other to tell us our duty again, and who will show us the way to heaven as well as tell us that there is such a place."[77]

Ironically, a poignantly moving image of Barton is also found in the laconic notation for October 3, 1778, by the irrepressible diarist Christopher Marshall. Marshall casts a cold, patriotic eye on what was to become Thomas Barton's last pilgrimage, the beginning of his aborted journey home, in actuality his final two-year transit to the grave: "this morning, I presume, Parson Barton moved off the last of his effects, in two covered wagons."[78]

8
Martyr

There are Thousands here, who have made Sacrifices to Britain that will astonish Posterity.— Let them not be called <u>Friends;</u>— —let them be called <u>Martyrs</u>.

—Thomas Barton

P ENNSYLVANIA'S DECISIVE ENFORCEMENT OF ITS REVISED TEST ACT IN 1778 effectively terminated the SPG effort in that province for the duration of the war. Except for a handful of clerics, we know little of the daily circumstances of most of its missionaries after that year: journals and letters have become lost; the exchange of communications between the SPG and its missionaries was extremely difficult; and censorship by the Pennsylvania government had a repressive effect on the SPG correspondents. The Philadelphia clergy who initially conformed, William Smith, William White, and Jacob Duché, however, never became submerged under the obscurity that overtook most of the others. Daniel Batwelle, too, left a trail of sorts after his arrest and imprisonment, for poor health and a fierce determination to flee America drove him to address a number of letters and petitions to various officials, and many of these have survived in government archives. As a victim who forced himself on the attention of the bureaucrats, we can follow Batwelle up to his becoming a Loyalist refugee in 1778.[1] And Barton, in New York, fighting the illness that was soon to kill him, heroically persevered. In a faltering, shaky hand that betrayed his physical infirmity, he reported needed intelligence to the society: the deaths of fellow SPG missionaries Philip Reading, Aeneas Ross, and George Craig; the trials of Traugott Frederick Illing, Episcopalian and Lutheran minister who served, among other charges, William Smith's new town of Huntingdon (or Standing Stone) located at the remote confluence of the Juniata River and Standing Stone Creek, and of William Frazer of New Jersey, both too isolated to send or receive mail.[2] His handful of letters permits us to piece together a narrative that epitomizes the fates of other SPG missionaries driven from their congregations into exile and dying or awaiting opportunity to embark on the ships which would return them to Great Britain.

By the middle of December 1778, Barton had settled his affairs enough to write of his changed circumstances.[3] His last extant report sent two years earlier (November 25, 1776) summarizes the major challenges that had confronted and eventually forced him and his wife out of Pennsylvania. New York itself was a haven for Loyalist refugees, with at least two of Barton's Pennsylvania colleagues also living there, Daniel Batwelle, from the Conewago settlements in York county, and Philadelphian William Stringer, who had dropped from sight after 1776. He had to depend on the hospitality of his wife's family, the Bards, and he possessed no funds beyond the little his congregations had given him and what he had raised through selling his furniture, having been unable, or choosing not, to draw upon his salary since October 1775.[4] Feeling duty-bound to remain in America until informed otherwise, he requests authorization "To quit America . . . as it is my wish, & shall ever be my study, to do nothing that may have even the appearance of Undutifulness or disrespect to that truly venerable body."[5]

Barton's January 8, 1779, letter to the SPG, a much longer piece, reads more like an official report or *notitia parochialis* than a simple communication of recent news. Expanding on his earlier missive, he informatively provides exact numbers of baptized. He explicitly details his ordeals, significant witness that the Revolution had not diminished the zealous performance of his mission. His situation is acute, indeed, for notwithstanding the moneys given him by his former congregations and the small sums he had raised, he must now survive the expenses of a "very expensive City." Two probabilities sustain him: namely, that before his money becomes exhausted, "I shall be enabled either to return to my Children & Churches, or to obtain the Society's Permission to quit this ungrateful Country altogether; and, under their benevolent Patronage & Influence, to solicit some humble Appointment in England; where, I trust, my Fidelity in their Service, for near 24 Years, will recommend me to Something, that may place me above Want in my declining Days."[6] The first of his hopes, return to Pennsylvania, was no empty flourish: it sustained him until his death one-and-a-half years later. More realistically, however, he worked to flee his near-poverty and the uncertainty of life in New York by sailing for Great Britain.

More broadly, Barton dramatically recalls the calamities that have destroyed the society's mission in the American colonies. His impassioned chronicle of suffering and death evokes the afflictions of Christian martyrs throughout history. Indeed, he explicitly insists on this likeness. Let the thousands who have suffered, he says, "not be called <u>Friends</u>;— let them be called <u>Martyrs</u>." The clergy, "in particular, have suffered beyond Example; and, indeed, beyond the Records of any History, in this Day of Trial.— Most of them have lost their All." They have, literally, lost their all, for several colleagues have "(from Grief & Despondency it is said) paid the last debt of Nature": Philip Reading, Aeneas Ross, and George Craig, "besides several in the Northern Colonies." Because they conformed to strict neutrality in political affairs and refused to compromise their religious principles, all "suffer'd a Persecution as cruel as the Bed of Procrustes."

Meditating on those priests—friends and martyrs both—Barton appears to obtain inspiration. His money almost run out, dependent on his in-laws, grievously cut off from his children, wracked with the physical agonies that were slowly killing him, he discovers the spiritual fortitude to affirm a future that would, in the event, never be. Although one may be tempted to dismiss it as the gesture of a man clutching desperately to whatever would preserve the last shreds of belief, throughout his missionary life, even amid the most perilous days following Braddock's defeat, he consistently iterated faith in the ultimate victory of his church. During this period of persecution, Barton's phrasing suggests that he has acquired sustaining inspiration from St. Paul's vision of Christian martyrdom. Paul wrote: "the sufferings of this present time are not worthy to be compared with the glory which shall be revealed in us. . . . For we are saved by hope: but hope that is seen is not hope: for what a man seeth, why doth he yet hope for? But if we hope for that we see not, then do we with patience wait for it."[7] Echoing Paul's insight into the paradoxes of suffering and salvation, of losing and winning, and of a hope beyond hope, Barton celebrates his own conviction in the church's survival, one ungrounded in practical eventualities of this world. "Notwithstanding," he writes, "the gloomy Cloud that now hangs over us, I cannot, for my own Part, let go the pleasing Hopes, that we shall return to our Charge, & have the pleasure to see the Church of England flourish in America, with encreasing Lustre."

Later that January, Barton learned that his eldest son, William, had returned safely from London, where he had been studying law. Responding to John DeHart of Elizabeth-town, New Jersey, who had passed on William's request to his father that he return to his parish, Barton expresses unabashed incredulity: "What he can mean by this request, I am totally at a loss to understand."[8] His earlier expectancy of returning to his charge was evidently of a different order altogether from the one envisioned by

William, who must have urged or expected his father to swear the test oath. He launches into a lengthy and thorough review of the events and reasoning that compelled him to reject compromising with and capitulating before "every worldy consideration" that might tempt him to violate his conscience. Indeed, he perceives no way of returning to "all that are most dear to me" "without being subject to an abjuration, which I cannot take." Reiterating a theme unifying all his communications dating from the Revolutionary period, he insists that "the proper duties and profession of a minister of the gospel should, in my opinion, never lead him into the field of politics," a caveat reinforced perhaps by his experience during the Paxton-Boys disturbances. His "own scruples" enforce a "stricter tie upon me, than any that could be made by oaths or tests." Perhaps recognizing how carried away he has become, he abruptly concludes the letter by apologizing to De-Hart for "troubling you on this subject."

In the wisdom of the proverb, there is more here than meets the eye. Barton's apparent shock over William's request, his detailed justification for his decision—the most thorough that has survived—his evident embarrassment at having set down what he felt had to be said—these add up to intimate some tension between Barton and his eldest, presumably most knowledgeable, son. What might have been its source?

Preserved among the minutes of Pennsylvania's Supreme Executive Council are several petitions by Paul Zantzinger, Barton's son-in-law, and William Barton requesting permission "to pass to Elizabeth-Town, to meet his [sic] father on private business"[9] and for Barton and his wife to return to Pennsylvania.[10] Usually, the council withheld its permission, but twice, on February 18, and April 14, 1780, it acted favorably. In his biography of Rittenhouse, moreover, William wrote of the April 14 meeting, the only one he mentions, that "this indulgence was obtained . . . chiefly through the friendship of the late general Joseph Reed, then president of that body; and, in pursuance of this passport, sanctioned by general Washington, the desired interview was had with Mr. and Mrs. Barton, at Elizabeth-Town, a very short time before the death of Mr. Barton."[11] Without guile, William Barton admits that his successful suit occurred largely because of "the friendship of the late general Joseph Reed, then president of that body." He had a "connection" and relied upon it to obtain a favorable ruling. We can reasonably ask several additional questions at this juncture: why would the son of a proscribed and banished Loyalist, a young man recently returned from England, be granted a passport out of Pennsylvania? Why did the executive council refuse throughout a full year and then abruptly assent? And finally, why would a young man studying law in England, offspring of a proclaimed traitor, be allowed to return to the commonwealth in the first place? What William conceals is that he had an even more powerful ally on the council, Vice President George Bryan, a man known perhaps for greater radical beliefs and inflexibility than Joseph Reed.[12]

As early as March 1779, Zantzinger and William Barton were working to obtain the council's passport. That the council did not grant its permission until February of the following year may have been due in great part to Zantzinger's reputation as an opportunist, lukewarm in his support of the Revolution. Bryan makes this evident in a letter to George Washington, to whom the council had redirected the petition. The executive council, Bryant advises,

> ever watchful of the public safety & happiness, think it behooves them to communicate to you, their suspicions, that Mr. Paul Zanzinger [sic] of the Burrough of Lancaster, in this State, merchant, who is lately gone hence for Camp, has a design of getting liberty to pass into New York. For this purpose He will probably set forth his desire to visit his father-in-law the Rev[d] Mr. Thomas Barton, now in that City. . . . I would suggest that Mr. Zanzinger is a Trader, who has never manifested much attention to the present contest, & very likely to be drawn by interested views to a mart where European merchandizes are sold at prices inviting to men who seek profit merely.[13]

Coupled with Zantzinger's dubious motives is Thomas Barton's history as a traitor, one recently confirmed for Bryan by a report that Barton has lately accepted "a chaplaincy in a British Regiment at New York . . . & thus [has] actively" joined "the Enemy."[14]

Complicating the negative assessment of these two men is Bryan's perception of William Barton. Apparently the latter enjoyed at very least the council's tentative favor: "Mr. Z., is probably accompanied by a son of Mr. B[s], a young gentleman, lately returned from England, where he has been weaned of all fond attachment to that corrupted Country, & brought to see the happiness & independence of North America in their proper light & connection. Young Mr. Barton is a much clearer character with us, than his Brother-in-law, & as such I venture to mention him."[15] In a world less complicated than that experiencing a revolution which was also a civil war, the authorities would probably have denied permission to Zantzinger and approved Barton. But they chose to withhold their approval from both throughout 1778.

Known to be unequivocally committed to the revolutionary cause, young Barton was to establish his reputation more securely and in time win assent for both himself and Zantzinger to visit their father in Elizabeth-town. Thomas Barton's incredulity over his son's request that he return to Pennsylvania, however, implies more than his knowledge of William's political predilections: it intimates as well that Thomas knew or suspected that his son's request probably carried with it an expectation that Thomas would relent by taking the oath and forswearing his earlier pledge to the king, for only by doing so would he be allowed back into Pennsylvania—his passport had declared clearly enough that he was "not to return again." When, therefore, he writes that he is "totally at a loss to understand" what William "can mean by this request," Barton in effect expresses disbelief over his son's presumed expectation that he repudiate his earlier stand—thus, the elaborate review of his original decision and his insistence once more on the integrity of his conscience: "I cannot therefore comprehend, how I can consistently return, before this interdict is cancelled; or some assurance given me, that I may again unite and live quietly with my family, *without being subject to an abjuration, which I cannot take.*"[16] In effect, Barton tells DeHart, and by implication his son, that lawyer William should know his father's resolve better than he apparently does.

Bryan's letter dates from March 1779; William Barton and Paul Zantzinger's petitions continued to appear, without positive results, until February 1780, at which time, and in April as well, the council approved their request. We may conjecture that although Zantzinger might have done little to redeem his reputation in the eyes of the executive council, William Barton's continuing good behavior and efforts on behalf of the American cause confirmed Bryan's original estimation of him. Very possibly, William actually pressured his father to take the Test Oath, maybe at the council's prompting. Knowing how much Thomas Barton longed to rejoin his scattered children,[17] the council might have anticipated that William would be able to exploit this vulnerability and bring about a reversal. Authorizing his journey to New Jersey in 1780, having until then repeatedly rejected the petitions, might represent, then, one more twist in the screw to obtain Thomas Barton's support, certainly a bright feather in the state's newly tailored cap of liberty if it could obtain it. But if the council indeed manipulated William Barton to persuade his father to recant, it was to be disappointed in Thomas.

Thomas Barton's attempt to distance his religious convictions from the political world faltered after his reply to DeHart. Recent military and political developments nurtured in Barton a kind of false trust in the justice of worldly events. History, he affirms in his next letter to the society, has conspired to force "A Majority of the People . . . to see, that They have been made only the Tools of despotic Authority: They begin to feel the Tyranny of their masters and secretly wish for a Deliverance."[18] A number of reversals experienced by "the sons of Treason . . . have thrown them into such

Consternation, that one spirited Campaign would crush and put an End to Rebellion in America."

As if to punish him for fostering this false (because political and worldly) hope, for ignoring Paul's insight into the nature of a hope that can be seen, for submitting once again to the essential naiveté that had disabled him so often in the past, his health collapsed. From about May into October, he lived on Staten Island "in Search of Health," availing himself of less crowded, more hygenic surroundings and of salubrious exposure to cleaner air, salt water, and sunshine. Eventually returning to New York, "which my Physicians tell me is the best Place at this Season," he wrote to the Reverend William Frazer, more or less cut off in New Jersey from contact with the society, to apprise him of recent developments and news of moneys now available to him. A distinct contrast to the clear, gracefully formed characters of Barton's calligraphy before 1778, the penmanship of this letter discloses a hand barely able to hold pen, of fingers painfully pushing the quill through each shakily executed word. It is all the more revealing, then, that Barton writes without evident self-pity and even with some humor.

Opening the epistle with news that a letter Frazer had addressed him has not arrived, he turns the loss into an Irish joke, noteworthy for its evidence that Barton considered himself Irish (rather than Anglo-Irish or of English ancestry): "I have not receiv'd the Letter which you address'd to me by M^r. MacFarquhar, & therefore (tho' an *Irishman*) cannot undertake to *answer* it."[19]

Barton's October 25, 1779, letter to the society is his final surviving communication. It depicts the terrible pass to which his wordly life had come, even as it witnesses the spiritual renewal he experienced as he drew to the end. It also indirectly discloses how isolated the society had become from actual events in America and from an appreciation of the adversities her missionaries had to endure almost daily.

The pathos of Barton's opening paragraph reminds us how needful being well-regarded and loved were to him. The New York City of October 1779 was in many respects a poor substitute for the world wherein he had been able to count on a vital network of support and affection, from proprietor down to peer to dependant. He writes as a man starved for the good word and for unambiguous evidence of warm appreciation. "Amidst the publick Calamities that surround me, & the Calamities I feel myself," he replies to the new secretary's, Dr. William Morice's, recently arrived letter, "Nothing could afford me greater Comfort than the, 'Society's Approbation of my Conduct,' under the difficult Trials I had to encounter.—I beg [to] pledge myself to that Ven^ble. Body that it shall be the Pride & Study of my Life, to merit the Sustenance of their favourable Opinion of me."[20] In part, Barton

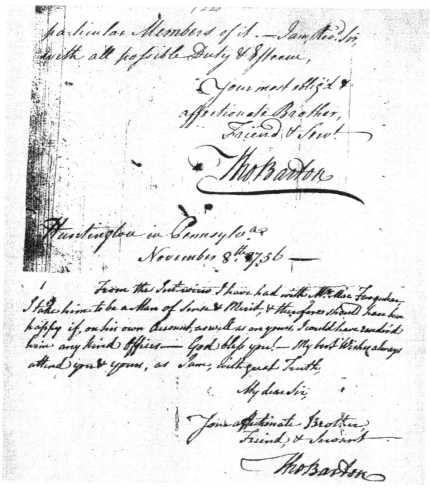

Comparison of Thomas Barton's signatures, November 8, 1756, and January 8, 1779, revealing the effects brought on by illness and the stresses to which he was subjected during the last part of his life. (SPG Letter Books, Series B, vol. 21: 31. Courtesy of the United Society for the Propagation of the Gospel, United Kingdom; and Society Miscellaneous Collection, the Historical Society of Pennsylvania, respectively.)

must also declare his obedience in this hyperbolic way to prepare his superior for his declining to respect the "Society's Direction" that he carry the Anglican mission into Huntingdon, Long Island. Unknown to his superiors in London, "A very formidable & violent Banditti from Connecticut are frequently making Incursions into the Eastern Parts of Long-Island, particularly to Huntingdon, where they plunder, commit Robberies, carry off such Families & Persons as are not their Friends."[21] He also pleads his "ill State of Health" as justification for avoiding this responsibility.

One infers that Dr. Morice's letter must have crushed Barton's expectations. He had anticipated the society's leave to return to Great Britain, and when the long-awaited missive arrived, it bore not the desired authorization but instead "Directions" dispatching him into the no-man's-land of eastern Long Island and to perils far worse than any he had experienced yet.

Barton must have perceived transparently that his fate had been sealed. He asks that the society honor bills in the amount of £250 he had drawn against his back pay, held in security in London at his request. When he had "first mentioned that Matter" of saving his yearly salary, he still anticipated, he says, the prospect of joining his family, for British armies appeared poised to invest areas of Pennsylvania beyond those surrounding Philadelphia, but "the Termination of our Resorces at a remoter Distance than ever" now required that he use the money. Allowing that some letters may have disappeared, Barton's resignation here, coupled with references to his earlier anticipation that he would use the money held for him should he reunite with his family contradicts his January 8, 1779, expectation that he would need "that little Fund . . . in Case I should be reduced to the disagreeable Necessity of leaving America."[22] That earlier prospect, implicitly accepted by his very silence in the later epistle, is no longer feasible.

Possibly alluding to Morice's request that he write "'concerning the Church & the distressed Ministers of it'" (Barton is quoting here), he promises to speak of it in his next. But for whatever reason—did he anticipate there might not be another occasion?—he cannot withstand the opportunity to describe the church's dilemma, and, at the same moment, to voice his own sanguine perception "that she will, one Day, rise triumphant & be the Glory of the New World." That he could write hopefully with so "many Discouragements . . . present[ing] themselves to my View" registers a resilience of spirit altogether remarkable. His church's values promise its resurrection: namely, "her Modesty & Peaceableness" and "the general Conduct of her Clergy" that will recommend her "to the Esteem & Attention of the People, as soon as their present Passions & Prejudices cool & subside." Here as throughout these final letters Barton stresses the temperance which the Church of England has always stood for and her clergy have tried to inculcate among her people, an ideal which of course attracted "Wrath, Bitterness, & Persecution" from those hostile to moderation, the die-hard patriots. His own personal testimony to the transfiguring potency of faith concludes the discussion: "Should the Church of England, at the Conclusion of these Troubles, be a *little* cherished by *Government,* as she has greatly been so by the Society, (without whose Patronage she must have been totally extinct in America,) she will certainly flourish & grow more than ever. These Hopes & this Belief furnish me with the best Consolation I now enjoy, & I will cherish them 'till I die."[23] We have no reason to believe he did otherwise than he promised.

Following the April 1780 meeting, William Barton and Paul Zantzinger again petitioned the Supreme Executive Council, "praying leave for the Reverend Thomas Barton & Wife to return from New York, or the Petitioners to go into that City."[24] The petition was "rejected Unanimously." The brothers-in-law tried once more on May. 19, Rather than record the rejection tersely this time, the minutes set forth the council's full rationale: "*Ordered,* That the many and great inconveniences which must attend the examples, as well as from the impropriety of the thing itself, the Council cannot, consistent with their duty to the publick, grant the said petition."[25]

In the meanwhile, Barton had booked passage on a ship, resigned to closing the circle of his career by returning to Great Britain. Before the ship sailed, however, he died on May 25.[26]

In its Tuesday, May 30, 1780, issue, New York's Tory newspaper, the *Royal American Gazette,* printed in its obituary the notice that Thomas Barton's "remains were interred in the chancel of St. George's Chapel." The full text of the *Gazette*'s obituary reads as follows:

On Thursday the 25th inst. departed this life, aged 50 years, the Reverend Thomas Barton, A.M., the Society's Missionary for Lancaster, in the province of Pennsylvania. This worthy clergyman was distinguished by a generous openness of temper, and liberality of sentiments; which, joined to an exemplary conduct, and indefatigable zeal in discharging the duties of his function, gained him the love and esteem of his parishioners, who greatly respected him during his residence amongst them for 21 years. His unshaken loyalty, and attachment to the constitution, drew upon him the resentment of the rebels, and exposed him to many hardships. The violence of the times compelled him at last to leave his numerous family, and take refuge in this city; where he bore a tedious and most painful sickness with fortitude and resignation; and died in firm expectation of that immortality and glory, which are the exalted privileges of sincere Christians.

On Friday last, his remains were interred in the chancel of St. George's Chapel.[27]

Evidently, none of his children attended the funeral. When St. George's Church was demolished, his body was transferred to New York's Trinity Church Cemetery. The marker now lost, Thomas Barton's remains lie somewhere near the intersection of 155th Street and Broadway.[28]

Appendix

Introduction

THOMAS BARTON WAS A COMPULSIVE WRITER OF LETTERS. TODAY, HIS surviving correspondence may be found in the Pennsylvania State Archives; in the various collections of the Historical Society of Pennsylvania; in the archives of both the Protestant Episcopal Church in America and the United Society for the Propagation of the Gospel in the United Kingdom (identified throughout this biography by the initials of its older designation, the SPG); in the William Smith papers at the University of Pennsylvania; in the Sir William Johnson papers in the New York State Library; and in anonymous letters to the *Pennsylvania Gazette,* recognizable as his by reason of subject matter and distinctive style. Many of course have been lost or destroyed, the most regrettable loss being his lenghty exchange with his brother-in-law, David Rittenhouse.[1] The SPG archives alone preserve no less than 37 documents in Barton's hand, nearly all of which are official reports he was required to submit regularly. From this collection, I have selected 6 of the most informative and characteristic documents embracing the beginning through the end of his American experience.

Barton's November 8, 1756, letter to the secretary of the SPG in London details his early vocational aspirations, the frustration of those hopes, and the stop-gap defensive measures he participated in during his first year-and-a-half's residence (May 1755–November 1756) in what was then termed the Bermudian or Conewago Creek settlement. As a record of life during that anxious time, his long report has no parallel among the surviving documents of either Cumberland or York counties. It was a time when the bloodied tomahawk reigned and imminent death haunted the dark line of trees edging one's little fields of flax and wheat. *Memento mori,* "remember that you must die"—this was the long-venerated maxim that preachers exhorted their congregations to meditate upon daily and that Thomas Barton incorporated into his own personal seal (see Chapter 3, p. 69).

If Barton's November 8, letter to the SPG provides us with a unique witness to frontier life the year following Braddock's defeat, his 1758 journal of the Forbes expedition also has no equal. Indeed, one can read the collected letters of General John Forbes, Colonel Henry Bouquet, and Colonel George Washington, and one can examine as well the Forbes campaign documents and correspondence scattered throughout the Pennsylvania archives and elsewhere, but none will give as connected and revealing and succinct a narrative, even in its present incomplete form, as that preserved in Barton's journal of that campaign, one of the principal events that helped turn the course of the French and Indian War around in Britain's favor.[2]

In 1758 the British made a concerted effort to destroy the formidable staging points that had helped France achieve its great military advantage—Louisbourg in Nova Scotia, Fort Ticonderoga in the Adirondacks, Fort Frontenac on Lake Ontario, and Fort Duquesne on the Forks of the Ohio (site of today's Pittsburgh). In his journal, Barton duly notes General James Abercromby's disastrous failure at Ticonderoga, and the other resounding British triumphs at Louisbourg and Frontenac. The taking of Fort Duquesne was the business of Brigadier-General John Forbes's expedition, an undertaking that was in many ways one of the most arduous and heroic military actions of British colonial history. Thomas Barton's journal preserves for us a vivid, though incomplete, record of that march through virgin forests and laurel jungles, and over the daunting Alleghenies by an army numbering over 6,000, not a few of whom, like Barton himself, had made their homes along Bermudian, Conewago, 'Possum, and Marsh Creeks of then York county.

Barton's chronicle also provides a running commentary on General Forbes's poor health, which further added to the expedition's difficulties. Throughout the campaign, Forbes was bed-ridden with several debilitating and ultimately mortal afflictions that often required his remaining far behind the main army and leaving his field command in the capable hands of the Swiss-born Lieutenant-Colonel Henri Bouquet. Even when he felt well enough to move forward, Forbes had to be carried in a litter slung between two horses, as Barton records in his journal. In this way, the expedition's commander heroically inspired his troops on to ultimate victory. Forbes died March 11, 1759, three months after the fall of Fort Duquesne and was buried in Philadelphia's Christ Church.

We find also in the journal, as we would expect, details of the campaign itself: movements of troops (including a few details of the activities of officers from Barton's area and even occasionally members of his own congregations, most notably, Archibald McGrew and Robert Callender); encounters with hostile Indians; the unpredictable arrivals and departures of Indian allies; graphic descriptions and assessments of the various forts and depots supporting the expedition (including the only extant measurements of Benjamin Chambers's fortification at the settlement still bearing his name, Chambersburg); comments on morale; and bits of gossip relating to officers and their rivalries with one another. Consistent with the literary practice of contemporary travelers and explorers, he also occasionally incorporated into his diary shorter journals set down by those who had reconnoitered the territory through which the army had to move. What we perhaps do not anticipate is the evidence, explicit and inferential, of Barton's growing repugnance with the business of how frontier warfare was often conducted.

Because Barton's journal bears unique witness to one of the most important events to occur within pre-Revolutionary Pennsylvania, it is frustrating, indeed, puzzling, to the modern reader that, in its present form, the chronicle is unfinished, breaking off two months before Forbes's army, demoralized and marching at the edge of despair, garnered the unexpected news that the French, in even worse straits than itself, had blown up Fort Duquesne and retreated. William Hunter, the first to edit Barton's journal, has convincingly argued that the only known extant manuscript of Barton's journal, now in the Historical Society of Pennsylvania, bears evidence of being a later, revised draft of earlier notes.[3] Why Barton never finished revising and transcribing we cannot determine, a puzzle made especially perplexing insofar as some evidence suggests that Barton remained with the expedition possibly as late as January of 1759. Chapter 2 of this biography explores how Barton's personal disillusionment with the callous ethical behavior of many of the troops may help explain the journal's abrupt breaking off before the actual investment of Fort Duquesne. Barton's revision cannot be dated. If, however, he undertook the effort in 1763/64, troubling developments in Lancaster during those years might also help us appreciate his abandoning the project.

Like his November 8, 1756, letter to the SPG, Barton's November 16, 1764, report is a mixed affair, intimating both something of the turbulence of the times and the personal pressures to which Barton had to respond. Significantly, the poor health that later complicated his discharging his duties already plays its role in undermining his early ministerial efforts in Lancaster.

Two subjects dominate this *notitia parochialis*. The first focuses on the religious turmoil Lancaster microcosmically reflected. The Great Awakening, now in full swing throughout the colonies, was challenging Barton's resources to the limit. Although he had effected a kind of alliance among Lancaster's more formal, liturgical dominations—he defines himself as a kind of coordinator among the Anglicans, the Lutherans, and the German Reformed—they were clearly losing ground to the "Swarm of Sectaries" which have been attracting vast numbers of converts to "their strange & novel Doctrines." Even traditional Presbyterianism, long an enemy to Anglican interests, is beset from without by "all the other Sects," as well as from within by factionalism in the form of Seceders, New Lights, and Convenanters. Whistling in the dark, as it were, Barton retreats into a security for which he has little justification, but to which he committed himself throughout the remainder of his career: "the Church of England . . . must prevail at last . . . amidst all the Rage & Wildness of Fanaticism." Blind to the forces amassed against his church, he even foresees "the Establishment of Episcopacy in America."

The second significant subject Barton addesses almost in passing—Pontiac's War and, relatedly, the Paxton Boys' massacre in Lancaster of helpless Susquehannock (Conestoga) Indians protected by the Crown. Barton's almost perfunctory notice of Henry Bouquet's expedition against Pontiac, along with his astonishingly brief allusion to "the Murder of the Indians in this Place, & the different Insurrections occasion'd by this inhuman Act," invites the questions and speculation addressed in chapter 5. Reading carefully between the lines of this report, the reader cannot avoid perceiving that Barton's concluding, veiled threat to resign from the society is no empty, last-minute gesture: despite his occasional, if forced, optimism, the entire letter intimates that vocationally, economically, culturally, Barton had at the end of 1764 reached a decisive turning point in his life.

The American colonies' break with the mother country complexified Barton's dilemma beyond anything he might have foreseen in 1764. The turmoil following the Declaration of Independence prevented his writing the SPG until November 25, 1776. That letter's brevity (uncharacteristic of Barton), together with its terse, rushed recording of the persecutions already besetting Barton and his Anglican colleagues, intimate the haste with which he seeks to exploit an opportunity to dash a letter off to the society. The report bears poignant witness to the determination of Pennsylvania's die-hard patriots either to coerce the Church of England into supporting the revolutionary government or to suppress it.

The May 20, 1778, petition of the SPG missionaries, in Barton's hand, over his signature, and most probably authored largely by him, futilely appeals to the supposed libertarian and humanitarian ideals of the new state's revolutionary government. Summarizing the plight of Pennsylvania's (mostly) itinerant SPG ministers, the petition, ignoring such notable exceptions as the fierce Tory-supporter Daniel Batwelle and the wealthy William Smith, sets forth a picture of an impecunious clergy selflessly dedicated to the twin ideal of preserving civil order and fulfilling its spiritual charge.

Nine days following the date of the collective appeal for toleration, Barton publicly acknowledged the inevitable. His communication of May 29, 1778, petitions Pennsylvania's Supreme Executive Council for safe conduct out of the state. No simple, humble request, Barton draws upon—almost playfully at times—a variety of rhetorical strategies, including hyperbole and irony, to justify his leaving Pennsylvania and, as he surely knew, all his children.

In poignant contrast to the clear penmanship distinguishing his earlier correspondence, the shaky, painfully executed hand of Barton's last letters registers the toll his persecutions and rapidly failing health have had upon him. His report of January 8, 1779, rehearses the narrative he had already written of, carefully documenting the time immediately before fleeing to New York City. Added to that, his present destitution, wherein he has been surviving on the generosity of his in-laws, drives him to appeal for the three years of back pay due him. Additionally, he passes on intelligence concerning the deaths of Pennsylvania colleagues during those troubled years and the continuing trials of two other missionaries too isolated to communicate with the society. Notwithstanding the self-pity he cannot suppress nor the bleak realities everywhere besetting the Church of England, Barton assures his superiors in London (but most of all perhaps himself) that there remains "sufficient Power & Spirit still in the Nation, which . . . will deliver us from the Tyranny that has scourg'd us for so long."

The final letter presented here, October 25, 1779, climactically dramatizes Barton's continuing battle to survive rapidly deteriorating health, this in part to justify to the SPG his declining its astonishing request that he undertake missionary work on Long Island, which is now infested with "A very formidable & violent Banditti from Connecticut." Following a paragraph wherein he tries to resolve several financial loose ends, he concludes once more with the hopeful expectation that the church in America "will, one Day, rise triumphant & be the Glory of the New World."

TEXTUAL NOTE

William A. Hunter notes that Barton's manuscript journal of the Forbes expedition, preserved by descendants from his first son, William, was purchased by the Historical Society of Pennsylvania at an auction in 1970.[4] Hunter transcribed and annotated the manuscript for publication in *The Pennsylvania Magazine of History and Biography* (4 [1971], 431–83). With permission of the Pennsylvania Historical and Manuscript Commission, which oversees Hunter's estate, and the Historical Society of Pennsylvania, I have used Hunter's reprint for my copy text, comparing it closely with the original manuscript at HSP.

Silently, Hunter modernized the original's punctuation, substituting periods for Barton's dashes or simply deleting them altogether. As Barton's numerous manuscript letters demonstrate, however, he consistently employed the dash (of varying lengths) or the period with the dash to end a sentence; he also frequently used dashes where we normally use commas to set off clauses and phrases. Barton's practice is not unique in eighteenth-century writing: Barton's colleague the Rev. Charles Woodmason (most probably also Anglo-Irish) consistently favored the dash; and Laurence Sterne (another Anglo-Irishman), for example, similarly utilizes the dash throughout his novels *Tristram Shandy* and *A Sentimental Journey,* as well as in his personal correspondence. Used consistently throughout a long piece of writing, the dash suggests spontaneity, abruptness in transition, even perhaps haste, although the present manuscript, as Hunter has convincingly argued, represents a draft written somewhat later and more carefully than the presumed original that was set down during the expedition. To reproduce Barton's eighteenth-century style accurately, I have restored Barton's original punctuation and capitalization.

Hunter's reprint contains several misreadings of the manuscript text. In a few other instances, Hunter inadvertently dropped words and lines. Without comment on Hunter's minor omissions and errors, I have silently supplied the correct readings, but noted where I have restored longer lines of text missed in his transcription.

Hunter's notes are plentiful and thorough. They offer the reader invaluable explanation and clearly identify Barton's numerous allusions and references to soldiers involved in the expedition. They also clarify mistakes and irregularities in Barton's text. With permission of *PMHB,* I have therefore retained Hunter's footnotes in their entirety. Only occasionally do I correct an error or oversight.[5]

In a number of instances, I felt that additional notes were needed, as were glosses of obscure words or comments or allusions to items of interest to local history. To distinguish these notes from Hunter's, I have used square brackets containing the further attribution "Ed." to set off my interpolations from Hunter's insertions.

Barton's correspondence offers editorial problems of another order. Uniformly, and notwithstanding his unusually clear hand, they disclose evidence of haste and poor health. Additionally, binding of archival copies often concealed or obscured text in the extreme left and right margins. In instances where the original text is difficult to read or construe, I have tried to supply the correct reading. In this, I have consulted the excerpted, modernized transcriptions published by William Stevens Perry,[6] who evidently had access to the letters before they were bound. Other times, I have offered what strikes me as the best reading. Again, all such editorial interpolations are set off within square brackets.

Appendix A:
November 8, 1756, Report to the Society
for the Propagation of the Gospel in Foreign Parts

Rev^d. Sir,[1]

It gives me a real Concern that I have never been able to send you any Account since I enter'd upon my Mission till now. Our Distresses Here have been such, that in short, I knew not what to write or what to do: These Considerations will I hope still support me in your Esteem, & incline the Honble. Society to Pardon me.—As I intend to be the more particular now, to atone for my past Silence; I foresee a long Letter, & must therefore bespeak your Indulgence.—

After a short & very agreeable Passage, I arriv'd at Philadelphia about the 16th. of April 1755; And immediately wrote to the People of Huntington,[2] who came generously with their Waggons, & brought away my Effects.—As soon as I settled my Affairs & visited my Friends, I set out for this Place about the latter End of May; where I was receiv'd with a hearty Welcome; and was much pleas'd to find the poor People fill'd with Gratitude, under a due Sense of the weighty Obligations they were under to the Honble. Society for the Favours confer'd upon them.—And what pleas'd me still more, was, to hear that they had struggled hard to keep alive some Sense of Religion among their Children, by meeting every Sunday & getting one of the Members to read Prayers to them.—

My first Business was to visit & make myself acquainted with the State & Numbers of the three Congregations at York, Huntington, & Carlisle. And having settled Wardens & Vestry-Men in each, they all met & according to their Numbers agreed mutually that I should officiate three Sundays in Six at Huntington, two at Carlisle, & one at York.—Upon hearing that within the Limits of my Mission, there

---

Original is no. 1 in the SPG Letter Books, Series B, vol. 21, Bodleian Library of Commonwealth and African Studies, Rhodes House Library, Oxford, U.K. (Reprinted courtesy of the United Society for the Propagation of the Gospel.)

[1] Identified by Barton on the last page as "The Rev^d. D^r. [Philip] Bearcroft," secretary of the SPG.
[2] Huntington township (in then York, now Adams, county), site of Christ Church.

were large Numbers of the Communion of the Church of England, in the Settlements of Canogochieg, Shippensburg, Sheerman's-Valley, West-Penn's-Borough, & Marsh Creek;—I determin'd to visit each of these Places four Times a year to prepare them for the Sacrament of the Lord's Supper, & to baptize their Children.—

I had the Pleasure to see my Hearers encrease daily; which amounted to such a Number in a few Weeks at Huntington, that I have been sometimes oblig'd to preach to them under the Covert of the Trees.—And when it was my Turn at Carlisle, I am told that People came 40, 50, & some 60 Miles.—The Dissenters also (who are very numerous in these Parts) attended constantly; & seem'd well dispos'd; always behaving themselves decently & devoutly.—The more rational Part of them appear well reconcil'd with our Church; & some of the Principal of them offer'd generously to subscribe to me.—

I now Began to consider myself (as the Rev^d. M^r. Provost Smith[3] expresses it in a Letter to me) "As One who had advanc'd to the very Frontiers of the Messiah's Kingdom, & among the first who had unfolded his everlasting Banners in the remotest Parts of the West."[4]

From the Advantage of my Situation bordering upon Nations of Savages, I entertain'd strong Hopes that it might please the Lord to make me a happy Instrument to subject some of these poor ignorant Creatures to the Kingdom of God, & of Jesus Christ. And hearing that a Number of them were come down from the Ohio to Carlisle, to dispose of their Furr & Deer-Skins, I made it my Business to go among them, & endeavour as much as possible to ingratiate myself into their good Opinion. Next Morning I invited them to Church; & such of them as understood any English came, & seem'd very attentive the whole Time.—When I came to visit them in the Afternoon, those that had been at Church, brought all their Brethren to shake Hands with me;–And pointing often upwards discours'd with one another some Time in their own Language. I imagine they were telling them what they had heard; & indeed I observ'd them to be pleas'd with the Relation.—

This gave me Reason to think that the Indians were willing to be instructed, & were susceptible of good Impressions: And if they found Missionaries divested of sinister & selfish Motives, they could easily be prevail'd upon to exchange their Savage Barbarity for the pure & peaceable Religion of Jesus. Just when I was big with the Hopes of being able to do Service among these tawny People,—we receiv'd the melancholy News, that our Forces under the Command of General Braddock, were defeated on the 9th. of July, as they were marching to take Duquesne, a French Fort upon the Ohio.—This was soon succeeded by an Alienation of the

---

[3] The Reverend William Smith, provost of the Philadelphia Academy, later the College of Philadelphia.
[4] Barton published William Smith's letter in full in his *Unanimity and Public Spirit: a Sermon Preached at Carlisle and Some Other Episcopal Churches in the Counties of York and Cumberland soon after General Braddock's Defeat* (Philadelphia, 1755).

Indians in our Interest:—And from that Day to this, poor Pennsylvania has felt incessantly the sad Effects of Popish Tyranny, & Savage Cruelty!—A great Part of five of her Counties have been depopulated & laid waste; & some Hundreds of her sturdiest Sons either murder'd, or carried into barbarous Captivity!—

At a Time of such publick Calamity & Distress, you may easily conceive, Rev^d. Sir, what must be my Situation, whose Fortune it was, to have my Residence in a Place, when these Grievances were felt most.—I repine not however at my Lot in being plac'd here; but rather esteem it a Happiness, since I hope I may say, God has enabled me to do some Service to our pure Protestant Religion, in Spite of its most inveterate Enemies.—

Tho' my Churches, are Churches militant indeed, subject to Dangers & Trials of the most alarming Kind; yet I have the Pleasure every Sunday (even at the worst of Times) to see my People coming crowding with their Muskets on their Shoulders; declaring that they will dye Protestants & Freemen, sooner than live Idolaters & Slaves.—The French King has rather serv'd than injur'd the Protestant Cause in these Parts: for the People have seen so much of the cruel Barbarities of those, who call themselves the Subjects & Allies of his Most Christian Majesty, that they detest the very Name of Popery.—

Among a People thus dispos'd, I should think myself extremely happy, were they barely able to keep me above Want; which at present indeed they are not. —It is but a little Time since these Counties were erected.[5] They were chiefly settled by poor People who not being able to purchase Lands in the interior Parts of the Country, came back where they were cheap.—Many of them were so low at first, that two Families were generally oblig'd to join in fitting out one Plough; And before they could raise a Subsistence, were necessitated to run in Debt for a Stock, & for what maintain'd them in the Interim.—As soon as they became industrious, the fertile Soil gave them an Hundred-fold, & in a little Time rais'd them to Affluence & Plenty.—When they were just beginning to feel the Comforts, & taste the Fruits of their Industry, a barbarous & cruel Enemy came, & ruin'd them!—The County of Cumberland has suffer'd particularly, & the Condition of its remaining shatter'd Inhabitants is truly deplorable!—Many of them are reduc'd to real Poverty & Distress;—groaning under a Burden of Calamities; some having lost their Husbands; some their Wives, some their Children,—And all the Labour of many Years! In this Condition (my Heart bleeds in relating what I am an Eye Witness to) they now wander about, without Bread of their own to eat, or a House to shelter themselves in from the Inclemency of the approaching Winter!—They have left many thousand Bushels of Wheat & other Grain behind them in their Barns & Storehouses; which must become a Spoil to the Enemy, while the just Owners of it must either beg or starve! Since I sat down to write this Letter, I have receiv'd Accounts, that a poor Family had fled for Refuge into this County above six Months ago,

[5] York county was erected on August 9, 1749, Cumberland on January 27, 1750.

where they have remain'd ever since; but finding they could not subsist,—chose a few Days ago to run the Risque of returning Home to enjoy the Fruits of their Labour, where they had not Time to unlode their Cart, before they were seiz'd by Indians, & murder'd!—

Carlisle is the only Remains of that once populous County;—They have a Garrison of about 100 Men; but how long they will be able to defend themselves is very uncertain, as the Enemy have threaten'd that Place in particular.—They still have their Share of my Ministrations, & seem extremely thankful to the Honble. Society upon whose Bounty I am chiefly supported.

By the Reduction of Cumberland, the County of York is become the Frontier:—And should the Enemy carry their Ravages this far, I shall be a considerable Sufferer; for upon my Arrival at Huntington, I found the Glebe still under its Native woods, & the People not able to make any Improvement upon it.—This put me under a Necessity of purchasing a small Plantation, & building on it at my own Expense;[6] by which Means I embarrass'd myself in Debt, in Hopes the People would assist me in paying for it, which indeed they promis'd to do: But this dismal Turn in our Affairs renders it impracticable.—From York I have still less to expect, as the Town is chiefly inhabited by Dutch, & not many of our Communion among them.—Upon the whole, I believe the People will be able to do very little for me, till we have some favourable Change.—I do not design, Rev^d. Sir, by any Thing I have said, to derogate from the Merit of my good Parishioners;—That would be ungrateful, as I have Reason to think that they are a worthy, well-dispos'd, & kind Sort of People, who profess the greatest Friendship & Esteem for me, & am persuaded would willingly do any Thing in their Power to afford me an easy Support & Maintenance.—

This Mission in a few Years would have vyed with the ablest in this Province, As it was in a flourishing State, and could not contain less [than] 2,000 Persons, Members of the Church of England. But so melancholy is the Transition, that it cannot afford to build one Church; So that I officiate sometimes in a Barn, sometimes in a Wastehouse; or wherever else Convenience offers.—

I have baptized since my Arrival 160 Infants, 10 Adults, & an Indian Girl who has been brought up in a Christian Family since her Infancy, after due Examination & Instruction. The Number of my Communicants is 58, which I have but little Expectation of encreasing, till this Storm is blown over.—But I assure you, Rev^d. Sir, no Endeavours of mine shall be wanting to bring many to Righteousness. —Whatever Hardships or Discouragements may attend my Ministry, I hope I shall ever keep in View the Importance of my Undertaking; and always strive to answer the pious & laudable Designs of the Honble. Society in appointing me their Missionary; by doing all in my Power to promote the Glory of Almighty God, & the

---

[6] In Reading township, near Mud Run.

Salvation of Mankind.—I receiv'd lately from the Hands of D^r. Jenney[7] the Society's Instructions to their Missionaries in North America,[8] which are very seasonable & justly adapted to our present Circumstances; And, if duly observ'd, & properly enforc'd, may do infinite Service to our bleeding Country.—

I have often observ'd, & indeed regreted it as a Misfortune, that our Missionaries in this Part of the World are so little acquainted with one another:—And though in the 12th. Instruction of the Society's Collection of Papers, it is recommended to them to "keep up a Brotherly Correspondence, by meeting together at certain Times, as shall be most convenient for mutual Advice & Assistance"; yet no such Thing is observ'd, & I dare affirm that many of them have never had an Opportunity of conversing with four of their Brethren since they left England.— How many Advantages we shall lose by such a Neglect at this Time of publick & emminent Danger, I shall submit to the Judgment of the Honble. Society.—

M^r. Provost Smith has been lately up here to settle Free-Schools,[9] who is the only Episcopal Clergyman, beside M^r. Secretary Peters,[10] that I have had the Happiness of seeing in these Counties since I came into them.—M^r. Smith has been pleas'd to communicate to me the Honble. Society's Designs to extend their Care to the Instruction of Indian Children at the Academy in Philad^a.—[11] Which good Scheme I believe M^r. Smith will heartily endeavour to put into Execution, & do every Thing in his Power to make it answer the glorious Ends propos'd by it. If I can assist him in any Part of it, he shall always find me ready & willing to do it.— Happy had it been for us had this Scheme been resolv'd upon many Years ago: For it is probably from the Neglect of this necessary Duty of instructing the Indians, that these Colonies derive the greater Part of the Miseries they now sadly groan under.—

While the French were industrious in sending Priests & Jesuits among them, to convert them to Popery, we did nothing but send a Set of abandon'd profligate Men to trade with them, who defrauded & cheated them; And practic'd every Vice among them that can be nam'd, which set the English & the Protestant Religion in such a disadvantagious Light, that we have Reason to fear they detest the Name of both.—

It is said by some of our Brethren who have lately escap'd from Captivity, that they heard the Indians say, they thought it no Sin to murder the English, but rather a meritorious Act; And if it was a Sin, the French had old Men among them who

---

[7] The Reverend Doctor Robert Jenny was rector of Christ Church, Philadelphia.

[8] *Instructions from the Society for the Propagation of the Gospel in Foreign Parts, to Their Missionaries in North-America* (London, 1756).

[9] Possibly a reference to the free schools proposed for Anglicizing the children of German-speaking Pennsylvanians. See above, Chapter 4, pp. 86–88. The paragraph (as in this letter's third-last paragraph), however, otherwise focuses on "the Instruction of Indian children," suggesting that Barton may also refer to missionary schools for Indian children.

[10] The Reverend Richard Peters, Pennsylvania provincial secretary.

[11] That is, the Philadelphia Academy.

could forgive all Sins.—Others observe that they cross'd themselves every Night & Morning, & went to Prayers regularly:—That they often murmur'd & said, the English it was true had often made them trifling Presents, but that they took Care they should never carry them many Miles before the Traders came after them to cheat them, giving them only a little Rum in Return.—Whereas the French always paid them well for their Skins &c^a., built Houses for them, instructed their Children, & took Care of their Wives when they went to War.

By such Neglect & such Treatment have we forfeited an Alliance that would, in all Probability, have secur'd to us a quiet Enjoyment of our Possessions, & prevented the dreadful Consequences of a Savage War.—

Several Sachims or Indian Kings, in their Treaties formerly with this Government, earnestly sollicited that no Europians should be permitted to carry Rum to their Towns;—Upon which an Act was pass'd by the Governor & Assembly of this Province, prohibiting any Person under a Penalty of Ten Pounds, to sell, barter, or give in Exchange, any Rum or other Spirits, to or with any Indian within the Province:—But the Difficulty of producing Proof against Offenders, as they were chiefly far back in the woods, where they could deal clandestinely, out of the View of any but themselves;—made this Act not answer for the good Intentions of the Legislature.—So that the Traders still continued to sell strong Liquors to the Indians, whereby they were often cheated & debauch'd, to the great Dishonour of Almighty God, Scandal of the Christian Faith, & Hindrance of propagating true Religion among them.—Yet I don't despair but some Methods may be fallen upon to reclaim them;—And make them sensible that their Attachment to the English will be their truest Interest & greatest Happiness.

And indeed (in my humble Opinion) Nothing can promise fairer to pro-duce these happy Effects, than this Scheme propos'd by the Honble. Society.—In the Conversion of Indians, many Difficulties & Impediments will occur, which Europian Missionaries will never be able to remove. Their Customs & Manner of Living are so opposite to the Genius & Constitution of our People that they could never become familiar to them.—Few of the Indians have any settled Place of Habitation, but wander about, where they can meet with most Success in Hunting:—And whatever Beasts or Reptiles they chance to take, are Food to them.—Bears, Foxes, Wolves, Raccoons, Pole-Cats, & even Snakes, they can eat with as much Chearfulness as Englishmen to their best Beef & Mutton.—But such Hardships are easily surmounted, & such an austere Life made agreeable, by such as from their Infancy have been accustom'd to them.—So that Indian Boys educated at the Academy under the care of able Masters,—Where they can be visited by their Relations, & taught every Thing necessary for them to learn, at an easier Expence than in any of the Universities in Europe, will be the fittest to be employ'd in this grand & glorious Work, & the most likely to succeed in it.—

However defective these Thoughts may be, I have ventur'd, Rev^d. Sir, to communicate them freely; And if I have luckily dropt any Hint that can be improv'd to the Advantage of this important Scheme, I shall esteem it a Happiness; As I shall always think it my Duty to pay the highest Regards to the Honble. Society's Directions.

I might justly incur the Censure of Ingratitude, did I conclude this Letter without presenting my most hearty Thanks, which I sincerely do, to that Honble. Body for appointing me their Missionary.—And I shall ever retain a grateful Sense of the many Friendships & Favours wherewith I was honour'd when in London, by particular Members of it.—I am, Rev^d. Sir, with all possible Duty & Esteem,

Your most oblig'd &
affectionate Brother,
Friend & Servt.

Tho Barton

Huntington in Pennsylv^a.
November 8th. 1756

The Rev^d. D^r. Bearcroft

Appendix B:
Journal of an Expedition to the Ohio, commanded by His Excellency Brigadier-General Forbes; in the Year of our Lord 1758

FRIDAY, 7th of July, receiv'd the Governor's[1] Commission appointing me Chaplain to the 3[d] Battalion of the Pennsylvania Regiment, commanded by Colonel Mercer;[2] with a Letter from the Secretary[3] apologizing for my not having the Preference of the other two.—[4]

Wednesday, July 12th. Set off from my own House in York County,[5] & reach'd Carlisle that Night, where I receiv'd the General's Letter,[6] with an invitation to attend the Troops under his Command; & promising me his Protection & Encouragement.—

Thursday, 13th. Waited on the General, & return'd him Thanks for the Honor he

---

Barton's original manuscript is at the Historical Society of Pennsylvania. (Reprinted here courtesy of HSP.)

[1] William Denny, lieutenant governor 1756–59. His reform of the Pennsylvania troops, about the end of 1757, had merit, but he was in other respects an inept executive.

[2] Hugh Mercer had served as major in Col. John Armstrong's 1st Battalion before being promoted to colonel of the new 3[d] Battalion.

[3] Richard Peters, secretary of the Provincial Council. See Hubertis Cummings, *Richard Peters: Provincial Secretary and Cleric, 1704–1776* (Philadelphia: University of Pennsylvania Press, 1944).

[4] For the 1st Battalion, Charles Beatty was commissioned as of June 9; for the 2[d], John Steel, as of June 10. Barton's commission was dated June 11, the dates conforming to the order of the battalions.

[5] In the present Huntington [correctly, Reading—Ed.] township, Adams county. Barton had been in Carlisle on July 7, though this is not indicated in his journal entry for that date.

[6] [John] Forbes to Barton, Carlisle [July 9; see above, p. 45].

John Forbes, colonel of the 17th Regiment of Foot, had come to America in 1757 with Lord Loudoun, the newly appointed British commander in North America. In December of that year, William Pitt replaced Loudoun with Maj. Gen. James Abercromby, directed Maj. Gen. Jeffery Amherst to lead an attack on Louisbourg, and gave Forbes the southern command, with orders to attack Fort Duquesne. For a biographical sketch, see Alfred P. James, *Writings of General John Forbes* (Menasha, Wis.: the Collegiate Press, 1938), ix–xii.

172

did me.—

July 14th & 15th.Waited at Carlisle in Expectation of marching with the General.–
Sunday July 16th. Preach'd to the Officers &Cª from Eccles: 8-11.—[7]
July 17th 18th & 19th. Still waited for the General, who intended every Day to march,[8] but was detain'd by Expresses coming frequently to him with disagreeable Accounts from General Abercrombie at Ticonderoga.—[9]
Friday[10] July 20th. Being tir'd with waiting at Carlisle, set out for Rays-Town[11] in Company with Major Shippen[12] escorted by a Detachment of the Virginia Light-Horse.—[13] A good Road through shallow barren Land much broken with Stones & little Hills led us to Shippensburg a small poor Town about 20 Miles from Carlisle, where we arriv'd the same Evening.—Here we found Captain Hay[14] with the Train of Artillery, & Captain McKenzie[15] with 300 Highlanders encamped on a low Piece of Ground on the East Side of the Town,—call'd Dunbar's Encampment.[16] At a little Distance from the Centre of the Town, is Fort-Morris,[17] a trifling Piece of Work with 4 Bastions, & about 120 Feet Square:—It does not appear that a Vauban[18] had any

---

[7] "Because sentence against an evil work is not executed speedily, therefore the heart of the sons of men is fully set in them to do evil." Perhaps Barton had in mind the French four-year occupation of Fort Duquesne.

[8] On July 18 Barton wrote Richard Peters that "I intend to set off tomorrow": *Pennsylvania Archives* [cited hereafter as *PA*], 1st Series, 3:450–52.

[9] Abercromby, Forbes's superior, attempted an invasion of Canada by way of Lake Champlain ,but the campaign bogged down before Fort Ticonderoga.

[10] Correctly, Thursday; the error in days persists through July 24.

[11] Now Bedford. The name is deceptive; Forbes wrote, on July 10, that "in Raestown there is not one single house; The place having its name from one Rae, who designed to have made a plantation there several years ago" (James, *Writings*, 140–41). John Ray, an Indian trader, had sold his claim to Gerrard (or Garret) Pendergrass, who settled there but was driven off by the Indians.

[12] Joseph Shippen, Jr., was the son of Edward Shippen of Lancaster and the brother-in-law of Colonel Burd, under whom he had served at Fort Augusta. Major in Burd's 2ᵈ Battalion, he was brevet lieutenant-colonel in the regiment. Some of his letters on the 1758 campaign have been published in the *Pennsylvania Magazine of History and Biography* (cited hereafter as *PMHB*) 36 (1912): 385–463.

[13] Part of the troop of forty men drawn from the 1st Virginia Regiment and commanded by Robert Stewart, who was captain of a company in that regiment.

[14] Capt. Lt. David Hay of the Royal Regiment of Artillery.

[15] Probably Capt. Hugh McKenzie of the 1st Highland Battalion, which also included Capts. Alexander and Roderick McKenzie.

[16] Col. Thomas Dunbar, of the 48th Regiment, who succeeded Braddock in command after the latter's defeat and death in July 1755, led Braddock's troops on their subsequent march to Philadelphia, in the course of which they reached Shippensburg by August 17 (Dunbar to Gov. Morris, *Colonial Records* [cited hereafter as *CR*], 6:595).

[17] One of two forts (the other was at Carlisle) ordered built by Gov. Robert Hunter Morris (for whom it was named). On receipt of the news of Braddock's defeat, it was regularly garrisoned by Pennsylvania troops after September, 1756. The site is on present Burd Street, in the northern part of town: see William A. Hunter, *Forts on the Pennsylvania Frontier, 1753–1758* (Harrisburg: The Pennsylvania Historical and Museum Commission,1960), 450–63.

[18] Sebastien le Prestre de Vauban (1633–1707), the French military engineer whose writings on fortification were classics.

Hand in laying it out.—Lodg'd at the Sign of the Indian-Queen, kept by M[r] Campbel,[19] where we met with good Entertainment.—

Saturday[20] *July 21*[st]. Preach'd this Morning at 8 O'Clock A.M. at the Request of the Commanding Officer,[21] from 2 Chron: 14.—1 1.—[22] Set off from this Place at 10, & in about 2 Hours reach'd Col: Chamber's,[23] where we met with a kind Reception, & a very generous & hospitable Entertainment.—This Gentleman's House is surrounded by a Stockade of 300 Feet in Length, & 90 in Width. It has a pleasant Stream of Water runing thro' it, & is full of small Huts built by the Inhabitants, who fled there from the Ravages of the Enemy.—[24] At a small Distance from the Fort are 2 Cataracts, call'd the Falling Springs, which tumble down a Precipice into Canogocheaque.—This Water is of such a Quality that Wood, Clay, Straws &C that lie any Time in it, are petrified, & sometimes incrusted with a hard Stone.—M[r]. Chambers informed me that in digging a Pit for a Saw-Mill he found Snail-Shells quite whole above 15 Feet under Ground.—This Place is distant from Shippensburg 10 Miles: The Road good, but the Land, thro' which it passes, not extraordinary.—Set off from M[r]. Chambers's about 4 Oclock,— good Road, & some good Land,—reach'd Fort Loudon[25] at 7—This Place is 14 Miles distant from the last mention'd.—The Fort is a poor Piece of Work, irregularly built, & badly situated at the Bottom of a Hill Subject to Damps & noxious Vapours.—

It has something like Bastions supported by Props, which if an Enemy should cut away, down tumbles Men & all. At little Distance from the Fort appears Parnel's–Nob, a round Hill of great Height.—The Fort is properly a square Ridout of 120 feet.—Here I found Captain Harding with 380 Royal Americans.—[26] camp'd there

[19] Francis Campbell, of whom Gov. Morris had written Gov. Horatio Sharpe, on January 7 [1755], that George Croghan "informs me that there is one Francis Campbell, a Storekeeper at Shippensburg who was bred for the church as he has heard among the Roman Catholicks, but has the Character of an honest, inoffensive man" (*PA*, 1st Series, 2:114. The letter is misdated 1754).

[20] Correctly, Friday.

[21] Presumably Capt. James Sharp of the 3[d] Battalion, Pennsylvania Regiment. Sharp was ordered on June 18 to take post at Shippensburg, where he remained until July 23, when he joined Col. John Armstrong on his march to Raystown with the last Pennsylvania companies. Sharp was not among the officers who signed the July 4 petition [see above, p. 44] for a Presbyterian chaplain.

[22] "...help us, O LORD our God; for we rest on thee, and in thy name we go against this multitude."

[23] Benjamin Chambers, at the present Chambersburg, Franklin county. He had been a colonel in Franklin's Association of 1747–48 (*PA*, 5th Series, 1:24).

[24] Chambers' own account of this "private fort" is quoted in Hunter, *Forts*, 556.

[25] Built in November 1756, by Pennsylvania to replace a temporary post at McDowell's Mill (present Markes, Franklin county). Forbes, on July 10, described it and Fort Lyttelton as consisting of "only two or three houses each, inclosed with a Stockade of 100 feet square" (James, *Writings*, 141). Named for the Earl of Loudoun, then the British commander in North America, the fort's site was one and a half-miles southeast of the present village of Ft. Loudon. It is now owned by the state and administered by the Pennsylvania Historical and Museum Commission (Hunter, *Forts*, 463–73). A drawing of a frontier post with bastions of the kind here described appears in *American Heritage* 22 (December 1970): 98.

[26] Capt. Ralph Harding was in command at Fort Loudoun about June 16 to July 23. This is the full strength of the four companies, which arrived at Raystown on July 27–28.

all Night, & was well treated by the Officers.—

Sunday,[27] *July 22ᵈ.*—March'd about 8 O'Clock this Morning.—Cross'd a Branch of Canogocheague Creek—Came to a Spring, where we sat down & eat some Bread & Cheese—Cut Locust Bushes for the Horses, & after resting about an Hour took Horse, & pursued our Journey to Fort Littleton[28] 18 Miles distant from Loudon— Where we arriv'd about 6 that Evening—The Road between these two Places is extremely bad—And Nothing to be seen but Mountains, & Hills, & Wrecks of Waggons, & Flower Casks &Cᵃ.—At Littleton we found Captains McPherson & Hamilton[29] encamp'd with 2 Companies of the Pennsylvania New Levies—This Fort is a regular & well-plan'd Square Stockade of 126 Feet—The Situation pleasant & advantagious—Remain'd here all Night, & lay with Major Shippen upon the Ground in a Soldiers-Tent— Great Rains & Thunder before Day—found myself all wet when I awak'd in the Morning.—

Monday[30] *July 23ᵈ.*— Set out at 10 O'Clock—Something like a level Country appears—& good Road to Sidling-hill, to the top of which you ascend after many Windings & Turnings—Sidling-Hill distant from Littleton 9 Miles—The Road now proves bad for 4 or 5 Miles—Now the Road gets better—some good Land—Met a prodigious Number of Waggons convoying Provisions, Amunition &Cᵃ to Rays Town.—Halted at a Spring. Made some Punch, eat Bread & Cheese—Set out again & reach'd Juniata Crossing[31] that Night—distant from Sidling-Hill 9 Miles.—Here we found Captain Morgan[32] encamp'd with some Companies of the Pennsylvania Regiment.—A small Fort just erected, & the Ford of Juniata piqueted in, in Order to protect Waggons &Cᵃ in passing—Stay'd at this Place all Night. Lay without a Bed, or any Covering but a Single Blanket.—[33]

Tuesday,[34] *July 24ᵗʰ* March'd about 8 OClock this Morning—The Road good— Some extraordinary Land & rich Bottoms, with here & there a little Hill.—Met with

---

[27] Correctly, Saturday.

[28] Begun in November 1755, at the present Fort Littleton, Fulton county, as one of four forts designed by Gov. Morris to form a defensive line west of the Susquehanna and named for Sir George Lyttelton, then chancellor of the exchequer. A purported plan published in William H. Egle, *An Illustrated History of the Commonwealth of Pennsylvania* (Harrisburg: DeWitt C. Goodrich, 1876), is an altered plan of Fort Ligonier (see Hunter, *Forts*, 410–24).

[29] Capts. Robert McPherson and Thomas Hamilton of the 3ᵈ Battalion, Pennsylvania Regiment.

[30] Correctly, Sunday.

[31] West of Breezewood, Bedford county, north of the point at which the present highway crosses the Juniata's Raystown Branch. Bouquet had stopped there June 21-24 on his march to Raystown.

[32] Capt. Jacob Morgan of Col. Burd's 2ᵈ Battalion had commanded at Fort Lebanon, near the present Auburn, Schuylkill county, 1756–58. Morgan now commanded at the Crossings, as Barton's journal shows, at least until July 24; he probably was relieved soon afterward.

[33] Fort Juniata, the first post constructed by Forbes's troops on their advance toward Fort Duquesne, was laid out on June 21 by engineer Capt. Harry Gordon. A rough (apparently preliminary) plan for the fort is in S. K. Stevens, et al., eds., *The Papers of Henry Bouquet*, 6 vols. (Harrisburg: the Pennsylvania Historical and Museum Commission, 1951–94), 2: after page 128 (referred to hereinafter as *BP*).

[34] Correctly, Monday. With "Tuesday July 25ᵗʰ," which follows, Barton resumes the correct dating.

fine Grass about 4 Miles from the Crossing—turn'd out our Horses to feed upon it—After resting 2 Hours, pursu'd our Journey to Snake-Spring,[35] where we cut Locust-Bushes for the Horses, & refresh'd ourselves with Punch, Bread, Cheese & dry Venison—After a Stay of about an Hour, set out again for Rays Town distant from the Crossing 12 Miles—Where we arriv'd in good Health about 4 OClock in the Evening— Waited on the Commanding Office[36] by whom I was receiv'd in a very friendly Manner—All the other Officers treated me likewise with much Respect.—Here I found about 1,800 Men—a fine Fort,[37] & Store-Houses—with two Encampments surrounded by Breast-Works.—

Tuesday July 25th. Arriv'd a Number of Pack-Horses with Flower &C, escorted by 30 Highlanders & a Company of Pennsylvania New Levies—

Wednesday, July 26th. Nothing worth Notice happen'd this Day.—[38]

Thursday-July 27th. A Number of Pack Horses arriv'd, escorted by 40 Royal Americans under the Command of a Lieutenant.—This Day arriv'd an Express from Carlisle—

Friday 28th July— 4 Companies of Royal Americans arriv'd, which, with the 40 that came Yesterday, make 380.—[39] Arriv'd 2 Companies of the Pennsylvania New Levies.—Colonel Burd set out to view the Roads with a Lieut: & 25 of the Light Horse.—[40]

Saturday 29th July— Arriv'd in Camp Sir John St Clair—[41] as did likewise Colonel Washington[42] escorted by Captain Stewart[43] & Part of his Troop of Light-Horse. —He was conducted in by Col: Bouquet who went out to meet him with a Party of

---

[35] Now Snake Spring Valley Run, which enters the Raystown Branch from the north, about one and a half-miles west of Everett, Bedford county.

[36] Col. Henry Bouquet, who had arrived there with some 800 men on June 24.

[37] Begun June 28, it was known as Raystown (Reas Town) until December 1, 1758, when Forbes named it in honor of the Duke of Bedford.

[38] On July 26, Bouquet wrote Forbes that "I am expecting some pack horses any day. As yet there has come only a brigade of ninety, very poor" (*BP*, 2: 278). These presumably are the brigades that arrived on July 25 and 27.

[39] Apparently the total effective strength of the four companies of Col. Bouquet and Capts. Ralph Harding, Francis Landers, and Thomas Jocelyn. Under Harding's command, they had left Fort Loudoun on July 23.

[40] Col. James Burd, 2d Battalion, Pennsylvania Regiment. Bouquet had written Forbes on July 26 that "I have asked Colonel Burd to go tomorrow with Rhor [*sic*] to the summit of the mountain [Allegheny] in order to determine the straightest line from here to the foot of the incline" (*BP*, 2:277). For engineer Ensign Charles Rohr's report of the reconnoiter, see ibid., 294.

[41] Lieutenant colonel in the 60th (Royal American) Regiment, serving as deputy quarter-master general, an appointment (overslaugh) that properly exempted him from exercising command. He had left Carlisle on July 21 (*BP*, 2:267).

[42] Col. George Washington, commanding the 1st Virginia Regiment. On July 25, he had written Bouquet suggesting a conference at Raystown; Bouquet, replying two days later, had suggested meeting at the blockhouses midway between Raystown and Fort Cumberland (*BP*, 2:274, 281); for the blockhouses, see also Barton's journal entry for September 6.

[43] Capt. Robert Stewart.

the Pennsylvania Troop.—[44]

Sunday July 30th 1758— Preach'd from 2 Chron: 14-11[45] to about 3000 Men—in the Presence of Col: Bouquet—Governor Glenn,[46] & all the Officers.—This Evening Col: Washington with 2 Companies of the Virginia Regiment set off for Fort Cumberland to provide Regimentals [*uniforms*].—

Monday July 31st 1758— About 100 Men being Part of the 2 Companies of North Carolina Troops arriv'd under Command of Major Waddle.—[47] An Alarm at 7 OClock P.M. When a Soldier belonging to Major Lewis[48] of Virginia came running into Camp wounded in the Head, Arms, Thighs, Hand, & Leg—He reports that being in Search of Horses about 4 Miles from Camp—3 Indians appear'd to him who endeavor'd to take him Prisoner, but finding him resolute; 2 of them endeavor'd to[49] shoot him; but their Guns Flashing, he shot at the first whom he saw drop—Upon which the 2d ran up to him with a Sword & Tomahawk & strove to kill him—But he warded off the Blows, & knock'd down his Antagonist, & gave him several Thumps with the Butt of his Gun, which he thinks near finish'd him— Before he had Time to perfect the good Work begun, the 3d fell upon him with a Sword, Knife, & Tomahawk, & wounded him in the Manner above mention'd— He struggled with & knock'd down this Fellow—but hearing a rustling in the Bushes he was oblig'd to run—& got into Camp in a bloody Condition.—

Tuesday August 1st—1758— A Party who went out this Morning with the above Person say, that they found his Hat cut thro' in many Places—That they discovered Tracks & Blood, & found Something like the Impression of a Person in Agony— They & the Cherokees who went with them return'd fully convinc'd that the Fellow reported Facts, & behav'd like a Briton.—Sir John St Clair & Colonel Burd set off

[44] The 1st and 2d Battalions of the Pennsylvania Regiment each had a troop of light horse, modeled after the Virginia troop. Capt. William Thompson commanded that in the 1st Battalion; Capt. John Hambright, that in the 2d Battalion.

[45] Note that this was the same text, if not the same sermon, used at Shippensburg on July 21.

[46] James Glen, governor of South Carolina, 1738–56, was a relative of Forbes. He volunteered his help in dealing with the southern Indians who were in demand as scouts and irregulars. Forbes had sent him from Philadelphia to Fort Cumberland to negotiate with the Cherokee Indians, after which he had come to Raystown on July 13. Forbes's will, dated February 13, 1759, named Glen as executor.

[47] This day Bouquet wrote Forbes that "Two North Carolina companies are arriving at the camp, reduced to 96 men, including countless invalids; and tomorrow we shall have the third from Cumberland 46 men strong" (*BP*, 2:292). Maj. Hugh Waddell's and Capt. John Paine's companies had marched up from Fort Loudoun, Pa.

[48] Maj. Andrew Lewis, of Washington's 1st Virginia Regiment. The episode that follows was reported to Forbes by Bouquet in a letter of this same date (*BP*, 2:293).

[49] [Hunter omitted "take him Prisoner, but finding him resolute; 2 of them endeavor'd to" —Ed.]

this Day with 200 Men to reinforce Major Armstrong[50] who was sent some Time ago to take Possession of a Post over the Allegeny Mountains, call'd Drowning Creek—[51] A number of Pack-Horses loaded with Provisions, Tools &C were sent with them.—A Party of Maryland Troops consisting of about 190 Men arriv'd in Camp under Command of Capt: Dagworthy.[52]

Wednesday, August 2ᵈ.— Five Indians, who set out from hence some Time ago in order to take a View of Fort Du Quesne, return, & report that they lay near that Place a considerable Time in Hopes of taking a Prisoner, but that no Person came out of the Fort.—That the Day they came away some Troops march'd in, but can't give any distinct Account of their Numbers.—[53]

This Afternoon a Party consisting of 40 Men arriv'd from Fort-Augusta commanded by Lieut: Broadhead.—[54]

Thursday, August 3ᵈ. Colonel Burd who had been out viewing the Road-Cutters, return'd with a small Party into Camp & brought with [him] some large Gooseberries from the Allegeny Mountain, where they grow naturally.—[55]

Arriv'd a Company from N: Carolina by Way of Winchester & Fort Cumberland.—[56]

Friday, August 4ᵗʰ. Arriv'd Colonel Armstrong with about 40 Men.—[57]

Saturday, August 5ᵗʰ. A Detachment of 523 private Men, 20 Serjeants, 20 Corporals, 3 Drummers march'd out of Camp with 3 Day's Provision, Commanded by L.

---

[50] Maj. George Armstrong of Col. Mercer's 3ᵈ Battalion was previously a captain in his brother John Armstrong's battalion. On July 23, Bouquet had sent Maj. Armstrong with one hundred men to reconnoiter the way toward Fort Duquesne and to set up a post between the Allegheny Mountain and Laurel Hill as a base for opening the road. Unwilling to rely on Armstrong's judgment, Bouquet sent the present party (which included engineer Rohr) to review Armstrong's report.

[51] The present Quemahoning Creek. Maj. Armstrong built a breastwork at Kickenapaulin's, near the southern end of the present Quemahoning Reservoir. It was garrisoned until about September 10.

[52] Capt. John Dagworthy was later designated lieutenant colonel by Forbes to command the Maryland companies. Barton refers to him by his new rank in entries for August 29 and later. See note 121.

[53] The report of these (Cherokee) Indians is summarized by Bouquet in a letter of August 3 to Forbes (*BP*, 2:313).

[54] Charles Brodhead, who had served on the eastern Pennsylvania frontier, was an officer in Col. Armstrong's 1ˢᵗ Battalion. Capt. Levi Trump, of Burd's 2ᵈ Battalion, wrote Gov. Denny on July 19 from Fort Augusta that "General Forbes...ordered me to Draught forty of the best men belonging to Col. Burds Batallion, and send them to him with Two Officers, of the best men belonging to Col. Burds Batallion, and send them to him with Two Officers, (viz.) Lieut Brodhead, & Ensign Holler" (*PA*, 1st Series, 3:480).

[55] Burd had set out August 1, as noted in the entry for that date. Bouquet reports his return to Forbes, August 3 (*BP*, 2:311), and Bouquet to Washington, August [3] (ibid., 343, where dated c. August 9).

[56] This was Capt. Andrew Bailey's company; see note 47.

[57] Col. John Armstrong, of the 1ˢᵗ Battalion, Pennsylvania Regiment, had left Carlisle on July 20, "with the last of the Provincials, being part of the three Companys, Consisting of about thirty-five [men] Each" (*PA*, 1st Series, 3:483).

Colonel Stevens,[58] Major Lewis, 10 Captains, & 20 Subalterns, with Orders to proceed to the Road Cutters.—

This Afternoon arriv'd the Artillery[59] consisting of 6 Brass-Cannon—12 Pounders—4 D° of 6 [pounders]—one 8-Inch Mortar—Two 8-Inch Hoitzers [Howitzers]—a small D°—and 12 Cohorns;—With 138 Waggons —70 belonging to the Train—20 to the Hospital,—and the Rest Loaded with Provisions &C.—

Sunday, August 6th. By an Express from Juniata we have Accounts, that 2 Waggoners on their Return from hence were kill'd & scalp'd by a Party of Indians, between the Crossing of Juniata & Fort Littleton, & 2 made Prisoners.—[60] Whereupon a Party of 30 White Men & 15 Indians were detach'd towards Franks-Town[61] in Order if possible to head the Enemy, & 'tis expected some of them will proceed to the Ohio.

Captain Patterson,[62] who set out the 27th of last Month with 5 Men, to take a View of Fort Du Quesne, returns this Day, & reports that he lay some Time before that Place, but that the Fogs, which were very thick during his Stay, prevented his making any valuable Discoveries;—That he saw no Person, nor heard no Drums tho' he was within a Quarter of a Mile of the Fort;—That a Cannon was fir'd every day about 12 OClock; that he saw no Cows, Horses, or any other Sort of Cattle; nor even the Tracks of any;—That he saw a larg Number of Battoes on the opposite Side of the River, but as there were great Freshes, he could not get over to make Discoveries there;— He adds that the Enemy have cut down large Trees all round the Fort to prevent the Approach of our Troops—And that upon discovering the Tracks of at least 100 Men bending their Course towards the Frontiers, he was oblig'd to retreat sooner than he expected.—

Monday, August 7th. Sir John St Clair & Colonel Burd return'd with a small Party from the Allegeny-Mountain.—[63] Sir John brought from thence a Piece of Stone-Coal, which appears to be as good as any in England.—A small Party of Indians with 6 White Men set off this Day towards Du Quesne.—[64] Baptiz'd a Child.—

---

[58] Lt. Col. Adam Stephen of Washington's 1st Virginia Regiment took post at Edmund's Swamp, northeast of the present Buckstown, Somerset county. See Bouquet Orderly Book (*BP*, 2:671), under date of August 4.

[59] Bouquet reported its arrival in his letter of August 8 to Forbes (*BP*, 2:333). Col. Armstrong had accompanied it from Shippensburg to Fort Loudoun, arriving there on July 23 (ibid., 272).

[60] Bouquet gives fuller details in his letter of August 8 (ibid., 332). Three sutlers' wagons, unescorted, were attacked east of Sideling Hill.

[61] A former Indian settlement near the present Hollidaysburg, Blair county. For the detachment's orders, see Bouquet Orderly Book, under date of August 6: "Two Subalterns & two Parties of 15 Volunteers each of the Virginia & Pennsylvania Regiments to go immediately out with the Indians & to carry Provisions for 8 days in Rice & Flour" (ibid., 672).

[62] Capt. James Patterson of Col. Armstrong's 1st Battalion. For his report on the present mission, see ibid., 327–29.

[63] Their return is noted in Bouquet's letter of August 8 to Forbes, previously cited.

[64] It was headed by Ensign Colby Chew of the 1st Virginia Regiment, as appears by the journal entry for August 20.

Tuesday, August 8th. Arriv'd an Express with Accounts, that the Indians had attack'd a Party near Fort Littleton, & had wounded 2 Men, but were repuls'd.—[65] About 200 Men return'd from Road-Cutting.—200 of the Virginia Troops arriv'd from Fort-Cumberland with a Number of Waggons for Baggage, Provisions &C.—

This Morning before Day Light, about 40 Cherokee-Indians who had liv'd here for some Time, & had receiv'd the best of Treatment, besides very valuable Presents—basely deserted us, without acquainting any person with their Design.—[66] The Commanding Officer led out the Troops this Afternoon a Mile into the Woods, & there exercis'd them in Marching, & Countermarching &C.

Wednesday, August 9th.— This Afternoon spent in the Field as Yesterday. —

Thursday, August 10th. The Virginian Troops who lay here some Time, with a Company of the Lower-County-Troops, march'd to join Col: Stevens on the Road. —[67] This Afternoon was spent in exercising the Troops, in running & firing in the Indian Manner.—

Friday, August 11th.— 240 Pack-Horses set out with Flour for Major Armstrong & his Party at Drowning-Creek.—[68] It appears from the Commissary's Books, that 4030 Persons draw Provisions this Day.—The troops are led to the Field as Yesterday, & exercis'd in the same Manner.—Arriv'd an Express from the General, with Accounts, that Admiral Hawke had met with the French-Fleet, & taken several Men of War, & dispers'd the Rest.—[69] Heavy Rains this Night.—

Saturday, August 12th. Arriv'd this Day 10 Waggons from Fort Frederick in Maryland, with 60 Barrels of Irish-Beef.—A Corporal and 3 Light-Horse arriv'd this Evening with Letters to Colonel Bouquet from the General.—[70]

Sunday, August 13th.— A cold Morning.—A large Piece of Ground sow'd with

---

[65] A convoy coming to Raystown, escorted by thirteen men, was attacked west of Sideling Hill. Reported in Bouquet's letter of August 8, previously referred to (*BP*, 2:332).

[66] Bouquet's letter of August 8 sets their number at fifty. For the report of these Indians' arrival at Fort Loudoun, on August 10, see Capt. Lewis Ourry to Bouquet, August 11 (ibid., 358–59).

[67] On this date Bouquet wrote to Washington that "Capt Posey's Company is marched upon the Road, and as the Small Pox broke out some days ago in your Reg^t I have Sent all wth Col. Stephens over Allegheny Hill" (*BP*, 2:350). Capt. John Posey commanded a company of artificers in the 2^d Virginia Regiment. Lt. Col. Stephen was at Edmund's Swamp, where these Virginians joined him on the evening of August 12 (ibid., 363).

[68] See the journal entry for August 1, with notes 50 and 51.

[69] On April 3, Vice Admiral Sir Edward Hawke had found a French fleet, loaded with supplies for Louisbourg, near La Rochelle on the west French coast and had inflicted heavy damage on it. References to the encounter appeared in the *Pennsylvania Gazette* for July 27 and August 3. Forbes's letter of August 9 to Bouquet (*BP*, 2:344–45), presumably carried by this express, does not mention this news, which may have reached Carlisle too late for inclusion.

[70] Probably the letters dated August 10 from Francis Halkett and Lewis Ourry published in *BP*, 2:346–47. The former refers to enclosed papers, probably including the *Pennsylvania Gazette*, and the latter reports Admiral Hawke's success.

Turnip'-Seed, & harrow'd in this Day.—[71] At 3 O'Clock, the Troops are led to the Field as usual, & exercis'd in this Manner—Viz.—They are form'd into 4 Columns 2 Men deep, paralel to, and distant from, each other about 50 Yards:— After marching some Distance in this Position, they fall into one Rank entire forming a Line of Battle with great Ease & Expedition.— The 2 Front-Men of each Column stand fast, & the 2 Next split equally to Right & Left, & so continue alternately till the whole Line is form'd.—They are then divided into Platoons, each Platoon consisting of 20 Men, & fire 3 Rounds; the right-Hand Man of each Platoon beginning the Fire, & then the left-hand Man; & so on Right & Left alternately till the Fire ends in the Center:—Before it reaches this Place, the Right & Left are ready again.—And by This Means an incessant Fire kept up.—When they fir'd six Rounds in this Manner, they make a sham Pursuit with Shrieks & Halloos in the Indian Way, but falling into much Confusion; they are again drawn up into Line of Battle, & fire 3 Rounds as before; After this each Battalion marches in Order to Camp.—

Baptiz'd a little Girl of 10 Years of Age, the Daughter of a Soldier.—

Monday, August 14th.— This Morning the Tents &C were cover'd with a Hoar-Frost; & some say there was Ice.—It is so excessive Cold, that we are make large Fires in & round the Encampments to moderate the Air.—

It is reported in Camp that 6 Captains with 70 Men set off from Fort Cumberland the 11th Inst to make Discoveries of the Enemy's Proceedings at Du Quesne.—[72] This evening Sir Allen MacClain with another Captain, 5 Subalterns, & 200 Highlanders & Royal-Americans marchd towards the Allegeny to join Col: Stevens on the Road.—[73] A Party of Carolinans were order'd to Juniata to relieve Captain Mc.Knight.—[74]

Tuesday, August 15th. A wet Morning, & continued raining most Part of the Day. —Arriv'd this Evening from Fort Augusta—Mr. Dunlap,[75] & brought with him

---

[71] In the manuscript the words "this Day" are written large, presumably to note the impropriety of doing this work on a Sunday.

[72] Washington wrote from Fort Cumberland on August 13 that "I detachd Captn McKenzie with 4 Officers & 75 Rank and file" (*BP*, 2:364). The officer named is Capt. Robert McKenzie of the 1st Virginia Regiment.

[73] Capt. MacLean commanded one of the three "additional companies" of the Highland Battalion. By August 16 he was at the foot of the Allegheny Mountain. The other captain was perhaps Alexander McKenzie, of the Battalion (but see note 16, *BP*, 2:372–73). Orders of August 14 specified "Two Capts 5 Subs 6 Serjts & 200 Rank & File, no Drummer; of the R. Americans & Highlanders to march over the Allegheney [Mountain]" (ibid., 677).

[74] Orders of August 13: "One Capt two Subalterns 2 Serjts 2 Corps & 50 private[s] of the North Carolina Troops are to march To Morrow Morning to Juniata to relieve the Garrison there, which is to march to Rays Town" (*BP*, 2:677). The captain was Andrew Bailey.

[75] James Dunlap. See Forbes to Bouquet, Carlisle, August 9, and Bouquet to Forbes, August 18 (*BP*, 2:344, 378).

Captain Ambust[76] the Son of Teedyuscung the famous Delaware Chief, accompanied by 2 other Delaware Indians. The Cherokees who were here receiv'd them into Friendship by smoaking a Pipe with them, & giving them Victuals.—

Wednesday, August 16th. A Dark cold Morning.— Colonel Armstrong with the 1st. Battalion of the Pennsylvanian Regiment march'd to reinforce the Troops[77] at Loyal-Hanning.—[78]

Thursday August 17th. Receiv'd Advice that the General on his March from Carlisle to this Place, was taken ill at Shippensburg, & relaps'd into the Flux, which confines him to his Bed.—[79] The commanding Officer receives the Public Prints[80] this Day, from whence we learn that the French come to the South Side of Lake George & have form'd a regular Encampment, & had 300 Battoes on the Lake.— We also learn that Major Rogers[81] had march'd with 2000 Men to make a Diversion in our Favor.—We further learn that a Number of Spaniards with a New Governor &C were arriv'd at Augustine, & were there fortifying themselves contrary to a solemn Treaty.—

Friday, August 18th. A fine clear Morning & a Warm Day.— At 4 OClock P.M. Major Armstrong,[82] Captain Callender,[83] & Captain Shelby[84] a Volunteer from Maryland, with 2 Volunteer Lieutenants (Kidd & Stoddart)[85] & 50 Men, 25 of which are Volunteers with Shelby, all set off together to make further Discoveries of the Enemy's Number, Strength, & Operations at Du Quesne:—And it is said by some Persons that an attack upon that Place this Season chiefly depends upon the

---

[76] Otherwise Hambus or Ambrose. Barton errs in identifying him as a son of Teedyuscung. Four Indians were in the party: Hambus, Teedyuscung's son (probably the one known as John Jacob), and two others. For Teedyuscung, see Anthony F. C. Wallace, *King of the Delawares: Teedyuscung, 1700–1763* (Philadelphia: University of Pennsylvania Press, 1949). The Delaware and Cherokee tribes were not on friendly terms.

[77] Orders of August 14: "The 1st Battalion of the Pennsa Regiment to March to Morrow Morning" (*BP*, 2:678). This departure evidently was delayed a day.

[78] The subsequent site of Fort Ligonier, now Ligonier, Westmoreland county. No troops were stationed there at this date, though engineer Ensign Charles Rohr had been sent on August 15 to select a site for a post there. Col. Armstrong's men worked at opening the road between the Allegheny Mountain and Laurel Hill.

[79] See Forbes to Bouquet, Shippensburg, August 15 (*BP*, 2:366–68).He was detained there until September 6.

[80] The *Pennsylvania Gazette* for August 10 includes the reports that follow, datelined New York, August 7, and citing as authorities a letter of August 2 from Albany and an express from South Carolina.

[81] Robert Rogers, captain of a company of rangers operating in the vicinity of Lake Champlain.

[82] Maj. George Armstrong had returned a day or two before from "Drowning Creek," when he delivered a letter of August 15 from Lt. Col. Stephen (*BP*, 2:370).

[83] Capt. Robert Callender of Col. Armstrong's 1st Battalion, Pennsylvania Regiment.

[84] First Lt. Evan Shelby in Capt. Alexander Beall's company resigned May 31, 1758, to raise his company of volunteers. Thirty of his men arrived at Fort Loudoun on August 4 (*BP*, 2:317–18).

[85] First Lt. Thomas Stoddart resigned May 31 from Capt. Francis Ware's company to hold the same rank under Capt. Shelby; John Kidd, ensign in Capt. John Dagworthy's company, resigned June 29 to become second lieutenant under Shelby.

Intelligence they shall bring.—[86]

Saturday, August 19th. A Clear, sharp Morning, & a warm Day.—Colonel Bouquet accompanied by many Gentlemen, & escorted by a Party of Light-Horse set out to view the new Road over the Allegeny-Mountains.—The same Day they return, & report that the Road far exceeded their Expectations, & that some Waggons had already pass'd the Mountain, each carrying 20ᶜ Weight.—[87]

Burried a Virginian Soldier this Day.—He was launch'd into a little Hole out of a Blanket, & there left naked.—And when I remonstrated against the Inhumanity as well as Indecency of it, a Serjeant inform'd me that he had Orders not to return without the Blanket.—Upon which I got some small Bushes cut, & thrown over him, till I perform'd the Service.—

Near 400 Persons are now in the Hospital, sick of Fluxes, Diarrhoas, Agues, Fevers, Small-Pox &C.—

Sunday, August 20th. Preach'd before the Commanding Officer & all the Troops from these Words in Jeremiah 23-10—"Because of Swearing the Land mourneth."— After Sermon—Baptiz'd the Child of a Soldier.—

Arriv'd last Night Ensign Colby Chew of the 1ˢᵗ Virginia Regiment, who set off from hence with a Party of White Men & Indians on the 7ᵗʰ Instant to make Discoveries at Fort Du Quesne,—& produces his Journal in the following Words:—[88]

[Ensign Colby Chew's Report]

"Monday, August 7ᵗʰ Set out from Rays Town by Order of Colonel Bouquet with a Party of Indians & white Men to make Discoveries of the Strength & Situation of Fort Du Quesne.—Proceeded this Night as far as the Shawanes Cabbins, about 8 Miles, S.80 W—

"*Tuesday the 8th* continued our Course along the old trading-Path.— Cross'd the Alleghany-Ridge, & encampt at Edmond's Swamp, 12 Miles—N. 70 W.—

"Wednesday 9ᵗʰ March'd about 9 Miles N. 60 W. to Quamehony-Creek, at which Place we continued Thursday & Friday the 10ᵗʰ & 11ᵗʰ Proceeded early in the Morning.—Cross'd the Laurel Ridge, & arriv'd at an old Encampᵗ at the Loyal Hannan Town, 15 Miles N. 55 W.

"*Saturday 12th* continued our Journey along the old trading-Path for 10 or 12 Miles; or for the most Part along the low Grounds of Loyal Hannan, which sometimes turn'd off the River, & cross'd some Ridges & the Points of Hills.— The high

[86] Maj. Armstrong's return and his lack of success are recorded in the journal entry for August 30. See also Bouquet to Governor [Denny], August 31 (*BP*, 2:450–51).

[87] For Bouquet's report on his inspection of the road, see Bouquet to Forbes, August 20 (*BP*, 2:391), and to Washington, August 21, ibid., 404.

[88] Another copy of Chew's report, differing in a few words, has been published in *BP*, 2:400–3. The original, in the Library of Congress's George Washington Papers, appears in Stanislaus Murray Hamilton, *Letters to Washington* (Boston: Houghton Mifflin, 1899–1902), 3:39-43.

Land is well timber'd; the low Grounds on the River, & in general on all the Creeks very thick & bushy.—Discover'd this Day some fresh Tracks of Indians, 15 Miles N—60W.—

"*Sunday the 13th*. March'd very early, & continued till 10 O'Clock, when the Indians discovering fresh Tracks of the Enemy, halted to conjure.[89]—The Low Grounds still thick & bushy.— Sent out Scouts, who stay'd till Dark; which oblig'd us to encamp there all towards Du Quesne. About an Hour before Sun-Set, heard the Report of 12 Cannon (as we imagin'd) at the French-Fort, 5 Miles N. 8o, W.—

"*Monday, 14th*. Continued our March & sent out Scouts, who return without discovering any Tracts, except those that went along the Path, which cross'd over many Ridges well timber'd.—Heard the Firing of several Guns.—Our Course 7 Miles, near W^t.—

"*Tuesday, 15th*. March'd very early, & at about 8 Miles from last Encampment, got into a large Path coming from the Nor'ward into the old trading Path, where we discover'd the Tracts of a large Number of Indians going both Ways.—Several Horses, some of which were shod, pass'd along this Road Yesterday towards Du Quesne.—We are of Opinion that the Guns which we heard Yesterday were fir'd by some of these Parties.—The Path is good:—The Ridges low & well timber'd; but all the Branches very thick with Crab-Trees & white Thorn; 12. Miles W.—The Provisions being near spent, the Indians held a Council of War, in which it was determin'd that all, except 5 Indians, Serjeant Vaughan & myself, should return.—

"*Wednesday, 16th*. Proceeded on our Way, being now only 7 in Number, & arriv'd at a Place where a larg Party of Indians (I believe about 100 in Number) had been encamp'd about 10 Days before.—They clear'd about 5 or 6 Feet Square very clean, & left there 5 Pieces of Bark with a Pipe full of Tobacco on each Piece.—This Place distant from our last Encampment about 6 Miles:—The Path but indifferent, crossing many Ridges:—The Course about N.80.W.—

"N.B.: The Hills are lost in this Place; And we find a plain level Country from hence to Du Quesne.—Here we quit the old trading-Path, & march'd 3 Miles N.W.—Then turn'd S.W. Cross'd the Path, & kept a Course S.70 W^t., till we were within 2 Miles of Du Quesne.—Turn'd to the N°. of W., & came to an old Indian. Town[90] on Ohio about 1 ½ Mile off the Fort, where I had a good Prospect up & down the River.—From hence we discover'd some Cattle grazing on an Island down the River, & hid ourselves in a Thicket, till the Indians by Magic & Conjuration pry'd into our Fate; after which we advanc'd within a ¾ of a Mile of the Fort; Then turn'd S.E. & ascended a Stony Ridge, when the Chief Warrior took his conjuring

[89] [Evidently, the Indians resorted here to magical divination to determine what might be going on and even perhaps for protection. See below the entry for Wednesday, August 16, for a more detailed description of this "conjuration."—Ed.]

[90] Shannopin's Town was named for a Delaware chief who died before 1751. "Old" in this usage means "former" or "abandoned."

Implements, & ty'd them about the Neck of 3 Indians, & told them they could not be hurt.—Round my Neck he ty'd an Otter's Skin, in which the Conjuring Tools had been kept: And round the Serjeant's Neck he ty'd a Bag of Paint that had been kept with them in the Bagg.—He then assur'd us that we were proof against Balls, for that those Things would protect us.—He then order'd us to strip off to our Britch Clouts & Moccosons; shook Hands with us, & bid us go on & fight like Men, for Nothing could annoy us.—The first View I had of the Fort was from the Banks of the Ohio, but at a great Distance.—We saw a Battoe & two Cannoos, in which were Indians fishing.—We were at this Time in a Pasture fenced in with Trees cut down one on another. We discovered by the Tracts that this Pasture (the furthest Part of which is not above ¾ of a Mile from the Fort) was much frequented by Indians.—Nevertheless I continued in the Pasture, from whence I could make no great Discoveries, except of the Number of Tents, till about Sun-Set; At which Time I inform'd the Indians that I was desirous they would accompany me to the Top of a Ridge that ran directly towards the Fort:—But they dislik'd the Proposal, & refus'd my Request; being in great Hopes of getting Scalps; However seeing me determin'd to go, & having proceeded on towards the Place, they follow'd me.— From the Top of this Ridge I had an extraordinary good View of the Fort.— Scarce 1/2 a Mile from it 50 or 60 Tents were pitch'd on the River Ohio:—And on the Monangahela there were several Houses, about 100 Yards from the Fort.—In this River I could discover no Battoes or Cannoes; Nor could I discover any new Works about the Fort.—I imagine the Men parade in the Fort as I saw them going in at Retreat-Beating; and am of Opinion the Number of French-Men do not exceed 300. —The Indians kept a continual hooping & hallooing; but I could not discern their Camp;—unless the Tents mention'd above were for them, which I judg'd were design'd for them from the first; for the People which I saw there appear'd by their Looks, Noise &Cᵃ to be Indians.—I could see no Sign of a Camp or any Buildings on the other Side of the Rivers.—After Dark the Indians got to Singing & Dancing; & by their Noise, I judge them to be about 50 in Number; all which the Cherokees inform'd me were Shawanese.—

"As I have taken a Draught of the Fort & Place, as well as I could upon a separate Paper, I shall make no Mention of it here.—[91] This Day's March, had we kept the Path, would have been about 12 Miles;[92] The course about N. 80 W.—The Ohio runs about S—20 W.—The Monangahela at the Mouth runs near E.—From the Top of this Ridge, I remov'd to another Place nearer the Monangahela, but could make no further Discoveries.—

"From this Place we return'd back to the Head-Warrior; & after some Consultation agreed to return Home;—Upon which we march'd about a Mile & encamp'd near the Old-trading-Path.— We heard the Indians singing & dancing all Night.—

---

[91] This map, accompanying the manuscript report in the Washington Papers, was not published with it.
[92] The copy published in *BP*, 2:403, has, incorrectly, "42 miles."

"*Thursday the 17th*. At the Dawn of Day we began our March, which we continued very fast till one O'Clock; in which Time we travell'd near 30 Miles, & overtook the Party which we order'd back when our Provisions grew scarce.— We then halted to refresh ourselves, after which we continued our March together; & having advanc'd 12 Miles farther, we encamp'd for that Night.—Within 2 Miles of Our Encampment we discovered some fresh Tracks coming from the Westward.—

"*Friday 18th*. Pursued our March, following the Tracks which we discovered last Night.—The low Grounds & Branches, which I made Mention of in the former Part of this Journal, are much deprest, liable to be overflow'd, & consequently very moist & soft: —So that I am afraid a Road through them will be but indifferent for Carriages.—We follow'd the Tracks till Night, & encamp'd within 4 Miles of Major Armstrong's Post at Quimahony-Creek.—

"*Saturday the 19th*, March'd early in the Morning, & arriv'd in Camp, where we found it was Ensign Allan's Party that we track'd; And that they had arriv'd in Camp the Night before."[93]

Monday, August 21st. The Accounts of General Abercrombie's Retreat confirm'd this Day;—[94] His Character & Behaviour is openly traduc'd, & it is said that he has been dragged thro' the Streets of New York, & burnt in Effigie.—As it is yet uncertain in Camp, whether this be owing to some Misrepresentation to the Populace, or bad Conduct in himself, Our Officers seem to mention it with Caution & Prudence.—Lieutenant Hodgson[95] of the Lower Counties on Delaware arrives from Fort Cumberland with 30 Men belonging to that Government.

Tuesday, 22d. Arriv'd from Fort Cumberland the Remainder of the Maryland Troops commanded by Captains Alexander & Joshua Bell, & Captain Ware.—[96] They report that 2 Indians arriv'd at Fort Cumberland a little before they left it with 2 Scalps, which they took near Fort Du Quesne.—But their Veracity & Honesty seems to be question'd.—Large Parties are still kept busy at Work, in digging a Trench round the Fort; covering such Parts of it as are expos'd; & making a Covert-Way to command the Water, which runs in a pleasant Stream under the Fort &Cᵃ.—

Wednesday, 23d.The Second Battalion of the Pennsylvania Regiment, commanded by Col: Burd;—The Remainder of the Royal Americans commanded by

[93] A copy of Ensign John Allen's report appears in *BP*, 2:324–26. He had set out from Quemahoning Creek on August 8, and returned there on August 18.

[94] Abercromby's difficulties following his unsuccessful attack of July 8 on Ticonderoga are referred to in Forbes' letter of August 18 to Bouquet (*BP*, 2: 382–84).

[95] Second Lt. Robert Hodgson of Capt. (later Maj.) Wells's company.

[96] Washington wrote from Fort Cumberland on August 19 that "A party of abᵗ 90 Marylanders under Captⁿ Beal Escorting a few Store Waggons, is this Momᵗ, arriv'd. I shall forward them to Rays Town to morrow" (*BP*, 2: 389–90). The captains were Alexander and Joshua Beall and Francis Ware.

Captain Joceleyn;[97] & 4 Companies of Highlanders commanded by Major Grant[98] march this Day with 4 Pieces of Cannon[99] towards Loyal-Hannon.—[100] Sir Allen MacClain returns this Day with a Party of Highlanders & Pennsylvanians from Road Cutting.—[101] He informs that the Men are in high Spirits, & that all Things go on well.—

The Pennsylvanians who return'd with Sir Allen receive Orders to march back again To-Morrow Morning.[102]

Thursday August 24th. Nothing extraordinary To-Day.—The working Parties are still kept busy;—Barracks & Hospitals are erecting—Large Pieces of Ground are plow'd & sow'd with Turnips; and a New Slaughter-House & Ovens are built.— Orders are given out that no Man presume to fire a Gun within a Mile of the Camp.[103] A Party arrives this Evening from Fort Cumberland, & brings in with them 308 Head of Beef-Cattle.—[104]

A perfect Harmony & Union subsists thro' the whole Camp: And Colonel Bouquet gains more & more upon the Affections of the People.—

Friday, August 25th. Captain Bosomworth,[105] Superintendant of Indian Affairs in the Western District, receives Accounts by Express from Fort Cumberland, That Captain Bullen, the Famous Catawba-Chief, always strictly attach'd to the British Interest, who call'd himself the Irishman, (his Father being of that Nation) was treacherously kill'd & scalp'd within a Mile of the Fort, by 5 Delawares who deceiv'd him by calling out, they were Cherokees & Friends.—Another Warrior was shot at the same Time; & a Young Squaw receiv'd a Shot in her Arm.—[106]

Saturday, August, 26th. A Damp foggy Morning.—Remov'd our Camp to a

---

[97] Capt. Thomas Jocelyn.

[98] James Grant, senior of the two majors of this corps.

[99] Two 12-pounders and two 6-pounders, according to Bouquet, besides 8 cohorns (*BP*, 2:392); compare the total reported by Barton in his entry for August 5.

[100] This was the detachment that actually took post at Loyalhanna, a move anticipated by Barton on August 16. The orders had been given out on August 21 (*BP*, 2:680). Bouquet estimated the total force at 1,500, some of whom would join en route: 300 Royal Americans, 400 each of the Highlanders, the Virginians, and the Pennsylvania 2ᵈ Battalion.

[101] A few days before, Bouquet had thanked MacLean and Maj. Lewis for their work on the road over the Allegheny Mountain (*BP*, 2:391).

[102] As ordered on this date: "The Detachment of the 2ᵈ Battⁿ Pennsᵃ Regᵗ that came to Day, to march To Morrow Morning & join their Corp" (*BP*, 2:681).

[103] This does not appear in the orderly book under this date; however, an order against firing about the camp was reiterated on August 25 (*BP*, 2:681–82).

[104] References to this convoy illustrate some problems of logistics: of 468 beeves that left Winchester, 9 were killed on the way to Fort Cumberland, 48 were lost, and 321 arrived there on August 23; Washington kept 90 and sent off the rest on August 25; 308 reached Raystown (*BP*, 2:416, 425).

[105] Capt. Abraham Bosomworth of the Royal American Regiment. He had helped attract southern Indians to join the expedition and on June 14 had brought twenty-nine Cherokees to Fort Loudoun. From there he went to Fort Cumberland, arriving by July 13, and then on to Raystown a few days later.

[106] See Washington to Bouquet, Fort Cumberland, August 24, in *BP*, 2:416. The second man killed is identified as Capt. French, also a Catawba.

pleasant Ridge S. of the Fort about 100 Yards, fronting the Artillery.—[107] The Field Officers in pitching their Tents, contend for Rank with some Warmth;—Some claiming it from the Seniority of their Troops; & Others from the Age of the Charters of their respective Provinces.—The Disputes however are settled by Col: Bouquet, & Major Waddle of Carolina takes the Right of the Provincials.—

Sunday, August 27th. A dark Morning, but a very sultry Day.—Preach'd at 11 O'Clock P.M. from the 144th Psalm & 3d Verse, to all the Troops.—[108]

Arriv'd this Evening from Fort Cumberland, 60 Waggons, chiefly loaded with Indian Corn,[109] escorted by 40 Soldiers commanded by Ensign Finney[110] of Major Well's Corps.—[111] Arriv'd at the same Time 54 Indians of the Catawba, Tuscarora, & Ottawaw Nations.—[112] They greatly lament the Loss of their brave Captain Bullen.—As soon as they laid down their baggage, one of their Chiefs made a Speech in English (which many of them Talk tolerably well) to the following Effect:—"This is the 3d time we have left our Country to revenge the Death of our Brothers, whose Bones we have seen scatter'd at Monangahela.—Our Success has not been equal to our Zeal, & the Reason is, we had too far to travel to the Enemy; And our Provisions being generally spent before we could reach their Borders, we were oblig'd to return before we could kill or scalp.—But now we desire to go to Loyal Hannon; from whence we can proceed to Fort Du Quesne, & return the next Day.—This, we say, we desire as well to revenge the Death of our Brothers the English, as that of our brave lamented Captain Bullen.—"

Some of them before they arriv'd in Camp painted with Black, & solemnly vow'd to kill Amboust Teedyuscung's Son[113] & the other two Delaware Indians who lately arriv'd from Fort Augusta:—For, said they, "We believe the White People are mad to entertain & give Presents not only to our Enemies, but their own."—But the Wretches had left the Camp a few Days before, & so fortunately sav'd their Lives.—[114]

---

[107] Orders of August 24: "The 2d Camp is to be removed To Morrow Afternoon between the Artillery & Highland Camp"; on August 25: "The Tents to be struck in 2d Camp to Morrow morning, as soon as they are dry, pack'd up and pitched in the new Camp" (*BP*, 2:681–82).

[108] "Lord, what is man, that thou takest knowledge of him! or the son of man, that thou makes account of him!" Is this an allusion to the contention of the previous day?

[109] Bouquet had written Washington on August 26 that "I expect to day your Convoy wth the Indians" (*BP*, 2:426).

[110] Second Lt. Archibald Finney of Capt. Benjamin Noxon's company (*PA*, 5th Series, 1:232).

[111] Maj. Richard Wells, commanding the Lower Counties troops.

[112] Barton errs in his identification of the third Indian nation. They were not Ottawas, a pro-French people living near the Great Lakes, but the Nottoways, an Iroquoian group from Virginia, related to the Tuscaroras. Washington had written Bouquet on August 24 that "The Rest of the Cuttawbas, & What Nottoway's and Tuscarora's that are here sets [sic] out to Morrow with the Waggon's for Rays Town" (*BP*, 2:416). Bouquet wrote Burd on August 29 that "We have a Reinforcemt of 52 Indians" (ibid., 445).

[113] Amboust and Teedyuscung's son were different persons.

[114] Bouquet had written Forbes on August 26 that "The Delawares have returned to Shamoken and Wyoming" (*BP*, 2:425).

A number of Pack Horses set off this Morning, loaded with Provisions for the Troops at Loyal Hannan—

Monday, August 28ᵗʰ.— A foggy Morning, & a very sultry Day.—About 11 O'Clock A.M. One of the 12 Pounders was fir'd to satisfy the Curiosity of the Indians, who were much pleas'd, & express'd great Admiration at it.—Arriv'd an Express from the General to Col: Bouquet,[115] by whom Captain Young Paymaster to the Pennsylvania Troops,[116] receives a Letter from Mʳ Secretary Peters— informing him that Louisbourg had actually surrendered on the 26ᵗʰ of July;—that we had taken above 4000 French Prisoners; & that during the Seige we had lost but 300: —That the famous Rogers had engag'd the Enemy 600 to 600, & had beat them & brought in 70 Scalps:—And, that the Duke of Mal'bro was landed in France, —had taken & destroy'd Sᵗ. Maloes, & was carrying Terror & Desolation along the Coast.—

The Indians are all drunk this Evening, which makes them very troublesome.—

Thursday, August 29ᵗʰ. A clear Morning.—Wind at N.W. pretty cold, & like a Fall-Day.—20 Men commanded by Captain Allen[117] set off To-Day to escort a Number of Waggons to Carlisle.—Ensign Jones[118] set off to Juniata with 30 Men to guard the Paymaster[119] to his Majesty's Troops.—

This Evening arriv'd in Camp Lieutenant James Reily[120] of the Maryland Troops, commanded by Lieuᵗ. Colonel Dagworthy;[121] & gives the following Intelligence.—

---

[115] Presumably he carried Maj. Halkett's letter of August 26 to Bouquet, published in *BP*, 2:428–29. Forbes's letter of August 28 (ibid., 439–41) could not have arrived so soon. A postscript to Halkett's letter reports the fall of Louisbourg and Rogers' success. The news contained in Peters's letter appeared in the *Pennsylvania Gazette* for August 24, but recorded that Marlborough could not attack St. Malo.

[116] Capt. James Young, commissary of the musters and paymaster in the Pennsylvania Regiment.

[117] Capt. Lt. Samuel Allen of Col. Armstrong's 1ˢᵗ Battalion. Gov. Denny designated himself colonel in chief of the Pennsylvania Regiment and, as such, nominal captain of a company in the 1ˢᵗ Battalion, with Allen as captain lieutenant (*PA*, 5th Series, 1:128–29). Orders of August 28 called for a detachment consisting of "Capᵗ Allen, 1 Sergᵗ & 30 men of the Draughts from the 1ˢᵗ, Battⁿ Pennᵃ Rᵗ to march To Morrow Morning" (*BP*, 2:684).

[118] John Jones of Capt. John Singleton's company of new levies assigned to the 2ᵈ Battalion, Pennsylvania Regiment. Orders of August 28 directed "A Subaltern 1 Serjᵗ & 30 Rank & file of the line to march to morrow morning to Juniata who are to escort from thence a Brigade of Waggons to the Camp—& the Pay Master General" (*BP*, 2:684).

[119] Thomas Barrow. On August 18 Bouquet had complained to Forbes that "We haven't a sou, and if Mr. Barrow does not join us quicklv, we shall no longer be able to pay anyone" (*BP*, 2:381).

[120] First Lt. in Capt. Joshua Beall's company; subsequently wounded September 14 in Grant's defeat; recommended by Bouquet, October 20, for an ensigncy in the Royal American Regiment (*BP*, 2:509, 577). Barton had not named him among the officers sent out on August 18.

[121] Forbes wrote Bouquet on August 28 that "Governʳ Sharp has just asked a favour of me that I could not well refuse which was to allow him to make Capᵗ Dagworthy a LieuᵗColonel of the Maryland troops, and he is accordingly appointed by a Commission I sent him this night" (*BP*, 2:440). His new rank was published at Raystown in orders of August 30 (ibid., 685). Since Forbes's letter cannot have been carried from Shippensburg by the 29ᵗʰ, Barton must have written this entry later.

[Lt. James Reily's Report]

"Friday August 18^(th). [sic] 1758 Set out from Rays Town by Order of the Commanding Officer with 8 Men to make Discoveries of the Strength & Operations of the Enemy at Fort Du Quesne, & if possible to take a Prisoner.

"At Quimahony I join'd Major Armstrong with upwards of 100 Men, with whom I proceeded to within 25 Miles of Du Quesne.—Here we held a Consultation & agree'd, that Captain Potter[122] & I should proceed with 6 Men each, & make what Discoveries we could;—That Major Armstrong with the Remainder should advance slowly after us, & lie in Ambush at a Place call'd the four-Mile Branch within 6 Miles of the French Fort:—M^r. Potter & I, after making some Discoveries, were to fire upon a Party of the Enemy in Order to draw them into the Ambush where Major Armstrong lay.—Big with the Prospect of Success we push'd on piloted by one Ferguson[123] a Serjeant in the Pennsylvania Service. Cross'd Braddock's Road, steering a Course near S—and ascended a Ridge that ran towards the Monongahela, where the Pilot told us we should have a good View of the Fort. Having gain'd the Top of the Ridge, I soon discover'd his Mistake; and advancing to the Point of it, climb'd up into the Top of a Tree, from whence I saw the Hill that overlooked the Fort, bearing N.W. & Distant by Computation 3 Miles.—Unwilling to trust the Issue of so important an Enterprize to a Man who had once led me astray, I requested of Captain Paris[124] to lead the way by the Direction & Assistance of a Person known by the Name of French Peter;[125] which occasion'd some little Disputes between Captain Potter & myself.—From this Place I advanc'd, by Direction of my New Guides, towards the Hill that overlooks the Fort, & cross'd it about Dusk.— It being too dark to make any Discoveries, I descended into a little Valley or Branch, where I found a good Spring, & lay down till 1 O'Clock, at which Time the Moon rose, & awak'd me to Action.—I proceeded 2 Miles N. up the River, & came upon a little Branch leading to Shinnopin's Town, where I halted till Morning; Then went on to Braddock's Road, where there is a muddy Spring with a small Stream running from it.—Here we found a large Encamping-Place, where Peter told us the French often came out as an Advance Guard from the Fort.— After having refresh'd ourselves, Captain Potter desir'd the Officers, to come to a

---

[122] James Potter of the 1^(st) Battalion, Pennsylvania Regiment. As subaltern in Col. Armstrong's own company, he normally would have been designated captain lieutenant; but Governor Denny's assumption of a captaincy in this battalion gave that rank to Samuel Allen. Potter's rank of captain was "provisional," as published in orders of June 17 (*BP*, 2:656).

[123] Possibly James or John Ferguson, both sergeants in Capt. James Patterson's company of the 1^(st) Battalion.

[124] Capt. Richard Pearis of Maryland had set out from Raystown with a dozen volunteers. He returned to Quemahoning on August 28 (*BP*, 2:378, 437).

[125] Not otherwise identifiable. Indians commonly received such European labels; Capt. Peter, Capt. John Peter, William Peters, and Old Peter are mentioned among Ohio Indians of this period.

Counsel of War with him, in which it was resolv'd by the Majority—That it was best to return to the Party left behind in Ambush:—And this Argument advanc'd in Favor of it—That as we were so near the Fort our Tracks would soon be discovered, which must prove fatal to us.—In Consequence hereof all return'd except Corporal Madden[126] & myself—For having an independent Command, & not thinking that the Discoveries we had made were sufficient to recompense the Toils & Fatigues we had undergone; I determined to proceed farther, & desir'd Captain Paris to request of Major Armstrong to halt till 12 or 1 O'Clock, at which Time I should endeavour to be back.—I proceeded on, & got to the Top of a Nob on the Ridge that overlooks the Fort, placing the Corporal as a Centinel, while I was taking a View of the Place. But the Fogs being very thick, I remain'd here near 2 Hours, during which Time I heard now & then the Firing of Platoons; the Barking of Dogs; the Ringing of Horse-Bells; & the incessant Strokes of about 40 or 50 Axes on the opposite Side of the River.—As soon as the Fogs clear'd away, the Corporal cry'd out, See! See! Yonder's the Fort!—Upon which I saw the Colours flying, & advanc'd to the Point of the Hill, but could have no favourable Prospect: From hence I proceeded S.E. to another Ridge which I expected would bring me nigher the Object I wanted to view.—Here I had just a Glimpse of the Fort; but finding myself much expos'd, having Nothing to cover me but low Shrubs which scarcely came Breast-high, I order'd the Corporal to stand Centinel, charging him if he discover'd any Body nigh [at] Hand to Acquaint me with it, that we might endeavour to take him; And then advanc'd to the Point of the Ridge, where I had a good Prospect of the Fort.—The Pickets are so so [sic] high that I could not see the Roofs of the Houses that are within.—I saw 2 Streets of Tents with 25 or 30 Tents in each Street, pitch'd upon the River Ohio, & several Persons going in & coming out of them. Near to the Fort is a large Pasture, where I discover'd small Companies of Two's & Three's sauntering about, with a great Number of Horses grazing but no Cattle of any other Sort.—Upon hearing a Person firing within ¼ of a Mile of me, I went back to the Corporal & ask'd him if he would go along with me and endeavour to take him Prisoner, who inform'd me there were Two; But telling him we were a Match for that Number, he very chearfully & resolutely agree'd to go.—When we came to the Place where we thought we heard the Firing, our Disappointment was great in finding they were on the opposite Side of the River.—Soon after I heard a Bell which inspir'd me with fresh Hopes that I should not come away Empty-handed, & that some Horses at least would fall a Prey to me.—Finding after some Search that all my Schemes were unsuccessful, I resolv'd to return to the Place where I left the Party in Ambush, where I arriv'd about 12 O'Clock agreeable to Appointment—But all were gone!—I immediately strip'd off to my Shirt & Moccassons, lest I might be track'd & pursued.—Continued my March at the Rate of 4 Miles an Hour, & overtook the Party above 20 Miles from

[126] Mordecai Madden of Capt. Alexander Beall's Maryland company.

Du Quesne.—Here I found Captains Callender & Haslet[127] with all the Men except 16, which they inform'd were gone back to make Discoveries—Major Armstrong with 12 to cross the Monongahela & view the S. Side of the Fort;— Captain Potter with 4 to go down the River;—And that Captain Shelby with 25 Men would endeavour to cross the Ohio.—In a little Time after one of Armstrong's Party arriv'd, to acquaint us that the Major was tir'd, & order'd us to halt for him; And immediately he & his Party came in, & reported that they had endeavour'd to cross the River, & had waded Breast-high, but found the Ford too deep.—We then proceeded to within 12 Miles of Loyal-Hannan: And next Morning early Captain Potter with his Party arriv'd, & reported that the Fogs prevented their getting a View of the Fort; and that Captain Shelby finding the Fording at Shinnoppins too high, had gone to the Old Chartiers-Town[128] in Order to cross there.— Pursued our Journey together till we came to Major Lewis's Camp[129] where I left all except my own little Party with whom I arriv'd at Rays-Town, August 29th. 1758."

Wednesday August 30th. Major Armstrong & Captain Callender return'd this Day from their unsuccessful Scout, & are coldly receiv'd by the Commanding Officer.—The Former is much censur'd & blam'd by every Body—And the Latter, by being subject to the Command of a superior Officer, stands excus'd.—[130] Orders are issued that no Man presume to sell or bestow Liquor to the Indians.—[131] Ensign Jones returns from Juniata with the Deputy-Paymaster to the Regulars.—Arriv'd an Express who confirms the Accounts of the Surrender of Louisbourg to his Britannick Majesty—[132] adding that Brest is block'd up.—In Company with Major Waddle Commander of the Carolina Troops, I climb'd to the Top a very high Mountain E.S.E. of the Camp, & distant about 2 Miles.—[133] We reach'd the Summit with much Difficulty, clambering from Rock to Rock the whole Way, for nearly 2 Hours.—A very extensive Prospect opens to our View—The Allegeny [Mountain] bearing W.N.W. of us—We fir'd each of us a Gun, & then return'd to Camp greatly fatigued.—

It is said that the General unable to ride, and determin'd to proceed at all Events,

---

[127] Capt. John Haslet of the 2d Battalion, Pennsylvania Regiment.

[128] At the present Tarentum, Allegheny county. This settlement was named for Peter Chartier, son of Martin Chartier and leader of a Shawnee band that removed from the lower Susquehanna to the Ohio after 1730.

[129] Maj. Lewis took command of the Virginia road builders after Sir John St. Clair placed Lt. Col. Stephen under arrest, following a quarrel (*BP*, 2:430–38). Apparently his camp was near Quemahoning.

[130] Maj. Armstrong was severely censured by Bouquet in a letter to Gov. Denny, (*BP*, 2:450–51).

[131] This is entered in the orderly book as a repetition of Gen. Forbes's orders (*BP*, 2:684).

[132] Forbes wrote Bouquet on August 28 that "I have heard no more of Louisbourg but as it is most certainly taken, I would make a *feu de joy* to put the Whole Army in Spirits" (*BP*, 2:441). Louisbourg had fallen to General Amherst on July 26.

[133] Evitts Mountain.

had order'd a Litter to be made to carry him with the more Ease.— This Evening a warm Dispute happen'd between Major _____ [134] and Captain _____ which was happily ended by flinging a few Bottles & Glasses, charg'd with Billings-gate-Ammunition,[135] such as Rascal, Scoundrel & Cᵃ.

Thursday August 31ˢᵗ. A cold, rainy Day.—A 6-Pounder was fir'd 8 Times—as a Preparative to our Rejoicings for the Reduction of Louisbourg.—

An Express arriv'd from Sir John Sᵗ. Clair at Loyal Hannan, but the Contents does not transpire.—[136] Old Keeshity an Indian strongly attach'd to the British-Interest came in from Fort Du Quesne, & brings with him 3 Ohio-Indians.—He produces a very distinct Draught of the Place; & the whole of his Intelligence seems much in our Favor.—[137]

This Evening the Commanding-Officer receiv'd 2 Letters from Frederick Post a Dutchman—now in an Indian-Town upon Ohio—with very favourable Ac-counts.—[138] Every Thing promises Success; and it is generally believ'd that Du Quesne will fall an easy Conquest.—

Friday September 1ˢᵗ. Rain all Last Night, & the greatest Part of this Day.—At 5 O'Clock P.M. A grand Feu de Joye[139] for the Success of our brave Men at Louisbourg; When 3 Royal Salutes were fir'd from 3 Twelve-Pounders; And all the Troops being drawn up in a Single Line, which cover'd the greatest Part of the Camp, fir'd 3 Rounds of small-Arms—The whole ended with 3 Huzzas, & a "God Save the King."—[140]

Saturday September 2ᵈ. Accounts in Camp that Lieuᵗ. Kidd, a Gentleman in the Maryland-Service, who went some Time ago[141] to make Discoveries about Du

---

[134] Maj. Armstrong?

[135] [An obscure reference probably denoting some kind of blank ammunition, possibly manufactured at a factory in or near the Billingsgate ward of London.—Ed.]

[136] Presumably in reply to Bouquet's letter of August 28 (*BP*, 2:435–36), but not found among Bou-quet's papers. A letter from Sir John to Col. Burd, written the morning of August 29, places him "4 Miles West of Kikeny Pawlings" (Shippen Family Papers, Correspondence, 3:221, HSP).

[137] A pro-British Onondaga Indian who had lived on the Ohio before the war, Kishaty (or Ogaghradirha) had been at Fort Augusta since 1756, and accompanied Col. Burd to Raystown. He set out from there on August 11 to get information at Fort Duquesne (*BP*, 2:354). On his return he met Burd (advancing to Loyalhanna) at Quemahoning on August 29. Writing to Bouquet the next day, Burd reported that "the Indian Gishaty…gave the Major [*James Grant*] & self a draught of F: Du Quesne which he drew with my Pincel before us & I inclose you the same" (ibid., 448).

[138] There can be little doubt that one of these letters was that published in *BP*, 2:371 (tentatively dated c. August 15), apparently sent from Logstown (the present Ambridge) on August 24. See Post's journal for this date in Reuben Gold Thwaites, ed., *Early Western Travels, 1748–1846* (Cleveland: A. H. Clark, Co., 1904), 1:201. The other letter from Post presumably is the one he wrote for the Indians, alluded to at the end of the letter in *BP*, 2:371.

[139] [That is, a bonfire.—Ed.].

[140] See Forbes's letter quoted in note 136. Orders of August 31 directed "All the Troop's to be under Arms tomorrow at 3 o'Clock P.M. & to march to the usual Place of Exercise…to make a *Feu de Joye* for the Conquest of Louisbourg" (*BP*, 2:685).

[141] On August 18; see Barton's entry for that date.

Quesne, & thought to be taken or kill'd, was safe arriv'd at one of our Advanc'd Posts.— M[r]. Clayton[142] a discreet young Gentleman, who out of a Spirit of Zeal for his King & Country came upon the Expedition a Volunteer, taking a Ride this Evening with Captain Hambright[143] of the Light-Horse, was unfortunately shot thro' the Os Humeri[144] by M[r]. Hambright's Gun going off accidentally, which in all Apearance gives him as much Pain as the real Sufferer—The Mornings now are generally very cold & foggy,—which bring on Fevers and Agues fast.—

Sunday September 3[d]. Preach'd from these Words in Nehemiah—4—14—"Be ye not afraid of them: Remember the Lord which is great & terrible, & fight for your Brethren, your Sons & your Daughters, your Wives & your Houses,"— Present the Commanding Officer, Governor Glen, Sir Allen MacClain, & the whole Troops.[145] Visited the Hospitals, where I found a great Number in a very low State, & was told that many dye.—A Party set off this Morning, to escort a number of Pack-Horses with Flour, & some fat Bullocks to Loyal-Hannan.—A Conference is held this Afternoon with the Indians, who give us great Assurances of their Fidelity & Attachment to our Interest.—[146]

Monday, September 4th. Lieu[t]. Colonel Dagworthy with 100 of the Maryland-Troops; Major Waddle with 48 of the Carolina troops; Captain Gooding[147] with 60 Men from the Lower-Counties; and Captain Trent[148] with a Number of Indians, of the Catawba, Ottaway,[149] & Tuscarora Nations set off towards Fort Du Quesne, to take Possession of an advantagious Post[150] near that Place, & to make what Discoveries they can of the Operations of the Enemy.—The Cherokees, after receiving all the Presents they expected, refus'd to go, & are for returning to their own Country, which gives us small Hopes of receiving any Advantages from that Nation.

Sir John S[t]. Clair arriv'd in Camp from Loyal Hannan, & seems much dissatisfied

---

[142] Probably David Clayton, who in 1759 was commissioned an ensign in the 2[d] Battalion, Pennsylvania Regiment.

[143] John Hambright served previously at Fort Augusta. He was now captain of a troop of horse in the 2[d] Battalion, Pennsylvania Regiment.

[144] [The humerus or long bone in the upper arm extending from the shoulder to the elbow.—Ed.].

[145] Orders of this date: "The Troops to attend Divine Services at 10 o'Clock, A.M" (*BP*, 2:686).

[146] With exceptions noted in the following day's entry.

[147] Jacob Gooding, Jr., replaced Capt. Benjamin Noxon.

[148] William Trent served as a captain of a company raised in Pennsylvania for service in New York during King George's War (*CR*, 5:177–78). In 1754 he commanded a Virginia militia company sent to the Forks of Ohio, where, on April 18, his ensign was forced to surrender a hastily-built and unnamed fort to a greatly superior French force.

[149] Not Ottawas, but Nottaways.

[150] Known unofficially as "Dagworthy's Camp" or "Grant's Paradise," about nine miles down Loyal-hanna Creek from the present Ligonier. This place was temporarily considered as an alternate site for the fort finally built at Ligonier. It was garrisoned briefly but abandoned after Maj. Grant's defeat on September 14 near Fort Duquesne.

with some Field-Officers there, who contended with him about Rank—[151] Captain MᶜPherson with 100 Men set off to shorten the New Road.—A 6-Pounder after being mounted on a New Carriage—was fir'd 3 Times. The Wadden struck thro' a Sutler's Tent, & made a great Hole.—

Thursday September 5ᵗʰ. A Pleasant Day. Drew, & witness'd the Will of a certain Gentleman, going upon the Expedition.— Sir John acquaints me this Morning that he "is going into the Inhabitants to look for Waggons, in which if he should not succeed, the Expedition must go to the D____ ["] He strongly solicitted me to acompany him; and at last Desir'd me to write to a Gentleman of my Acquaintance who had a great Influence over the Dutch, & might be of much Service to him in getting Waggons:—I wrote to the Gentleman, & am in Hopes Sir John will find him very useful.—[152] Governor Glen, Sir John Sᵗ. Clair, & Captain Young set off together towards the Inhabitants escorted by 30 Light-Horse.—Colonel Bouquet set out for Loyal Hannan guarded by the Remainder of Captain Hambright's Troop;—And Colonel Mercer takes the Command in his Absence.—[153] It is said that 500 Waggons at least are now wanted for the Expedition.—

Wednesday September 6ᵗʰ. Having a Curiosity to see Fort Cumberland—[154] I set off about 8 OClock this Morning for that Place in Company with Captain Cameron,[155] Doctor MacClain,[156] & some other Gentlemen.—The Road is good thro a fine rich Valley hem'd in by a Ridge of high Mountains on each Side.—[157] At the Distance of about 8 Miles from Rays-Town, is a large Bason of Water springing out of the Ground, mostly hid by Sedge, Rushes & Cᵃ.—2 Miles farther are many Acres of dead Trees, said to be kill'd by Caterpillers:—4 Miles from thence are 3 fine Springs, & on a Pleasant rising-Ground near them, 2 Block-Houses with Bastions, built in such a Manner as to flank each other.—They were erected by Major Lewis to defend the Road-Cutters from sculking Parties of the Enemy.—[158] Upon our Entrance we found a Shot-Bag, & a Handkerchief full of

[151] The reference probably is to Sir John's quarrel with Lt. Col. Stephen on August 24.

[152] Sir John's errand (and Young's part in it) is discussed in Bouquet to Forbes, September 4 (*BP*, 2: 468-70). Forbes's sequent letter of September 9 to Governor Denny appears in *CR*, 8:167-69, and *PA*, 8th Series, 6:4829–4832. The outcome was a piece of legislation, signed on September 20, entitled "A Supplement to the Act, entituled, An Act for regulating the Hire of Carriages to be employed in his Majesty's Service."

[153] In a letter of September 4 to Washington, Bouquet refers to "Colonel Mercer who will have the Command here" (*BP*, 2:476–77); and the orderly book notes, under date of September 5, "Orders given by Col° Mercer" (ibid., 686).

[154] At the present Cumberland, Md.

[155] Allan Cameron of one of the three "additional companies" of the 1ˢᵗ Highland Battalion.

[156] Lauchlin MacLeane, surgeon with the 1ˢᵗ Highland Battalion, visited Fort Cumberland because of Col. Byrd's proposal that he direct the surgeon's mates of the Virginia troops (*BP*, 2:368–69).

[157] Cumberland Valley is the present Bedford Valley, between Wills Mountain on the west and Evitts Mountain on the east, not to be confused with the Cumberland Valley in the present Cumberland and Franklin counties.

[158] Near the present Centerville, Bedford county, halfway between Raystown and Fort Cumberland.

Limes.—At some small Distance upon the Road, one of our Men found a Jacket & Hat;—And in one of the Houses where Fires had been made, were many Tracks in the Ashes—& Human-Excrement just fresh. Here we refresh'd ourselves, & din'd hearty.—Distant from this Place about 12 Miles, are 8 or 10 large-natural Pits, call'd the Sink-Holes, which receive the Rains & Waters from the Tops of the Mountains; & after running a considerable Way under Ground, gush out into Springs & little Rivulets. Reach'd Fort Cumberland about 7 OClock the same Evening.—S.S.W. of Rays-Town, & distant 34 Miles.—Here we found Colonel Washington encamp'd with 850 of the Virginia Troops; from whom we had a very polite Reception, & generous, hospital Entertainment.—Lieu[t]. Colonel Mercer,[159] who commands the Second Regiment during the Sickness of Col. Byrd,—[160] treated us in the same Manner.

I spent Next Day in Viewing the Place: The Situation is pleasant enough, almost quite surrounded with high Mountains. Upon a rising-Ground in the Fork of Potowmack & Wills-Creek stands the Fort, which is a trifling Piece of Work.—It was originally a Square-Stockade of 100 Feet with 4 Bastions;— but so ill put up, & the Timber so small, that General Braddock declar'd he could make a better with Rotten-Apples.—Since his Time some Improvements have been made—On the Outside of the Stockade, a Sort of Battery has lately been added, which covers about 3 Sides of the Fort—It is made of Square Logs—fill'd with Earth—about 20 Feet thick & 12 high—with a dry Ditch not finish'd.—There are 10 Embrasures with an Iron-4-Pounder planted in each—It is so irregular that I believe Trigonometry cannot give it a Name.—No Part of it will defend the other, & I heard a judicious Gentleman say—He "would rather fight with 50 Men out of it, than with 100 in it."—If it is design'd as a Defence against Cannon, the Spot where it stands is ill chose; For about 300 Yards N.W. of it is a fine Hill, which entirely commands it; & in my Opinion here should be the Fort.—[161] About 400 Yards S.S.W. of it is another Hill on the Virginia Side of Potowmack, from whence it might easily be annoy'd.—On the Top of this Hill is a large Store-house built by the Ohio Company,—[162] which at present serves as a Hospital, & here a Guard of 30 Men is kept, who pass & repass the Powtomack in a Flat—This River at the Ferry runs N.E and by E—About 50 Yards lower it bends round a Point of Land, & receives Will's Creek in the Elbow.—Wills' Creek at the mouth runs S.S.W. After the Junction of

---

[159] George Mercer of Col. William Byrd's 2d Virginia Regiment.

[160] Washington had written Bouquet on September 2 that "Col° Byrd is very Ill" (*BP*, 2:466).

[161] A plan of Fort Cumberland, sent by Gov. Dinwiddie to the Board of Trade in 1755, has been several times republished and appears in Lawrence Henry Gipson, *The British Empire before the American Revolution*, 6: *The Great War for the Empire* (New York: Knopf, 1946), facing p. 51.

[162] Completed in 1751 by the Ohio Company of Virginia. The same company built a store-house at the present Brownsville, Fayette County, in 1754 and was the original sponsor of the attempt to build a Virginia fort at the Forks of Ohio in the same year.

Wills' Creek,[163] Potomack runs S.—forming an Isthmus, which at the Distance of 5 Miles from the Bent is not above 4 Miles Over.—

On the Banks of Potowmack about 40 Yards from the Fort are several fine Gardens fenc'd in, which supply the Garrison with all Kinds of Vegetables.—The Barracks are mean, & ill contriv'd.—About 100 Yards S.W. of the Fort, is a large Square Post with a Piramidical Top, & a Plate of Lead with the following Inscription nail'd to one Side of it—

"To the Memory

Of Serjeant W^m. Shaw, Serjeant Tim^y. Shaw, Jer^a. Poor, & Jam^s. Cope Soldiers Of the 1st Virginia Regiment, this Monument is erected: To testify the Love & Esteem paid them by their Officers, for their Courage & gallant Behaviour.—

Nov: 1756—They went with 11 Catawbas to gain Intelligence, & in the First Encounter with the Enemy met with the success their Courage deserv'd Incited by this Advantage, & fir'd with a Noble Ambition to distinguish Themselves: They engag'd a Party of the Enemy hard by Fort Du Quesne And fell gloriously fighting bravely, being greatly overpowered by
Superior Numbers.
In Premium Virtutis Erigendum curavit[164]

Adamus Stephen"

Some of these Men afterwards return'd, & are now Officers in the Virginia Service.— They are perhaps the first who ever saw their own Monument, & read their own Epitaph—[165] It appears by a Draught of General Braddock's Route, which Colonel Washington honor'd me with a Sight of—That the Course from Fort Cumberland to Du Quesne is W.N.W. 56 Miles—Then N.N.W. 60 Miles—

Having spent Thursday, Friday, & Saturday very agreeably at this Place—I preach'd at 7 O'Clock on Sunday Morning[166] by Desire of Col. Washington from

---

[163] [The line "Wills Creek...Junction of Wills' Creek" was dropped in Hunter's transcription.—Ed.].

[164] [The terse Latin here makes translating this difficult. Carl A. Rubino of Hamilton College and John Barry of University College, Cork, suggest the following: "He saw to the erection of this monument as a reward for valor."–Ed.]

[165] A copy of the foregoing inscription was published in April, 1788, in *The Columbian Magazine* as "an extract from the journal of an officer on General Forbes's expedition," and is reprinted in William H. Lowdermilk, *History of Cumberland, (Maryland) from the Time of the Indian town, Caiuctucuc, in 1728, up to the Present Day* (Washington: James Anglim, 1878), 266–67. The text is introduced with the words, "About one hundred yards from Fort Cumberland, is a large square post with a pyramidical top, having a plate of lead, with the following inscription nailed on one side of it, viz"; and it is followed by the observation, "Risum teneatus!—*Some of these men,* afterwards *returned,* and are now officers in the Virginia service." The almost unaltered quotations from Barton's journal clearly identify it as the source of the text as published.

[166] September 10, 1758.

Nehemiah 4—14.[167] And About 9 O'Clock set out for Rays Town with my worthy Friend Captain Cameron—where we arriv'd about 7 that Evening.—

Here we found the Troops much dejected:—An Expedition for this Season seems to be despair'd of:—Accounts that the General had relaps'd into his Disorder, & was dangerously ill at Fort Loudoun:—[168] Only 20 Day's Provision now in Camp, & a Demand from Fort Cumberland for Part of it to be sent thither:—The Cattle purchas'd in Virginia are very poor, & their Beef scarcely fit to eat:—And no Prospect of getting Waggons, tho' 500 are immediately wanted to forward the King's Service—The Season is far advanc'd—The Leaves begin to fall; the Forage to wither—& cold Nights to approach.—All these Circumstances concur to damp our Spirits, & make us uneasy.

Monday September 11th A hoar Frost this Morning.—Arriv'd To Day 43 Waggons loaded with Provisions & Forage, & 42 Pack-horses with D° escorted by a Party under Command of Lieut. Snider.—[169] 30 Pack-horses went to Fort Cumberland with Flour, guarded by a Party under Ensign Jones.—[170] Accounts from Loyal Hannan are, that a Serjeant with 6 Men who had been viewing Du Quesne had return'd with 3 Horses which they took out of a Penn near that Place; that soon after 6 Indians came to Loyal Hannan, & retaliated the Affront—They attack'd 4 Men in a Pasture, 2 of which ran away immediately—the other 2 fought bravely—but they kill'd & scalp'd one (a Highlander) & carried off the other (a Virginian) Prisoner.—[171] That Colonel Dagworthy had march'd with 300 Men to take Possession of a Post 14 Miles beyond Loyal Hannan.—[172] That Major Grant with 750 Men consisting of Highlanders; Royal Americans, & Virginians was gone upon a Secret Expedition towards the Ohio—[173] Sir Allen MacClain inform'd me the Scheme was to draw a Party if possible into an Ambush, & if they succeeded, to march directly to Logs-Town 14 Miles below Du Quesne, where several Families of French and Indians resided, & put all to the Sword;—[174] And that a Light-

---

[167] "And I looked, and rose up, and said unto the nobles, and to the rulers, and to the rest of the people, Be not ye afraid of them: remember the Lord, *which is* great and terrible, and fight for your brethren, your sons, and your daughters, your wives, and your houses."

[168] Paymaster James Young returned to Raystown on September 9 with news that Forbes had arrived at Fort Loudoun on the 3d but had suffered a relapse that same night (Young to Bouquet, Raystown, Sept. 10, *BP*, 2:489).

[169] Jacob Snyder of the 1st Battalion, Pennsylvania Regiment.

[170] Probably John Jones in Capt. John Singleton's company of "new levies" assigned to the 2d Battalion, Pennsylvania Regiment. (There was also an Ensign Samuel Jones in Capt. William Biles' company in the 3d Battalion.) See the Orderly Book for September 10: "Two Subs 2 Serjts 2 Corporals & 30 private to escort Pack Horses to Fort Cumberland tomorrow morning" (*BP*, 2:688).

[171] See Bouquet to Forbes, Camp at Loyalhanna, Sept. 11 (*BP*, 2:489–92), where this episode is related.

[172] Actually the "advantagious Post" referred to by Barton on September 4. The distance now given is too great.

[173] This was the undertaking that ended in Grant's defeat near Fort Duquesne on September 14.

[174] This objective of the expedition is not mentioned in official explanations of the affair made after the event. See especially, Bouquet to Forbes, Camp at Loyal Hannon, Sept. 17 (*BP*, 2:513–14).

Horse-Man who had been sent Express by Sir John S[t]. Clair from Loyal Hannan, & thought to have deserted—was found in the woods a perfect Skeleton, having lost his Way, & wander'd about the Wilderness several Days without any Food, except what Nature threw in his Way—He is however likely to do well, & brought in all the Papers safe.—[175]

Tuesday September 12th. A cold foggy Morning—Fires are made Up & down the Camp which become highly necessary not only to moderate the Air, but to dissipate the unwholesome & gross Vapours & Fogs to which this Place is greatly subject.— Last Night one of the 3 Ohio-Indians who came in a few Days ago with Keeshity—treacherously deserted, & it is thought he will immediately proceed to Fort Du Quesne to give the French Intelligence of our Proceedings.—[176] Captains Bosomworth & McKee[177] set off To Day for the Advanc'd-Posts, with a Party of the dastardly, ungrateful Cherokees.—

Wednesday September 13th. Captain Blackwood[178] with 35 Men arriv'd from Fort Littlton.—M[r] Bartholemew came from Loyal Hannan with a Brigade of empty Waggons.—Lieu[t]. Quicksell[179] set off With 20 Men to escort a Number of Pack-Horses loaded with Flour for the Advanc'd Posts.—Ensign Jones return'd from Fort Cumberland with his Party, who acquaints us that Governor Sharp[180] was arriv'd at that Place with 200 of the Maryland Militia to garrison the Fort while the VirginiaTroops are employ'd upon the Expedition.—

Thursday September 14th. The State of Provisions is now so low, that Commissary Clark[181] is dispatched to the Inhabitants to forward some immediately.—

The King's Hospital contains this Day 137 Sick Persons.—Many of our Provin-

---

[175] Thomas Glen of Capt. William Thompson's troop of light horse disappeared August 29 on his way from Loyalhanna to Raystown, and was assumed to have deserted to the French. He arrived at Raystown on September 9 (*BP*, 2:449, 488).

[176] See the journal entry for August 31.

[177] Thomas McKee, an Indian trader, was known as Captain McKee from his service in Benjamin Franklin's Association of 1747–48 (*PA*, 5th Series, 1:24). He commanded a garrison at Fort Hunter, north of the present Harrisburg, in the first four months of 1756. On September 10 Captain Bosomworth wrote Bouquet from Raystown that "the Interpreter to the Indians" (probably McKee) had been sick since the 5th, but that he intended "marching to morrow or the next day at farthest with all the Cherokee & Ohio Indians to join the others at the Advanced Post" (*BP*, 2:486).

[178] John Blackwood of the 3[d] Battalion, Pennsylvania Regiment. He and most of his company had been at Reading until about May 20, when they left for Raystown.

[179] Joseph Quicksel of Capt. Jacob Orndt's company of the 2[d] Battalion, Pennsylvania Regiment. Identification as a lieutenant probably results from Orndt's being commissioned, as of 2 June 1758, as major in the 1st Battalion. Orders were given on September 13 that "Ensign Quicksel with 20 Men of the 2[d] Batt[n] Penns[a] R[t] just arrived from Lyttleton is to proceed to Loyal Hannon, as an Escort to Pack Horses" (*BP*, 2:689).

[180] Horatio Sharpe, Governor of Maryland 1753–69.

[181] Daniel Clark. Col. Mercer wrote from Raystown on September 14 that "M[r] Clark is gone to the Settlement to hurry up the live Stock & other Provisions there" (*BP*, 2:505); on September 23 Capt. James Sinclair wrote from the same place that "Mr Clark is returned from Carlile, he has brought us a hundred & fifty Bullocks" (ibid., 539).

cial Officers got drunk this Night; broke their Shins in returning Home, & were upon Crutches thro' the Camp next Day.—

Friday September 15th 1758— General Forbes arriv'd in Camp this Day,[182] carried in a Sort of a Sedan-Litter between 2 Horses;—& guarded by Captain Thompson's Troop of Light Horse, & Colonel Montgomery with 100 Highlanders.—He was in a low State, yet a great Satisfaction & Pleasure appear'd in his Countenance upon finding himself at Rays Town with his Troops.—The Roads were crowded with People to see him, whom he saluted with a Smile as he pass'd along—And they in their Turn discover'd a secret Joy upon seeing him:—He was conducted to the Highland-Camp by a Number of Gentlemen who went 5 or 6 Miles to meet him, where a pretty little Territ[183] with a good Chimney, lin'd within with Boards, & without with Oil-Cloths, was prepar'd for him.—[184] The Troops seem to [be] inspir'd with fresh Spirits upon the General's Arrival, & a Chearfulness appears in every Face.—[185]

A Party set off in the Morning for Loyal Hannan commanded by Capt. McPherson & Ensign Jones, with 100 Bullocks & 200 Sheep for the Troops there.—A Number of Pack Horses return'd from the above Place escorted by Lieu[t]. Prentice[186] with a Party in Order to carry up Flour.—The State of Provisions at that Place is so low, & the Pack Horses so much abus'd that the Artillery-Horses are oblig'd to be loaded with Flour & sent up this Evening.—

Saturday September 16th. This Afternoon the 3 additional Companies of Highlanders commanded by Sir Allen MacClane, Captain Cameron, & Captain Robinson march'd to join the Forces at Loyal-Hannan.—[187] About the same Time Colonel Washinton arriv'd in Camp from Fort Cumberland escorted by Captain Stewart's

[182] The date of arrival is confirmed by the Bouquet orderly book, where the final entry of this date is prefaced with the notation, "General Forbes's Orders" (*BP*, 2:689); and letters of Col. Mercer to Washington, September 15 (Hamilton, *Letters to Washington*, 3:102), and of Forbes himself to Bouquet, September 17 (James, *Writings*, 212; *BP*, 2:522) give the same date. However, Forbes to Sharpe, dated September 16 (James, *Writings*, 211) places the General at Juniata the night before. The simplest explanation seems to be that letters that Forbes drafted or dictated in the evening may have been written out and dated the following day with no change in wording. There are other examples of Forbes's letters that are similarly misdated.

[183] [An obscure usage, related to *torret, turret,* "a small tower," therefore possibly denoting a circular "hut," a word cited by Hunter in the next note—"the Gen[ls] Hut."—Ed.].

[184] Engineer Harry Gordon had declined, on July 22, to prepare accommodations for Forbes (*BP*, 2:259). In December, when the campaign had ended, Capt. Lewis Ourry took possession of "the Gen[ls] Hut" (ibid., 631–32).

[185] Forbes's poor health, his long delayed march to Raystown, and consequent anxiety regarding the success of the campaign are the chief defense for Bouquet's authorization of Maj. Grant's unfortunate action against Fort Duquesne, an affair of which Forbes was only imperfectly informed by Bouquet's letter of September 11 (*BP*, 2:489–92). Grant was defeated the day before Forbes's arrival at Raystown, but the news was not received there until four days later.

[186] John Prentice of the 1st Battalion, Pennsylvania Regiment.

[187] Capt. James Robertson (not Robinson).

Troop of Virginia Light-Horse.—

About 7 OClock P.M. there was Thunder & Lightning, which is the first that has been seen or heard since we came to Rays-Town, tho' we have had heavy Gusts frequently—After Night there was a heavy Rain, but it did not last long.—Very sultry all Night.—It is said that the Troops at Loyal Hannan told Colonel Bouquet they would be willing to eat Leaves provided the Expedition would go on.—And it is to be hop'd these brave Men will get an Opportunity to display their Courage & Zeal for their King & Country.—

Sunday September 17th. By Order of the General preach'd to all the Troops at 11 O'Clock P.M.—from S^t. John's Revelation 2^d. Chap & 5th. Verse.—[188] About 1 OClock arriv'd an Express from Philad^a. with Accounts that Col. Bradstreet had taken & destroy'd Fort Frontenac;—burnt all the French Shipping on Lake Ontario; and got Possession of Furs, Skins, &C to the Value of 70,000 £ Sterling—That the Indians were surprisingly alter'd for the better; & that Col. Bradstreet had gone down the River S^t. Lawrence, with a Design, it is thought to attack La Galette.[189]

Col. Washington return'd to Fort Cumberland with the Escort that came with him.—

Late this Evening Lieu^t. Evans[190] of the Royal Americans came from Loyal Hanning with a Party guarding a Number of empty Waggons.—

Monday, September 18th. A very cold Morning—At 12 O'Clock P.M—A grand Feu de Joye for the Success of his Majesty's Arms against Fort Frontenac, when 3 Twelve-Pounders were fir'd 7 Rounds each; which was repeatedly answer'd by Vollies of Small Arms from the different Camps.—[191] Lieu^t. Craighead[192] return'd from the Allegeny, where he was sent to escort Horses loaded with Flour for ye Advanc'd Posts.—In the Evening a Number of Pack Horses were sent to Fort Loudoun to bring up Flour, guarded by a Number of Draughts who are to take Post at Fort-Juniata under the Command of Capt. Aston & 2 Subalterns.—[193]

Tuesday September 19th.— Went out about 2 Miles into the Woods with 2 Offi-

---

[188] "Remember therefore from whence thou art fallen, and repent, and do the first works; or else I will come unto thee quickly, and will remove thy candlestick out of his place, except thou repent." The relevance of the text is not obvious.

[189] A captain in the Royal American Regiment, John Bradstreet was made a lieutenant colonel by William Pitt, who authorized his attack on Fort Frontenac following Abercromby's defeat at Ticonderoga. Frontenac, which controlled the entrance into the St. Lawrence River from Lake Ontario, surrendered on August 27. The news was added as a postscript to Forbes's letter of September 17 to Bouquet (*BP*, 2:524).

[190] John Evans.

[191] Forbes's intention to "fire a *feu de joye* here to morrow" is expressed in his letter of September 17. Official orders for September 15–20 are unavailable; the Bouquet orderly book, published in *BP*, 2: 656–90, terminates with the orders of September 14. The manuscript Forbes orderly book in the Toner Manuscript Collection, Library of Congress, begins with orders of September 21.

[192] Patrick Craighead of Capt. Charles McClung's company, 3^d Battalion, Pennsylvania Regiment.

[193] George Aston (or Ashton) of the 3^d Battalion, Pennsylvania Regiment.

cers to fowl, & Shot some Pidgeons.—While we were out we hear'd 24 Cannon fired in Camp, & imagining that an Express had arriv'd with some joyfull Accounts—we return'd & found that the Gunners were only practising.—In a few Minutes after arriv'd an Express from Loyal Hannan with the melancholy News that Major Grant, who on the 9th. Inst. set off with 800 Men towards Fort Du Quesne, was defeated near that Place about 5 Days ago.—[194] All the Particulars of that unhappy Affair that are yet come to Hand, are as follow—That on the 13th. Inst. at Night 300 Men dress'd in White Shirts, commanded by Captain McDonald[195] went to the Fort; & that Mr. Rohr[196] an Engineer measur'd the Walls & took a Draught of it:—That they burnt many Huts about the Fort, & even attempted to force the Pickets, without being challeng'd by a Centinel or any other Person—That the Centinels upon the Walls, at the Time our Men were employ'd in this Manner, cry'd out in English—"Turn out the Relief, All's Well."—[197] On the 14th. in the Morning Major Grant order'd the Revallee to be beat, & soon after began his March towards the Fort with Drums beating, Pipes playing &Ca.,—That he stay'd before the Place a considerable Time before he met with any Disturbance; At last the Enemy rush'd out in great Numbers (some say 1000) dress'd in White Shirts in Imitation of our Men the Night before, & attack'd the Highlanders and Royal Americans who at this Time were advanc'd within 300 Yards of the Fort under Command of Major Grant. Major Lewis who was left with the Baggage a Mile behind, press'd forward with the Virginians, as soon as he heard the Attack begin, & left Captain Bullet[198] to take Care of the Baggage in his Stead.—That they fought obstinately & boldly on both Sides for above an Hour; & that the Highlanders gave Way first & could not be rallied again; That the others kept firing & retreating till they reach'd the Place where Captain Bullet was with the Baggage; And that as soon as Major Lewis fell,[199] Bullet fill'd his Place with great Resolution & Bravery, running about, & praying the Men to stand & fight; but having lost at this Time above 250 Men, they could not be prevail'd upon, & immediately retreated as fast as possible; & by the Assistance of some Horses which Capt. Shelby took from the French-Pastures on the other Side of the River, carried off all the Wounded.—In this Action the Royal-

[194] For accounts of this affair by participants, see Grant to Forbes, n.d. (c. September 22), in *BP*, 2: 499–504, and the journal of Thomas Gist (the "Ensign Guest" of *BP*, 2:509) in *PMHB* 80 (1956): 289–93. Accounts based on information from participants appear in the correspondence of Washington, Bouquet (*BP*, 2:513–17), Joseph Shippen (*PMHB* 36 [1912]: 462–63; *BP*, 2:527–28), and others.

[195] William McDonald of the 1st Highland Battalion, later reported "Killed or missing" (*BP*, 2:508).

[196] Ensign Charles Rohr of the Royal American Regiment was also "Killed or missing." He was to have made a plan of the fort (see Bouquet to Forbes, September 11, *BP*, 2:490), but it seems unlikely that he actually did so.

[197] Whatever the source of Barton's account of operations on the night of the 13th, it is not supported by other reports and is not very convincing. His narrative of the action on the 14th, however, is in better agreement with other accounts.

[198] Thomas Bullitt of the 1st Virginia Regiment.

[199] Reported "Killed or missing," Lewis was taken prisoner with Maj. Grant (*BP*, 2:504).

Americans lost 4 Officers & 35 Soldiers:—The Highlanders 10 Officers & 131 Men:—The Virginians 6 Officers &103 Men:—The Carolinians 4 Men & no Officer:—The Marylanders 1 Officer & 27 Men:—The Lower Counties 2 Men & no Officer:—And the Pennsylvanians 1 Officer & 18 Men.—[200] Captain Bullet was the last that left the Field, & seeing Major Grant sitting on a Log without a Wound or any Hurt, & ask'd him if he Could not come away; but he absolutely refus'd, saying his "Heart was broke."— Upon which Captain Bullet left him, & knows not what became of him afterwards.—

Captain Armstrong[201] arriv'd this Evening from Loyal Hannan with 100 Men of the first Battalion, guarding 80 Sick to the Hospital, 2 of which dy'd the Night he arriv'd.—A General Court Martial sat this Day to try a Number of Men for Desertion.—[202]

Wednesday September 20th. An Express arriv'd from the East-ward: but Nothing transpires. Lieu[t]. MacMartin[203] of the Highlanders arriv'd from Fort Cumberland with 40 Men.—Lieu[t]. Evans of the R-Americans set out with a Party to escort 114 Pack-Horses loaded with Provisions for the Advanc'd Posts, & one Waggon with Powder & Ball.—Major Campbell[204] arriv'd this Evening from the Crossings of Juniata with a large Party of Highlanders.—Orders are issued that no Officer for the future shall appear in a Blanket Coat.—[205] The General rid out this Afternoon in his Litter to view the Fort, Camps, Breastworks &C[a].—

Thursday September 21st. Colonels Washington & Byrd arriv'd from Fort Cumberland with the Remainder of the 2 Virginia Regiments, consisting of about 1000 Men.—Captain Ghist[206] & I rid out 7 Miles to meet them, & finding Colonel Washington Afoot, I dismounted, & walk'd the whole Way with him to Camp.— Colonel Byrd who had just arose from a Sick-Bed, & Doctor M ᶜClain, who had been taken ill at Fort Cumberland, were carried in Litters made in Imitation of the

---

[200] This is consistent with a list published in *PA*, 5th Series, 1:253–54, except that the Virginians lost 61 men, not 103; the latter is the number who returned not wounded. The less accurate copy in *BP*, 2: 508–9, reports 187 Highlanders lost, and no Virginians (instead of 131 and 61), yet it arrives at the same total of 278.

[201] William Armstrong, a brother of Col. Armstrong, served in the 1ˢᵗ Battalion, Pennsylvania Regiment. Col. Armstrong wrote Bouquet from Stony Creek, on September 17, that "Capt Armstrong proceeds with the Waggons & Sick for Reas' Town" (*BP*, 2:525).

[202] The court, "whereof Col° Mercer is Presid[t]," met again on September 23. It tried ten men, all but one for desertion; two were acquitted, including one of the alleged deserters; of the guilty, three were sentenced to be whipped, five to be shot (Forbes orderly book, September 22–24).

[203] Cosmo McMartin.

[204] Alexander Campbell, second major of the 1ˢᵗ Highland Battalion, was presumably ordered up to replace Maj. Grant, now a prisoner.

[205] Orders for this date are not available.

[206] Christopher Gist, acting as an Indian agent for Virginia, claimed to have secured the services of the Catawba, Tuscarora, and Nottaway Indians mentioned in the entries for August 27 and September 4 (*BP*, 2:210–11, 214, 354).

General's.—[207] Ensign McDowel[208] arriv'd from Fort Littleton with a Party escorting 54 Waggons & 84 Pack Horses loaded with Provisions & Forage.—An Officer & 30 Men are sent with a Flag of Truce to Fort Du Quesne with private Instructions.—[209] Mr Basset an Engineer is sent to oversee the Repairing of the Roads between Forts Loudoun and Littleton.—[210] The Express receives Orders to carry no private Letters out of Camp.—

Friday September 22ᵈ. Receiv'd a Letter from Colonel Dagworthy at Loyal Hannan with the Particulars of Major Grant's Expedition.—

An Elk is brought into Camp, which weighs near 400ˡᵇ.—The Horns are very large; & the Flesh like that of a Bull.—The Officers of the 3ᵈ. Battalion practise the manuel Exercise under the Direction of the Serjeant Major.—Captains Blackwood & Stone are sent to view the Roads at Dunning's Narrows.—[211]

Colonel Dagworthy is re-call'd from his Post on the Waters of Kiskiminitas[212] to join the Forces at Loyal Hannan.—

Ensign Finny of the Lower Counties, is promoted to a Lieutenancy in the same Corps & Mʳ. George Wells Son of Major Wells, a young publick-spirited Volunteer, to an Ensigncy in Captain Gooding's Company.—[213] Orders issued that a Detachment consisting of 1 Capt., 3 Subalterns, 4 Serjeants, & 70 Men be posted upon the different Roads leading to Camp, at about a Mile Distance; to stop all Straglers, Soldiers & others going to, or coming from Camp without proper Passes or Licenses—They are to patrole Day & Night to watch scouting Parties of the Enemy.—[214]

Saturday September 23ᵈ.— A Party commanded by Capt. Boyd[215] & 2 Subalterns are sent to escort 60 Waggons loaded with Provisions to the Advanc'd Posts.— Another Party sent to the same Places commanded by Captain Armstrong & Lieuᵗ.

---

[207] See the entry for September 6.

[208] William McDowell of Capt. Thomas Hamilton's company of the 3ᵈ Battalion, Pennsylvania Regiment.

[209] The officer was Ensign Archibald Blane, of the Royal Americans. Bouquet's orders to him, dated September 19 at Loyalhanna, were to deliver a letter to the French commander. The orders, a copy of Bouquet's letter, and DeLigneris' reply, dated September 22 at Fort Duquesne, are published in *BP*, 2:525–26, 533.

[210] Lt. Thomas Basset of the Royal American Regiment. His mission, as reported by Forbes to Bouquet, was to repair the road between Fort Loudoun and Fort Juniata (*BP*, 2:537).

[211] Capt. Ludwick Stone of the 3ᵈ Battalion, Pennsylvania Regiment. Dunnings Narrows were east of Raystown, where the Juniata breaches Evitts Mountain, just below the mouth of Dunnings Creek.

[212] "Dagworthy's Camp."

[213] Wells was promoted from private.

[214] Orders of this date specify two detachments of this size, one to guard roads to the west, north, and northeast; one to guard those to the cast, south, and southwest (Forbes orderly book, September 22).

[215] Robert Boyd of the 3ᵈ Battalion, Pennsylvania Regiment.

Prentice, with 164 Pack Horses loaded with Flour.—[216] Two Highland Officers who were in the Action with Major Grant arriv'd, & give much the same Accounts we had before.—The Guards take Post upon the different Roads, agreeable to Yesterday's Orders.—Captain Young with the military Chest goes forward, guarded by 40 Men of the 3ᵈ. Battalion of the Pennsylᵃ. Regᵗ.—Lieuᵗ. Johnson[217] arriv'd from Carlisle with Part of Capᵗ. Blackwood's Company escorting 115 Bullocks, & 39 Sheep.—About 2 OClock P.M. fell very large Hail Stones— Soon after it lighten'd, thunder'd, & rain'd—In the Night many Flocks of wild-Geese flew over Camp towards the Southward.—

Sunday September 24ᵗʰ. Mʳ Monro[218] Chaplain to the Highland Regiment preach'd to all the Troops from 2 Sam. 10 Chap: & 12 Verse.—[219] Captain Eastburn[220] return'd from Loyal Hannan, sick.—Receiv'd Orders from Major Halket[221] to attend John Hannah Soldier in the 1ˢᵗ. Virginia Regᵗ., Thomas Williams Soldier in the Maryland-Companies, Benjamin Murphy, & Salathiel Mixon of the N. Carolina Companies, & John Doyle of the Pennsylvania Regiment, who are all adjudg'd to suffer Death by the general Court Martial, whereof Col. Mercer was President, & orderd by the General to be shot at 7 O'Clock on Tuesday Morning next.—[222] Captain Steuart of the 1ˢᵗ. Virginia Regᵗ. who was in the Action with Major Grant, reports, that it will be extremely difficult to make a Road from Loyal Hannan to Fort Du Quesne; while Capᵗ. Callender, & some others report the Contrary, & say, that an excellent Road may be made, & that they will undertake with 500 Men to open one in 5 Days fit for any Carriages to pass; such a one as Waggons may easily travel with 20ᶜ each.—[223]

Captain MᶜGrew[224] set off to take Post at Juniata-Fort in Room of Captain Aston,[225] who is charg'd with Disobedience of Orders, & sent for to make his Defence.—

Monday September 25ᵗʰ. At 6 O'Clock this Morning visited & pray'd with the

---

[216] Orders for September 22 direct "the Detachmᵗ of yᵉ 1ˢᵗ Battallⁿ of Pensylᵃ Regᵗ to march to morrow as an Escort to provisions for Loyall Hannon" (Forbes orderly book). Capt. James Sinclair wrote from Raystown on September 23 that he had sent, under two escorts, 55 wagons and 160 pack horses (*BP*, 2:539).

[217] William Johnson of Capt. John Blackwood's company of the 3ᵈ Battalion, Pennsylvania Regiment.

[218] Henry Monro.

[219] "Be of good courage, and let us play the men for our people, and for the cities of our God: and the LORD do that which seemeth him good."

[220] Robert Eastburn of a company of "new levies" assigned to the 2ᵈ Battalion, Pennsylvania Regiment.

[221] Francis Halkett, a captain in the 44ᵗʰ Regiment of Foot, served as Gen. Forbes's aide-de-camp.

[222] Results of the court martial of September 19 and 23 were published in orders of September 24, where Mixon appears inaccurately as "Sallateell Nicholson" and Doyle is more precisely identified as of "Capᵗ Pattersons Compʸ" (James Patterson; Forbes orderly book).

[223] The argument of the two captains illustrates the sustained dispute between Virginia and Pennsylvania over the practicality of a direct (Pennsylvania) road from Raystown to the Ohio.

[224] Archibald McGrew of the 3ᵈ Battalion, Pennsylvania Regiment.

[225] See the entry for September 18.

Prisoners, who have not yet receiv'd their Sentence.—About 2 OClock P.M. arriv'd Capt. Patterson with 40 Men wounded in the late unhappy Action[226] some were carried in Litters, & some on Horses.—Ensign Kirkpatrick who had been accidentally shot thro' the Knee at Loyal Hannan, Lieu^t. Bryan & Lieu^t. Lattimore,[227] came in at the same Time in a bad State of Health.—[228]

Receiv'd an Invitation from Major Halket Aid du Camp, to dine this Day with the General, who was very facetious[229] & in high Spirits at Table, tho' extremely weak & in a low State of Health:—He enquir'd much into the Moral State of the Army; declar'd he was concern'd at not being able to attend Divine Service; & that he was sorry I had so disagreeable an Office upon my Hands at present, as that of attending Persons under Sentence of Death.—Much was also said about the Expedition, which is not proper to mention.—An Express arriv'd from Philad^a. with Advices from England—We learn that our Affairs in Germany are in a good State;—That the Duke of Malbro is return'd to England, & that the Minister is not pleas'd at his Coming so soon &C^a.—[230]

Visited the Prisoners in the Evening, who I found in Tears under terrible Apprehensions of approaching Death.—I pray'd with them; & examin'd into the State of their Souls, & their Preparations for Eternity;—but to my great Mortification found very little Sense of Religion in any of them. Before I left them an Officer came in with the General's Pardon to John Hannah, Thomas Williams, Benjamin Murphy & Salathiel Mixon, who seem'd more affected and more penitent at the Thoughts of Living than the Thoughts of dying; They were immediately discharg'd.—[231]

Thomas Keinton[232] came from Loyal Hannan with 70 Horses;—About the same

---

[226] Grant's defeat on September 14.

[227] Lts. John Bryan and Robert Latimore and Ensign David Kirkpatrick were among the signers of the July 4 petition for a Presbyterian chaplain [see above, p. 44]. Bryan and Kirkpatrick were of Captain John McClughan's company from the Lower Counties. Latimore served in the Pennsylvania Regiment (*PA*, 5th Series, 1:267).

[228] Following this, a line of the manuscript—apparently "Din'd with the General"—has been erased and written over.

[229] [That is, "agreeable, polished" or more likely "sprightly, jocular, witty," an attitude not expected in one suffering as did Forbes.—Ed.].

[230] This presumably refers to Marlborough's return to England in early July with forces that had operated near St. Malo on the north coast of Brittany but had failed to take that place.

[231] "John Hannah Soldier belonging to the 1st Virg^n Reg^t Thomas Williams of the Maryland Comp^ys Benjn Murphy & Salateel Mixon of the N^o Carolina Comp^ys ordered by the Sentence of a Genl Court Martial to be shot tomorrow morning for desertion But their Officers from some favorable Circumstances and in hopes that the flagrant Example now before them of the Grossness of their Crimes in Cheating & Robing their King & Country will have a proper Influence upon their future Conduct, have Appeald to the Genl to pardon them; He therefore freely grants their request & orders them To Join their respective Corps to morrow after the Execution in hopes that it may have the desir'd Effect" (Forbes orderly book, September 25).

[232] Thomas Kinton or Kenton, a Pennsylvania Indian trader, apparently first licensed in 1748. For references to him in 1759, see John W. Jordan, ed., "Journal of James Kenney, 1761–1763," *PMHB* 37 (1913): 1–47.

Number are discharg'd, being render'd unfit for Service.—It is said that some of our Grass-Guards upon hearing the Cackling of Wild-Geese at Night, ran into Camp, & declar'd they had heard the Voice of Indians all around them.—

Tuesday September 26th. Very early this Morning visited & pray'd with John Doyle, who is to be shot to Death at 7 O'Clock P.M. [sic, A.M. intended].—He told me he was brought up a Papist; & as his Conscience never supply'd him with sufficient Reasons to renounce that Profession, he was resolv'd to dye one—yet as he made no Doubt but the Prayers of good Men would avail much, he beg'd of me to stay with him the few Minutes he had to live, & attend him to the Place of Execution; to which I agreed.—In a little Time came in the Provost,[233] & pin'd a Paper to his Breast with these dreadful words—Viz—

"Camp at Rays Town September 26th. 1758

"John Doyle, a Soldier in Captain Patterson's Company in the Pennsylvania Reg¹., is to be shot to Death for Desertion."—

I walk'd with him to the Place of Execution, surrounded by a strong Guard.— He behav'd with uncommon Resolution;—exhorted his Brother-Soldiers to take Example by his Misfortunes;—To live sober Lives;—to beware of bad Company;—to shun pretended Friends, & loose wicked Companions, "who, says, he, will treat you with Civility & great Kindness over a Bottle; but will deceive & ruin you behind your Backs:"—But above all he charg'd them never to deser¹.—When he saw the Six Men that were to shoot him, he enquir'd if they were good Marks-Men; and immediately strip'd off his Coat, open'd his Breast, kneel'd down, & said— "Come Fellow-Soldiers, advance near me—do your Office well, point at my Heart,—for God's Sake do not miss me, & take Care not to disfigure me."—He would suffer no Handkerchief to be ty'd over his Face, but look'd at his Executioners to the last, who advanc'd so near him that the Muzzles of their Guns were within a Foot of his Body.—Upon a Signal from the Serjeant Major they fir'd, but shot so low that his Bowels fell out—his Shirt & Breeches were all on Fire, & he tumbled upon his Side;— rais'd one Arm 2 or 3 Times, & soon expir'd. A shocking Spectakle to all around him; & a striking Example to his Fellow Soldiers.—[234]

[William Hunter added the following as the conclusion to his 1971 reprint of Barton's journal:

---

[233] Of the military police.
[234] Here, abruptly, the journal ends, with almost three quarters of its last page left blank.

EPILOGUE

(Forbes orderly book, September 28, 1758, Toner Manuscript Collection, Library of Congress.)

As the late example of Doyle who was shot to Death for Desertion by Sentence of a Genl Court Martial & the Clemency shown the others will it is hoped have a good effect upon the rest of the Army in preventing that Scandalous & infamous crime of Desertion by which they bring sure Ruin to themselves & shew their endeavours of betraying their Country to their Enemies; the General therefore flatters himself that their will be no such thing for the Future & that though he is sensible that the Men have gone through a great deal of Fatigue during this Campaign, yet the remainder being so Short & the advance posts of the Army almost at ye Enemyes Nose the Genl therefore with great confidence depends upon the Mens Alicrity & Steadiness in Carrying on the rest of the Service that we may shew our Enemys the danger of Rousing Brittons fired & animated with Love of their King & Country.

He therefore entreats & recommends to the whole that Considering the few numbers our Army Army [*sic*] consists of & the many Labourious & fatigueing Steps that are to be executed) everyone in his Station will Contribute all in his power to the forwarding of the Service with Alicrity & pleasure as every one must be Sensible that a good Understanding & a Mutual Cement of Hands & Hearts will most Certainly be the most surest means of a Completion to all our wishes, that is success over our Enemys & the Support & prosperity of these Provinces.

Genl Forbes has been pleasd to Release all the prisoners in the Fort & the different Corps are to send for them accordingly.]

Appendix C:
November 16, 1764, Report to the Society
for the Propagation of the Gospel in Foreign Parts

Rev^d. Sir,[1]

The Letter which you did me the Honour to write to me on the 6th. of November 1763—came by Way of New York, where it was detain'd till about six Weeks ago —It was my Duty to have wrote you sooner, which I should have done, had not the constant Engagements of my Office, a Crowd of Family Avocations, & frequent Indispositions of Body (occasion'd by the Fatigues & Colds I suffer) interrupted me—I beg Leave at this Time to address you; and to lay before the Ven^ble. Society a full State of my Mission, together with such Remarks as I have made in my Itinerantcy—

This Mission then takes in the whole of Lancaster County (80 Miles in Length, & 26 in Breadth,) Part of Chester County, & Part of Berks; So that the Circumference of my stated Mission only is 200 Miles—The County of Lancaster contains upwards of 40,000 Souls;—Of this Number not more than 500 can be reckon'd as belonging to the Church of England; The Rest are German Lutherans, Calvinists, Mennonists, Moravians, New-Born, Dunkars, Presbyterians, Seceders, New Lights, Covenanters, Mountain-Men, Brownists, Independents, Papists, Quakers, Jews &c. —Amidst such a Swarm of Sectaries, all indulg'd & favour'd by the Government, it is no Wonder that the National Church should be borne down.—[2] At the last Election for the County, to chuse Assemblymen, Sheriff, Coroner, Commissioners, Assessors &c., 5000 Freeholders voted, & yet not a single Member of the Church

---

Original is no. 14 in the SPG Letter Books, Series B, vol. 21, Bodleian Library of Commonwealth and African Studies, Rhodes House Library, Oxford, U.K. (Reprinted courtesy of the United Society for the Propagation of the Gospel.)

[1] Identified by Barton as the "Rev^d. D^r. [Daniel] Burton," secretary for the SPG.
[2] Barton's catalogue reflects the religious ferment, known as the Great Awakening, that was sweeping the colonies at this time. For a discussion of the awakening's impact upon Lancaster during the years c. 1740–c. 1770, see Jerome H. Wood, Jr., *Conestoga Crossroads: Lancaster, 1730–1790* (Harrisburg: Pennsylvania Historical and Manuscript Commission, 1979), 196–203.

was elected into any of these Offices.—Notwithstanding these and the like Discouragements, I have the Satisfaction to assure the Hon[ble]. Society, that my People have continued to give Proofs of that Submission & Obedience to Civil Authority, which it is the Glory of the Church of England to inculcate: And whilst Faction & Party Strife have been rending the Province to Pieces, they behav'd themselves as became peaceable & dutiful Subjects, never intermiddling in the least—Suffer me to add, Sir, that in the Murder of the Indians in this Place, & the different Insurrections occasion'd by this inhuman Act, not one of them was ever concern'd—Justice demands this Testimony from me in their Favour; as their Conduct upon this Occasion has gain'd them much Credit & Honour—Upon the whole, the Church of England visibly gains Ground throughout the Province—The Mildness and Excellency of her Constitution, her Moderation & Charity, even to her Enemies, And (I hope I may be indulg'd to say) the indefatigable Labours of her Missionaries, must at Length recommend her to all, except those who have an hereditary Prejudice & Aversion to her.—

The German Lutherans have frequently in their Coetus's[3] propos'd a Union with the Church of England; & several of their Clergy, with whom I have convers'd, are desirous of addressing his Grace, my Lord Archbishop of Canterbury, & my Lord Bishop of London, upon this Subject.—A large & respectable Congregation of Dutch Calvinists[4] in Philadelphia, have already drawn up Constitutions, by which they oblige themselves to conform to the Canons & Constitutions of the National Church; and to use her Liturgy & Forms, & none else, provided they be approv'd of, & receiv'd at Home; and that my Lord Bishop will grant Ordination to such Gentlemen as they shall present to him.—

The Germans in general are well affected to the Church of England, & might easily be brought over to it—A Law obliging them to give their Children an English Education (which could not be deem'd an Abridgement of their Liberty, as British Subjects) would soon have this Effect.—

The Presbyterians are in much Disrepute with all the other Sects, & seem to be at a Stand—They gain no Accessions, except from the Importations of their own Society from the North of Ireland—And yet what is strange, Numbers of their young Men are daily emancipated by the Colleges of New England and the Jersey,[5] who are licens'd by their Presbyteries, & sent by Scores into the World, in Search of a Flock:—But they are a People who are unsteady, and much given to Change; fond of Novelty, & easily led away by every kind of Doctrine.—This disposition will ever be a Bar to their Encrease.—The Seceders[6] are making great Havock

---

[3] That is, *synods*.

[4] Or German Reformed.

[5] That is, New Jersey.

[6] At this time, the Presbyterian denomination was represented by the primary, conservative tradition of Scottish and Ulster-Scottish, "Old Light," Calvinism and several splinter groups identified by Barton—the Seceders, the Covenanters (or Reformed Presbyterians), and the New Lights. One of the principal

among them, & are proselyting[7] them by Thousands to their Opinions:—These last however, are a Set of Men who, under a Monarchical Government, I think, cannot submit long;—Their Interest, upon their own Principles, must undoubtedly destroy itself—

The Church of England then must certainly prevail at last—She has hitherto stood her Ground amidst all the Rage & Wildness of Fanaticism; and whilst Methodists & New Lights have roam'd over the Country, "leading captive silly Women"; and drawing in Thousands to adopt their strange & novel Doctrines, the Members of this Church (a few in Philadelphia excepted) have "held fast the Profession of their Faith without wavering"—And, if depriv'd as she is of any legal Establishment in her Favour, & remote from the immediate Influence & Direction of her lawful Governors the Bishops, she has stood unmov'd, & gain'd a respectable Footing—What might be expected if these were once to take Place?—[8]

The Establishment of Episcopacy in America has been long talk'd of, & long expected; And I humbly beg the Hon[ble]. Society's Pardon, if I should take the Liberty to observe, that this could never, in any former Time, be introduced with more Success than at present—[9] Many of the principal Quakers wish for it, in Hopes it might be a Check to the Growth of Presbyterianism, which they dread; And the Presbyterians, on the other Hand, would not chuse to murmur at a Time, when they

areas of conflict involved the Westminster Confession of Faith, which served as a fundamental statement or standard of belief for mainstream Presbyterianism. The Seceders and Covenanters, objecting to what they perceived as doctrinal "laxity," rejected the Westminster Confession particularly on the principle of grace, and disputed "issues of lay patronage of church livings" (Andrew R. Holmes, *The Shaping of Ulster Presbyterian Belief and Practice, 1770–1840* [Oxford: Oxford University Press, 2006], 5. While both groups broke away from the governing synod (although differing on the issue of evangelicalism, which Covenanters embraced), the more moderate, liberal New Light movement, inspired by "Enlightenment sensibilities" (ibid., 138), did not seek separation from the governing synod. The fine doctrinal distinctions among these groups are far more complex than space permits clarifying.

[7] That is, *proselytizing.*

[8] Barton's friend and colleague William Smith offers a picture of what might take place: "When M[r]. Whitfield first came to these Parts, among several of his Doctrines many run away with that of an instantaneous sort of Conversion or *new Light*, the signs of which were Falling into Fits, Faintings, &c., &c.— To such an enthusiastic Pitch many well-meaning Persons of a warmer Temper could no Doubt work themselves up, & might, perhaps, mistake, their own Enthusiasm for the inward Operations of the holy Spirit" (William Smith to the Rev. Samuel Chandler, April 1755, *Historical Collections Relating to the American Colonial Church*, ed. William Stevens Perry, vol 2: *Pennsylvania* [Hartford, Conn.: the Church Press, 1871], 552).

[9] Principally for political reasons, the establishment in North America of an administrative hierarchy involving bishops was feared by most other Protestant denominations and for this reason it was much debated within the Church of England itself. Wood, *Conestoga Crossroads*, 201–2, citing a 1769 Barton letter, reveals what a volatile subject this was at the time. For a more general discussion of what Wood terms the "bishop controversy," see John Frederick Woolverton, *Colonial Anglicanism in North America* (Detroit: Wayne State University Press, 1984), 220–33. From existing evidence, Barton is surely mistaken in his optimism here. The first bishop of the Protestant Episcopal Church in America, Samuel Seabury, was ordained after the American Revolution.

are oblig'd to keep fair with the Church whose Assistance they want against the Combinations of the Quakers, who would willingly crush them—I hope to be indulg'd, if, with all Humility, I should further observe, that it is thought, the Lands lately belonging to the Romish Clergy in Canada, are sufficient to support a Bishop in America & a Number of Missionaries in the new Conquests, without adding to the Burden of the Mother Country; and that his Majesty, if properly applied to, would be graciously pleas'd to appropriate them to this Use.—[10] These Things perhaps have been already mention'd to, & consider'd by the Society:—But the Affection which I bear to the Church of England, would not suffer me to omit any Hint, that I thought might be an Advantage to her.—

As it will be my highest Ambition in Life to spend & be spent in promoting the Kingdom of Christ, I shall think it the Duty & Glory of my Office, whenever a Door is open'd, to preach the "glad Tidings of Salvation" to the unenlighten'd Heathen around me;—But the Time for doing this, seems yet at a Distance.—The Indian War still rages;[11] And the Fierceness & Barbarity of these faithless Wretches at present strike a Dread & Terror upon any Attempts of this Kind—Colonel Bouquet[12] is now at the Head of a large Body of Troops in the Heart of their Country; and it is hop'd will reduce them to such Terms as they will not for the future dare to violate—Whenever this is done, Missionaries may be able, under the Influence & Direction of Heaven, to bring Numbers of these poor Infidels to the Knowledge of the true God, and to embrace the Gospel of his blessed Son— Notwithstanding the Hardships & Difficulties that must unavoidably attend this great Work, I shall never refuse to bear my Part in it, when Prudence & a Prospect of Success shall invite to it.—I have already a very laborious Part in the Vineyard, as will appear from the following View of the different Churches under my pastoral Care—

The Town of Lancaster contains about 600 Houses, and is a very respectable & wealthy Place.—It has a large & elegant German Lutheran Church, a Calvinist Church, a Moravian Church, a Quaker Meeting, Presbyterian Meeting, a Popish Chapel, constantly supplied by Jesuitical Missionaries—besides the Church under my Care, which is a Stone Building, with a handsome Steeple, & neatly finish'd within—The Grave Yard is enclos'd with a good Stone Wall, cover'd with Cedar Shingles—About 30 Families attend this Church; the Presbyterians, & such of the Germans as understand English, attend also occasionally when they happen to have no Service of their own—To this Church belongs a Parsonage house, which rents for £15. Currency, which is about £8//10 Sterling.—My Communicants here are 25—

The Church of Caernarvon is 20 Miles E. N. E. of Lancaster, on the Verge of

---

[10] Barton refers to British territorial gains after its victory over France in the Seven Years' War.

[11] Pontiac's War, which began in 1763.

[12] Colonel Henry Bouquet, whom Barton knew from the Forbes campaign of 1758, commanded the expedition to relieve western Pennsylvania and the Ohio valley.

Berks County—This is a large Edifice, & has a good Appearance, the Front being built of hewn Stone; It is well pew'd, & has a Side & End-Gallery—The Grave Yard is secur'd by a Stone Wall, cover'd with Poplar & pitch'd—The Families belonging to this Church are between 50 and 60, all of Welsh Extraction—For the Summer Season People of different Denominations attend here, many of which come a great Way, so as often to make up a Congregation of near 500 Persons— This Church has a small Glebe (bequeathed to it by a worthy Member deceas'd) which rents for £5 Curr^{cy}.—My Communicants here are about 40—Mr. Nathan Evans, whom I mention'd in a former Letter to the Society, as a generous Bene-factor to the Congregation of Caernarvon, is since dead—But as he has left several Sons behind him in affluent Circumstances, it is hop'd they will be induc'd to fol-low the Example of their worthy Father.

The Church of Pequea is in Chester County, 18 Miles E. and by S. of Lan-caster—This is likewise a Stone Building, furnish'd within with neat Pews, Pulpit & Desk—A Stone Wall encloses the Grave Yard, but is not yet cover'd—The Congregation here consists of about 50 Families, besides Numbers of Dissenters who constantly attend—The Communicants are 30—A Glebe of 100 Acres of Land belongs to this Church, which rents for £10, Curr^{cy}.—

At these Churches I officiate Sunday about alternately, And have never, to my Knowledge, been absent once, even in the severest Weather, except detain'd by Sickness; to which I was always happy enough to be a Stranger till of late—I have baptiz'd within this Twelvemonth 115 Infants, 12 White Adults & 2 Black ones —Four or five of these were Converts from Quakerism—The Rest were such, whose Parents had belong'd to the Church, but dying early, they neglected this Sac-rament, til rous'd to consider the great Necessity of it—They all came to the Font well prepar'd, & were able to give a good Account of their Faith—The Catechetical Instructions to my young People are never omitted—And here I have the Pleasure to acknowledge the Receipt of the Catechisms sent for their Use; for which, in their Name, I return many Thanks; They were very acceptable, & I am persuaded will be useful—They have already advanc'd so far into Lewis's Exposition[13] as to be able to say one half by Heart—But I am sorry to observe, that there were not Books enough for the Number of my Catechumens, who encrease every Day—I must therefore take the Liberty to request 50 Copies more, with a few Prayer-Books for the poorer Sort—At the same Time, permit me, Rev^d. Sir, to request for myself a Set of M^r. Berriman's Sermons,[14] which I have never seen, tho' I am told they have been sent over for the Use of the Missionaries—

Besides these stated Duties, I am often call'd 10, 15, or 20 Miles to visit the

---

[13] Several editions of John Lewis's (1675–1747) exposition, *The Church Catechism explained by way of Question and Answer, and confirmed by Scriptural Proofs*, had been published by 1764.
[14] Various collections of William Berriman's (1680–1750) sermons were available, the most recent in an edition of 1763.

Sick, bury the Dead &c. which greatly adds to my Fatigue—My Itinerantcy also bears heavy upon me, in my present State of Health—The Churches of New London & Whiteclay Creek[15] demand a Share of my Labours—I wish I could attend them oftener than I do—The former is 35 Miles from me, & has about 20 Families belonging to it—The latter upwards of 50 Miles, & has (I think) 60 Families— This Church was formerly an Appendage to the Mission of New Castle; but has long been neglected; And I would beg Leave to assure the Ven[ble]. Society that no Congregation deserves more to be taken Care of—They are an orderly religious People.—They have a large & convenient Church; and are willing to contribute liberally towards the Support of a Missionary.—From a View of their Numbers, & the decent regular Appearance they made when I officiated among them, I am induc'd to become a Petitioner in their Behalf.—A prudent Clergyman settled between these two Churches, I have every Reason to believe, would soon make a flourishing & valuable Mission here.—I would therefore humbly hope, that whilst the Ven[ble]. Society are labouring to propagate the Religion of Christ amongst their remote & destitute Fellow Creatures, these worthy People will be thought worthy their Notice, and in Time share in their Beneficence.

I return my most grateful Acknowledgments to the Society for their kind Indulgence in giving me Leave to remove to another Mission, for the better Preservation of my Health.—I am not only animated by the Countenance I have always had the Honour to receive from that great, & truly venerable Body, but encourag'd & supported under all my Pastoral Cares:—And it shall be the great Endeavour of my Life, never to prove unworthy of the Notice they have been pleas'd to take of me, or deficient in any of the Duties that can reasonably be expected from me;—But the Peace of my Mind, & the Prospect of doing Good being dearer to me than any other Consideration; I should chuse to continue with a People whom I love & value, had I any Prospect of supporting my Family—My Ambition aspires at Nothing more than what will purchase me a Freedom from Want, from low & abject Dependence—Even this cannot be obtain'd here—I am oblig'd to live in a Place, where every Necessary of Life must be purchas'd at a most extravagant Rate—I have 11 in Family, a Wife, 7 Children & 2 Servants, which with all the Oeconomy & Frugality I can make Use of, cannot be maintain'd under £150 Sterling p[r] Annum—And I do   assure the Hon[ble]. Society I seldom receive above £100, including their own generous Allowance—It is the Misfortune of a Missionary, that let his Behaviour be what it will, or let his People entertain ever so good an Opinion of him, to their Courtesy he stands for a Maintenance, And very few will be found generous enough to tax themselves for this Purpose—As to the Fees which

---

[15]Barton wrote the SPG of these churches on November 10, 1766: "The People of Whiteclay Creek…are building a large Brick Church in the Town of New Port [Delaware]; & will engage, in conjunction with New London [Chester County, Pennsylvania], to purchase a Glebe, & raise £30 Sterling a Year towards the Support of a Missionary" (SPG Letter Books, Series B, 21:17).

Missionaries might receive by Marriages, these generally fall into the Hands of Magistrates, & Separatist Teachers—in this Affair we are much abus'd, & have great Cause of Complaint—There is in this Town a German Surgeon (who had formerly been a Calvinist Preacher, but for some ill Conduct was suspended & disgrac'd.)[16] This Man (I am well assur'd) marries about 300 Couple in a Year, which must be worth £150 p[r] Annum to him—He has no Cure of Souls, & is a Person of bad Principles—He often marries People belonging to my Churches, which creates much Uneasiness, as the Validity of such Marriages are often disputed—If it should be ask'd why this Man should have the Preference given to him, before a regular Clergyman, I answer—No License, or Publication is by him thought necessary—No Questions are ask'd; & no Examination enter'd into, to know whether the Consent of Parents be obtain'd &c.—And besides this, they are sure to have it kept a secret as long as they please.—Tho' this Person has been long look'd upon as a publick Nuisance, yet he has been suffer'd to go on—I beg to be inform'd by the Hon[ble]. Society, what Measures I ought to pursue under this Grievance, to obtain Redress.—

Whether a Removal to another Mission would be of any Advantage to me, I know not.—I make no Doubt but in most of them, I should find it difficult to support such a Family as mine, & to educate my Children—I shall ever esteem it my highest Honour that I have been employ'd in the Society's Service; But if the Prospect of Indigence should at any Time compel me to retire, I would humbly hope that their Protection & Countenance will be continued to me—

This Letter, I expect will will [sic] be deliver'd to you by the Hon[ble]. M[r]. Hamilton, the late worthy Governor of this Province, now a Member of the Society —[17] This Gentleman is well acquainted with the State of this Mission, & has been a very liberal & generous Benefactor to the Church in Lancaster—The Rev[d]. M[r]. Peters Rector of the Churches in Philad[a]., who is now in England, has been often kind enough to visit the Mission, & has preach [sic] in the different Congregations —To this Gentleman I am much indebted for many valuable Favours—No Man has taken more Pains to be acquainted with the State of Religion in America, or can furnish

---

[16] Barton refers here to John Bartholomew Rieger (1707–69), who served German Reformed congregations until his dismissal. Charles H. Glatfelter succinctly summarizes Rieger's controversial career: Rieger "also practiced medicine.... In [1762] some members of the Seltenreich congregation charged before the coetus that Rieger had not been truthful in reporting to a justice of the peace the cause of death of a man whom a wealthy Lancastrian had hit on the head with a stone.... The coetus told Rieger to give up the ministry and, in effect, removed him from membership. Continued as an independent minister" (*Pastors and People: German Lutheran and Reformed Churches in the Pennsylvania Field, 1717–1793* [Breinigsville, Pa.: Pennsylvania German Society, 1980], 1:108–9). Glatfelter also cites Barton's November 16, 1764 letter. Joseph Henry Dubbs offers as another reason for Rieger's unpopularity "his intimate relations with the Moravians" (*The Reformed Church in Pennsylvania* [Lancaster, Pa.: Pennsylvania German Society, 1902], 103).

[17] James Hamilton (1710–83), the founder, with his father, Andrew, and later proprietor of Lancaster, served as lieutenant-governor of Pennsylvania, 1748–54, 1759–63, and 1771.

the Society with better Information concerning it—

I shall draw for half a Year's Salary due at Christmas in Favour of Mess[rs]. Simon & Henry Merchants in this Place;[18] And I request the Ven[ble]. Society to allow the Payment of my Bill—

I beg your Pardon, Sir, for trespassing upon your Time with so long a Letter—I was led into this Fault by a well meant Zeal, & I hope you'll indulge it—

Suffer me to offer my Duty & most respectful Service to the Hon[ble]. Society; And to declare with what real Respect & Esteem

I have the Honour to be, Rev[d]. Sir,
Your faithful Brother, and
Most obedient humble Serv[t].

Tho Barton

Lancaster in Pennsylvania,
November 16th. 1764. —

---

[18] Joseph Simon (prominent in Lancaster's Jewish community) and William Henry (the famed gunsmith and for a while a communicant of St. James's church) had formed a partnership to sell from their "store at the corner of King Street...near the Court House a wide variety of hardware items" (Wood, *Conestoga Crossroads*, 99).

Appendix D:
November 25, 1776, Report to the Society
for the Propagation of the Gospel in Foreign Parts

Lancaster in Pennsylvania Novr. 25. 1776.

Revd Sir,[1]

Amidst the dreadful Conflict, which has rent this once happy Country to Pieces, it was impossible for me to indulge my Inclination in keeping up a regular Correspondence with the Society—All Intercourse between England & this Colony has, for above a Twelvemonth, been entirely cut off; so that there was no Channel, thro' which could a Letter pass, except by going almost an Anson's Voyage,[2] & being subject to be open'd, scrutiniz'd, & perhaps return'd back for the Censures of the Congress.—I must commit even this to the Hands of Fortune, having no better Conveyance than by Way of New York, where I shall send it by one of the British Officers, who have long been confin'd in this place as Prisoners of War, & are now releas'd upon the <u>Demand</u> of General Howe.—

As I would not trespass upon your Patience, nor distress your Humanity, I shall avoid entering into a Detail of Politics——I only beg Leave to hint that that [sic] the Calamities of America, brought on by a few ambitious & designing Men here, & which might have been prevented if Lord Howe's conciliatory Propositions had

---

Original is no. 31 in the SPG Letter Books, Series B, vol. 21, Bodleian Library of Commonwealth and African Studies, Rhodes House Library, Oxford, U.K. (Reprinted courtesy of the United Society for the Propagation of the Gospel.)

[1] Identified by Barton as the "Rev. Dr. [Richard] Hind," secretary to the SPG.
[2] George Anson (1697–1762), British admiral who purged the admiralty of laxness and corruption. He also acquired a reputation for perseverance, discipline, and infinite resourcefulness, partly as a result of his expedition of 1740–44 (the voyage Barton refers to). Commanding a squadron of six poorly outfitted ships, Anson was sent late in the season to attack Spanish possessions in South America. By 1743, he had lost all but five ships in his command. Nonetheless, he attacked and seized an immensely rich Spanish treasure galleon, the *Nuestra Señora de Covadonga* on June 20, 1743, then circumnavigated the globe to become a rich man from his prize money.

been accepted, are great beyond Description, and that it has been my Misfortune, among many others, to share in them.—

I have been oblig'd to shut up my Churches, to avoid the fury of the Populace, who would not suffer the Liturgy to be us'd, unless the Collects & Prayers for the King & royal Family were omitted, which neither my Conscience, nor the Declaration I made & subscrib'd, when ordain'd, would allow me to comply with:—And, altho' I used every prudent Step to give no Offence, even to those who usurp'd Authority & Rule, & exercised the severest Tyranny over us, yet my Life & Property have been threaten'd upon meer <u>Suspicion</u> of being unfriendly to, what is call'd, the American Cause—Indeed every Clergyman of the <u>Church of England</u>, who dar'd to act upon proper Principles, was mark'd out for Infamy & Insult;—In Consequence of which the <u>Missionaries</u> in particular have suffer'd greatly—Some of them have been drag'd from their Horses;— —assaulted with Stones & Dirt;— —duck'd in Water;— —oblig'd to flee for their Lives;— —driven from their Habitations & Families;— —laid under Arrests, & imprison'd![3]—I believe they were all (or, at least, most of them) reduc'd to the same Necessity, with me, of shutting up their Churches—It is, however, a great Pleasure to me to assure the Venerable Society that, tho' I have been depriv'd of the Satisfaction of discharging my <u>publick</u> Duties to my Congregations, I have endeavour'd (I think not unsuccessfully) to be beneficial to them in another Way.—I have visited them from House to House regularly; instructed their Families; baptiz'd & catechiz'd their Children; attended their sick, and perform'd such other Duties in <u>private</u> as aton'd for my Suspension from <u>publick Preaching</u>.—I think it my Duty to inform the Society that these are the Principles I acted upon— —If I have acted wrong (in not using the Liturgy in that maim'd & mangled State, in which, it is said, some of my reverend Brethern us'd it, rather than shut up my Church <u>pro Tempore</u>) I hope the Society will attribute my Faults to the Strictness of my Attachment to what I thought, my Duty, and so forgive me—I should have been very happy to have had their Advice and Direction on so critical an Occasion—But that was impossible to be obtain'd.—I now believe the Day is near at hand, when the Churches will be open, & I shall again enter on my <u>publick Duties</u>—I shall then do myself the Favour to be more particular in my Address to the Ven[ble]. Society—At present therefore I shall only add that, tho' I have Nothing to subsist on, but the gratuitous Offerings of my Congregations, who have been very kind to me, I have not been able to draw for my Salary; nor can I do it now, as the Money struck by Congress (which is the only Money now current among us) is so depreciated, that I should run a Risque in receiving it.—

---

[3] Barton here refers to the recent experiences of the Rev. Daniel Batwelle, SPG itinerant minister in Cumberland and York counties. As recorded by Samuel Johnston (November 25, 1776, SPG Letter books, Series B, 21:45), on a journey to York in September of 1776 to obtain provisions for his family, Batwelle was set upon by "a Number of People…, all Germans," who seized his horse and eventually "soused him in the Water" of Codorus Creek "several times." Drenched thus, he was made to "run from Town…about twelve Miles before he got dry Cloths."

My Son[4] will call on you before he leaves London—By him I request you will favour me with the 3 last Abstracts; & with such Instructions as the Ven[ble]. Society may think necessary for me, to which I shall pay the most tacit [?][5] Attention —I beg they will be assur'd of my Zeal for the Dignity as much as Interest of the Church,— —of my best Endeavours to promote the Design of my Appointment; and of all that Duty & Affection which I justly owe them—

I have the Honour to be, with Particular Respect.
Rev[d]. Sir,
Your oblig'd, & most obedient humble[?] Serv[t].

Tho Barton

P.S. The present Spirit of the Times will not admit of a <u>Publication</u> of some Parts of this Letter, at least so as to have the writer of it known.—

---

[4] Barton's eldest son, William (1754–1817), was studying in England during this time.
[5] In the extreme left margin, this word is difficult to read, but *tacit*—"understood but unspoken or unexpressed"—seems to fit the meaning and the letters that can be made out.

Appendix E:
May 20, 1778, Case of the Protestant Episcopal Missionaries of Pennsylvania, Addressed to the Consideration of the Honorable Assembly of Said State, Now Met in Lancaster

The Missionaries were appointed, and sent to America, by a Society in England, composed of the first Personages in the Kingdom, who were erected and settled into a Corporation by Charter, granted in the Year 1701, by the great Deliverer King William III.

This Society having the Management and Disposal of large sums of Money, collected in England, "towards the Maintenance of a Learned & orthodox Clergy, and the making such other Provision as might be necessary for the Propagation of the Gospel in Foreign Parts," have, for upwards of 70 Years, expended near £5000 p^r: Annum in America. They became the Patrons of their Missionaries, and have enabled them to preach the Gospel in some places "wholly unprovided of a Maintenance for Ministers and the publick Worship of God."

The Missionaries, by the Nature of their Appointment, are mostly <u>itinerant</u>: Being neither limited or fix'd to any particular Nation, they are often called, by the Duties of their Office, not only into different Counties[,] but into different States.

Upon being sent Abroad, they receive from the Society these Instructions, viz.[:] "To recommend Brotherly Love and Christian Charity" particularly among <u>all</u> Protestant Inhabitants of the District or Colony where they exercise their Ministerial Functions; To inculcate Submission to Government and Obedience to Authority, <u>not only for Wrath but also for Conscience Sake</u>; To exhort their People faithfully and chearfully <u>to pay Tribute to whom Tribute is due</u>; And to take special Care to give no Offence to the Civil Government, by intermedling in Affairs not relating to their own Calling or Function."[1]

Original is no. 32 in the SPG Letter Books, Series B, vol. 21, Bodleian Library of Commonwealth and African Studies, Rhodes House Library, Oxford, U.K. (Reprinted courtesy of the United Society for the Propagation of the Gospel.)

[1] Although the quotation marks suggest Barton is quoting directly and exactly from the official *Instruction from the Society for the Propagation of the Gospel in Foreign Parts, to Their Missionaries in North-America* (London: Edward Owen, 1756), 4–6, omitted text, changes in pronouns (second person

In Conformity to these Instructions, the Missionaries, included in this Case, (For they are not authorised, nor will they presume to speak of any others) beg Leave to declare, (with an Appeal to Heaven and their Consciences for the Truth of the Declaration,) that they have not <u>intermedled</u>, directly or indirectly, in the present melancholy Contest, nor done any Act or Thing inimical to the Liberty or Welfare of America.

Bound by every Tie of Duty to their Ecclesiastical Superiors at Home, affectionately attach'd to the Interest and Prosperity of this Country, and exempted by their Office, from taking any active Part on either Side, they have considered themselves under Moral obligations, and have made it their Study to give no offence to either of the contending Parties.

The Missionaries having never derived any Advantages from American <u>Establishments</u>, or settled Revenues, are generally in humble Circumstances: And being now, from the Nature of the present Controversy, suspended from the <u>full</u> Exercise of their Ministerial Functions here; and from even the Priviledge of visiting such of their Congregations as reside in different Counties;—Forbid by the Principles of their Profession, and the Cannons of the Church, to which they belong, from accepting or following any Calling in Office <u>Civil</u>, <u>Military</u>, or <u>Commercial</u>, they must be reduced to disabilities of procuring the common Necessaries of Life for themselves & Families, were the Society's Bounty to be withdrawn.

It is unnecessary to say more upon this Subject. The Wisdom of the Honorable Assembly will more fully point out the peculiar Hardships of the Missionaries in particular, should they under the above Circumstances suffer the Penalties of an Act, intituled [sic] "An Act for the further Security of the Government."

Having the Happiness of addressing themselves to Christians & Protestants who will pay due Regard to <u>religious Scruples</u>, however different they may be from their own, the Missionaries hope that they will be permitted Candidly to avow they cannot, in Conscience, abjure "the King of Great Britain his Heirs and Successors," nor totally dissolve their connections with the Countries that gave them Birth;—From which they have hitherto drawn their chief Support;—And to which alone they must look up for their future Maintenance.

The Missionaries therefore Flatter themselves that, while their Publick and private Conduct shall intitle or recommend them to the favor of America, they may be allowed the same Indulgence, which Missionaries, both Protestant and Papists of all Christian Nations, have experienced.—

The Protestant Missionaries from Denmark to Tranquebar,[2] in the East Indies, received favor and Protection from the Natives, tho' not Professors of the Religion

---

to third), etc., indicate that he is doing so without indicating elisions and changes intended to adapt the original to his exposition.

[2] Or Tharangamdai, India, the site of a colony founded by the Danish East India company in 1645. In 1706, Lutheran clergy established the first Protestant mission in India.

of Christ.– –The Swedish and Moravian Missionaries send to America, were permitted not only to exercise their Functions, but even to Purchase lands &^{ca}., for the Support and Endowment of their Missions, without being constrained to Swear Allegiance to the Government then in being.

The Popish Missionaries have ever enjoyed the same Privileges in all the different Countries they have visited.—The great Mogul has allowed them Protection and Liberty of Conscience in all his vast Dominions.– –Throughout Asia and Africa, the Philipine Islands, and the Isles call'd the Ladrones[3] in the South Seas, they are suffered to exercise all the Duties of their Function[s] without binding themselves to any of those Countries by the Sanction of Oaths and Tests.

These Things are not mentioned with any Design of dictating or pointing out Rules of Conduct for the Honorable Assembly; but only to mark the Policy (at least) which all nations have used in encouraging and protecting Men, set apart for the Purposes of Religion and Morality.

The Protestant Episcopal Missionaries, therefore, of Pennsylvania have reason to expect they will not be View'd in a less favorable light; and therefore pray that the Honorable Assembly will consider their present distress'd situation, and relieve them in such manner as their own Wisdom and Humanity shall dictate: – –And it shall be the Prayer of the Missionaries, that the "Peace of God which passeth all Understanding, may keep their Hearts and Minds in the Knowledge and Love of God, and of his Son Jesus Christ our Lord, and that the Blessing of God Almighty, the Father, the Son, and the Holy Ghost may be amongst them and remain with them Always!—

Signed in behalf of himself, and the rest of the Protestant
Episcopal Missionaries of Pennsylvania—

Tho Barton

Lancaster May 20th: 1778.

Missionary of Lancaster —

---

[3] A chain of islands located in the Pacific Ocean halfway between New Guinea and Japan.

Appendix F:
To the President, & Supreme Executive Council of the Commonwealth of Pennsylvania, The Petition of Thomas Barton, of the Borough of Lancaster, Clerk

Sheweth;

That during a Period of 27 Years, your Petitioner hath resided in America, an inoffensive, and (he hopes he may be allowed to say) an useful Member of Society; as will appear by many publick Testamonials, with which several of the first Characters in it have been pleased to honour him.

That in Conformity to the Instructions given by the Incorporated Society for the Propagation of the Gospel in Foreign Parts to their Missionaries, viz. "To recommend Brotherly Love & Christian Charity, particularly among all Protestant Inhabitants of the District & Colony where they exercise their Ministerial Functions;.... To inculcate Submission to Government & Obedience to Authority, not only for Wrath,[1] but also for Conscience sake; and to take special Care to give no Offence to the Civil Government, by intermeddling in Affairs not relating to their own Calling or Function";[2]....And Likewise in Obedience to the divine Precept of the Apostle, "To obey them that have the Rule over us,"[3] Your Petitioner declares, with an Appeal to Heaven for the Truth of the Declaration, that he hath ever considered it a moral Obligation, & made it an invariable Rule of his Conduct,

---

Original text is in Records of Pennsylvania's Revolutionary Governments, microfilm, roll 36, frames 438-40. Barton's title ("Clerk") identifies him as a member of the clergy, a cleric.

[1] *Not only for Wrath*, "not merely for fear of punishment."

[2] Barton here cites from the SPG's *Instructions from the Society for the Propagation of the Gospel in Foreign Parts to Their Missionaries in North-America* (London: Edward Owen, 1756), 4–5.

[3] *The Apostle*, that is St. Paul: "Obey them that have the rule over you, and submit yourselves." It may be that Barton cites Paul with pointedly cautionary irony, for the verse continues: "for they watch for your souls, as they that must give an accounting" (Hebrews, 13:17). Barton's next paragraph's "Your petitioner (who has the happiness of addressing himself to Advocates of religious as well as civil Liberty," certainly speaks ironically to Barton's persecution for religious conviction.

"as much as in him lay, to live peaceably with All Men";.....And therefore has not intermedled directly or indirectly in the Present melancholy Contest; nor done any Act or Thing inimical to the Freedom or Welfare of America. – – – – –

That, bound, as he is, to this Country, by Interest and Affection, by the dearest & tenderest Ties on Earth, it was his Hope and his Wish that the like Conduct would have secured to him the future Confidence of it, & allowed him the Pleasure of a Connection with it, to the latest Period of his Life – – – –But finding by a late Act of Assembly, intitled "An Act for the better Security of the Government,"[4] that he must suffer a Seperation not only from this State, but also from a dear & much beloved Child; except upon Conditions to which no earthly Consideration can prevail with him by consent;– – – –And being here, in Effect, suspended from the full Exercise of his Ministerial Function;– – – –restrained from even visiting such Families of his Congregations as reside in different Counties, as many of them do; – – – –having a young & large Family wholly dependant on him; deprived of every Prospect, when the Society's Bounty shall be withdrawn, of procuring any competent Maintainance;– – –And forbid by the Principles of his Profession, & the Canons of the Church to which he belongs, from accepting or following any Calling, or Office civil, military, or commercial, Your Petitioner, (who has the Happiness of addressing himself to Advocates of religious as well as civil Liberty,) hopes he may be permitted to avow, that he cannot in Conscience "abjure the King of Great Britain, his Heirs, & Successors"; nor totally "dissolve" his Connections with the Country that gave him Birth,– – –Where many of his Relations yet re-side;...from which he has hitherto drawn his chief Support; & to which he must now look up for his future Maintainance. —

Reduc'd to this sad Alternative, Your Petitioner, rather than violate a religious Scruple, "chuses to sell his Estate, and retire out of the State;" and therefore "prays" that the Honble. President & Supreme Executive Council will grant him "Leave to sell & convey his Estate" accordingly; that he take the earliest & most convenient Opportunity of returning to Ireland, the Place of his Nativity, where he trusts the Indulgence of a kind Providence will raise up New Friends, & allow him to end his Days in the free & peaceful Exercise of his Office, & the good Opinion of his Countrymen & Fellow Citizens.— — — —

And your Petitioner, (instructed & disposed to offer Intercessions for all Men) will ever pray &^ca.

Lancaster, May 29th. 1778. —

---

[4] The Pennsylvania General Assembly passed this test act, a more stringent version of earlier legislation, on April 1, 1778.

Appendix G:
January 8, 1779, Report to the Society
for the Propagation of the Gospel in Foreign Parts

New York, January 8th. 1779.

Rev^d. and Worthy Sir,[1]

By the Rev^d. M^r.Stringer,[2] who, a few Days ago, took his Passage on Board the Amazon, I did myself the Favour to write you a long Letter enclosing a Number of Papers, to explain to the Venerable Society the Reason of my long Silence, & of my being, at present, in this place.

I now embrace this Opportunity of representing the State of my Mission, & what Duties I was enabled to perform for two Years past.— — —The Society are already well acquainted that I had 3 stated Churches to attend, Viz. One at Lancaster, where I resided, another at Pequea, in the County of Chester, 19 Miles distant; and the third at Caernarvon, on the Borders of the County of Berks, 20 Miles distant. — — —The Souls, belonging to these 3 Churches, amounted to about 1050, exclusive of a number of others, who constantly join'd in our Worship.— — —Upon the Declaration of Independency,[3] when I saw myself excluded from the publick Duties of my Office, I visited my People from House to House; &, by private Instruction, Exhortation &c., endeavoured to render myself as useful as possible.—I had the Pleasure to find that this Method, of Meeting in Secret, &, as it were, by Stealth, having Somewhat the Appearance of the Persecution of the primitive Christians, it had these good Effects, it kindled & encreas'd their Zeal, & united them the closer together.—In this Way therefore I perform'd with much Satisfaction till a Law

Original is no. 36 in the SPG Letter Books, Series B, vol. 21, Bodleian Library of Commonwealth and African Studies, Rhodes House Library, Oxford, U.K. (Reprinted courtesy of the United Society for the Propagation of the Gospel.)

[1] Identified by Barton as the "Rev^d. [Richard] Hind," secretary for the SPG. Unknown to Barton, however, Hind had retired in 1778.
[2] William Stringer, evidently Irish, ministered to Philadelphia's St. Paul's church 1773–77.
[3] That is, the Declaration of Independence.

passed, enacting that "no Male white Inhabitant, above the Age of 18, who had not taken the Test,[4] should, under the Penalty of Imprisonment, go out of the County in which he resided."—Thus circumstanc'd, as a great Part of the Country Congregations resided in different Counties, which cut off my Communication with them, & theirs with me, all I could do was, to attend near the Confines of these Counties, where I was met by the Women (who are not subject to the Penalties of the Law) with their Young Ones to be catechized, & their Infants to be christened: And under these melancholy Restrictions I have somtimes [sic] baptized, above 30 in a Day. — —In the two last Years I baptized 347 Children, including those of the Military, who were placed amongst us, and 23 Adults.— —Eleven of the latter were baptiz'd in one Day, the Day I took my Departure.—Under the severest Oppressions, & the greatest Indignities that could be offer'd to the Rights of Freemen, the Behaviour of the Congregations of Pequea & Caernarvon has been such as will ever endear them to me.— —They have all (4 excepted) uniformly & steadily retain'd their Attachment to British Government, & their Affection & Loyalty to their Sovereign. — — —Their Attention likewise to myself ought to be mention'd;——When they found that I could not, except at the Expence of Honour & Conscience, continue with them any longer, having, at this Time, no Alternative left, but to "renounce the King, his Heirs & Successors, or to depart the State," they made a generous Collection among themselves, presented me £50, with what Arrears were due to me; and took a House at Caernervon for my Children, remov'd them from Lancaster, with kind Assurances that they should be supported, till it might please God to unite us again.— — —With this Sum, & what arose from the Sale of my Furniture, in my Pocket, I am now in this very expensive City; cherish'd, however, by some Hopes that, before it is quite expended, I shall be enabled either to return to my Children & Churches, or to obtain the Society's Permission to quit this ungrateful County altogether, and, under their benevolent Patronage & Influence, to solicit some humble Appointment in England; where, I trust, my Fidelity in their Service, for near 24 Years, will recommend me to Something that may place me above Want in my declining Days.—

In the Midst of my Struggles, in these Times of Difficulty and Distress, to support a large & helpless Family, I never, till now, had it in my Power, for upwards of 3 Years, to draw for my Salary, or any Share of the Collections made for the American clergy—As my Fate & Destination are, at present, precarious & uncertain, let me humbly request the Venerable Society to secure that little Fund, in such Manner as they may think best & most advantageous for me; as I shall probably have no other Source to apply to, in Case I should be reduc'd to the disagreeable Necessity of leaving America.— —I likewise beg they will be pleas'd to remember that M[r]. Graham, Schoolmaster in Lancaster, having neglected his School for an

---

[4] See above 143–47 for a discussion of Barton's responses to Pennsylvania's use of a loyalty oath to obtain political conformity.

Office under Congress, was discharg'd from their Service about this Time Twelve-month;—And that I paid him the whole of his Salary up to Christmass 1777, amounting to £15 Sterling, for which I took his Receipt; & a Bill drawn upon the Treasurer in my Favour for that Sum, which I hope the Society will allow to be added to my other Monies.—

The Clergy of America, the Missionaries in particular, have suffer'd beyond Example, and, indeed, beyond the Records of any History, in this Day of Trial.— — —Most of them have lost their All; many of them are now in a State of melancholy Pilgrimage & Poverty; & some of them have lately (from Grief & Despondency it is said) paid the last Debt of Nature.— —Among the latter, I am just informed, are M^r. Reading of Appoquinaminck, M^r. Ross of Newcastle, and M^r. Craig of Chester,[5] be-sides several in the Northern Colonies.— — —We may well exclaim, <u>Quis Furor, O Cives!</u>[6]— —What have we done to deserve this hard Treatment from our former Friends & Fellow Citizens?— —We have not intermedled with any Matters incon-sistent with our own Callings & Functions.— — — —We have studied to be quiet, & give no Offence to the present Rulers.— —We have obey'd the Laws & Government, now in Being, as far as our Consciences, and prior Obligations would permit.— —We know no Crime that can be alledg'd against us, except an honest Avowal of our Principles can be deem'd such; And for these have we suffer'd a Persecution as cruel as the Bed of Procrustes.— — —[7]

But, notwithstanding the gloomy Cloud that now hangs over us, I cannot, for my own Part, let go the pleasing Hopes, that we shall return to our Charge, & have the pleasure to see the Church of England flourish in America, with encreasing Lustre.—I am fully persuaded there is sufficient Power & Spirit still in the Nation, which, whenever properly exerted, will deliver us from the Tyranny that has scourg'd us so long.— —It is easy for those who may have an interest in laying Faults committed by themselves, upon others, "to mislead by false Misrepresentations"— These are Men, who have ungenerously asserted that "his Majesty has no Friends in America"; than which Nothing can be more unjust or untrue— —There are Thou-sands here, who "have made Sacrifices to Britain that will astonish Posterity.—Let them not be called <u>Friends</u>;— —let them be called <u>Martyrs</u>.—They have clung around

---

[5] Philip Reading had charge of St. Anne's church, Appoquinimink, Delaware, 1746–82. Aeneas Ross (1739–82) came to Bucks county, Pennsylvania, in 1740 and died in New Castle, Delaware, 1783. George Craig, who ministered to St. James's in Lancaster before Barton's incumbency, also died after Barton's 1779 letter, sometime after 1783, while serving at St. Martin's church, Marcus Hook, then Chester county. The isolation and poor communication among the missionaries at this time explain Bar-ton's mistakes about the deaths of Ross and Craig.

[6] "What fury, O citizens!" or "What madness is this, O citizens?": an oft-cited quotation from Lucan (Marcus Annaeus Lucanus, AD 39–65), *Bellum Civile*, 1.8.

[7] In the Greek myth, the bandit Procrustes forced passersby to lie on an iron bed, which he had adjusted to prevent their fitting perfectly: thus, if they were too short, he was "justified" in forcibly stretching them to conform; if too long, he amputated their legs. As a parable, the story suggests the arbitrary use of power to exact conformity—here, political conformity.

the Neck of their Parent State, with all the Tenderness & Sympathy of filial Duty & Affection"; some of whom have suffer'd even unto Death for their Loyalty; And there are many Thousands more, who only wait for some Security to evince their zealous & unshaken Attachments.——I could say much upon this Subject, but I ought to beg your Pardon for having already gone so far beyond my Line, & ventured on the Field of Politics——They are a disagreeable Topick, & shall therefore be dis-miss'd. —

But, before I conclude, permit me the Liberty to mention two of my Brethren, who have it not in their Power to write; and whose present Situation claim's [sic] the Ven[ble]. Society's Notice & Pity.—The first is M[r]. Frazer of Amwel,[8] as worthy a Man as lives, who has been strip'd of almost all he possess'd, by the Rebel Army; and being left in Circumstances too low to enable him to remove, is oblig'd to submit to daily Threats & Insults, & to throw himself upon the Generosity of his People for the Support of a young & growing Family———The second is M[r]. Illing,[9] a German, who, about 7 or 8 Years ago, receiv'd Ordination from my Lord Bishop of London, and came to America without any Appointment, or Allowance.—He set-tled in the Back Parts of Pennsylvania, where he became Very useful, by faithfully discharging the Duties of his Office; both in English & Dutch, to a large Number of People, whose Contributions altogether, perhaps, never amounted to £30 Sterling p[r] Annum, and for 2 Years past, would not been sufficient to keep him alive, had he not receiv'd Relief from private Beneficence. It would not become me to point out what should be done for them.—I only beg Leave to represent them as good Men, zealously attach'd to the Church of England, & the Interest of Great Britain, & as being now in Distress.—

I shall be unhappy till I hear from you—Be pleas'd to direct to me[10] at D[r]. Bard's,[11] New York;——to present my best Duty & Respect to the Society; and al-ways to believe that I am, Rev[d]. Sir, with the truest Affection & Esteem,

Your much obliged Brother, Friend, & Serv[t].

Tho Barton

N.B. Please to consider Part of this Letter as private. — — —

---

[8] The Scot William Frazer began his American mission in 1767 in Amwell (Hunterdon), New Jersey. He died in Trenton in 1795.

[9] Traugott Frederick Illing began his career as a Lutheran minister in Elizabethtown, Lancaster county, in 1758. He appears to have been ordained as an Anglican priest about 1772 but continued serving Lutheran churches as well. In 1779, he took charge of St. Peter's Anglican church in Middletown.

[10] That is, "direct correspondence to me."

[11] The Bards were related to Barton's second wife, Sarah DeNormandie of New York City.

Appendix H:
October 25, 1779, Report to the Society
for the Propagation of the Gospel in Foreign Parts

New York, October 25th. 1779.

Rev^d. Sir,[1]

The very obliging & polite Letter, which you did me the Honour to write to me on March 4th., did not reach me before September 12th., due to the tedious Passage of the Fleet, by which it came; & to some Delays after. I embrace the earliest <u>direct</u> Conveyance that has since offer'd, to make you a Tender of my Respects & best Thanks for the kind Notice you have been pleas'd to take of me.– –Amidst the publick Calamities that surround me, & the private Calamities I feel myself, Nothing could afford me greater Comfort than the "Society's Approbation of my Conduct," under the difficult Trials I had to encounter.––I beg [to?] pledge myself to that Ven^{ble}. Body that it shall be the Pride & Study of my Life to merit the continuance of their favourable Opinion of me.

It would give me great Pleasure to be able to comply with the Society's Directions, with Respect to my "occasionally visiting Huntingdon, [Long Island,]" but in the present State of that Country, that is impossible, without running a very great Risque of being, at least, made a Prisoner—A very formidable & violent Banditti from Connecticut are frequently making Incursions into the East Parts of Long-Island, particularly to Hungtindon [sic], where they plunder, commit Robberies, carry off such Families & Persons as are not their Friends.—As to "any other Place where I can safely perform my Duty," be assured I shall be happy in attending; & shall omit no Opportunity that offers for the Discharge of my Function.—My ill State of health obliged me to spend last Summer in Staaten-Island, for the Benefit of Bathing & Exercise; where I read Prayers, & preach'd very often, & baptized several Children; but many Parts of that Island being likewise infested by the

Original is no. 37 in the SPG Letter Books, Series B, vol. 21, Bodleian Library of Commonwealth and African Studies, Rhodes House Library, Oxford, U.K. (Reprinted courtesy of the United Society for the Propagation of the Gospel.)

[1] Identified by Barton as the "Rev^d. M^r. [William] Morice," secretary of the SPG.

Enemy, I could visit only particular Places.—I intend to go over there occasionally, & try to do all the Good I can.—

I ought to be, & always shall be, grateful to you for the generous [&?] very kind Offer you make me of your "Services" with Respect to the Money in the Society's Hands.—When I first mentioned that Matter, I entertained [very, many?] sanguine Expectations that I should soon be released from my present unhappy Situation, & returned to my Family & Churches; in which Case it would have been my Choice to have left my Money in England for its <u>Security,</u> (for, indeed, I cannot think any Thing secure in this miserable & distressed Country, in its present Situation;) but my Disappointment in that Expectation, & now viewing the Termination of our Reso[u]rces [?] at a remoter Distance than ever [?], I am under a Necessity of drawing for the whole of it; & therefore have remitted Bills, by this Conveyance, in Favour of Mark Cramer, Esqr., Merch^t. in London for £250 Sterling, due this Day, exclusive of M^r. Graham's Bill of £15 Sterling, which I paid him, as will appear from his Letter, herewith sent you.—You will be pleas'd to observe, Sir, that my last Bill upon the Society was drawn October 16th. 1775, for £40. Stir^g. in Favour of M^r. Paul Zantzinger,[2] that I never drew since, till now; & therefore hope the Society will honour this Draught.—

I have already troubled you with so long a Letter, that I must omit, to the next Opportunity, what I wish to say to you "concerning the Church & the distressed Ministers of it:"—This shall be the Subject of my next; [?] Permit me, however, just to mention that, notwithstanding the present depress'd & persecuted State of the Church of England here, & the many Discouragements which, at this Time, present themselves to my View, I am still sanguine enough to hope & believe that she will, one Day, rise triumphant & be the Glory of the New World.—The Evidence she has uniformly given of her Moderation & Peaceableness, & the general Conduct of her Clergy throughout the whole of this violent Contest, must, at length, recommend her & them to the Esteem & Attention of the People, as soon as their present Passions & Prejudices cool & subside;— —particularly to those who (where she has been <u>silenced</u>) have never heard any Thing from the Pulpit, but angry Invectives against the best of Sovereigns; treasonable Declamations against the best of Governments; Wrath, Bitterness, & Persecution against peaceable & innocent People.— —Should the Church of England, at the Conclusion of these Troubles, be a <u>little</u> cherished by <u>Government</u>, as she has greatly been so by the Society, (without whose Patronage she must have been totally extinct in America,) she will certainly flourish & grow more than ever.—These Hopes & this Belief furnish me with the best Consolation I now enjoy, & I will cherish them till I die.—

I am extremely happy to think that I can correspond with the present Secretary of the Society with the same Freedom, & have Reason to expect the same Favour

---

[2] Barton's son-in-law (1744–1817), married to his daughter, Esther, Barton's second child.

& Indulgence, which I had the Honour to enjoy from his two immediate worthy Predecessors.—Be assured that I shall endeavour to deserve your Friendship & Attention; & that I am, with my most dutiful & affectionate Respects to the Venerable Society,

Rev^d. Sir,
Your much obliged Brother,
& very humble Servant,

Tho Barton

Abbreviations

CR	*Colonial Records* (full title: *Minutes of the Provincial Council of Pennsylvania*)
EAS	*Early American Studies*
HSP	Historical Society of Pennsylvania
JPH	*Journal of Presbyterian History*
PA	*Pennsylvania Archives*
PH	*Pennsylvania History*
PHMC	Pennsylvania Historical and Museum Commission
PMHB	*Pennsylvania Magazine of History and Biography*
SPG	Society for the Propagation of the Gospel in Foreign Parts (modern designation: United Society for the Propagation of the Gospel)
WMQ	*William and Mary Quarterly*

Notes

INTRODUCTION

1. Although Richard Hooker, ed. *The Carolina Backcountry on the Eve of the Revolution: the Journal and Other Writings of Charles Woodmason, Anglican Itinerant* (Chapel Hill: Published for the Institute of Early American History and Culture by the University of North Carolina Press, 1953) gives Woodmason an English origin, David Doyle, *Ireland, Irishmen and Revolutionary America, 1760–1820* (Dublin: Published for the Cultural Relations Committee of Ireland by the Mercier Press, 1981) identifies Woodmason as Anglo-Irish (58).

2. See, for example, David Doyle, *Ireland, Irishmen,* and Kerby A. Miller, *Emigrants and Exiles: Ireland and the Irish Exodus to North America* (New York: Oxford University Press, 1985); and Kerby Miller, Arnold Schrier, Bruce D. Bowling, and David N. Doyle, *Irish Immigrants in the Land of Canaan: Letters and Memoirs from Colonial and Revolutionary America, 1675–1815* (New York: Oxford University Press, 2003).

3. Bernard Bailyn, *The Ordeal of Thomas Hutchinson* (Cambridge, Mass.: Harvard University Press, 1974), viii.

4. Ciaran Brady, ed., *Worsted in the Game: Losers in Irish History* (Dublin: Lilliput Press, Ltd., 1989), 7–8.

5. Among others, Owen Ireland, "The Ethnic-Religious Dimension of Pennsylvania Politics, 1778–1779," *WMQ*, 3rd series, 30 (1973), has noted that "by the third year of Independence, the Scotch-Irish Presbyterians and their Calvinist allies were in charge of the state. Once in power, they . . . enacted loyalty oaths to disable political and religious neutrals and opponents of the patriotic movement, and replaced the Anglican-oriented College of Philadelphia with their own Presbyterian-dominated University of Pennsylvania" (425).

More broadly, David Hawke, *In the Midst of a Revolution* (Philadelphia: University of Pennsylvania Press, 1961) notes of the radical Constitutionalist faction that "they set out to make a sharp break with the past, with almost every tradition that had ruled Pennsylvania politics for nearly a century" (190).

For a general discussion of Philadelphia's role in the colonial Enlightenment, see Nina Reid-Maroney, *Philadephia's Enlightenment, 1740–1800: Kingdom of Christ, Empire of Reason* (Westport, Conn.: Greenwood Press, 2001).

6. John F. Woolverton, *Colonial Anglicanism in North America* (Detroit: Wayne State University Press, 1984), 214.

7. Henry F. May, *The Enlightenment in America* (New York: Oxford University Press, 1976), 80.

8. Owen S. Ireland, *Religion, Ethnicity, and Politics: Ratifying the Constitution in Pennsylvania* (University Park: Pennsylvania State University Press, 1995) provides useful background on the rise of Pennsylvania's Constitutional party.

CHAPTER 1. WATCHMAN ON THE WALLS

1. The term *Episcopalian* was not widely used officially until the American Revolution in order to avoid unpatriotic connotations of *Anglican,* a word generally suggesting things relating to England or the English nation.

2. Marsh Creek is west and south of today's Gettysburg. In May of 1775, the traveler Philip Vickers Fithian described it as "a fine Brook; its rich Banks are lined with tall Sycamores" (*Philip Vickers Fithian: Journal, 1775–1776; Written on the Virginia-Pennsylvania Frontier and in the Army Around New York,* ed. Robert Greenhalgh Albion and Leonidas Dodson [Princeton: Princeton University Press, 1934], 9).

3. Petition of the Inhabitants of the Townships of Huntington and Tyrone . . . on the West Side of the River Susquehanna, October 3, 1748, SPG Letter Books, Vol. 16, no. 116 (also included in William Stevens Perry, ed., *Historical Collections Relating to the American Colonial Church,* vol. 2: *Pennsylvania* [Hartford, Conn.: The Church Press, 1871], 254–55).

4. Ibid.

5. Before 1755, the SPG missionaries serving Lancaster—Richard Locke and George Craig—had occasionally visited Christ Church.

6. Andrew Montour, also called Henry, was the eldest son of the famous Indian interpreter Madame Montour, who claimed descent from a Huron and one of the governors of Canada. Andrew, whose Indian name was Sattelihu, figures prominently in Pennsylvania history as an interpreter, scout, and officer in the French and Indian wars. In the words of historian C. Hale Sipe (*The Indian Wars of Pennsylvania,* 2nd ed. [Harrisburg: the Telegraph Press, 1931]: "A town, a creek, an island, a county, a mountain range—all in Pennsylvania—are named for him and his mother" (171). William Buchanan of Lurgan township, Cumberland (now Franklin) county, contributed significantly to the defense of that area. John Harris was the influential owner of the strategically important ferry at the site of today's Harrisburg.

7. Hans Hamilton, first sheriff of York county, was a prominent landowner who served in various ranks, including that of lieutenant colonel, in the militia and the Pennsylvania Regiment. John Pope, assemblyman and justice of the peace, was disciplined in 1756 by the Menallen Friends' Meeting for participating in military actions against the Indians. David McConaughy was a mill-owner, provisioner/victualer, and officer in the militia and the Pennsylvania Regiment. All were residents of western York county and near-neighbors of Barton.

8. Thomas Barton to Governor Robert Hunter Morris [?], November 2, 1755, *CR,* 6:675.

9. Thomas Barton to the Secretary, November 8, 1756, SPG Letter Books, Series B, vol. 21, no. 1.

10. Ibid.

11. Several documents show John Steel and Andrew Bay to have been active in the defense of Cumberland and York counties. See, for example, William Smith's November 1, 1756, letter to the Bishop of Oxford (*Historical Collections,* ed. Perry, 2:556), where Smith credits Barton and "two worthy Presbyterian Ministers" with setting martial examples for their people. In addition, the Minutes of the General Council of Cumberland County, October 30, 1755 (Lamberton Scotch-Irish Collection, 1:23, HSP), includes the names of Bay and Steel as attending the war council.

12. Barton's 142–acre plantation was located in Reading township, south of Mud Run, on the site of today's Ebersole farm along state Rt. 394. (I thank Arthur Weaner for this information.)

13. Thomas Barton to Richard Peters, July 30, 1755, Peters Papers, 4:36, HSP.

14. Prefatory Letter in Thomas Barton, *Unanimity and Public Spirit* (Philadelphia, 1755), xiii.

15. William Smith to the Bishop of Oxford [November 1, 1756], *Historical Collections,* ed. Perry, 2:556.

16. Ibid.

17. Thomas Barton to the Secretary, November 8, 1756, SPG Letter Books, Series B, vol. 21, no. 1.

18. William Barton, *Memoirs of the Life of David Rittenhouse* (Philadelphia: E. Parker, 1813), 101–2.

19. Ibid., 102.

20. Pulman Collection, April 16, 1778, vol. 90, folios 353/3, College of Arms, London.

21. See Evelyn Philip Shirley, *The History of the County of Monaghan* (London: Pickering, 1879), 274.

22. Pulman Collection, fols. 353/3.

23. Donald M. Schlegel of Columbus, Ohio, has done considerable work on clarifying the Barton (co. Monaghan) genealogy and that of the Tenison family, into whose possession most of Capt. William Barton's estate passed (manuscript draft, "The Barton Estate and Lough Baun in County Monaghan"). See his article "The Barton Estate and Lough Bawn in County Monaghan," *Clogher Record* 15 (1995): 110–21.

24. William Barton, *Memoirs,* 102.

25. See Henry F. May, *The Enlightenment in America* (New York: Oxford University Press, 1976), 80–86, for a discussion of Smith as "one of the major figures of the Moderate Enlightenment."

26. Albert Frank Gegenheimer, *William Smith: Educator and Churchman, 1727–1803* (Philadelphia: University of Pennsylvania Press,1943), 36–41.

27. Thomas Barton to Thomas Penn, February 28, 1757, Penn Papers, Official Correspondence, 8:239, HSP: "I shar'd too liberally of your Goodness when in London, to doubt of your Interest (which I know is great) with the Society, in my Behalf; which claims more than my Thanks."

28. *A Calendar of Ridgely Family Letters, 1742–1899, in the Delaware State Archives,* vol. 1, ed. Leon deValinger, Jr., and Virginia E. Shaw (Dover: Delaware Public Archives Commission,1948), 84.

29. See R. Lloyd Praeger, *Some Irish Naturalists* (Dundalk: W. Tempest,1949), 48–49. Among the more intriguing parallels between Thomas and Richard Barton is their mutual fascination with the petrifying properties of certain bodies of water. See also Charles W. Rutschy, Jr., "Thomas Barton's Collection of Minerals," *PH* 8 (1941): 148–50; and Barton's Forbes expedition journal (reprinted below in Appendix B), July 21, where Barton describes Falling Spring in the vicinity of today's Chambersburg..

30. Alfred W. Newcombe, "The Appointment and Instruction of S.P.G. Missionaries," *Church History* 5 (1936): 347–48.

31. Cited in John Calam, *Parsons and Pedagogues: the S.P.G. Adventure in Education* (New York: Columbia University Press, 1971), n. 19, 75.

32. Frederick L. Weiss, *The Colonial Clergy of the Middle Colonies, New York, New Jersey and Pennsylvania, 1628–1776* (Worcester, Mass.: Genealogical Publishing Co., 1957), 175.

33. John F. Woolverton, *Colonial Anglicanism in North America* (Detroit: Wayne State University Press, 1984), 90.

34. Carl Bridenbaugh, *Mitre and Sceptre: Transatlantic Faiths, Ideas, Personalities, and Politics, 1689–1775* (New York: Oxford University Press,1962), 57.

35. See May, *Enlightenment,* 76–78, and Woolverton, *Colonial Anglicanism,* chapter 9.

36. Cited in Woolverton, *Colonial Anglicanism,* 89.

37. (London, 1756).

38. Ibid., 3.

39. Ibid., 4–5.

40. Ibid., 5.

41. Ibid.

42. Ibid., 6.

43. Ibid., 8.

44. Woolverton, *Colonial Anglicanism,* 90.

45. Ibid.

46. The initiative implied by the 1748 petition by the people of Conewago makes it likely that they later sought out Barton. Indeed, the Reverend Richard Locke of Lancaster wrote in 1746 of being apprised by "a Person of Contwager [i.e., Conewago]," of the congregation's "want of a Clergyman" (Richard Locke to the Secretary, October 16, 1746, SPG Letter Books, Series B, vol. 14, no. 199). Newcombe ("Appointment and Instruction") notes that such arrangements were common: "The petitioners frequently asked for the services of a particular missionary, possibly one about to go to England for ordination and appointment or one already on the way" (350).

47. See David Noel Doyle, *Ireland, Irishmen and Revolutionary America* (Dublin and Cork: Published for the Cultural Relations Committee of Ireland by the Mercier Press, 1981), 37–39, 58–60; and Kerby A. Miller, *Emigrants and Exiles: Ireland and the Irish Exodus to North America* (New York: Oxford University Press,1985), 149–52, 158–60, and 376–77, and also Kerby Miller, Arnold Schrier, Bruce D. Boling, and David N. Doyle, *Irish Immigrants in the Land of Canaan: Letters and Memoirs from Colonial and Revolutionary America, 1676–1815* (New York and Oxford: Oxford University Press, 2004), and especially for a discussion of Barton's career, 487–99.

48. Miller, *Emigrants and Exiles,* 150.

49. Ibid., 151.

50. Doyle, *Ireland,* 37.

51. Ibid., 58–59.

52. Ibid., 51.

53. Ibid., 54 and 56.

54. For a study of the movement of Anglo-Irish Quakers to the frontier, see Albert Cook Myers, *Immigration of the Irish Quakers into Pennsylvania* (Swarthmore: Albert Cook Myers, 1902).

55. Statistics are far from accurate, but Doyle, *Ireland* estimates that "in 1715 Ulster had a population of 600,000, one third Scottish stock, with up to 130,000 English stock Anglicans and over 270,000 Irish Catholics" (58).

56. See the following wherein Barton advocates the cause of fellow Irishmen: the Reverend Philip Hughes: Thomas Barton to William Smith, August 24, 1755, S, I, 14–6–53, the Francis Lister Hawks Manuscript Collection, Records of the General Convention, Archives of the Episcopal Church, U.S.A., Austin, Texas; Mr. Popham: Thomas Barton to Sir William Johnson, December 2, 1767, *The Papers of Sir William Johnson,* 13 vols. (Albany: State University of New York, 1921–62), 5:843–48; William Andrews: Thomas Barton to Sir William Johnson, November 6, 1769, ibid., 7:239–40.

57. Doyle, *Ireland*, 38.

58. John Callam, *Parsons and Pedagogues*, 104–7, 206–7, discusses the difficult financial circumstances faced by SPG teachers, who probably received better stipends than the
"average" educator such as Barton at that time. Calam writes that "Society pedagogues had
every reason to fear their financial future" (105).

59. Doyle, *Ireland*, 59.

60. Owen S. Ireland has written: "By the middle of the eighteenth century these groups,
along with numbers of German church people and sectarians, had assembled in Pennsylvania, where the liberal franchise made them all participants in politics. The erosion of the
initial Quaker hegemony, the Anglicanization of the Penn family and the proprietary interest, the precarious position and the missionary status of the Anglican church, the political
awakening of the Germans, and the influx of Scotch-Irish Presbyterians, especially the virtual torrent of middle-class exiles from Ulster after mid-century, combined to create a
volatile political mixture. Competition between the assembly and the proprietary governor
in the 1760s, itself based partly on religious differences, contributed to widespread political mobilization, while vigorous, not to say brutal, electoral contests exacerbated ethnic and
religious conflicts" ("The Crux of Politics: Religion and Party in Pennsylvania, 1778–
1789," *WMQ*, 3rd Series, 42 [1985]: 470). See also Wayne L. Bockelman and Owen S. Ireland, "The Internal Revolution in Pennsylvania: an Ethnic-Religious Interpretation," *PH* 41
(1974): 125–59.

61. R. J. Dickson, *Ulster Emigration to Colonial America, 1718–1775* (London: Routledge and Keegan Paul, 1966), evaluates the relative importance of perceptions of religious
oppression and actual economic forces in trying to appreciate the emigration from Ulster;
see especially chapters 2 and 3.

62. See, for example, the petition from Lancaster, November 1, 1755, *PA*, 1st series,
2:450–51.

63. Minutes of the General Council of Cumberland County, October 30, 1755, Lamberton Scotch-Irish Collection, 1:23, HSP.

64. William A. Hunter, *Forts on the Pennsylvania Frontier, 1753–1758* (Harrisburg: the
Pennsylvania Historical and Museum Commission,1960). For more recent general discussions of frontier fort building in colonial Pennsylvania, see Louis M. Waddell, "Defending
the Long Perimeter: Forts on the Pennsylvania, Maryland, and Virginia Frontier: 1758–
1765," *PH* 62 (1995): 171–95, who advances an additional purpose for the building of forts,
one he defines as the "loadstone principle": "forts were deliberately placed beyond the settlements so that the war could be drawn—as by a loadstone—toward them, sparing the settled communities from the violence" (180). Whereas Virgina tended to reinforce heavily
settled communities by erecting forts in their midst, Pennsylvania instead sought to protect
its frontier settlements by inviting attacks on somewhat remotely situated fortifications.
Says Waddell: "the great expense of the isolated, elaborate works at Fort Pitt and Fort Augusta can only be understood in the light of this concept" (ibid.). Also see R. S. Stevenson,
"Pennsylvania Provincial Soldiers in the Seven Years' War," *PH* 62 (1995): 196–212.

65. Ibid.

66. Officers of the Provincial Service, 1755, *PA*, 5th series, 1:31.

67. Robert L. Bloom writes in *History of Adams County, Pennsylvania, 1700–1990* (Gettysburg: Adams County Historical Society, 1992): "Tradition exists that a fort was erected
just north of Arendtsville, another in Butler Township, one between Two Taverns and Bon-
neauville, another near Gulden's in Straban Township, and one located in Latimore Township. It seems hardly possible that such forts, if indeed they had been built in the central and

eastern parts of the county, would have provided much protection to Adams Countians to the west" (n.5, 18).

The present author has learned that a blockhouse, possibly the above-mentioned one "in Butler township," was erected on 'Possum Creek, at the point where Stone Jug Road crosses it and near the site where David McConaughy, active in local defense, had a mill. This would have been a few miles from Christ Church.

68. Hans Hamilton to [?], April 4, 1756, *PA,* 1st series, 2:611–12.

69. *Forts,* 391.

70. Thomas Barton to Richard Peters, August 22, 1756, *PA,* 1st series, 2:756.

71. Thomas Barton to Governor William Hunter Morris, August 21, 1756, *PA,* 1st series, 2:755.

72. William Denny to [?], July 21, 1757, *PA,* 1st series, 3:235.

73. Hunter, *Forts,* 392.

74. Armstrong's official report is perhaps the best; see Colonel John Armstrong's Account of the Expedition against [the] Kittanning, 1756, September 14, 1756, *PA,* 1st series, 2:767–75. See also William A. Hunter, "Victory at Kittaning," *PH* 23 (1956): 376–407; and James P. Myers, Jr., "Pennsylvania's Awakening: the Kittanning Raid of 1756," *PH* 66 (1999): 399–420.

75. Robert Hunter Morris to [?], September 1756, Gratz MSS., Case 15, Box 18, HSP.

76. Hunter, "Victory at Kittanning," 404–5.

77. Thomas Barton to Thomas Penn, Feb. 28, 1757, Penn Manuscripts, Official Correspondence, 8:239, HSP.

78. Ibid. Hunter, "Victory at Kittanning," 406–7, also notes Barton's cautious tone.

79. Thomas Barton to William Smith, September 23, 1756, *Historical Collections,* ed. Perry, 2:560.

Interestingly, Armstrong separates several elements that occur in Barton's version and speaks of Jacobs more laconically, compelling one to wonder what actually transpired. In one place, Armstrong writes generally of an unnamed Indian who, asked to surrender, "said he was a Man and would not be a Prisoner." Later he describes only how "Capt Jacob[s] tumbled himself out at a Garret or Cock Loft Window, at which he was Shot." See Armstrong's Account of [the] Expedition against Kittanning, September 14, 1756, *PA,* 1st series, 2:769.

80. Ned Landsman, "Roots, Routes, and Rootedness: Diversity, Migration, and Toleration in Mid-Atlantic Pluralism," *EAS* 2 (2004): 269–309, identifies this fascination with martyrdom as inhering in Scots and Ulster-Scots culture. Writing of the Paxton Boys' pamphlets, Landsman notes that "the language was one of martyrdom and resistance, deriving from nearly ubiquitous popular traditions that long circulated in Ulster and western Scotland" (296).

Students of Irish history will also recognize the ideal as one often used to characterize Irish resistance to British power, a theme culminating in many of W. B. Yeats's works, particularly his "Easter 1916," as well as in several works by Padraig Pearse.

81. Thomas Barton to Richard Peters, April 11, 1758, *PA,* 1st series, 3:377.

82. See Richard Baird's Deposition, May 12, 1758, *PA,* 1st series,, 3:396–97.

83. See *PA,* 5th series,, 1:128–31.

84. George Stevenson to Richard Peters, April 30, 1758, *PA,* 1st series, 3:384.

85. Richard Peters to George Stevenson, May 3, 1758, *PA,* 1st series,, 3:386–87.

Peters also mentioned several names of local interest: Archibald McGrew, Thomas Armour, Robert Stevenson, Joseph Armstrong, David M'Conoway (i.e., McConaughy), Thomas Minshall, Benjamin Smith, and Hans Hamilton.

86. Ibid., 387.

87. George Stevenson to Richard Peters, May 21, 1758, *PA,* 1st series, 3:401.

88. See David Curtis Skaggs, *The Poetic Writings of Thomas Cradock, 1718–1770* (London: University of Delaware Press,1983), 38–39.

89. Thomas Barton to Thomas Cradock, August 10, 1759, Cradock Papers, Maryland Historical Society.

90. *PA,* 5th series, 1:128–31, lists the officers for the Third Battalion.

91. See James P. Myers, Jr., "The Reverend Thomas Barton's Conflict with Colonel John Armstrong, Ca. 1758," *Cumberland County History* 10 (1993): 3–14, particularly 5–9.

92. See *PA,* 5th series, 1:177.

93. In his Journal, July 7, 1758, Barton wrote of receiving "the Governor's Commission appointing me Chaplain to the 3[d] Battalion of the Pennsylvania Regiment . . . with a Letter from the Secretary apologizing for my not having the Preference of the other two."

94. Officers of the Third Battalion, Pennsylvania Regiment, to General Forbes, July 4, 1758, GD 45/2/33/2, Dalhousie Muniments, Scottish Record Office.

95. John Armstrong to Richard Peters [?], July 8, 1758, *PA,* 1st series, 3:447.

96. Members of the Episcopal Churches in the Counties of York and Cumberland, Pennsylvania, to General John Forbes, July 5, 1758, GD 45/2/56, Dalhousie Muniments, Scottish Record Office.

97. General John Forbes to Thomas Barton, July 9, 1758, copied by Barton for Richard Peters, July 18, 1758, Society Collection, HSP.

98. John Armstrong to Richard Peters, October 3, 1758, *PA,* 1st series, 3:551.

99. In March 1765, Captain James Smith and his company of local militia—the "Black Boys," so-called because they blackened their faces to conceal their identities—waylaid and destroyed a convoy sent out from Philadelphia and carrying contraband goods for trading with the Indians on the justification that the prohibited tomahawks, guns, powder, scalping knives, etc., would be used against the people of the frontier.

100. Robert Grant Crist, "John Armstrong: Proprietor's Man," Pennsylvania State University Ph.D. dissertation, 1981, examines Armstrong's fall from power; see 156–58 and chapter 8 (161–92).

101. Samuel Chew to Charles Ridgely, September 5, 1754, *A Calendar of Ridgely Family Letters, 1742–1899,* ed. deValinger, and Shaw, 1:84.

CHAPTER 2. "TREATED LIKE A CRIMINAL"

1. Thomas Barton to William Smith, October 28, 1755, S, I, 19–6–58, the Francis Lister Hawks Manuscript Collection, Records of the General Convention, Archives of the Episcopal Church, USA.

2. *Unanimity and Public Spirit,* A SERMON Preached at CARLISLE, And some other Episcopal Churches in the Counties of *YORK* and *CUMBERLAND,* soon after GENERAL BRADDOCK'S Defeat, Published by particular REQUEST. By the Reverend Mr. *THOMAS BARTON,* MISSIONARY to the said CHURCHES. To which is prefixed, A LETTER from the Reverend Mr. *SMITH,* Provost of the College of *Philadelphia,* concerning the Office and Duties of a *Protestant Ministry,* especially in Times of public Calamity and Danger, was published by Franklin and Hall, Philadelphia, September 1755.

3. Thomas Barton to William Smith, October 28, 1755, S, I., 19–6–58, Hawks MS. Collection, Episcopal Archives.

4. William Smith to the Archbishop of Canterbury, October 22, 1755, *Historical Collections Relating to the American Colonial Church,* 2: *Pennsylvania,* ed. William S. Perry (Hartford: the Church Press, 1871), 558.

5. That is, Barton's small plantation situated south of Mud Run, Reading township, in present-day Adams county. The glebe lands adjoining Christ Church in Huntington township had not yet been cleared.

6. Thomas Barton to Richard Peters, July 30, 1755, Peters Papers, 4:36, HSP.

7. Anticipating exactly such criticism, Smith sought to neutralize it at the outset. See, for example, "A Letter," *Unanimity,* vi–vii, where he promises "to strip such Objections of their false Varnish, and shew that to admit them in their full Force, tends evidently to involve the World in *Error* and *Slavery.*"

8. Richard Peters to Thomas Penn [?], September 16, 1756, Penn Papers, Official Correspondence, HSP.

9. William Smith to the Bishop of Oxford, [November 1, 1756], *Historical Collections,* ed. Perry, 2:556.

10. Albert Frank Gegenheimer, *William Smith: Educator and Churchman, 1727–1803* (Philadelphia: University of Pennsylvania Press, 1943), 127–36, details Smith's controversial career during these years.

11. William Smith to the Archbishop of Canterbury, October 22, 1755, *Historical Collections,* ed. Perry, 2:558.

12. Ibid.

13. Ibid. Here and elsewhere (for example, William Smith to the Bishop of Oxford [November 1, 1756], *Historical Collections,* ed. Perry, 2:556) Smith maintains that his initial letter, which supposedly inspired Barton, was duly published with Barton's sermon; yet the printed letter, because it also comments on Barton's sermon, is actually a later, expanded version of the original (Horace W. Smith, *Life and Correspondence the Rev. William Smith,* 2 vols. [Philadelphia: A. George, 1879–80], 1:110–18, reprints the original letter to Barton).

14. Preface, *Unanimity,* iii.

15. See Gegenheimer, *William Smith,* 198–200, for several contemporary assessments.

16. *Unanimity,* v.

17. Ibid.

18. Ibid., vi. Evidently, Smith is here quoting directly from some source.

19. Ibid., xiii.

20. Ibid.

21. Ibid., xiv.

22. Ibid., xiv–xv.

23. Ibid., ix.

24. Ibid., xvi.

25. Ibid., 10.

26. Ibid., 4.

27. The Paxton Boys' affair has attracted considerable discussion. The following selections provide an introduction to the significant issues: Brooke Hindle, "The March of the Paxton Boys," *WMQ,* 3rd Series, 3 (1946): 461–86; Krista Camenzind, "Violence, Race. And the Paxton Boys," in *Friends and Enemies in Penn's Woods: Indians, Colonists, and the Racial Construction of Pennsylvania,* ed. William A. Pencak and Daniel K. Richter (University Park, Pennsylvania: Penn State University Press, 2004), 201–20; James E. Crowley, "The Paxton Disturbance and Ideas of Order in Pennsylvania Politics," *PH* 37 (1970): 317–

39; and Daniel K. Richter, *Facing East from Indian Country: a Native History of Early America* (Cambridge, Mass.: Harvard University Press, 2001), 201–8.

28. *Unanimity,* 6.

29. Ibid., 7.

30. Ibid., 9–10.

31. Ibid., 13–14.

32. Thomas Barton to the Secretary, November 8, 1756, SPG Letter Books, Series B, vol. 21, no, 1.

33. Barton wrote: "I receiv'd lately . . . the Society's Instructions to their Missionaries in North America, which are very seasonable & justly adopted to our present Circumstances; And if duly observ'd & properly inforc'd, may do infinite Service to our bleeding Country" (ibid.).

34. *Instructions,* 4–5.

35. Ibid., 5.

36. He does speak of his military activities elsewhere, however; see, for example, Thomas Barton to Richard Peters, April 11, 1758, *PA,* 1st series, 3:377.

37. Thomas Barton to the Secretary, 8 November 1756, SPG Letter Books, Series B, vol. 21, no. 1.

38. The correspondence is catalogued in the Hawks MS. Collection, Episcopal Archives, as follows: (1) Barton to Smith, S, I, 14–6–53/ 15–6–54/ 16–6–55/ 18–6–57/ 19–6–58; S, III, 51–67–25; and (2) Smith to Barton, S, I, 17–6–56.

These are apparently the letters William S. Perry laconically refers to (2:567) in a note in his *Historical Collections* as being concerned with Barton's published sermon; he fails to comment on their significance.

39. William Smith to Thomas Barton, October 9, 1755, S, I, 17–6–56, Hawks MS. Collection, Episcopal Archives.

40. Roberts's sermon was apparently popular enough to justify at least six editions in 1745, published in Dublin and Belfast as well as London.

41. (London, 1745).

42. Thomas Barton to William Smith, October 19, 1755 and October 28, 1755, S, I, 18–6–57 and S, I, 19–6–58, Hawks MS. Collection, Episcopal Archives.

43. Thomas Barton to William Smith, October 28, 1755, S, I, 19–6–58, Hawks MS. Collection, Episcopal Archives.

44. Ibid.

45. Thomas Barton to William Smith, August 15, 1755, S, I, 14–6–53, Hawks MS. Collection, Episcopal Archives.

46. Ibid.

47. The publication was advertised in Franklin's *Pennsylvania Gazette,* September 25, 1755, 135, and October 2, 1755, 142.

48. Thomas Barton to William Smith, October 28, 1755, S, I, 19–6–58, Hawks MS. Collection, Episcopal Archives.

49. Barton's paranoia is discussed below in chapter 6.

50. Thomas Barton to William Smith, October 19, 1755, S, I, 18–6–57, Hawks MS. Collection, Episcopal Archives.

51. Thomas Barton to William Smith, October 28, 1755, S, I, 19–6–58, Hawks MS. Collection, Episcopal Archives.

52. See Thomas Barton to Thomas Penn, April 7, 1758, Penn Papers, Official Correspondence, 9:21, HSP, wherein Barton speaks of having requested "some Time ago . . . to be remov'd; & it is with Concern that I am oblig'd to renew my Application."

53. Thomas Barton to William Smith, November 2, 1755, *Historical Collections,* ed. Perry, 2:559.

54. William Smith to Thomas Barton, October 9, 1755, S, I, 17–6–56, Hawks MS. Collection, Episcopal Archives.

55. William Smith to the Archbishop of Canterbury, October 22, 1755, *Historical Collections,* ed. Perry, 2:557–58; Richard Peters to Thomas Penn, 16 September 1756, Penn Papers, Official Correspondence, 4:36, HSP; William Smith to the Bishop of Oxford, [November 1, 1756], *Historical Collections,* ed. Perry, 2:555–7; William Smith to the Secretary, November 1, 1756, ibid., 562–64; and William Smith to the Secretary, November 5, 1756, ibid., 565–66.

56. Thomas Barton to William Smith, October 28, 1755, S, I, 19–6–58, Hawks MS. Collection, Episcopal Archives.

57. It is difficult to envision Smith acting as he did without Peters's knowledge and, at least, tacit approval.

58. For a discussion of this, see James P. Myers, Jr., "Thomas Barton's Conflict with Colonel John Armstrong, ca. 1758," *Cumberland County History* 10 (1993): 5–9.

Chapter 3. *Memento Mori*

1. William A. Hunter, ed., "Thomas Barton and the Forbes Expedition," *PMHB* 95 (1971): 438, speculates that Barton might have "decided soon after the date of this final entry to terminate his military duties."

2. Ibid., 437.

3. *Pennsylvania Gazette,* December 14, 1758, no. 1564; and December 21, 1758, no. 1565.

4. Thomas Barton to the Secretary, 21 December 1759, SPG Letter Books, Series B, vol. 21, no. 4.

5. John Armstrong to [Richard Peters?], July 8, 1758, *PA,* 1st series, 3:447 (my emphasis).

6. Ibid.

7. Barton, "Journal," in the Appendix B to this volume, 172.

8. Thomas Barton to Richard Peters, July 18, 1758, Society Collection, HSP.

9. Ibid., 451.

10. Address of the Members of the Episcopal Churches of York and Cumberland Counties to General Forbes, July 5, 1758, GD 45/2/56, Dalhousie Muniments, Scottish Record Office.

11. John Armstrong to [Richard Peters ?], July 8, 1758, *PA,* 1st series, 3:447.

12. See Armstrong's letter, ibid., written the same day Barton brought himself to Forbes's attention, July 8, 1758: "he won't suffer himself to be Call'd a Chaplain to the Battalion, nor act under the Governor's Commission."

13. John Forbes to Thomas Barton, July 9, 1758 [misdated 1759], included in SPG Letter Books, Series B, vol. 21, no.3.

14. Thomas Barton to John Forbes, July 8, 1758 [misdated 1759], included in ibid., vol. 21, no. 2.

15. Ibid.

16. Thomas Penn to Thomas Barton, March 21, 1761, *Records of the States of the United States, Pennsylvania,* microfilm, E 2b, reel 3, unit 2, 2 (my emphasis).

17. John Armstrong to Richard Peters, October 3, 1758, *PA,* 1st series, 3:551.

18. Ibid.

19. John Armstrong to [Richard Peters?], July 8, 1758, *PA,* 1st series, 3:447.

20. See above, 41.

21. Thomas Barton to Richard Peters, August 22, 1756, *PA,* 1st series, 2:756.

22. Thomas Barton to Richard Peters, February 6, 1756, *PA,* 1st series, 2:568.

23. MS 157, pt. 1, Salem County Historical Society, Salem, N. J. This is one of three MSS. sermons owned by the Salem County Historical Society, identifiable by reason of handwriting and style as Barton's. The society also possesses portions of Barton's baptismal records for the years 1770–74.

24. Journal, Wednesday, September 6th. Subsequent citations from Barton's Journal may be keyed to the appropriate dates in the Journal text, Appendix B below.

25. Ibid. One of those who read Barton's manuscript was the Dublin-born Philadelphia printer and bookseller Mathew Carey, who printed this account verbatim in the April 1788 issue of his *Columbian Magazine.* Carey probably obtained the journal through one of Thomas's sons, William or Benjamin Smith, who, with Carey, belonged to the American Philosophical Society (see Hunter's note 165, Appendix B, above, 197). Benjamin Smith Barton was also a member of Carey's Hibernian Society.

26. See Hunter's note 231, Appendix B, 206 below.

27. Journal, Monday September 26th, 207 below.

28. See Hunter's note 231, Appendix B, 206 below.

29. John Armstrong to Richard Peters, October 3, 1758, *PA,* 1st series, 3:551.

30. See the *Pennsylvania Gazette,* December 14, 1758, no. 1564, and December 21, 1758, no. 1565.

31. Thomas Barton to Richard Peters, July 5, 1763, Peters Papers, 6:10, HSP.

32. Thomas Barton to Thomas Penn, April 28, 1773, repr. in the Lancaster County Historical Society *Journal* 23 (1919): 107. Barton's "Observations upon Public Roads & Proposals" appeared in the *Pennsylvania Gazette,* February 20, 1772, no. 2252, over the signature "Clericus."

33. See particularly the letters from Carlisle or Cumberland county in the following issues of the *Pennsylvania Gazette:* July 29, 1756, no. 1440, 3; February 12, 1756, no. 1416, 3; and June 10, 1756, no. 1433, 2.

34. December 14, 1758, no. 1564.

35. *Pennsylvania Gazette,* December 21, 1758, no. 1565.

36. H. M. J. Klein and William F. Diller, *The History of St. James' Church (Protestant Episcopal), 1744–1944* (Lancaster: St. James' Church, 1944), 30.

37. Thomas Penn to Thomas Barton, March 12, 1761, *Records of the U.S., Pennsylvania,* E 2b, reel 3, unit 2, 3.

38. Ibid.

39. Thomas Barton's Records of Marriages, 1759, St. James's Episcopal Church, Lancaster, Pa.

40. Thomas Barton to Thomas Secker, March 12, 1757, Miscellaneous File no. 15212, York County Historical Society.

41. Thomas Barton to the Secretary, November 8, 1756, SPG Letters Books, vol. 21, no. 1.

42. William Smith to the Secretary, November 1, 1756, *Historical Collections Relating to the American Colonial Church,* vol. 2: *Pennsylvania,* ed. William S. Perry (Hartford: the Church Press, 1871), 564.

43. Ibid., 565.

44. Ibid.

45. Ibid.

46. Klein and Diller, *History of St. James' Church,* 11–24, discuss Locke's and Craig's troubled ministries at St. James's Church, Lancaster.

47. Richard Peters to [Thomas Penn ?], September 16, 1756, Penn Papers, Official Cor., 4:36, HSP.

48. Thomas Penn to Richard Peters, December 11, 1756, *Records of the U.S., Pennsylvania,* E 2b, reel 2, unit 3, 44.

49. Thomas Penn to Thomas Barton, December 7, 1756, *Records of the United States, Pennsylvania,* E 2b, reel 2, unit 3, 401.

50. Philip Bearcroft to William Smith, July 1, 1757, *Historical Collections,* ed. Perry, 2:566, and Thomas Penn to Thomas Barton, January 10, 1759, William Barton, *Memoirs of the Life of David Rittenhouse* (Philadelphia: E. Parker, 1813), 289.

51. Thomas Barton to Thomas Penn, April, 7, 1758, Penn Papers, Official Cor., 9:21, HSP.

52. Thomas Penn to Thomas Barton, January 10, 1759, cited in William Barton, *Memoirs of Rittenhouse,* 289.

53. Klein and Diller, *St. James' Church History,* 30.

54. Thomas Barton to Secretary Philip Bearcroft, December 21, 1759, SPG Letter Books, Series B, vol. 21, no. 4.

55. For a discussion of the early problems besetting the first two SPG missionaries and St. James's Church, see Klein and Diller, *History of St. James' Church,* 11–24.

Chapter 4. "A Swarm of Sectaries"

1. Few immigrants from Ireland seem to have been as restless as Barton's friend, the former Irish Roman Catholic and deputy to Sir William Johnson, George Croghan. For discussions of Croghan see, Albert T. Volwiler, *George Croghan and the Westward Movement, 1741–1782* (Cleveland: Arthur H. Clark Co., 1926); Nicholas B. Wainwright, *George Croghan: Wilderness Diplomat* (Chapel Hill: Published for the Institute of Early American History and Culture by the University of North Carolina Press, 1959); and Robert G. Crist, *George Croghan of Pennsboro* (Harrisburg: Dauphin Deposit Trust Co., 1965). Sir William Johnson himself, scion of the landed Irish McShane family of county Meath, also seems to have shared this trait. For discussions of Johnson's career, see Arthur Pound and Richard Edwin Day, *Johnson of the Mohawks: a Biography of Sir William Johnson, Irish Immigrant, Mohawk War Chief, American Soldier, Empire Builder* (New York: Macmillan, 1930); Milton W. Hamilton, *Sir William Johnson: Colonial American, 1715–1763* (Port Washington, N.Y.: Kennikat Press 1976); and Fintan O'Toole, *White Savage: William Johnson and the Invention of America* (New York: Farrar, Straus and Giroux, 2005);

Restlessness, "unrootedness," is one of the underlying themes in Patrick Griffin's *The People with no Name: Ireland's Ulster Scots, America's Scots Irish and the Creation of a British Atlantic World, 1689–1764* (Princeton: Princeton University Press, 2001).

2. From Lancaster, Barton also served parishes in Pequea and Caernarvon. He later acquired additional congregations, such as those in nearby Delaware at White Clay Creek and New London. Eventually his circuit embraced two hundred miles.

3. Thomas Barton to the Secretary, November 8, 1756, SPG Letter Books, Series B, vol. 21, no. 1.

4. Alexander Murray to the Secretary, January 25, 1764, *Historical Collections Relating to the American Colonial Church,* ed. William S. Perry, vol. 2: *Pennsylvania* (Hartford: The Church Press, 1871), 358.

5. Barton's persistent financial hardship was, of course, the legacy of most SPG missionaries in colonial America. For a perceptive discussion of this problem and its influence on the success, or lack thereof, with which the itinerants executed their responsibilities, see John Calam, *Parsons and Pedagogues: the S.P.G. Adventure in American Education* (New York: Columbia University Press, 1971).

6. Thomas Barton to the Secretary, December 21, 1759, SPG Letter Books, Series B, vol. 21, no. 4. This does not contradict his statement that he moved to Lancaster in May (see above, 78). Edward Shippen in a letter of August 31, 1759 to his son speaks of Barton's having difficulty in obtaining housing for his family (Shippen Letter Books, American Philosophical Society); hence his remark to Secretary Philip Bearcroft indicates that by, presumably, November, he had resolved the problem.

7. Ibid.

8. William Smith to the Secretary, July 20, 1762, SPG Letter Books, Series B, vol. 21, no. 249, refutes accusations of forgery.

9. Thomas Barton to the Secretary, July 6, 1761, SPG Letter Books, Series B., vol. 21, no. 7.

10. Ibid. (Barton's emphasis).

11. William Smith to the Secretary, July 20, 1762, SPG Letter Books, Series B, vol. 21, no. 249.

12. Smith's paying off Barton's debt is the measure of his friendship and esteem. Smith, already secure in his quest to become a wealthy man, had a reputation for miserliness and not paying his own bills. Thomas Firth Jones, who discusses this character flaw in his biography of Smith, cites contemporary testimony to Smith's bad reputation: "there was some justice to [Benjamin Franklin's] saying that Smith did not pay his bills. William—son of James [secretary of the province of Pennsylvania]—Logan wrote to a potential landlord of Smith's, 'He is accounted so very bad a pay master that it may be difficult for thee to get thy rent from him.' And Dr. [Benjamin] Rush, in his summation of Smith's life, said, 'He seldom paid a debt without being sued or without a quarrel'" (*A Pair of Lawn Sleeves: a Biography of William Smith [1727–1803]* [Philadelphia: Chilton Book Co., 1972], 44).

13. Thomas Barton to the Secretary, May 8, 1760, SPG Letter Books, Series B., vol. 21, no. 5.

14. The phrase is from the letter cited at the very beginning of this chapter: Thomas Barton to the Secretary, November 16, 1764, SPG Letter Books, Series B, vol. 21, no. 14.

15. Thomas Barton to the Secretary, December 6, 1760, SPG Letter Books, Ser. B, vol. 21, no. 8

16. Ibid. Although a Lutheran, Kuhn also enjoyed pew privileges at St. James Church.

17. Ibid. Some of his congregation's disdain might explain why he had to approach two of his wealthier churchwardens for financial relief for the church's sexton, John Street, and his family; see Thomas Barton to William Atlee and Jasper Yeates, June 22, 1769, Stauffer Collection, HSP.

18. *Pennsylvania Gazette,* March 12, 1761, no. 1681.

19. Ibid., July 6, 1761, no. 1698.

20. See their request submitted on October 18, 1762, reprinted in H. M. J. Klein and William F. Diller, *History of St. James' Church (Protestant Episcopal), 1744–1944* (Lancaster: St. James's Church, 1944), 37–38.

21. Ibid., 43–44.

22. Carl Bridenbaugh, *Mitre and Sceptre: Transatlantic Faiths, Ideals, Personalities, and Politics, 1689–1775* (New York: Oxford University Press, 1962), 134.

23. Samuel E. Weber, *The Charity School Movement in Colonial Pennsylvania* (New York: Arno Press, 1969), 32–33.

24. Thomas Barton to the Secretary, November 8, 1756, SPG Letter Books, Series B, vol. 21, no. 1.

25. William Smith to the Secretary, December 1, 1753, cited in Weber, *The Charity School Movement,* 27.

26. William Smith to the Bishop of Oxford, [November 1, 1756], *Historical Collections,* ed. Perry, 2:556 (my emphasis).

27. Weber, *Charity School Movement,* 27. Smith's letter reveals darker motives, one he shared with Franklin who, with Smith, deemed German migrants as "Palatine boors" and "the greatest of all dangers to Pennsylvania" (cited in Jones, *Pair of Lawn Sleeves,* 13). Smith carried the denunciation further: "'The distressing prospect of approaching darkness and idolatry' was among them, Smith warned. . . . 'liberty is the most dangerous of all weapons, in the hands of those who do not know the use and value of it. . . .'" (ibid., 12).

28. Barton appears not to have felt the extreme bigotry evident in Smith and Benjamin Franklin, who also advocated measures to integrate the Germans. His appeal for unity in his published sermon *Unanimity* implies a more-than-expedient feeling, while his agreement to allow the congregation of Bender's Lutheran Church to use Christ Church until they were able to erect their own building offers further evidence of his tolerance. The accord he achieved with the Reformed and especially the Lutherans in Lancaster, moreover, intimates a degree of mutual respect between these German denominations and Barton not evident in Smith and Franklin. Barton's attitude toward such German "enthusiasts" as the Moravians is another matter, but, again, the conflict here is more clearly rooted in doctrinal rather than simply ethnic sentiments.

29. Thomas Barton to the Secretary, November 16, 1764, SPG Letter Books, Series B, vol. 21, no. 14.

30. Ibid.

31. Weber, *Charity School Movement,* 53.

32. Ibid.

33. Thomas Barton to the Secretary, December 6, 1760, SPG Letter Books, Ser, B., vol. 21, no. 8.

34. Ibid.

35. See James Logan to John Penn, July 21, 1729, Logan Letter Books, 3:302, HSP: "you may easily believe there are some grounds for the common Apprehension of the People, that if some speedy Method be not taken, [the Scots-Irish Presbyterians] will make themselves Proprietors of the Province."

36. Thomas Barton to the Secretary, December 6, 1760, SPG Letter Books, Series B., vol. 21, no. 8.

37. Thomas Barton to the Secretary, November 8, 1762, *Historical Collections,* ed. Perry, 2:343.

38. Thomas Barton to the Secretary, June 28, 1763, SPG Letter Books, Series B, vol. 21, no. 13.

39. Thomas Barton to the Secretary, November 8, 1762, *Historical Collections,* ed. Perry, 2:343.

40. For remarks on indigo, see Thomas Penn to Thomas Barton, February 11, 1762, *Records of the States of the United States, Pennsylvania,* microfilm, E 2b, reel 3, unit 2, 107; on hemp, see Thomas Penn to Thomas Barton, March 21, 1761, 2; on potash, hemp, and flax, see Thomas Penn to Thomas Barton, April 11, 1764, ibid., unit 3, 48–49; on marble and iron manufactur-

ing, see Thomas Penn to Thomas Barton, ibid., 49–50; and Thomas Barton to Thomas Penn, February 11, 1762, *Records of the States, Pennsylvania*, E 2b, reel 3, unit 2, 107.

41. Thomas Penn to Thomas Barton, February 11, 1762, ibid., 108.

42. Jones, *Pair of Lawn Sleeves*, 84.

43. Thomas Penn to Thomas Barton, February 11, 1762, *Records of the States, Pennsylvania*, E 2b, reel 3, unit 2,108.

44. *Pennsylvania Gazette*, February 20, 1772, no. 2252.

45. Thomas Barton to Thomas Penn, April 28, 1773, repr. in "The Beginnings of Artificial Roads in Pennsylvania," Lancaster County Historical Society *Journal*, 23 (1919), 107. (This article also reprints Barton's original article in the *Pennsylvania Gazette*, 99–107.)

46. Thomas Penn to Thomas Barton, February 11, 1762, *Records of the States, Pennsylvania*, E 2b, reel 3, unit 2, 108.

47. *Charter, Laws, Catalogue of Books . . . of the Juliana Library Company* (Philadelphia, 1766), 56.

48. Thomas Penn to Thomas Barton, March 21, 1761 and September 27, 1765, *Records of the States, Pennsylvania*, E 2b, reel 3, unit 2, 2; and ibid., 314–15.

49. Thomas Firth Jones, however, reminds the modern reader that "in that day . . . the M.A. was awarded to all who held the B.A. for three years and came to apply for it" (*Pair of Lawn Sleeves*, 52).

50. Thomas Barton to the Secretary, 28, June, 1763, SPG Letter Books, Series B, vol. 21, no. 13.

51. Thomas Barton to Richard Peters, July 5, 1763, Peters Papers, 6:10, HSP.

52. Thomas Barton to the Secretary, June 28, 1763, SPG Letter Books, Series B, vol. 21, no. 13.

Chapter 5. "A Stark Naked Presbyterian"

1. The following provide background on the Paxton disturbances: Brooke Hindle, "The March of the Paxton Boys," *WMQ*, 3rd ser., 3 (1946): 461–86; John R. Dunbar, ed., "Introduction," *The Paxton Papers* (The Hague: Martinus Nijhoff, 1957), 3–51; Hubertis Cummings, "The Paxton Killings," *Journal of Presbyterian History* 44 (1966): 219–43; James E. Crowley, "The Paxton Disturbance and Ideas of Order in Pennsylvania Politics," *PH* 37 (1970): 317–39; James Kirby Martin, "The Return of the Paxton Boys and the Historical State of the Pennsylvania Frontier, 1764–1774," *PH* 38 (1971): 117–33; Peter A. Butzin, "Politics, Presbyterians and the Paxton Riots, 1763–64," *JPH* 51 (1973): 70–84; Alden T. Vaughan, "Frontier Banditti and the Indians: The Paxton Boys' Legacy, 1765–1775," *PH* 51 (1984): 1–29; Lorett Treese, *The Storm Gathering: the Penn Family and the American Revolution* (University Park: Pennsylvania State University Press, 1992), 29–47; James P. Myers, Jr., "The Rev. Thomas Barton's Authorship of *The Conduct of the Paxton Men, Impartially Represented* (1764), *PH* 61 (1994): 155–84; Patrick Griffin, *The People with no Name: Ireland's Ulster Scots, America's Irish, and the Creation of a British Atlantic World* (Princeton: Princeton University Press, 2001); Daniel K. Richter, *Facing East from Indian Country: a Native History of Early America* (Cambridge, Mass.: Harvard University Press, 2001), 201–8; and Krista Camenzind, "Violence, Race. And the Paxton Boys," in *Friends and Enemies in Penn's Woods: Indians, Colonists, and the Racial Construction of Pennsylvania*, ed. William A. Pencak and Daniel K. Richter (University Park: Pennsylvania State University Press, 2004), 201–20.

Richard Slotkin, *Regeneration through Violence: the Mythology of the American Frontier, 1600–1800* (Middletown, Conn.: Wesleyan University Press, 1973) offers a useful introduction to the general theme of frontier violence.

2. Dunbar, *Paxton Papers,* reprints twenty-eight of these works which he feels bear directly on the Paxton affair. He rejects another thirty-five as insufficiently concerned with the troubles. See *Paxton Papers,* 50.

3. However, W. H. Egle, *History of the Counties of Dauphin and Lebanon* (Philadelphia: Everts & Peck, 1883), 68, attributed it to the noted Philadelphia Presbyterian divine John Ewing. In this, he was followed by at least one historian of note, Hubertis M. Cummings, *Scots Breed and Susquehanna* (Pittsburgh: University of Pittsburgh Press, 1964), 135–37, and "The Paxton Killings," 243.

4. Although he makes a valiant attempt to explain Barton's writing of *The Conduct,* Marvin F. Russell, "Thomas Barton and Pennsylvania's Colonial Frontier," *PH* 46 (1979): 326–29, ultimately tries to justify the "inconsistencies and shortcomings" in part with Barton's confusion, "his own inner turmoil."

5. See William Barton, *Memoirs of the Life of David Rittenhouse* (Philadelphia: E. Parker, 1813), 146–50, where he discusses Rittenhouse's role in turning back the rioters.

6. David Rittenhouse to Thomas Barton, February 16, 1764, ibid., 147–49.

7. Franklin's *Narrative* is reprinted in Dunbar, ed., *Paxton Papers,* 55–75.

8. William Barton, *Memoirs of Rittenhouse,* 149–50, n. 47.

9. Ibid., 111–12, n. 23.

10. See H. M. J. Klein and William F. Diller, *The History of St. James' Church (Protestant Episcopal), 1744–1944* (Lancaster: St. James' Church, 1944), 30–32.

11. Abraham Neff to Thomas Barton, November 5, 1763, Lancaster County Deed, H 181, microfilm, Lancaster County Historical Society, Lancaster, Pa.

12. As the Crown's superintendent for Indian affairs, northern division, Sir William Johnson acted as guardian for the Conestogas, a handful of survivors of the once powerful Susquehannocks who had been nearly decimated by the Iroquois and Marylanders.

13. Thomas Barton to Sir William Johnson, "supposed May 1768," *Documentary History of the State of New York,* ed. E. B. O'Callaghan and B. Fernow (Albany: Weed, Parsons, & Co., 1851), 4:381–82.

14. Thomas Barton to Sir William Johnson, July 26, 1770, *The Papers of Sir William Johnson,* 13 vols. (Albany, 1921–62), 7:813.

15. "The Bartons of Lancaster in 1776," Lancaster County Historical Society *Journal* 52 (1948): 213–17.

16. "AN ANSWER, TO THE PAMPHLET Entituled [sic] the Conduct of the *Paxton Men,* impartially represented: Wherein the ungenerous Spirit of the AUTHOR is Manifested, &c. And the spotted GARMENT pluckt off" (Philadelphia, 1764); reprinted in Dunbar, ed., 317–37.

17. Dunbar ed., *Paxton Papers,* 334.

18. *Conduct of the Paxton Men,* 3.

19. Ibid.

20. Ibid., n., 3.

21. "A DECLARATION AND REMONSTRANCE OF the distressed and bleeding Frontier Inhabitants Of the Province of *Pennsylvania,* Presented by them to the Honourable the GOVERNOR AND ASSEMBLY of the Province. . . " (n.p., 1764); reprinted in Dunbar, ed., 99–110.

22. *Conduct of the Paxton Men,* 9 (my emphasis).

23. Ibid.

24. Ibid., 32.

25. I.e., John Trenchard and Thomas Gordon.

26. *Conduct of the Paxton Men,* 23.

27. Ibid., 34.

28. Thomas Barton to William Smith, October 28, 1755, the Hawks Manuscript Collection, Records of the General Convention, Archives of the Episcopal Church, U.S.A., S,I,19–6–58; Thomas Barton to William Smith, November 2, 1755, *Historical Collections Relating to the American Colonial Church,* William S. Perry, ed., vol. 2: *Pennsylvania* (Hartford. Conn.: the Church Press, 1871), 559; Barton to Richard Peters, July 5, 1763, Peters Papers, 6:10, HSP.

29. Thomas Barton to William Smith, September 23, 1756, *Historical Collections,* ed. Perry, 2:560.

30. Thomas Barton to the Secretary, November 8, 1756, SPG Letter Books, Series B, vol. 21, no. 1; Thomas Barton to the Secretary, June 28, 1763, ibid., no. 13; Thomas Barton to the Secretary, December 6, 1760, ibid., no. 8; Thomas Barton to the Secretary, January 23, 1766, *Historical Collections,* ed. Perry, 2:400.

31. Thomas Barton to the Secretary, November 16, 1764, SPG Letter Books, Series B., vol. 21, no. 14 (my emphasis).

32. Thomas Barton to Sir William Johnson, "supposed May 1768," *Documentary History of New York,* 4:382.

33. Not all Presbyterian frontiersmen viewed the Conestogas so hostilely. John Harris and the Rev. John Elder, for instance, were known for their moderation. Even the acclaimed Indian fighter, the "Hero of Kittanning," and Barton's old rival from Carlisle, Colonel John Armstrong, expressed what is probably a more accurate apprisal of the victims: "I should be very sorry that ever the people of this County [i.e., Cumberland] should attempt revenging their injuries on the heads of a few inoffensive superannuated Savages, whome nature had already devoted to the dust" (John Amstrong to Gov. John Penn, December 28, 1763, *PA,* 1st series, 4:152.

34. *Conduct of the Paxton Men,* headnote, 3.

35. Ibid., 30.

36. William Barton, *Memoirs of Rittenhouse,* 147, n. 47.

37. Cited in ibid., 148, n. 47.

38. Ibid., 101–2.

39. John D. Crimmins, *St. Patrick's Day: Its Celebration in New York and Other American Places, 1737–1845* (New York: John D. Crimmins, 1902); and Richard C. Murphy and Lawrence J. Mannion, *The History of the Society of the Friendly Sons of Saint Patrick in the City of New York, 1784 to 1955* (New York; [no publisher], 1962) discuss St. Patrick's cultural importance and popularity among all Irish immigrants of colonial America.

40. See above, 37, n. 56.

41. See Crimmins, *St. Patrick's Day,* 11, 18–19; and Murphy and Mannion, *History . . . of the Friendly Sons of St. Patrick,* 11–13.

42. Thomas Barton to the Rev. Mr. [William] Frazer, October 5, 1779, Society Collections, HSP.

43. Paralleling this stylistic analysis, Carla Mulford has analyzed Benjamin Franklin's authorship of the *Narrative of the Late Massacres.* See "*Caritas* and Capital: Franklin's *Narrative of the Late Massacres*," in J. A. Leo Lemay, ed., *Reappraising Benjamin Franklin: A Bicentennial Perspective* (Newark: University of Delaware Press, 1993), 347–58. See also

Lemay, *The Career of Benjamin Franklin, 1726–1776: New Attributions and Reconsiderations* (Newark: University of Delaware Press, 1986) for a general discussion of attribution of authorship based on stylistic analysis.

44. Barton's *Unanimity,* of course, was plagiarized from Samuel Roberts's 1745 sermon, thus complicating the stylistic analysis here. That said, it might be argued that Barton might have been attracted to Roberts's sermon in part because of stylistic affinities it shared with Barton's own prose and, further, that Barton himself might have continued to employ stylistic qualities he found felicitous in Roberts.

45. These adjectives might usefully be employed to help define William Smith's more sophisticated and varied style.

46. *Metonymy* denotes the figure of speech which uses the name of one thing for that of another closely associated with it, as in "fifteen guns" for "fifteen bandits." *Synecdoche* describes using a part for the whole, as in "hands" for, say, "cowboys."

47. Anglo-Irishman Laurence Sterne also employs the dash consistently to mark the ends of his sentences.

48. Thomas Barton to the Secretary, June 28, 1763, SPG. Letter Books, Series B, vol. 21, no. 13; Thomas Barton to Richard Peters, July 5, 1763, Peters Papers, 6:10, HSP; *Pennsylvania Gazette,* July 28, 1763, no. 1805.

49. Thomas Barton to the Secretary, November 8, 1756, SPG Letter Books, Series B., vol. 21, no. 1.

50. Thomas Barton to Thomas Penn, April 7, 1758, Penn Papers, Official Correspondence, 9:21, HSP.

51. Thomas Barton to the Secretary, November 8, 1756, SPG Letter Books, Series B, vol. 21, no. 1; and Thomas Barton to Richard Peters, July 5, 1763, 6:10, Peters Papers, HSP.

52. Thomas Barton to the Secretary, June 28, 1763, SPG Letter Books, Series B, vol. 21, no. 13. Figures of speech and patterns of alliteration link the extended passage from which this quotation is taken with parts of an anonymous letter to the *Pennsylvania Gazette* proclaiming the fall of Fort Duquesne in 1758, strongly suggesting the same author; compare these two citations: from the *Pennsylvania Gazette,* December 14, 1758, no. 1564: we are now "in the quiet and peaceable Possession of the finest and most fertile Country of America. . . . our Back Settlements, instead of being frightful Fields of Blood, will once more smile with Peace and Plenty"; and from [Barton],*The Conduct of the Paxton Men,* 16: those "who have so long suffer'd the Province to bleed beneath the *Savage Knife,* its fairest and most fruitful Fields to be deluged in Gore. . . ."

53. Thomas Barton to Thomas Penn, February 28, 1757, Penn Papers, Official Correspondence, 8:239, HSP.

54. Thomas Barton to Richard Peters, July 5, 1763, Peters Papers, 6:10, HSP; *Pennsylvania Gazette,* 28 July 1763, no. 1805; Barton to the Secretary, November 8, 1756, SPG Letter Books, Series B., vol. 21, no. 1; Barton to Thomas Penn, February 28, 1757, Penn Papers, Official Correspondence, 8:239, HSP.

55. Thomas Barton to William Smith, November 2, 1755, Perry, ed., *Historical Collections,* 2:559; Barton to William Smith, October 28, 1755, Hawks MS. Collection, S,I,19–6–58, Episcopal Archives; Thomas Barton, *Unanimity and Public Spirit* (Philadelphia, 1755), 13 and iii; Barton to the Secretary, November 8, 1756, SPG Letter Books, Series B, vol. 21, no. 1; Barton to Thomas Penn, April 7, 1758, Penn Papers, Official Correspondence, 9:21, HSP; Barton to Richard Peters, April 11, 1758, *PA,* 1st series, 3:377; Barton to Richard Peters, July 18, 1758, ibid., 3:452.

56. Thomas Barton to the Secretary, January 8, 1779, SPG Letter Books, Series B, vol. 21, no. 36; and Thomas Barton to the Secretary, October 25, 1779, ibid., no. 37.

57. The other, more complex alliterative patterns occurring throughout *The Conduct* merit careful comparison with Barton's established predilection for this technique.

58. Thomas Barton to the Secretary, November 8, 1756, SPG Letter Books, Series B, vol. 21, no. 1; Thomas Barton to the Bishop of Oxford, March 12, 1757, transcription, Miscellaneous File, no. 15212, York County Historical Society, York, Pa.; and *Pennsylvania Gazette,* July 28, 1763, no. 1805.

59. See Thomas Barton to the Secretary, November 8, 1756, SPG Letter Books, Series B, vol. 21, no. 1; Thomas Barton to Thomas Penn, February 28, 1757, Penn Papers, Official Correspondence, 8:239, HSP. Compare these with *The Conduct*'s author's speaking of himself: "I and my Neighbours have been melancholy Eye Witnesses" to "Scenes of Destruction & Desolation" (30).

60. Thomas Barton to Gov. Robert Morris, August 21, 1756, *PA,* 1st series, 2:755; Barton to Thomas Penn, February 28, 1757, Penn Papers, Official Correspondence, 8:239, HSP; Barton to Richard Peters, July 5, 1763, Peters Papers, 6:10, HSP; and *Pennsylvania Gazette,* July 28, 1763, no. 1805.

61. See note 44.

62. Thomas Barton, *Unanimity and Public Spirit,* 14.

63. Ibid., 15.

64. Ibid., 14–15.

65. Ibid., 14.

66. *Conduct of the Paxton Men,* 33.

67. Ibid.

68. For an account of William's life, see Milton Rubincam, "A Memoir of the Life of William Barton, A.M. (1754–1817)," *PH* 12 (1945): 179–93.

69. Rhoda Barber, "History of the Founding of Wrightsville," 1830, MS. in HSP.

70. Thomas Barton to the Secretary, November 16, 1764, SPG Letter Books, Series B, vol. 21, no. 14.

71. Ibid.

72. Ibid.

73. See above, 54–61.

74. *Proselyting:* "converting."

75. Thomas Barton to the Secretary, November 16, 1764, SPG Letter Books, Series B, vol. 21, no. 14.

76. Ibid.

77. Ibid.

78. Ibid.

79. Ibid.

80. Ibid.

81. Ibid.

82. Ibid.

83. Ibid.

84. Ibid.

85. A list of Johnson papers destroyed by fire includes the following note: "a letter from Thomas Barton declaring esteem and commending John Henry, gunsmith, who wishes to settle in Detroit" (*Johnson Papers,* 4:180). Placement of the note suggests the letter dates from about August 2, 1763. The Henrys were a prominent Lancaster family. William Henry

the artificer and gunsmith belonged for a time to Barton's congregation. Another mysterious early entry in the Johnson list involves Barton's *Conduct*. A later compilation of destroyed documents lists "a pamphlet called the *Conduct of the Paxtoners*" (*Johnson Papers*, 4:383). Because this last dates from April 1–3, 1764 and Barton's tract was issued sometime after March 17, 1764, it appears that Barton may have lost little time in sending a copy to Johnson. The only Paxton pamphlet apparently mentioned among the Johnson papers, one suspects that Barton sent Johnson, the Crown's Indian agent for the northern colonies who was renowned for his fairness and sympathy for the Indians, the copy to explain how he came to write it. The explanation, if that were the case, and Barton's dilemma might also have led to his being invited to Johnson Hall in the autumn of 1765. As the author of *The Conduct*, it is unlikely that Barton would have been welcomed at Johnson Hall unless Sir William possessed an understanding beyond what the pamphlet's surface allowed.

86. Thomas Barton to Sir William Johnson, October 7, 1765, *Johnson Papers*, 11:954–55. The letter was sent from New York City in the course of Barton's return from the Mohawk Valley.

87. In another tactic to register his impatience to leave, Barton gratuitously excerpted a letter from General Thomas Gage (July 12, 1765) in which Gage's response makes clear that Barton had inquired about a chaplaincy: "Sir, There is not at present any Chaplain nominated for the Garrison of Montreal; if you should think it for your advantage to accept of that in preference to the livings you now enjoy, you will please to acquaint me" (Thomas Barton to the Secretary, *Historical Collections*, ed. Perry, 2:401–2).

88. Thomas Penn to Thomas Barton, June 17, 1767, *Records of the States of the United States: Pennsylvania*, microfilm, E.2b, reel 4, unit 1, 132–34, refers to Barton's earlier wish to move to Maryland. See also William Smith to Sir William Johnson, June 22, 1767, *Johnson Papers*, 5:568–70.

89. Thomas Penn to Thomas Barton, September 27, 1765, *Records of the States, Pennsylvania*, E.2b, reel 3, unit 3, 314–5: "I was greatly pleased to hear you was [*sic*] recovered from a dangerous illness you were seized with in the Lower Counties [i.e., Delaware], and heartily wish you a continuance of your health and all other blessings; assuring you of all the good offices in my power."

90. Thomas Barton to James Burd, April 28, 1766, Shippen Papers, 6:147, HSP. One wonders if his participation in the pamphlet war were being bruited about the taverns and streets of Lancaster.

91. Thomas Penn to Thomas Barton, June 17, 1767, *Records of the States, Pennsylvania*, E.2b, reel 4, unit 1, 132–34; Thomas Barton to James Hamilton, May 9, 1768, Penn-Bailey Collection, HSP.

92. Thomas Barton to Sir William Johnson, May 1768, *Documentary History of New York*, 4:381–83; Barton to Richard Peters, June 2, 1768, Peters Papers, HSP, 6:58–59; Barton to Edmund Physick, December 18, 1770, reprinted in *PMHB* 4 (1880): 119.

93. William Smith did not return to Philadelphia until the spring of 1764; see Albert Frank Gegenheimer, *William Smith: Educator and Churchman, 1727–1803* (Philadelphia, 1943), 73.

94. Although he might have been speaking as the member of a party responding to the tactics of unscrupulous adversaries, Barton registers his distaste for dirty political campaigning in at least two letters. See Thomas Barton to Richard Peters, September 28, 1756, and October 2, 1761, Peters Papers, 4:74 and 5:103, HSP.

95. See Theodore Thayer, *Pennsylvania Politics and the Growth of Democracy, 1740–1776* (Harrisburg: the Pennsylvania Historical and Museum Commission, 1953); G. B. War-

den, "The Proprietary Group in Pennsylvania, 1754–1764," *WMQ,* 3rd ser., 21 (1964): 367–89; James E. Crowley, "The Paxton Disturbance," 336–37; James Kirby Martin, "Return of the Paxton Boys," 117–33, particularly 129–33; Peter A. Butzin, "Politics, Presbyterians and the Paxton Riots," 76–84; and Michael Zuckerman, "The Decay of Deference on the Provincial Periphery," *EAS* 1 (2007): 1–29. Joseph S. Foster, *In Pursuit of Equal Liberty: George Bryan and the Revolution in Pennsylvania* (University Park: Pennsylvania State University Press, 1994), 35–57, has also covered this development well.

96. Thomas Barton to Edmund Physick, December 18, 1770, reprinted in *PMHB* 4 (1880): 119.

97. See Rhoda Barber MS., HSP, and Robert Proud *The History of Pennsylvania, in North America . . .* (Philadelphia, 1798), 2:329. Benjamin Franklin was one of the first to propose that the Proprietary party colluded with the Paxtonians: "Why will the Government, by its Conduct, strengthen the Suspicions, (groundless no doubt) that it has come to a private Understanding with those Murderers, and that Impunity for their past Crimes is to be the Reward of their future *political* Services?" ("Preface to Galloway's Speech, 1764," in *The Papers of Benjamin Franklin,* ed. Leonard W. Labaree, Volume. 11: *January 1 through December 31, 1764* [New Haven and London, 1967], 305; see also 107 and 378.)

98. Dunbar, ed., *Paxton Papers,* 22–23.

99. See the satiric broadside "An Address of Thanks to the Wardens of Christ Church and St. Peters . . . in the Name of all Presbyterian Ministers in Pennsylvania" (Philadelphia, 1764).

100. *Answer to "The Conduct of the Paxton Men,"* in Dunbar, ed., *Paxton Papers,* 334.

101. Although Benjamin Franklin and Joseph Galloway lost their seats, Quakers effectively retained their majority in the Assembly. See Butzin, "Politics, Presbyterians, and the Paxton Riots," 83, and Crowley, "The Paxton Disturbance," 337.

102. See George Stevenson to William Henry, September 25, 1777, and John Carothers to William Henry, September 25, 1777, *PA,* 1st series, 5:634–35, for accusations that Barton knew of the conspiracy to seize the arsenals; and George Bryan to General Washington, March 5, 1779, *PA,* 1st series, 7:225–26, for denunciations of his Tory activities. The Tory plot is discussed below, 139–41.

CHAPTER 6. NO "CANTING PARSON"

1. John Penn to Sir William Johnson, December 31, 1763, *The Papers of Sir William Johnson,* 13 vols. (Albany: the University of the State of New York, 1921–62), 4:284–85.

2. For example, see the following letters in the *Johnson Papers:* Sir William Johnson to John Penn, January 20, 1764, 11:17–19; Sir William Johnson to Thomas Gage, January 27, 1764, 4:307–11; Sir William Johnson to John Penn, February 9, 1764, 4:322–24; Sir William Johnson to John Penn, February 27, 1764, 4:343; Sir William Johnson to Cadwallder Colden, January 27, 1764 and February 28, 1764, 4: 305–7 and 345–47.

3. See the note in the *Johnson Papers,* 4:180, indicating the letter as one destroyed by fire.

4. *Johnson Papers,* 4:383.

5. Ibid.

6. Francis Wade to Sir William Johnson, March 31, 1766, *Johnson Papers,* 5:140–42.

7. See Thomas Barton to Sir William Johnson, November 9, 1765, *Johnson Papers,* 4:867.

8. Thomas Barton to Sir William Johnson, October 7, 1765, *Johnson Papers,* 11:954.

9. Thomas Barton to Sir William Johnson, November 9, 1765, *Johnson Papers,* 4:28.

10. Thomas Barton to Sir William Johnson, November 30, 1765, Gratz Collection, Colonial Clergy, Case 8, Box 21, HSP.

11. See Charles W. Rutschky, Jr., "Thomas Barton's Collection of Minerals," *PH* 8 (1941): 148–50; and "The Reverend Thomas Barton, Amateur Scientist of Compassville, Pennsylvania," Pennsylvania Academy of Science, *Proceedings* 15 (1941): 200–3.

12. *Transactions of the American Philosophical Society* (Philadelphia, 1779), 1:338–39.

13. In addition to Rutschky's articles, the following offer general discussions of Barton's scientific activities and his role in supporting Rittenhouse's making of the Orreries: William Barton, *Memoirs of the Life of David Rittenhouse* (Philadelphia: E. Parker, 1813); Edward Ford, *David Rittenhouse: Astronomer-Patriot, 1732–1796* (Philadelphia: University of Pennsylvania Press, 1946); Howard C. Rice, Jr., *The Rittenhouse Orrery: Princeton's Eighteenth-Century Planetarium, 1767–1954* (Princeton: Princeton University Library, 1954); Brooke Hindle, *David Rittenhouse* (Princeton: Princeton University Press, 1964); and James P. Myers, Jr., "The Missionary and the Clockmaker: a Saga of Two Brothers-in-Law," *Pennsylvania Heritage,* 20 no. 1 (Winter 1994): 4–9.

14. Samuel Auchmuty was rector of Trinity Church in New York City, 1764–77.

15. Thomas Barton to Sir William Johnson, October 7, 1765, *Johnson Papers,* 11:955.

16. Thomas Barton to Sir William Johnson, November 9, 1765, *Johnson Papers,* 4:867.

17. Ibid., 866–67.

18. Ibid., 865.

19. Ibid., 867.

20. See the *Johnson Papers,* 4:877.

21. Thomas Barton to Sir William Johnson, October 31, 1766, *Johnson Papers,* 5:402.

22. Irish-born Cadwallader Colden was lieutenant governor of New York from 1761 to 1776, the year of his death. Something of a philosopher and scientist, he was known as a forceful defender of the crown's interests against encroachments by the colonial factions.

23. C. F. Pascoe, *Two Hundred Years of the S.P.G.: an Historical Account of the Society for the Propagation of the Gospel in Foreign Parts, 1701–1900,* 2 vols. (London: the SPG, 1901), 1:65–71.

24. Cited in Frank J. Klingberg, "Sir William Johnson and the Society for the Propagation of the Gospel (1749–1774)," *Historical Magazine of the Protestant Episcopal Church* 8 (1939): 5.

25. Ibid., 8–11.

26. Thomas Barton to Sir William Johnson, October 7, 1765, *Johnson Papers,* 11:955 (Barton's emphasis).

27. Sir William Johnson to Thomas Barton, November 7, 1765, *Documentary History of New York,* 4:361.

28. Daniel Burton to Sir William Johnson, May 26, 1766, *Johnson Papers,* 5:220–21.

29. William Smith's publication in 1753 of an ambitious educational plan, *A General Idea of the College of* Mirania; *With a Sketch of the Method of teaching* Science & Religion, *in several Classes . . . ,* brought him to the attention of Benjamin Franklin and Richard Peters and in time led to the founding of the Academy, later College, of Philadelphia, with Smith as its provost.

30. William Smith to Sir William Johnson, March 16, 1767, *Johnson Papers,* 5:511. See Thomas Firth Jones, *A Pair of Lawn Sleeves: A Biography of William Smith (1727–1803)* (Philadelphia and New York: Chilton Book Co., 1972), 6–12.

31. Ibid.

32. Ibid., 512.

33. Ibid., 513.

34. Ibid.

35. Sir William Johnson to William Smith, April 10, 1767, *Johnson Papers,* 5:528–32.

36. Ibid., 531.

37. Ibid.

38. Thomas Barton to the Secretary, November 10, 1766, SPG Letter Books, Series B., vol. 21, no. 17.

39. Ibid.

40. Ibid.

41. William Smith to Sir William Johnson, June 22, 1767, *Johnson Papers,* 5:569.

42. Ibid.

43. Ibid.

44. Thomas Barton to Sir William Johnson, July 22, 1767, *Johnson Papers,* 5:604.

45. Sir William Johnson to Thomas Barton, November 5, 1767, *Johnson Papers,* 5:775.

46. Thomas Barton to Sir William Johnson, that December 1767, *Johnson Papers,* 5:844.

47. For background on the Stump killings, see James Kirby Martin, "The Return of the Paxton Boys and the Historical State of the Pennsylvania Frontier, 1764–1774" *PH* 38 (1971): 122–24; and Alden T. Vaughan, "Frontier Banditti and the Indians: The Paxton Boys' Legacy, 1763–1775," *PH* 51 (1984): 8–13.

48. George Croghan to Sir William Johnson, February 7, 1768, *Johnson Papers,* 12:425.

49. Thomas Barton to Sir William Johnson, March 25, 1768, *Johnson Papers,* 6:171.

50. Thomas Barton to Sir William Johnson, May "supposed, 1768," *Documentary History of New York,* 4:381.

51. Thomas Barton to Sir William Johnson, 25 March 1768, *Johnson Papers,* 6:171.

52. Arthur Pound and Richard Edwin Day, *Johnson of the Mohawks: a Biography of Sir William Johnson, Irish Immigrant, Mohawk War Chief, American Soldier, Empire Builder* (New York: Macmillan,1930), 421.

53. Cited in H. M. J. Klein and William F. Diller, *The History of St. James' Church (Protestant Episcopal), 1744–1944,* (Lancaster: St. James' Church, 1944), 47.

54. Cited in ibid.

55. Ibid., 47–48.

56. Sir William Johnson to Daniel Burton, October 8, 1766, *Johnson Papers,* 5:389.

57. Richard Slotkin, *Regeneration through Violence: the Myth of the American Frontier, 1600–1860* (Middleton, Conn.: Wesleyan University Press, 1973), explores this myth on the frontier.

58. Sir William Johnson to Daniel Burton, November 8, 1766, *Johnson Papers,* 5:415.

59. Thomas Barton to Sir William Johnson, December 2, 1767, *Johnson Papers,* 5:845–46.

60. *Phiz:* a facial expression.

61. Ibid., 846.

62. Thomas Barton, Preface, *The Family Prayer-Book, Containing Morning and Evening Prayers for Families and Private Persons* . . . (Ephrata, 1767), 3–5. For a discussion of the prayer book, see William Frederick Worner, "Thomas Barton's Family Prayer Book," Lancaster County Historical Society *Journal* 34 (1930): 288–99.

63. Thomas Barton to Sir William Johnson, 2, December, 1767, *Johnson Papers,* 5:843.

64. Sir William Johnson to Thomas Barton, January 5, 1768, *Johnson Papers,* 6:66.

65. Thomas Barton to Sir William Johnson, November 6, 1769, *Johnson Papers,* 7:240.

66. Sir William Johnson to Thomas Barton, February 16, 1770, *Johnson Papers,* 7:391.

67. Ibid.

68. Thomas Barton to Sir William Johnson, March 31, 1770, *Johnson Papers,* 7:515.

69. Thomas Barton to Sir William Johnson, July 26, 1770, *Johnson Papers,* 7–811 (Barton's emphasis).

70. See Thomas Barton to Sir William Johnson, July 8, 1771, *Johnson Papers,* 8:181, replying to Sir William Johnson to Thomas Barton, February 28, 1771, *Documentary History of New York,* 4:438–39.

71. Johnson died in 1774.

72. Thomas Barton to Sir William Johnson, July 8, 1771, *Johnson Papers,* 8:181.

73. Ibid.

74. Petition of Thomas Barton to the Supreme Executive Council, May 29, 1778, Records of Pennsylvania's Revolutionary Governments, microfilm, roll 36, frame 438.

CHAPTER 7. "THE RAGE OF THE TIMES"

1. John Frederick Woolverton, *Colonial Anglicanism in North America* (Detroit: Wayne State University Press, 1984), 34.

2. Ibid.

3. David L. Holmes, "The Episcopal Church in the American Revolution," *Historical Magazine of the Protestant Episcopal Church* 47 (1978): 273–74.

4. As noted above in Chapter 4, n. 34, Provincial Secretary James Logan had voiced the same fear in 1729 to John Penn: "You may easily believe there are some grounds for the common Apprehension of the People, that if some speedy Method be not taken, [the Scots-Irish Presbyterians] will make themselves Proprietors of the Province" (James Logan to John Penn, July 21, 1729, Logan Letter Books, 3:302, HSP).

5. Owen S. Ireland, "The Crux of Politics: Religion and Party in Pennsylvania, 1778–1789," *WMQ,* 3rd series, 42 (1985): 472, has written in this respect that, the Presbyterian radicals "first attacked their old enemies (Quakers and Germans) with the Test Acts and then turned on their former Anglican allies by assailing the charter of the College of Philadelphia."

6. As noted in chapter 5, the improbable, if expedient, alliance between the Anglican proprietary and the Scots-Irish Presbyterians was both a late development and one that did not endure long after the 1763/64 Paxton-Boys disturbances.

7. The following explore this development: David Hawke, *In the Midst of a Revolution* (Philadelphia: University of Pennsylvania Press, 1961); Robert L. Brunhouse, *The Counter-Revolution in Pennsylvania, 1776–1790* (Harrisburg: Pennsylvania Historical and Museum Commission, 1971); Owen S. Ireland, "The Ethnic-Religious Dimension of Pennsylvania Politics, 1778–1779," *WMQ,* 3rd series, 30 (1973): 423–48; "The Crux of Politics: Religion and Party in Pennsylvania, 1778–1789," *WMQ,* 3rd series, 42 (1985): 453–75; Anne Ousterhout, *A State Divided: Opposition in Pennsylvania to the American Revolution* (New York: 1987); J. William Frost, *A Perfect Freedom: Religious Liberty in Pennsylvania* (Cambridge, Eng.: Cambridge University Press, 1990); and Joseph F. Foster, *In Pursuit of Equal Liberty: George Bryan and the Revolution in Pennsylvania* (University Park: Pennsylvania State University Press, 1994). Among the more recent of these to assess the impact of the radical faction, Frost has trenchantly summarized its attitude: "To the revolutionaries there could

be no bystanders when the fundamental liberties of a people were at stake. Pluralism and toleration in religion were good, but a religious dissent that threatened the war effort would not be acceptable. . . . At the very least, all citizens should support the government by declaring allegiance, paying taxes, using the new paper money issued to finance the war, and either serving in the militia or paying for a substitute" (66).

8. Edgar Legare Pennington, "The Anglican Clergy of Pennsylvania in the American Revolution," *PMHB* 63 (1939): 403–4, has shown that Pennsylvania lay precariously on a kind of seismic "line of cleavage" between those camps.

9. Pennington, "Anglican Clergy," 404.

10. Philip Reading of Apoquiniminck, died c. 1777; George Ross of New Castle, died sometime before 1779; and George Craig of Chester, died sometime before 1779.

11. Pennington, "The Anglican Church," 413.

12. A letter of June 30, 1775, signed by all six clergy—Richard Peters, Thomas Coombe, Jacob Duché, William Smith, William Stringer, and William White—reveals how they conformed to initial expectations by the patriots that they participate in a national day of fasting, prayer, and humiliation. Searching their consciences and "being at a great distance from the advice of our Superiors," the letter explains, ". . . We were the more willing to comply with the request of our Fellow-Citizens, as we were sure . . . that they did not even wish any thing from us inconsistent with our characters as Ministers of the Gospel of Peace" (cited in Pennington, 413–4).

Lest their compliance appear an oversimplification of the resolution implied here, Pennington notes that Richard Peters died within the year; Stringer returned to England; Coombe, refusing the test oath, also returned later; and Duché reversed himself, the first of several changes of mind (see Kevin J. Dellape, "Jacob Duché, Whig-Loyalist?," *PH* 62 [1995]: 293–305). Only Smith and White remained unfaltering in their commitment. Nonetheless, Smith's sincerity frequently fell under suspicion during the Revolution. The signatories affirm that prudence suggested they comply with the Congress and their own respective vestries: "the Time is now come . . . when even our silence would be misconstrued, and when we are called upon to take a more public part."

13. See The Clergy to the Bishop of London, October 6, 1775, William S. Perry, ed., *Historical Collections of the American Colonial Church*, vol. 2: *Pennsylvania* (Hartford, Conn.: The Church Press, 1871), 480–81.

14. Hawke, *In the Midst of a Revolution;* Ireland, "The Crux of Politics,"; and Ousterhout, *A State Divided,* detail the extent to which Pennsylvania employed coercion to bring about and enforce political uniformity during the Revolution.

15. Philip Reading to the Secretary, March 18, 1776, *Historical Collections,* ed. Perry, 2:482. Reading's first letter has survived and is to be found in the Gratz Collection, Colonial Clergymen, Box 24, Case 8, HSP.

16. Philip Reading to the Secretary, September 19, 1775, Gratz Collection, Colonial Clergymen, Box 24, Case 8, HSP.

17. Thomas Barton to the Secretary, March 1, 1775, SPG Letter Books, Series B, vol. 21, no. 26.

18. Esther Rittenhouse Barton died June 18, 1774.

19. Thomas Barton to the Secretary, March 1, 1775, SPG Letter Books, Series B, vol. 21, no. 26.

20. Ibid., June 10, 1775, SPG Letter Books, Series B, vol. 21, no. 28.

21. William Smith to the Secretary, July 10, 1775, *Historical Collections,* ed. Perry, 2:475.

22. A typical example of such a prayer may be found in the Litany from the 1775 English Book of Prayer (cited in Holmes, "The Episcopal Church," 288–89):

> That it may please thee to keep and strengthen in the true worshipping of thee, in righteousness and holiness of life, thy Servant *George,* our most gracious King and Governour; *We beseech thee to hear us, good Lord.*
>
> That it may please thee to rule his heart in thy faith, fear, and love, and that he may ever-more have affiance in thee, and ever seek thy honour and glory: *We beseech thee to hear us, good Lord.*
>
> That it may please thee to be his defender and keeper, giving him the victory over all his enemies; *We beseech thee to hear us, good Lord.*

23. Cited in Philip Reading to the Secretary, August 25, 1776, *Historical Collections,* ed. Perry, 2:484.

24. William White, *Memoirs of the Protestant Episcopal Church in the United States of America* (Philadelphia: S. Patter, 1820), 60–61.

25. Philip Reading to the Secretary, August 25, 1776, *Historical Collections,* ed. Perry, 2:483–84. Reading refers to the 1662 Oath of Uniformity. Holmes, "The Episcopal Church" (269), writes of the oath that it "bound all priests to perform public worship without change or mutilation according to the liturgy of the Church of England. This meant the verbatim reading of services of the Book of Common Prayer . . . all of which included prayers for the King, for the Royal Family, and for Parliament. . . . The reader should remember . . . that most Christians of the time believed that breaking an oath would cause divine retribution."

26. Philip Reading to the Secretary, August 25, 1776, *Historical Collections,* ed. Perry, 2:484.

27. Ibid., 484–85.

28. Ibid.

29. H. M. J. Klein and William F. Diller, *The History of St. James' Church (Protestant Episcopal), 1744–1944* (Lancaster: St. James' Church, 1944), 55.

30. Thomas Barton to the Secretary, November 25, 1776, SPG Letter Books, Series B, vol. 21, no. 31.

31. Ibid.

32. Thomas Barton to the Secretary, January 8, 1779, SPG Letter Books, Series B, vol. 21, no. 36.

33. Thomas Barton to the Secretary, November 25, 1776, SPG Letter Books, Series B, vol. 21, no. 31.

34. Thomas Barton to the Secretary, that January 1779, SPG Letter Books, Series B, vol. 21, no. 36.

35. Thomas Barton to the Secretary, December 15, 1778, *Historical Collections,* ed. Perry, 2:129.

36. Thomas Barton to the Secretary, November 25, 1776, SPG Letter Books, Series B, 21:31.

37. Ibid.

38. Frederick Lewis Weis, *The Colonial Clergy of the Middle Colonies, New York, New Jersey, and Pennsylvania, 1628–1776* (Worcester, Mass.: Genealogical Publishing Co., 1957), 175–76.

39. Jerome H. Wood, *Conestoga Crossroads: Lancaster, Pennsylvania, 1730–90* (Harrisburg: the Pennsylvania Historical and Manuscript Commission, 1979), 86 (Wood misreads the conspirator's name as "Shelby").

40. He solemnly "affirmed" rather than swore to the truth of his deposition; see Deposition of Daniel Shelly, September, 22, Records of Pennsylvania's Revolutionary Governments, 1775–1790, Record Group 27, in the Pennsylvania State Archives, microfilm, roll 12, frames 1093–94. That the Shellys of Shelly Island were Mennonites rather than Quakers was communicated to me by Leo Shelly, archivist of St. James's Episcopal Church and reference librarian at Millersville University.

41. Deposition of William Beckworth and Adam Laughlin, September 6, 1777, *P.A.*, 1st ser., 5:624–25; Supreme Executive Council to John Creigh, September 16, 1777, ibid., 628–29; John Carothers to William Henry, September 25, 1777, ibid., 634; and George Stevenson to William Henry, September 25, 1777, ibid., 635. See also Wood, *Conestoga Crossroads,* 86–87, for an account of this episode.

42. George Stevenson to William Henry, September 25, 1777, *PA,* 1st ser., 5:635.

43. Deposition of Daniel Shelly, Records of Pennsylvania's Revolutionary Governments, roll 12, frame 1093.

44. *Laws Enacted in a General Assembly* . . . (Philadelphia, 1777), 37–39.

45. John Carothers to William Henry, September 25, 1777, *PA,* 1st series, 5:634: "I am not personally acquainted with you."

46. Barton was invited to preach the dedicatory sermon: "The German Lutherans in this town have built one of the most elegant Churches in Pennsylvania; at the Opening of which they invited me to preach—I readily consented" (Thomas Barton to the Secretary, November 10, 1766, SPG Letter Books, Series B, vol. 21, no. 17).

47. For this discussion of Lancaster's wartime character and importance, I draw heavily on Wood, *Conestoga Crossroads,* 79–89.

48. Ibid., 81.

49. Wood, 85–87, describes several outbreaks and escapes.

50. Christopher Marshall, cited in Wood, *Conestoga Crossroads,* 86.

51. Edward Burd to Jasper Yeates, October 6, 1777, Yeates Papers, Correspondence, 1762–1780, HSP.

52. Edward Burd to Jasper Yeates, September 8, 1777, Yeates Papers, Correspondence, 1762–1780, HSP.

53. Sally Bard was a new in-law because of Barton's second marriage in 1776 to the former Mrs. Sarah DeNormandie of New York City.

54. Sally Bard to Mrs. Mary Bard, [January ?] 1776, cited in "The Bartons in Lancaster in 1776," Lancaster County Historical Society *Journal* 52 (1948): 215.

55. Ibid.

56. Ibid., 214.

57. Ibid., 215.

58. Testimonials of the Vestry of Bangor Church in Caernarvon and the Vestry of St. John's Church in the County of Chester for Thomas Barton, September 21/October 1778; and of the Vestry of St. James's Church, Lancaster, September 21, 1778, SPG Letter Books, Series B, vol. 21, nos. 33 and 34.

59. Klein and Diller, *History of St. James' Church,* 51–53.

60. Sarah Barton to Louisa DeNormandie, 1776, "The Bartons in Lancaster," 216.

61. Ousterhout, *A State Divided,* 161.

62. Ibid.

63. Ibid.

64. Cited in ibid., 161–62.

65. Coombe returned to England. Richard Peters had died in 1775, and William Stringer

returned in 1779. See Pennington, "Anglican Clergy," 412–18, for a discussion of the Philadelphia clergy's reaction to the coercive measures of the 1770s.

66. The Case of the protestant Episcopal Missionaries of Pennsylvania to the Assembly, May 20, 1778, SPG Letter Books, Series B, vol. 21, no. 32.

67. Ibid.

68. Thomas Barton to John DeHart, January 30, 1779, in William Barton, *Memoirs of the Life of David Rittenhouse* (Philadelphia: E. Parker, 1813), 280.

69. Ibid.

70. Petition of Thomas Barton to the Supreme Executive Council, May 29, 1778, Records of Pennsylvania's Revolutionary Governments, microfilm, roll 36, frame 438.

71. Records of Pennsylvania's Revolutionary Governments, roll 36, frame 438.

72. Lancaster County Deed Books, S 724 and 727 (August 26, 1778); recorded November 30, 1778.

73. Passport, September 17, 1778, preserved in the SPG Letter Books, Series B., 21:31.

74. Testimonials of the Vestries of the Bangor and St. John's Churches, September 21/October 1778, SPG Letter Books, Series B, vol. 21, no. 33.

75. Thomas Barton to the Secretary, January 1779, SPG Letter Books, Series B, vol. 21, no. 36.

76. Thomas Barton to Dr. Hind, December 15, 1778, Perry, ed., *Historical Collections, 5: Delaware,* 129. Barton's petition of May 29 raises an intriguing question: in his appeal, he refers to being made to "suffer *a Separation* . . . from a dear & much beloved Child; except upon Conditions to which no earthly Consideration can prevail with him to consent." What this separation from, presumably William, who was studying law in England, can mean is unclear.

77. Esther Atlee to William Atlee, October 7, 1778, cited in Klein and Diller, *St. James' Church History,* 58.

78. Christopher Marshall, October 3, 1778, cited in Theodore W. Jeffries, "Thomas Barton (1730–1780): Victim of the Revolution," Lancaster County Historical Society *Journal* 81 (1971): 60.

CHAPTER 8. MARTYR

1. See, for example, the following: Samuel Johnston to the Secretary, November 25, 1776, *Historical Collections of the American Colonial Church,* ed. William S. Perry, vol. 2: *Pennsylvania* (Hartford, 1871), 487–89; Deposition of William Beckworth and Adam Laughlin, September 6, 1777, *PA,* 1st series, 5:624–25; George Stevenson to William Henry, September 25, 1777, ibid., 635; Petition of Daniel Batwelle to John Hancock, October 1, 1777, Gratz Collection, American Colonial Clergy, Case 8, Box 21, HSP; John Hancock to the Pennsylvania Supreme Executive Council, October 30, 1777, ibid.; Petition of Daniel Batwelle, November 7, 1777, ibid.

2. Thomas Barton to the Secretary, January 8, 1779, SPG Letter Books, Series B, 21:36.

3. Thomas Barton the the Secretary, December 15, 1778, *Historical Collections,* ed. Perry, 2:129–30.

4. Thomas Barton to the Secretary, October 25, 1779, SPG Letter Books, Series B, 21:37.

5. Thomas Barton to the Secretary 15 December 1778, *Historical Collections,* ed. Perry, 2:129–30.

6. Thomas Barton to the Secretary, January 8, 1779, SPG Letter Books, Series B, 21:36.

7. Romans, 8:18–25.

8. Thomas Barton to John DeHart, January 30, 1779, cited in William Barton, *Memoirs of the Life of David Rittenhouse* (Philadelphia: E. Parker,1813), 279–80.

9. Minutes, Supreme Executive Council, April 14, 1780, *CR,* 12:317.

10. See *CR,* September 17, 1778, 11:579; February 18, 1780, 12:256; April 12, 1780, 12:257; April 14, 1780, 12:317; May 2, 1780, 12:339; May 19, 1780, 12:357; *PA,* 1st series, March 5, 1779, 7:225–26.

11. William Barton, *Memoirs of Rittenhouse,* 281, n. 54.

12. Joseph F. Foster, *In Pursuit of Equal Liberty: George Bryan and the Revolution in Pennsylvania* (University Park: Pennsylvania State University Press, 1994) offers a sympathetic reading of Bryan, although he still stresses Bryan's inflexible stubbornness.

13. George Bryan to George Washington, March 5, 1779, *PA,* 1st series, 7:225–26.

14. There is no evidence supporting this accusation. As his letters make transparently clear, Barton was too ill to discharge the duties of a regimental chaplain. Rather, the report Bryan alludes to probably confuses Barton with Batwelle, who indeed possessed such a commission.

15. George Bryan to George Washington, March 5, 1779, *PA,* 1st series, 7:225–26.

16. Cited in William Barton, *Memoirs of Rittenhouse,* 280; italics mine.

17. In his January 8, 1779 letter, Barton reported that "the Congregations of Pequea & Caernarvon . . . took a House at Caernarvon for my Children, remov'd them from Lancaster, with kind Assurances that they should be supported till it might please God to unite us again" (SPG Letter Books, Series B, 21:36).

18. Thomas Barton to the Secretary, February 1779, cited in A. H. Young, "Thomas Barton: A Pennsylvania Loyalist," Ontario Historical Society *Papers and Records* 30 (1934): 41.

19. Thomas Barton to William Frazer, October 5, 1779, Society Collection, HSP.

20. Thomas Barton to the Secretary, October 25, 1779, SPG Letter Books, Series B, 21:37.

21. Ibid.

22. Thomas Barton to the Secretary, January 8, 1779, SPG Letter Books, Series B, 21:36.

23. Thomas Barton to the Secretary, October 25, 1779, SPG Letter Books, Series B, 21:37.

24. Minutes, Supreme Executive Council, May 6, 1780, *CR,* 12:339.

25. Minutes, Supreme Executive Council, May 19, 1780, *CR,* 12:357.

26. Theodore W. Jeffries, "Thomas Barton (1730–1780): Victim of the Revolution," Lancaster County Historical Society *Journal* 81 (1977): 61.

27. Cited in Klein and Diller, *St. James' Church History,* 61. The thematic emphases, much of the vocabulary, and many of the stylistic turns suggest that Barton may himself have written most of the epitaph.

28. Ibid.

Appendix

1. This correspondence is known because William Barton cites from it extensively throughout his biography *Memoirs of the Life of David Rittenhouse* (Philadelphia: E. Parker, 1813).

2. The term *French and Indian War* denotes the conflict that took place in North America between Great Britain, France, and their various Indian allies, during the years 1754–63. The French and Indian War was actually part of a far vaster, worldwide conflict known as the Seven Years' War (1756–63), a violent conflict between Britain and France for imperial control of North America, India, Africa, the West Indies, and Europe itself. Its conclusion in 1763 left Great Britain the master of the North American continent. The victory, however, did not come easily or without painful cost, for, ultimately, the war ironically contributed to the Revolutionary War and Britain's losing her thirteen North American Colonies.

See Seymour Schwartz, *The French and Indian Wars 1754–1763: the Imperial Struggle for North America* (New York: Simon and Schuster, 1994) for a succinct, map-centered, history of the war. Walter Borneman, *The French and Indian War: Deciding the Fate of North America* (New York: HarperCollins, 2006) offers a more recent, thorough discussion,

3. See Hunter's introduction to his annotated transcription of Barton's journal, "Thomas Barton and the Forbes Expedition," *PMHB* 95 (1971): 431–39.

4. Ibid., 438.

5. For example, Hunter's note 5 mistakenly identifies Barton's residence as Huntington township, site of Christ Church's glebe-land. As Barton makes clear in various letters, however, he resided in Reading township, a fact confirmed by the survey in the Adams County Historical Society archives, and by William Barton in his biography of his uncle, David Rittenhouse.

6. *Historical Collections Related to the American Colonial Church,* vol. 2: *Pennsylvania* (Hartford, Connecticut: the Church Press, 1871).

Selected Bibliography

MANUSCRIPT COLLECTIONS

Adams County Historical Society.

American Philosophical Society.

Archives of the Episcopal Church, USA, Austin, Texas: Records of the General Convention, the Francis Lister Hawks Manuscript Collection (Thomas Barton-William Smith Letters).

Cumberland County Historical Society.

Historical Society of Pennsylvania: Etting Collections; Gratz Collection; Lamberton Scotch-Irish Collection; Penn Papers (Official Correspondence); Peters Papers; Shippen Family Papers; Stauffer Collection.

Lancaster County Historical Society.

Library Company of Philadelphia.

Pennsylvania Historical and Museum Commission, Division of Public Records, Harrisburg.

Presbyterian Historical Society, Philadelphia.

St. James Episcopal Church, Lancaster.

Scottish Record Office, Dalhousie Muniments, Edinburgh.

York County Historical Society.

MANUSCRIPT AND PUBLISHED PRIMARY SOURCES

"An Address of Thanks to the Wardens of Christ Church and St. Peters . . . in the Name of all Presbyterian Ministers in Pennsylvania." Philadelphia, 1764.

Barber, Rhoda. "History of the Founding of Wrightsville." *MS.* in HSP, 1830.

Barton, Thomas. *The Family Prayer-Book, Containing Morning and Evening Prayers for Families and Private Persons* . . . Ephrata, Pennsylvania, 1767.

———. *The Reverend Thomas Barton's Letter of 8 November, 1756 and Forbes Expedition Journal of 1758,* ed. James P. Myers, Jr. *Adams County History* 8 (2002): 4–63.

———. Three manuscript sermons. Salem, NJ: Salem County Historical Society.

Bouquet, Henry. *The Papers of Henry Bouquet,* ed. Sylvester K. Stevens, Donald H. Kent, and Autumn L. Leonard. vol. 2: Harrisburg: Pennsylvania Historical and Manuscript Commission, 1972.

A Calendar of Ridgely Family Letters, 1742–1899, in the Delaware State Archives, ed. Leon deValinger, Jr. and Virginia E. Shaw, vol. 1. Dover: Delaware Public Archives Commission, 1948.

Charter, Laws, Catalogue of Books . . . of the Juliana Library Company (Philadelphia, 1766).

Documentary History of the State of New York, ed. E. B. O'Callaghan, vol. 4. Albany: Weed, Parsons, & Co., 1851.

Fithian, Philip Vickers. *Philip Vickers Fithian: Journal, 1775–1776; Written on the Virginia-Pennsylvania Frontier and in the Army Around New York,* ed. Robert Greenhalgh Albion and Leonidas Dodson. Princeton: Princeton University Press, 1934.

Forbes, John. *Writings of General John Forbes, Relating to his Service in North America,* ed. Alfred P. James. Menasha, Wis.: the Collegiate Press: 1938.

Franklin, Benjamin. *The Papers of Benjamin Franklin,* ed. Leonard W. Labaree, vol. 11: *January 1 through December 31, 1764.* New Haven: Yale University Press, 1967.

Historical Collections Relating to the American Colonial Church, ed. William Stevens Perry. 5 vols. Hartford, Conn.: the Church Press, 1871–78.

Holmes, Andrew R. *The Shaping of Ulster Presbyterian Belief and Practice, 1770–1840.* Oxford: Oxford University Press: 2006

Johnson, Sir William. *The Papers of Sir William Johnson.* 13 vols. Albany: State University Press of New York, 1921–62.

Laws Enacted in a General Assembly . . . Philadelphia, 1777.

The Paxton Papers. Edited by John R. Dunbar. The Hague: Martinus Nijhoff, 1957.

Pennsylvania. *Laws Enacted in a General Assembly . . .* Philadelphia, 1777.

———. *Minutes of the Provincial Council of Pennsylvania . . .* [usually cited by binder's title of *Colonial Records*]. 16 vols. Harrisburg, 1838–53.

———. *Pennsylvania Archives,* 1st series, ed. Samuel Hazard. 12 vols. Philadelphia, 1852–56.

———. *Pennsylvania Archives,* 2nd series, ed. John B. Linn and William Henry Egle. 19 vols. Harrisburg, 1874–90.

———. *Pennsylvania Archives,* 3rd series, ed. William Henry Engle and George Edward Reed. 30 vols. Harrisburg, 1894–99.

———. *Pennsylvania Archives,* 5th series, ed. Thomas Lynch Montgomery. 8 vols. Harrisburg, 1906.

———. Records of Pennsylvania's Revolutionary Governments, 1775–1790, roll 36, frame 438.

The Pennsylvania Gazette, Philadelphia.

Records of the States of the United States, Pennsylvania, microfilm, E 2b, reel 3, unit 2, 2.

Rev. Thomas Barton (1728–1780) and Some of His Descendants and Some of Their In-Laws, compiled and collected by Stuart E. Brown, Jr. Berryville, Va.: Virginia Book Company, 1988.

Roberts, Samuel. *Love to Our Country, and Zeal for Its Interest . . . Preach'd to a Congregation of Protestant Dissenters at Salisbury on Sunday, October 6, 1745. . . . London, 1745.*

Society for the Propagation of the Gospel in Foreign Parts (now known as the United Society for the Propagation of the Gospel). Records of the Society for the Propagation of the Gospel, Letters, Series B, vol. 21: Pennsylvania, 1701–86. Micro Methods, Ltd., 1964.

Woodmason, Charles, *The Carolina Backcountry on the Eve of the Revolution: the Journal and Other Writings of Charles Woodmason, Anglican Itinerant,* ed. Richard Hooker. Chapel Hill: Published for the Institute of Early American History and Culture by the University of North Carolina Press, 1953,

SECONDARY MATERIALS

Bailyn, Bernard. *The Ordeal of Thomas Hutchinson.* Cambridge, Mass.: Harvard University Press, 1974.

Barr, Daniel P. "'A Road for Warriors': the Western Delawares and the Seven Years' War." *PH* 73 (2006): 1–36.

———. "Victory at Kittanning? Reevaluating the Impact of Amstrong's Raid on the Seven Years' War in Pennsylvania." *PMHB* 131 (2007): 5–31.

Barton, William. *Memoirs of the Life of David Rittenhouse.* Philadelphia: E. Parker, 1813.

"The Bartons in Lancaster in 1776." Lancaster County Historical Society *Journal* 52 (1948): 213–17.

Bockelman, Wayne L., and Owen S. Ireland, "The Internal Revolution in Pennsylvania: an Ethnic-Religious Interpretation." *PH* 41 (1974): 125–59.

Brady, Ciaran, ed., *Worsted in the Game: Losers in Irish History,* Dublin: Lilliput Press, 1989.

Bridenbaugh, Carl. *Mitre and Sceptre: Transatlantic Faith, Ideas, Personalities, and Politics, 1689–1775.* New York: Oxford University Press, 1962.

———. *Myths and Realities: Societies of the Colonial South.* Baton Rouge: Louisiana State University Press,1952.

Brunhouse, Robert L. *The Counter-Revolution in Pennsylvania, 1776–1790.* Harrisburg: The Pennsylvania Historical and Museum Commission, 1971.

Buck, Solon L. and Elizabeth H. *The Planting of Civilization in Western Pennsylvania.* Pittsburgh: University of Pittsburgh Press, 1939.

Butzin, Peter A. "Politics, Presbyterians and the Paxton Riots, 1763–64." *JPH* 51 (1973): 70–84.

Buxbaum, Melvin H. *Benjamin Franklin and the Zealous Presbyterians.* University Park: Pennsylvania State University Press, 1975.

Calam, John. *Parsons and Pedagogues: The S.P.G. Adventure in American Education.* New York: Columbia University Press, 1971.

Camenzind, Krista. "Violence, Race, and the Paxton Boys," in *Friends and Enemies in Penn's Woods.* Pencak and Richter, eds., 201–20.

Campbell, Alexander. "A 'nursery for soldiers to the whole world': Colonel James Prevost and the Foreign Protestant Military Migration of the Mid-Eighteenth Century." *PMHB* 129 (2005): 253–81.

Clements, William L. "Rogers's Michillimackinac Journal." American Antiquary Society *Proceedings* 28 (1918): 224–73.

Crimmins, John D. *St. Patrick's Day: Its Celebration in New York and Other American Places, 1737–1845.* New York: John D. Crimmins, 1902.

Crist, Robert G. *George Croghan of Pennsboro*. Harrisburg: Dauphin Deposit Trust Co., 1965.

———. "John Armstrong: Proprietors' Man." Unpublished PhD diss., Pennsylvania State University, 1981.

Crowley, James E. "The Paxton Disturbance and Ideas of Order in Pennsylvania Politics." *PH* 37 (1970): 317–39.

Cummings, Hubertis M. "The Paxton Killings." *JPH* 44 (1966): 219–43.

———. *Richard Peters: Provincial Secretary and Cleric, 1704–1776*. Philadelphia: University of Pennsylvania Press, 1944.

———. *Scots Breed and Susquehanna*. Pittsburgh: University of Pittsburgh Press, 1964.

Dellape, Kevin J. "Jacob Duché, Whig-Loyalist?" *PH* 62 (1995): 293–305.

Dickson, R. J. *Ulster Emigration to Colonial America, 1718–1775*. London: Routledge and Keegan Paul, 1966.

Dowd, Gregory Evans. *War Under Heaven: Pontiac, the Indian Nations, and the British Empire*. Baltimore: The Johns Hopkins University Press, 2002.

Doyle, David Noel. *Ireland, Irishmen and Revolutionary America, 1760–1820*. Dublin: Published for the Cultural Relations Committee of Ireland by the Mercier Press: 1981.

Dubbs, John Henry. *The Reformed Church in Pennsylvania*. Lancaster: The Pennsylvania German Society, 1902.

Dunaway, Wayland F. *The Scotch-Irish of Colonial Pennsylvania*. Chapel Hill: University of North Carolina Press, 1944.

Egle, William Henry. *History of the Counties of Dauphin and Lebanon*. Philadelphia: Everts & Peck, 1883.

———. *An Illustrated History of the Commonwealth. . . .* Harrisburg: DeWitt C. Goodrich, 1876,

Ford, Edward. *David Rittenhouse: Astronomer-Patriot, 1732–1796*. Philadelphia: University of Pennsylvania Press: 1946.

Foster, Joseph S. *In Pursuit of Equal Liberty: George Bryan and the Revolution in Pennsylvania*. University Park: Pennsylvania State University Press, 1994.

Frost J. William. *A Perfect Freedom: Religious Liberty in Pennsylvania*. Cambridge, UK: Cambridge University Press, 1990.

Gegenheimer, Albert Frank. *William Smith: Educator and Churchman, 1727–1803*. Philadelphia: University of Pennsylvania Press, 1943.

Gipson, Lawrence Henry. *The British Empire before the American Revolution, 6: The Great War for the Empire*. New York: Knopf, 1946.

Glatfelter, Charles H. *Pastors and People: German Lutheran and Reformed Churches in the Pennsylvania Field, 1717–1793*. vol. 1. Breinigsville, Pa.: The Pennsylvania German Society, 1980.

Griffin, Patrick. *The People with no Name: Ireland's Ulster Scots, America's Scots Irish and the Creation of a British Atlantic World, 1689–1764*. Princeton: Princeton University Press, 2001.

Hamilton, Milton W. *Sir William Johnson: Colonial American, 1715–1763*. Port Washington, N.Y.: Kennikat Press, 1976.

Hamilton, Stanislaus Murray. *Letters to Washington, and Accompanying Papers*. Boston: Houghton, Mifflin and Company, 1899–1902.

Hawke, David. *In the Midst of a Revolution.* Philadelphia: University of Pennsylvania Press, 1961.

Hinderacker, Eric, and Peter C. Mancall. *At the Edge of Empire: the Backcountry in British North America.* Baltimore: The Johns Hopkins University Press, 2002.

Hindle, Brooke. *David Rittenhouse.* Princeton: Princeton University Press, 1964.

———. "The March of the Paxton Boys." *WMQ,* 3rd series, 3 (1964): 461–86.

Holmes, David L. "The Episcopal Church in the American Revolution." *Historical Magazine of the Protestant Episcopal Church* 47 (1978): 273–4.

Hunter, William A. *Forts on the Pennsylvania Frontier, 1753–1758.* Harrisburg: The Pennsylvania Historical and Museum Commission, 1960.

———. "Thomas Barton and the Forbes Expedition." *PMHB* 95 (1971): 431–83.

Ireland, Owen S. "The Crux of Politics: Religion and Party in Pennsylvania, 1778–1789." *WMQ,* 3rd Series, 42 (1985): 453–75.

———. "The Ethnic-Religious Dimension of Pennsylvania Politics, 1778–1779." *WMQ,* 3rd series, 30 (1973): 423–48.

———. *Religion, Ethnicity, and Politics: Ratifying the Constitution in Pennsylvania.* University Park: Pennsylvania State University Press, 1995.

Jeffries, Theodore W. "Thomas Barton (1730–1780): Victim of the Revolution." Lancaster County Historical Society *Journal* 81 (1977): 39–64.

Jennings, Francis. *The Creation of America: through Revolution to Empire.* Cambridge, UK: Cambridge University Press, 2000.

Jones, Thomas Firth. *A Pair of Lawn Sleeves: a Biography of William Smith (1727–1803).* Philadelphia: Chilton Book Co., 1972.

Jordan, Francis Jr. *The Life of William Henry, of Lancaster, Pennsylvania.* Lancaster, Pa.: Press of the New Era Printing Co., 1910.

Ketcham, Ralph L. "Conscience, War and Politics in Pennsylvania, 1755–1757." *WMQ,* 3rd series, 20 (1963): 416–39.

Klein, H. M. J., and William F. Diller. *The History of St. James' Church (Protestant Episcopal), 1744–1944.* Lancaster, Pa.: St. James' Church, 1944.

Klett, Guy S. *Presbyterians in Colonial Pennsylvania.* Philadelphia: University of Pennsylvania Press, 1937.

Klingberg, Frank J. *Anglican Humanitarianism in Colonial New York.* Philadelphia: The Church Historical Society, 1940.

———. "Sir William Johnson and the Society for the Propagation of the Gospel (1749–1774)." *Historical Magazine of the Protestant Episcopal Church* 8 (1939): 4–37.

Kopperman, Paul E. *Braddock at the Monongahela.* Pittsburgh: University of Pittsburgh Press, 1977.

Landsman, Ned. "Roots, Routes, and Rootedness: Diversity, Migration, and Toleration in Mid-Atlantic Pluralism." *EAS* 2 (2004): 269–309.

Lemay, J. A. Leo. *The Career of Benjamin Franklin, 1726–1776: New Attributions and Reconsiderations.* Newark: University of Delaware Press, 1986.

———. *The Life of Benjamin Franklin,* 3 vols. Philadelphia: University of Pennsylvania Press, 2006–9.

———, ed. *Reappraising Benjamin Franklin: A Bicentennial Perspective.* Newark: University of Delaware Press, 1993.

Leyburn, James G. *The Scotch-Irish: a Social History.* Chapel Hill: University of North Carolina Press, 1962.

Lowdermilk, Will H. *History of Cumberland . . . together with a History of Braddock's Expedition.* Washington: James Anglim, 1878.

Marietta, Jack D. *The Reformation of American Quakerism, 1748–1783.* Philadelphia: University of Pennsylvania Press, 1984.

Martin, James Kirby. "The Return of the Paxton Boys and the Historical State of the Pennsylvania Frontier, 1764–1774." *PH* 38 (1971): 117–33.

May, Henry F. *The Enlightenment in America.* New York: Oxford University Press, 1976.

Merrell, James H. *Into the American Woods: Negotiators on the Pennsylvania Frontier.* New York: W. W. Norton, 1999.

Merritt, Jane. *At the Crossroads: Indians & Empire on a Mid-Atlantic Frontier, 1700–1763.* Chapel Hill: University of North Carolina Press, 2003.

Miller, Kerby A. *Emigrants and Exiles: Ireland and the Irish Exodus to North America.* New York: Oxford University Press, 1985.

———, Arnold Schrier, Bruce D. Bowling, and David N. Doyle. *Irish Immigrants in the Land of Canaan: Letters and Memoirs from Colonial and Revolutionary America, 1675–1815.* New York: Oxford University Press, 2003.

Moyer, Paul. "Violence, Race, and the Paxton Boys," in *Friends and Enemies,* ed. Pencak and Richter, 201–20.

Mulford, Carla. "*Caritas* and Capital: Franklin's *Narrative of the Late Massacres,*" in Lemay, ed., *Reappraising Benjamin Franklin,* 347–58.

Murphy, Richard C. and Lawrence J. Mannion. *The History of the Society of the Friendly Sons of Saint Patrick in the City of New York, 1784 to 1955.* New York: n.p., 1962.

Myers, Albert Cook. *The Immigration of the Irish Quakers into Pennsylvania.* Swarthmore, PA.: Albert Cook Myers, 1902.

Myers, James P., Jr. "The Missionary and the Clockmaker: A Saga of Two Brothers-in-Law." *Pennsylvania Heritage* 20 (Winter 1994): 4–9.

———. "Pennsylvania's Awakening: the Kittanning Raid of 1756." *PH* 66 (1999): 399–420.

———. "The Rev. Thomas Barton's Authorship of *The Conduct of the Paxton Men, Impartially Represented* (1764)." *PH* 61 (1994): 155–84.

———. "The Reverend Thomas Barton's Conflict with Colonel John Armstrong, ca. 1758." *Cumberland County History* 10 (1993): 3–14.

———. "*Unanimity and Public Spirit* (1755): Controversy and Plagiarism on the Pennsylvania Frontier." *The Pennsylvania Magazine of History and Biography* 119 (1995): 225–48.

Newcombe, Alfred W. "The Appointment and Instruction of S.P.G. Missionaries." *Church History* 5 (1936): 340–58.

O'Toole, Fintan. *White Savage: William Johnson and the Invention of America.* New York: Farrar, Straus and Giroux, 2005.

Ousterhout, Anne. *A State Divided: Opposition in Pennsylvania to the American Revolution* New York: The Greenwood Press, 1987.

Pascoe, C. F. *Two Hundred Years of the S.P.G.: an Historical Account of the Society for the Propagation of the Gospel in Foreign Parts, 1701–1900,* 2 vols. London: The SPG, 1901.

Pencak, William A., and Daniel K. Richter, eds. *Friends and Enemies in Penn's Woods: Indians, Colonists, and the Radical Construction of Pennsylvania.* University Park: Pennsylvania State University, 2004.

Pennington, Edgar L. "The Anglican Clergy of Pennsylvania in the American Revolution." *PMHB* 63 (1939): 401–31.

———. "The S.P.G. Anniversary Sermons, 1702–1783." *Historical Magazine of the Protestant Episcopal Church* 20 (1951): 10–43.

Pound, Arthur, and Richard Edwin Day. *Johnson of the Mohawks: a Biography of Sir William Johnson, Irish Immigrant, Mohawk War Chief, American Soldier, Empire Builder.* New York: Macmillan Co., 1930.

Praeger, R. Lloyd. *Some Irish Naturalists: a Biographical Notebook.* Dundalk, Northern Ireland: W. Tempest, 1949.

Proud, Robert. *The History of Pennsylvania, in North America. . . ,* 2 vols. Philadelphia: Zachariah Poulson, 1798.

Reid-Maroney, Nina. *Philadelphia's Enlightenment, 1740–1800: Kingdom of Christ, Empire of Reason.* Westport, Conn.: Greenwood Press, 2001.

Rice, Howard C., Jr. *The Rittenhouse Orrery: Princeton's Eighteenth-Century Planetarium, 1767–1954.* Princeton: Princeton University Library, 1954.

Richter, Daniel K. *Facing East from Indian Country: a Native History of Early America.* Cambridge, Mass.: Harvard University Press, 2001.

———. *Native Americans' Pennsylvania.* University Park: Pennsylvania State University Press, 2005.

Rubincam, Milton. "A Memoir of the Life of William Barton, A.M. (1754–1817)." *PH* 12 (1945): 179–93.

Rupp, I. Daniel. *History and Topography of Northumberland, Huntingdon, Mifflin, Centre, Union, Columbia, Juniata and Clinton Counties, Pa.* Lancaster, Pa.: G. Hills, 1847.

Russell, Marvin F. "Thomas Barton and Pennsylvania's Colonial Frontier." *PH* 46 (1979): 313–34.

Rutschsky. Charles W., Jr. "Thomas Barton's Collection of Minerals." *PH* 8 (1941): 148–50.

Schlegel, Donald M. "The Barton Estate and Lough Bawn in County Monaghan." *Clogher Record* 15 (1995): 110–21.

Shirley, Evelyn Philip. *The History of the County of Monaghan.* London: Pickering, 1879.

Sipe, C. Hale. *The Indian Wars of Pennsylvania.* Harrisburg: The Telegraph Press, 1931.

Skaggs, David Curtis. *The Poetic Writings of Thomas Cradock, 1718–1770.* London: University of Delaware Press, 1983.

Slotkin, Richard. *Regeneration through Violence: the Mythology of the American Frontier, 1600–1800.* Middletown, Conn.: Wesleyan University Press, 1973.

Smith, Horace W. *Life and Correspondence of the Rev. William Smith.* 2 vols. Philadelphia: S. A. George, 1879–80.

Stevenson, R. S. "Pennsylvania Provincial Soldiers in the Seven Years' War." *PH* 62 (1995): 196–212.

Thayer, Theodore. *Pennsylvania Politics and the Growth of Democracy, 1740–1776.* Harrisburg, Pa.: the Pennsylvania Historical and Museum Commission, 1953.

Thwaites, Reuben Gold. *Early Western Travel, 1748–1846.* 3 vols. Cleveland: A. H. Clark, Co., 1904–7.

Treese, Lorett. *The Storm Gathering: The Penn Family and the American Revolution.* University Park: Pennsylvania State University Press, 1992.

Tully, Alan, "Ethnicity, Religion, and Politics in Early America." *PMHB* 108 (1983): 491–535.

Vaughan, Alden T. "Frontier Banditti and the Indians: The Paxton Boys' Legacy, 1765–1775." *PH* 51 (1984): 1–29.

Volwiler, Albert T. *George Croghan and the Westward Movement, 1741–1782.* Cleveland: Arthur H. Clark Co., 1926.

Waddell, Louis M. "Defending the Long Perimeter: Forts on the Pennsylvania, Maryland, and Virginia Frontier: 1758–1765." *PH* 62 (1995): 171–95.

Wainwright, Nicholas B. *George Croghan: Wilderness Diplomat.* Chapel Hill: Published for the Institute of Early American History and Culture by the University of North Carolina Press, 1959.

Wallace, Anthony F. C. *King of the Delawares: Teedyuscung.* Philadelphia: University of Pennsylvania Press, 1949.

Ward, Matthew C. "An Army of Servants: the Pennsylvania Regiment During the Seven Years' War." *PMHB* 119 (1995): 75–93.

———. *Breaking the Backcountry; the Seven Years' War in Virginia and Pennsylvania, 1754–1765.* Philadelphia: University of Pennsylvania Press, 2002.

Warden, G. B. "The Proprietary Group in Pennsylvania, 1754–1764." *WMQ,* 3rd series, 21 (1964): 367–89.

Weber, Samuel Edwin. *The Charity School Movement in Pennsylvania.* New York: Arno Press, 1969.

Weis, Frederick Lewis. *The Colonial Clergy of the Middle Colonies, New York, New Jersey, and Pennsylvania, 1628–1776.* Worcester, Mass.: Genealogical Publishing Co., 1957.

White, William. *Memoirs of the Protestant Episcopal Church in the United States of America.* Philadelphia: S. Patter, 1820.

Wood, Jerome H. *Conestoga Crossroads: Lancaster, Pennsylvania, 1730–90.* Harrisburg: The Pennsylvania Historical and Museum Commission, 1979.

Woolverton, John F. *Colonial Anglicanism in North America,* Detroit: Wayne State University Press, 1984,

Young, A. H. "Thomas Barton: A Pennsylvania Loyalist." Ontario Historical Society *Papers and Records* 30 (1934): 33–42.

Zuckerman, Michael. "Authority in Early America: the Decay of Deference on the Provincial Periphery." *EAS* 1 (2003): 1–29.

Index

273